KT-244-706

WILL WE EVER KNOW THE TRUE STORY?

BLITZ EDITIONS

This material has previously appeared in partwork form as *Unsolved*

Published in this edition 1992 by Blitz Editions
an imprint of Bookmart Limited
Registered Number 2372865
Trading as Bookmart Limited
Desford Road, Enderby, Leicester LE9 5AD

Printed in Czechoslovakia

ISBN 1 85605 122 6

CONTENTS

THE SINKING OF THE BELGRANO

On 2 May 1982 the Argentine cruiser *General Belgrano* was sunk by a British submarine. Despite the huge loss of life, the action was applauded in Britain as a shrewd blow in the Falklands conflict; but as the facts began to emerge, disturbing doubts concerning the role of the British government in the incident were raised. For although it was claimed, at first, that the submarine commander had been acting on his own initiative in firing his torpedoes, it later transpired that the action had been authorised beforehand by Prime Minister Margaret Thatcher and her War Cabinet. PAUL FOOT looks at the course of events leading to the sinking and reaches some disquieting conclusions

On 2 April 1982 Argentine forces landed on the Falkland Islands and sparked off the conflict with Britain over the disputed sovereignty of the territory. Below: Argentine soldiers patrol the area around Port Stanley, the islands' largest settlement. Britain reacted to the invasion by despatching a large Task Force to the South Atlantic and on 1 May a Vulcan bomber made the first assault on Argentine positions by bombing the runway of Port Stanley's airport. Inset: an airport hangar engulfed in flames following the bomber's raid

EVER since the Argentines had invaded the Falkland Islands on 2 April 1982 war had been possible. As the huge British Task Force had lumbered southwards through the Atlantic, the US Secretary of State Alexander Haig, appointed as mediator in the dispute, had been conducting peace negotiations in Washington, Buenos Aires and London, but despite all his efforts the two sides had failed to reach any agreement. By the end of the month the Task Force was in striking distance of the Falklands and on Saturday 1 May it struck: at 4.23am local time, a Vulcan bomber, flying all the way from Ascension Island, bombed the runway at Port Stanley, the only sizeable village on the islands; later that day, ships from the Task Force approached the shore and shelled Argentine positions, and the first troops were put ashore by helicopter. The war, it seemed, had begun in earnest. And yet even at this late stage moves towards a peace settlement were in progress.

Shortly after midnight on 3 May, news of a fresh peace initiative reached London. 'Peruvian President Fernando

Shortly after midnight, news of a fresh peace initiative reached London

Belaúnde Terry said today that peace negotiations between Argentina and Britain were under way and that both countries had agreed in principle to cease hostilities,' read the Reuter's news agency report from Lima. 'He was speaking at a Press conference here on efforts to end the fighting between Britain and Argentina over the disputed Falkland Islands.' This was promising news indeed; however, at 1.10am a Downing Street Press officer issued a statement denying that Prime Minister Margaret Thatcher knew anything of any Peruvian peace plan. And at 1.58am, just an hour and a half after the first news of impending peace from Lima, came another, far more sensational Reuter's report: 'A British submarine torpedoed the Argentine cruiser *General Belgrano* in the South Atlantic last night . . . ' Throughout the day, further news of the incident emerged. According to the Ministry of Defence, the submarine commander had taken action under Article 51 of the United Nations Charter which allows any country to defend itself and its territory. The commander had acted on his own initiative, it seemed,

Below: *General Galtieri of the Argentine junta waves to cheering crowds from the balcony of Government House in Buenos Aires' Plaza de Mayo on 10 April 1982. The Argentine people have always held a firm conviction that the Falkland Islands – or the Malvinas – are the property of their country rather than of Britain and, following the April invasion, they were united in support of the hitherto unpopular junta for the first time. Only the previous month violent demonstrations against Galtieri and his dictatorship had raged in the capital but in April the people were demonstrating their backing of the Argentine troops (right). The legend across the flag – a replica of Britain's Union Jack – reads 'Dirty Pirates'*

and the cruiser had been sunk with huge loss of life. There would be no last-minute peace settlement now.

The House of Commons assembled after the Bank Holiday Monday on Tuesday 4 May. At once Defence Minister John Nott rose to give this statement on the sinking of the *General Belgrano*: 'This heavily armed surface attack group was close to the total exclusion zone and was closing on elements of our Task Force which was only hours away. We knew that the cruiser itself has substantial fire power, provided by 15-inch [38-centimetre] guns with a range of 13 miles [21 kilometres], and Seacat anti-aircraft missiles. Together with its escorting destroyers, which we believe were equipped with Exocet anti-ship missiles with a range of more than 20 miles [30 kilometres], the threat to the Task Force was such that the Task Force commander could ignore it only at his peril.' This important statement, made not in haste but some forty hours after the sinking, gave the clear impression of a dangerous move by a heavily-armed group of ships that was approaching the Task Force and was only hours away from it.

The most disturbing aspect of the news was that the *Belgrano* had been sunk *outside* the 200-mile [320-kilometre] 'total exclusion zone' – this maritime exclusion zone, imposed by the British forces, had come into effect on 12 April and Argentina had been warned that any ships or aircraft penetrating the zone would be liable to be attacked. Yet the *Belgrano* had been some 50 miles [80 kilometres] outside the zone when it was fired upon. Nonetheless, in Parliament on 5 May, John Nott and Margaret Thatcher gave further assurances that the cruiser, although outside

'I will admit proudly that it was us who sank the *Belgrano*'

the zone, had posed a major threat to the Task Force and it had been the clear duty of that force to sink it.

Just six weeks later, the Falklands War had been won by the British with relatively few losses. The sinking of the *Belgrano* had been by far the most bloody act of the conflict – the 368 crew members who perished made up more than a third of the war's total losses – but, in general, the decision to sink the cruiser was applauded in Britain as the first shrewd blow in a famous and swift British victory.

This view was forcefully put by Commander Christopher Wreford-Brown when his submarine *The Conqueror* – flying the Jolly Roger in accordance with service custom after sinking an enemy ship – sailed up the Clyde on its return to Faslane base in Scotland on 3 July. The captain told waiting journalists that in his view the sinking of the *Belgrano* had been entirely justified. Then he went on to insist strongly that he had been *ordered* to sink the enemy vessel, scotching the idea that he and he alone had decided to fire his torpedoes. 'I will admit proudly that it was us who sank the *Belgrano*,' the *Daily Telegraph* reported him as saying. 'I was under direct orders from Fleet Headquarters and they were confirmed by me before I went into the attack.' On 5 May John Nott had stated: 'The actual decision to launch a torpedo was clearly one taken by the submarine commander.' But according to the submarine commander himself, the order had come from Britain. From whom? It was not until 4 October that, in a rather curious government statement issued to the news agencies, it was 'confirmed' that the order to sink the *Belgrano* had come from the War Cabinet – Margaret Thatcher, John Nott, Deputy Prime Minister William Whitelaw and chairman of the Conservative party Cecil Parkinson – meeting at the prime minister's country residence Chequers on 2 May.

What were the reasons behind the War Cabinet's decision and why had they hitherto concealed their part in the attack? One man determined to find out was MP Tam Dalyell, a formidable campaigner on the Labour Opposition benches. An old Etonian who had represented the Scottish seat of Linithgow for twenty years, Dalyell had been one of the few dissidents on the Falklands issue. He had travelled widely in South America and had many friends and political colleagues there. He was a bitter opponent of the fascist regime in Argentina but saw himself as a friend of the Argentine people. He knew that one issue that united them all was their claim to sovereignty of the Falkland Islands – or the Malvinas as the Argentines called them. He had regarded the government's decision to send a Task Force to repel the Argentine invaders as an act of pure folly and clashed fiercely with the Labour front bench over the issue, losing his position as Shadow Spokesman on Science as a result.

As the new Parliamentary session got underway in late October 1982, Tam Dalyell started asking questions about the Falklands conflict in general and about the sinking of the *General Belgrano* in particular. He had been approached by a member of the crew of the *Conquerer* who had furnished him with vital and disturbing information about the submarine's position and course at the time of the engage-

Below: the last moments of the General Belgrano *captured in a photograph taken by a crew member from a red life raft (in the foreground). Other life rafts can be seen clustered in the icy waters around the cruiser's sinking hulk. The unleashing by the* Conqueror *of its fatal torpedoes had been no sudden decision. For in his exhaustive inquiries into the incident, MP Tam Dalyell discovered – from members of the submarine crew themselves – that the* Conqueror *had detected the* Belgrano *and her escorts, the* Hippolito Bouchard *and the* Piedra Bueno, *at around 4pm, local time, on Friday 30 April. The submarine closed in on the surface group at periscope depth and on the afternoon of 1 May – still a full day before the sinking – monitored the ships 'razzing' (re-fuelling at sea) from a distance of 4000 yards (3650 metres). At this point, the* Belgrano *and her escorts presented 'sitting duck' targets – so why, if the cruiser then posed a threat to the Task Force, was it not sunk at this time?*

ment, and in November, acting on this information, Dalyell asked the Ministry of Defence what the course of the *Belgrano* had been when it was sunk. Spokesman Peter Blaker replied: 'When it was torpedoed, the *Belgrano* was sailing on a course of 280 degrees.' This meant that the cruiser was not, as John Nott had asserted in the House of Commons the previous May, 'closing on' the Task Force. She was sailing away from it in exactly the opposite direction.

In one short sentence Mr Blaker seemed to have demolished the original explanation for sinking the *Belgrano*. If the ship was not 'closing on' the Task Force but sailing away from it, how could it have possibly posed a threat? In the same answer Blaker attempted to explain the motive for firing on the cruiser: 'Concerned that HMS *Conquerer* might lose the *General Belgrano* as she ran over the shallow water of the Burdwood Bank, the Task Force commander sought and obtained a change in the rules of engagement to allow an attack outside the 200-mile exclusion zone.'

'One thing that twenty years in the House of Commons develops in a man is the instinct to sense when one is being

When the Conqueror struck

On 26 April 1982 the *General Belgrano* left her operational base of Ushuaia in Tierra del Fuego for the last time. She had a crew of 1138 men and was under the command of Captain Navio Hector Elias Bonzo.

At 4pm on 2 May a third of the crew were at action stations, a third on stand-by and a third were resting. None of them were wearing anti-flash protection clothing. The first torpedo hit the cruiser amidships, ripping through four decks. A series of huge explosions was followed by a second hit, which struck the cruiser's prow. Of the 368 men who died, at least 330 were killed by the heat and blast of the explosions. Others perished in the freezing waters.

The survivors managed to launch 62 rubber rafts which carried them away from their sinking ship; there were moments of panic as the *Belgrano* listed and threatened to fall on top of the rafts; most of the men were covered in oil and their hands were slipping on the oars. Captain Bonzo was the last to leave the ship; he swam fifty feet (15 metres) through the icy sea and was hauled into one of the rafts.

A third torpedo had missed the *Belgrano* but had run on to hit one of her escort ships, the *Bouchard.* The torpedo failed to explode and *Bouchard* went in hot pursuit of the submarine. For an hour *Conqueror* darted away on a zig-zag course, then slowed and prepared to rise. A depth charge from the *Bouchard* shook the submarine and away it wriggled once more. Another hour later, with the destroyer finally shrugged off, *Conqueror* came to the surface and radioed her victorious news.

Meanwhile the *Belgrano's* rafts were carried by the fierce and biting wind south-east towards the ice of the Atlantic. The men huddled together for warmth. The following afternoon, 26 hours after the sinking, the first survivors were picked up.

'One thing puzzles me,' Captain Bonzo told Arthur Gavshon and Desmond Rice, authors of *The Sinking of the Belgrano,* some months later. 'You Anglo-Saxons are supposed to be so logical. As a mere Latin, I thought that a total exclusion zone must mean that if you were in it, then you got shot at. But if you were going to be shot at in any case, then, tell me, why have a total exclusion zone at all?'

It appeared that the government and the military were thinking up new excuses as they went along

Right: the Sun *newspaper celebrates the death of the* General Belgrano *with jingoistic glee. Below right: South Atlantic fleet positions on the day of the sinking. Below: Defence Minister John Nott (left) and Admiral Sir Terence Lewin are quizzed at a press conference about the movements and actions of the British Task Force. Nott's assertion, made in the House of Commons on 4 May, that the* General Belgrano*'s 'threat to the Task Force was such that the Task Force commander could ignore it only at his peril' would soon turn out to be far from the truth*

told something that is not quite right,' Dalyell later wrote. He started making inquiries about the Burdwood Bank and discovered that these shoals, which lie south-south-west of the Falklands, were very well surveyed. At its very shallowest, the Bank is 25 fathoms (150 feet/45 metres) below the surface of the sea; most of it is much deeper than that – 540 to 600 feet (165 – 180 metres). The draft of the nuclear submarine *Conqueror*, when fully submerged, is 55 feet (16·7 metres) and it was specifically designed to operate with all its equipment in the shallow waters of the Baltic. If the Argentine cruiser *had* sailed over the Burdwood Bank, the shallow waters would not for a moment have hindered the ability of the submarine to pursue it.

The revised explanation for the sinking of the *Belgrano*, then, seemed less than satisfactory. Suspecting that the Burdwood Bank had been thrown into the debate as a red herring, Dalyell again asked the Ministry of Defence the position of the cruiser when sunk. He was supplied with a precise answer: '55 degrees 27 minutes south, 61 degrees 25 minutes west.' But this meant that, when fired upon, the *Belgrano* was far to the south-west of the Burdwood Bank and steaming on a course that would have missed it by nearly 100 miles (160 kilometres). As Dalyell commented in a powerful speech on 21 December, it appeared that the government and the military were thinking up new excuses for the sinking as they went along. Or as the *New Statesman* was to put it: 'The official story has been constantly changing which is usually a sign that an account of events is being manufactured after the event to meet political requirements.'

The changing story had done little to arouse public concern, however; the picture that had emerged by the end of 1982 was one of a British submarine suddenly encountering an enemy vessel and of the commanders – both of the Task Force and the War Cabinet – deciding to take no chances as to the danger it threatened. The conflict had just begun, nerves were on edge, and there, suddenly, was an enemy ship. If you are involved in war, you have to defend yourself. This theory depended, of course, on the *suddenness* of the *Conqueror*'s discovery of the *Belgrano*. Every reaction of the government and the military at the time had indicated that the *General Belgrano* had been sighted only a short time before it was sunk. On 4 May John Nott had stated: 'The next day, 2 May, at 8pm London time, one of our submarines detected the Argentine cruiser *General Belgrano* . . .' Only minutes later the cruiser had been sunk. Then in November, the government published a White Paper: *The Falklands Campaign: The Lessons*. Paragraph 110 of the paper stated: 'On May 2, HMS *Conqueror* detected the Argentine cruiser *General Belgrano*.' But on 6 December Tam Dalyell asked the Ministry of Defence: 'At what time was contact with the *General Belgrano* first made by one of Her Majesty's submarines?' and back came the reply, from Peter Blaker: 'It would not be in the public interest to give this information.' The official line was changing again. In May and November the story was that the cruiser had been detected at 8pm on 2 May. But now, in December, disclosure of the time of contact was judged to be 'not in the public interest'. Why?

Already various theories and rumours about the incident were circulating.

The book *The Falklands War* by the *Sunday Times* Insight Team, published in November, stated that the submarine had contacted the cruiser a full day before the sinking. Then in May 1983, a West Country journalist, Geoffrey Underwood, published *Our Falklands War.* Several months earlier when the *Conqueror* had berthed in Plymouth, Underwood had managed to interview Wreford-Brown and in his book he quoted the submarine's commander as saying: 'We were asked to look for and find the *General Belgrano* . . . We located her on our passive sonar and sighted her visually early on the afternoon of 1 May' – again, the day *before* the sinking. Wreford-Brown went on: 'We took up a position astern and followed the *Belgrano* group for over thirty hours. We reported that we were in contact with her . . . We had instructions to attack if she went inside the total exclusion zone.' The order to attack outside the exclusion zone did not come, he disclosed, until the following day, 2 May, after the submarine had been following the cruiser for more than thirty hours.

This did terrible damage to the government's original explanation. For if the cruiser was a threat to the Task Force, it was a threat when first sighted and should have been sunk at once. If it was not a threat then, when guns were blazing and bombs were dropping all around Port

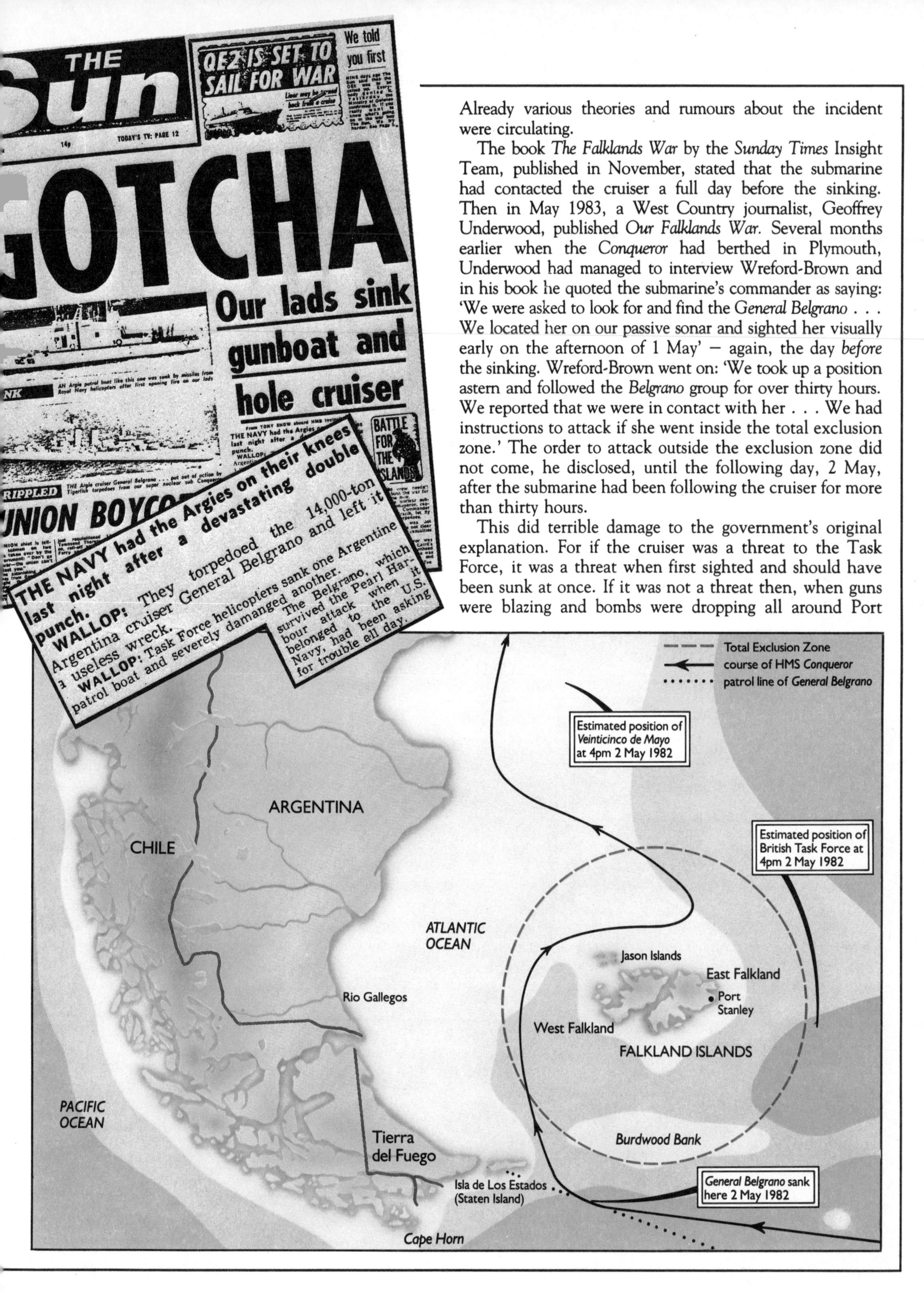

THE Sun

14p TODAY'S TV: PAGE 12

QE2 IS SET TO SAIL FOR WAR

We told you first

GOTCHA

Our lads sink gunboat and hole cruiser

AN Argie patrol boat like this one was sunk by missiles from Royal Navy helicopters after first opening fire on our lads

RIPPLED THE Argie cruiser General Belgrano . . . put out of action by Tigerfish torpedoes from our super nuclear sub Conqueror

UNION BOYCO

From TONY SNOW aboard HMS Invincible

BATTLE FOR THE ISLANDS

THE NAVY had the Argies on their knees last night after a devastating double punch.

WALLOP: They torpedoed the 14,000-ton Argentina cruiser General Belgrano and left it a useless wreck.

WALLOP: Task Force helicopters sank one Argentine patrol boat and severely damanged another.

The Belgramo, which survived the Pearl Harbour attack when it belonged to the U.S. Navy, had been asking for trouble all day.

Right: 26 hours after the Argentine cruiser went down, the first survivors were picked up from their rafts. Rescue operations went on well into the next day and of the crew of 1,138 men, 368 perished. Last to leave the holed ship had been its captain, Hector Bonzo, who at a press conference in Buenos Aires on 7 May (below right, speaking into microphone) hit out at the British action. Below: a Belgrano *survivor is reunited with his family*

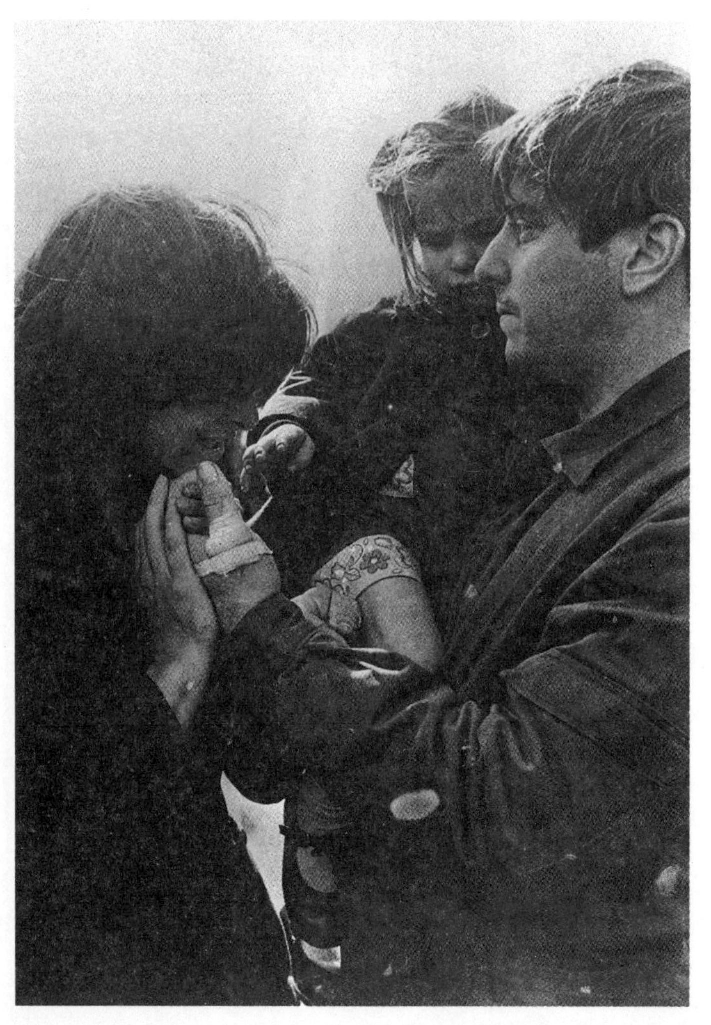

Stanley, how could it have been a threat thirty hours later after it had sailed away from the Task Force? The official view stated by Nott immediately after the attack and held to by government and military chiefs, seemed at best unlikely, at worst quite wrong. Why and how, then, had the *General Belgrano* been sunk? With suspicions aroused, those who doubted the government's frankness began to examine the events preceding the sinking in greater detail.

Almost all of Argentina's leading political figures in 1982 have since admitted that they were astonished by the British response to the seizure of the Falkland Islands. They had been led to expect that the British would huff and puff but would never go to war for a handful of people 8000 miles (13,000 kilometres) away. They watched the British armada as it made its way south with mounting apprehension yet they were stuck with the decision they had made. The ruling junta was hated throughout the entire middle and working class of Argentina. Its economic policy was in ruins; its reign of terror had not worked. The Falklands escapade was a desperate attempt to curry popularity and unite the nation behind the dictatorship. To abandon the islands without a shot being fired or a concession being agreed would have humiliated the junta beyond the point where it could survive. Yet all the offers of a peace settlement put to the Argentines by the American Secretary of State Alexander Haig demanded immediate withdrawal of forces from the islands without anything apparently to show for it.

The divisions and demoralisations within the junta increased as the British Task Force grew closer, and the bombardment around Port Stanley on the morning of 1 May created panic. Although the bombardment had caused little damage and the Argentine forces were still capable of defending the islands, the start of a shooting war against an enemy incomparably better trained and better equipped – and an enemy supported by most of the western world including the United States – removed many of the junta's earlier inhibitions about a settlement.

The immediate, reflex reaction of the hard-liners in the Argentine military, however, was to meet force with force. In their book *The Sinking of the Belgrano,* published in 1984, authors Arthur Gavshon and Desmond Rice provide a detailed account of events on the afternoon and night of 1 May and report that at 3.55pm local time, the Argentine aircraft carrier *Veinticinco de Mayo* received orders from Vice-Admiral Walter Allara, the Argentine Fleet Commander, to move towards the Task Force and engage it in action. This is confirmed by the findings of Dr Robert Scheina, an American academic specialising in naval operations who, in May 1983, wrote a paper on the Falklands War for the US Naval Institute Proceedings. The information in Scheina's paper was based on extensive interviews with the Argentine high command and he managed to describe the Argentine fleet movements in minute detail.

Scheina confirmed that on the afternoon of 1 May, not just the *Veinticinco de Mayo* but all the Argentine warships stationed north of the Falklands moved at top speed towards the Task Force to engage it. But, Scheina goes on to state, these movements definitely did *not* involve the *Bel-*

grano; the mission of the *Belgrano* group was twofold: 'They were to provide an early warning for the southern mainland and to be in a position to intercept any British reinforcements which might come from the Pacific. While on station, the cruiser plied back and forth between Isla do Los Estados and Burdwood Bank. Her operating area was outside the 200-mile total exclusion zone.

The *Belgrano*, then, sighted by the *Conqueror* early on Saturday afternoon 1 May, was never part of any intended attack on the Task Force but was simply working its way back and forth along a line well south and west of the Falkland Islands to head off any British ships that might come the other way – from the Pacific. Nor, realistically, could the *Belgrano* be thought to have been forming part of a 'pincer movement' with the *Veinticinco de Mayo*, as Rear-Admiral Sir John 'Sandy' Woodward, the Task Force commander, and various British ministers have speculated. As the captain of the *Belgrano*, Hector Elias Bonzo said later, it would have been a pretty odd sort of pincer movement with the prongs 350 miles (560 kilometres) apart. The *General Belgrano*, it seems, had specific orders to patrol a defensive line, and that is exactly what she did.

Meanwhile, on the Argentine mainland, there were strong moves for disengagement of hostilities to avoid an all-out war. At a meeting of divisional and brigade generals in the afternoon of 1 May, it was recommended that Argentina return to the negotiating table in an attempt to avert war. And at 8.30pm, report Gavshon and Rice, there was a top-level meeting at which at least two of the three-man junta were present. General Jose Vaquero, chief of the army staff, summed up the mood of the short meeting: 'No queremos guerra abierta' – 'We don't want open war.'

At once, orders went out to the Argentine fleet to withdraw. The most important orders, of course, were to the northern groups where the *Veinticinco de Mayo* could not get its Skyhawks into the air because of the light wind and the darkness. But the order went out also to the *Belgrano*: head for home.

Robert Scheina agrees with this general view, though he says the orders to withdraw were issued later, in the early hours of 2 May. Rear-Admiral Juan Jose Lombardo, Argentine Naval Commander South Atlantic, appearing on BBC television's *Panorama* in 1984, confirmed that orders to withdraw were issued, giving times a little later than Gavshon and Rice's and a little earlier than Scheina's. But whatever time the orders were given, the experts agree that signals to withdraw, sent out in code, had reached the *Belgrano* by first light on 2 May.

Consider then the feelings of the leader of the Argentine junta, General Leopoldo Galtieri, at around midnight on that May Day. His short-lived triumph was over; his fleet was withdrawing. His problem, which he contemplated morosely as the night went on and as he helped himself to more and more of his beloved 'Etiqueta' whisky, was how to escape catastrophe. At about 1.30am on 2 May, the telephone rang. At the other end of the line was Dr Fernando Belaúnde Terry, President of Peru. He offered a lifeline that Galtieri eagerly grasped.

The news that fighting had broken out over the Falkland Islands had caused consternation in the Torre Tagli, the ancient Foreign Office in Peru's capital Lima. The Peruvian foreign service is recognised as being the most able and the best-trained in South America. It has a tradition for peacemaking between belligerent parties. The civil servants there persuaded the Foreign Secretary, Dr Javier Arias Stella, a Fellow of the Royal Society of Pathologists in London, to intervene in the Falklands crisis. Peru, his staff reminded

Right: President Belaúnde Terry of Peru (centre), at a press conference in Lima's presidential palace on the evening of 2 May, announces the Falklands peace initiative worked out between Peruvian politicians and US Secretary of State Alexander Haig. Below: Argentine Foreign Minister Nicanor Costa Mendez (left) and the president Leopoldo Galtieri (right) were ready to accept the Peruvian peace proposals — but unknown to them any hopes of peace had already been sunk with the loss of the Belgrano

Galtieri's problem, which he contemplated morosely as the night went on, was how to escape catastrophe

him, had a long history of close association with the Argentine and good contacts in Embassies in the United States and Europe. Dr Arias Stella had urgent talks with President Belaúnde Terry and the two men decided to act. Dr Arias Stella rang the American Embassy and offered the whole diplomatic service of his country in the cause of peace. Belaúnde Terry, meanwhile, put through a call to President Ronald Reagan in Washington.

Reagan was out of town and so the call was re-routed to the home of Alexander Haig who had conducted the unsuccessful negotiations between Britain and Argentina over the past four weeks. Haig leapt at the Peruvian initiative. He and Belaúnde spent many hours on the phone that evening, talking, as Haig later testified, on 'an open telephone line'. They both agreed that they must find a version of peace plans that might be acceptable to both sides.

The key to the dispute was, of course, sovereignty over the Falkland Islands, which neither side was prepared to concede. Very well, suggested Belaúnde Terry, why not leave the matter of sovereignty undecided for the moment and accept that both sides had 'conflicting claims' to the islands? Would not such a formula at least allow a cease fire and withdrawal pending further discussions?

The other main problem, said Haig, concerned the fiercely patriotic islanders. Britain could hardly be expected to accept any settlement that did not take their feelings and their future into account. Another clause in any immediate peace treaty would have to deal with 'the points of view and interests of the islanders'.

By such discussions and concessions, Belaúnde and Haig hammered out a new peace plan. It included terms for an immediate cease fire, withdrawal of the entire Argentine army from the Falklands and withdrawal of the British Task Force from the area.

The new plan was a sensible and sensitive one. It gave tiny concessions to both sides without wounding the pride of either. It sought to stop the hostilities and bloodshed at once and to solve the problem of the administration of the Falkland Islands once and for all.

As he spoke to Alexander Haig in Washington, Belaúnde was not alone in the presidential palace; with him were Dr Arias Stella and Mr Manuel Ulloa Elias, the then prime minister and by far the most able politician in Peru's ruling conservative party. Ulloa also spoke to Haig and refined some of the points in the treaty.

Soon after midnight, Belaúnde phoned Galtieri with his plan. Galtieri, according to the Peruvians, was extremely friendly, enthusiastic and optimistic. He quarrelled with the odd word in the proposed treaty but the matters in dispute, he was sure, could be dealt with in the morning. On three of the four sides of the square, 1 May ended full of hope: in Washington, Lima and Buenos Aires, there was every expectation that a peace agreement could be reached.

But what was the British attitude? The only open sign of that came from the British Foreign Secretary Francis Pym who flew to Washington on 1 May, arriving early in the evening. At once Pym gave a press conference to waiting journalists who found him, as they reported in the next

Britain's claim to the Falklands

In 1690 Captain John Strong of the British Navy made the first landing on the islands and it was he who introduced the name Falkland after the treasurer of the Navy, Viscount Falkland. It was not until 1764, however, that the islands were inhabited for the first time when a small colony was established by the French on East Falkland. Two years later the French handed their colony to Spain, which then ruled what is now Argentina. Meanwhile, a fort had been established by the British on West Falkland and the islands had been formally claimed for the British Crown.

In 1770 the two colonies came to blows when five Spanish frigates forced the British out. After strong protests from the British government, a treaty was drawn up under which Spain agreed to allow Britain to re-establish a colony. But it was suggested at the time, and neither confirmed nor denied by the government, that there had been a secret agreement under which the British had agreed to abandon their claim to the Falklands forever – and in 1774 they packed up their colony and left altogether.

In 1816 the part of South America that is now Argentina declared itself independent of Spain and took charge of all Spanish territory in that area of the South Atlantic, including the Falklands. The British objected verbally but took no action until 1833 when two British frigates arrived to 'establish British claims to the islands'. The South American fishermen who inhabited the islands were ejected and a small population of British emigrants began to establish itself.

Sovereignty of the islands has been disputed in international courts and assemblies for the past 150 years but all attempts to settle the rival claims have foundered.

Right: British Foreign Secretary Francis Pym (left) with US Secretary of State Alexander Haig in Washington on the evening of 1 May. The British bombardment of Port Stanley had been carried out in order to 'concentrate the minds' of the Argentines on reaching a peace settlement, Pym told journalists and, he continued, 'No further military action is envisaged for the moment. . . '

day's papers, 'in ebullient mood'. Why had he come? To see if there was a final chance of peace by negotiation, Pym stated. What chance was there of that following the recent bombardment of the Falklands, he was asked. Every chance, replied Pym. The bombardment had been carried out in order to 'concentrate the minds' of the Argentines on reaching a settlement (in which, as we have seen, it was extremely successful). He went on: 'No further military action is envisaged for the moment, other than to make the exclusion zone secure.'

For the journalists at the press conference – as, indeed, for everyone who read them, Pym's words could have only one meaning. As the *Daily Mail* correspondent reported on 3 May: 'It was clear that the British fleet would not fire unless provoked by an Argentine attempt to breach the 200-mile exclusion zone.' The British hawk, in other words,

Left: British inhabitants of the Falkland Islands pose with their sheep dogs in 1924. Above: Port Stanley in the Twenties

A Labour government in 1968 and a Conservative government in 1980 both tried to float a 'lease-back' deal, handing sovereignty to the Argentines who would then lease it back to the islanders. Both times this solution collapsed under opposition from the islanders.

During the war of 1982, British Foreign Secretary Francis Pym stated: 'We are not in any doubt about our title to the Falkland Islands and we never have been.' This was very far from the truth. In 1829 the Prime Minister the Duke of Wellington had written: 'I have perused the papers respecting the Falkland Islands. It is not at all clear to me that we have ever possessed the sovereignty of these islands.' Several internal Foreign Office memoranda over the last eighty years have shown similar doubts about the legality of the British title. In 1936 the head of the American desk at the Foreign Office, John Troutbeck, wrote: 'The difficulty of the position is that our seizure of the Falkland Islands in 1833 was so arbitrary a procedure as judged by the ideology of the present day. It is therefore not easy to explain our possession without showing ourselves up as international bandits.'

had been called off for the moment in the hope that peace might be reached. No other interpretation can be put on the words of Mr Pym that night.

When Admiral Sir Terence Lewin, Chief of Staff of the British armed forces, and his other senior officers arrived early in the morning of Sunday 2 May at their command centre at Northwood, Middlesex, what did they know of the seemingly successful peace discussions of the previous evening? Nothing, they reply. Lord Lewin, as he now is, has consistently asserted that he had no idea of any of the dramatic events in Buenos Aires, Lima or Washington on 1 May. Yet in December 1983, a year and a half later, Tam Dalyell heard from what he claims is an impeccable source that the British government's crack signals intelligence unit at Government Communication Headquarters (GCHQ) at Cheltenham had picked up the orders to the Argentine ships to withdraw and had decoded them in two minutes. (In April 1984 MP Denzil Davies attempted to confirm this story with a written question to Mrs Thatcher; he was told that information gathered during the conflict regarding the movement of the Argentine fleet was classified 'in the interests of national security'.) GCHQ, Dalyell was assured, had also intercepted the discussions between Belaúnde and Haig on that 'open telephone line' and passed the received information on to the chiefs of staff.

Whether they had received news of the fresh peace initiative or not, by midday Sir Terence and his armed service chiefs were bowling along to Chequers where the prime minister was presiding over the War Cabinet. The military had a simple request; the Task Force had, they told Mrs Thatcher, John Nott, William Whitelaw and Cecil Parkinson, sighted an Argentine cruiser the *General Belgrano* and although the vessel was outside the total exclusion zone, it might pose a threat to the Task Force. Lewin later stated: 'It didn't matter what direction the *Belgrano* was going. She might just have been wasting time so as to be able to attack the Task Force at night. Critics who say she was steaming for home have no idea what they are talking about. I went straight to Chequers and called the War Cabinet into a side room and told them the situation. I said we could not wait. Here was an opportunity to knock off a major unit of the Argentine fleet.'

So the service chiefs asked for permission to alter the rules of engagement and sink the enemy cruiser outside the total exclusion zone. It was a request the prime minister and her War Cabinet colleagues, given the information that the *Belgrano* posed a major threat to the Task Force, could hardly refuse. The War Cabinet's unanimous decision was arrived at in a matter of seconds and the chiefs of staff hurried on their way back to Northwood.

The War Cabinet had agreed to the chief of staffs' request at 1pm yet the *General Belgrano* was not attacked until seven hours later. If, as the chiefs of staff had reported to Thatcher, Nott and the others, the cruiser posed a threat to the Task Force, why was it not sunk at the earliest available opportunity? There was no problem with communications; Lord Lewin has said publicly that Northwood was in direct and almost instant communication with the

Right: Britain's nuclear submarine Conqueror *sails triumphantly up the Clyde on its return to Faslane base in Scotland on 3 July. Below right: in accordance with naval custom after sinking an enemy ship, the craft flew the Jolly Roger — but instead of crossed bones, the macabre flag bore crossed torpedoes. Commander Christopher Wreford-Brown (centre) and his crew were warmly congratulated by Britain's Task Force commander, Rear Admiral Sandy Woodward, for their action in the South Atlantic. 'That cool and determined attack was typical of your whole patrol,' wrote Woodward. 'Well done. Bon voyage. Take a well earned break.' In sinking the* Belgrano, *the* Conqueror *had succeeded where the Japanese air force had failed four decades before. Three years after being built for the United States Navy in 1938 and christened the* Phoenix, *the cruiser had survived the Japanese raid on Pearl Harbor (below)*

Conqueror. Yet a member of the crew of the *Conqueror* has said that the order to fire did not come until just over an hour before the sinking. Why, if the cruiser was such a threat and the Cabinet had given permission to sink it, did the chiefs of staff wait at least six hours before relaying the attack orders to the submarine?

During those six hours the peace negotiations rushed along without faltering to what seemed like almost the perfect conclusion. At 1pm London time, as Mrs Thatcher was authorising the sinking at Chequers, it was 8am in Washington and Francis Pym and Alexander Haig were just getting up. At 10am the two men met for three hours of talks and then they had lunch.

Meanwhile President Belaúnde was pursuing his initiative in Lima. He had to attend a ceremonial parade for an hour and a half in the morning but for the rest of the time he kept the telephone lines to Washington and to Buenos Aires buzzing.

Galtieri and his advisers had decided that they did not like the expression 'points of view and interests' of the islanders in the Belaúnde-Haig initiative. The wording was changed, therefore, to 'needs and aspirations'. There were lengthy arguments about which four countries would be appointed to administer the islands. Galtieri rejected the idea that the United States should be in the group since America had come out in support of Britain over the original conflict. He suggested Canada instead. Venezuela

The old 'General'

At the time of the Falklands conflict in 1982, the *General Belgrano* was an old ship approaching retirement but its crew were proud of its distinguished fighting record. The cruiser was built in 1938 for the United States Navy and she was christened *Phoenix*. After trial runs, she sailed to her base at Pearl Harbor where she survived the Japanese bombing raid of December 1941 that brought America into the Second World War. During the war, *Phoenix* served in the South Pacific where she sank the Japanese battleship *Fuso* and gained nine battle stars for active service.

In April 1951 *Phoenix* was sold to the Argentine navy and was renamed *17 de Octubre* after the date, in 1945, when President Peron had come to power. In 1956, after the fall of Peron, the cruiser's name was changed again, to *General Belgrano*, after one of the leaders of the Argentine revolution of 1810. In the years before the sinking, the *Belgrano* was used mainly as a training ship; although equipped with some modern guns and signals equipment she was recognised as one of the most vulnerable ships in the Argentine fleet.

was chosen as a second country, West Germany a third and the fourth was left open.

During the morning, a draft treaty was drawn up by foreign office officials in Lima; its clauses kept being erased and amended as the day wore on. 'We became greatly excited,' said Dr Arias Stella. 'We really thought peace was at hand.' To the Peruvians, the two belligerent parties appeared to be negotiating with enthusiasm and purpose at only one remove. Belaúnde and Mr Manuel Ulloa Elias, the Peruvian prime minister, were acting, in effect, as agents for Galtieri and the junta while Haig was 'acting for' Pym who was in the same room for most of those vital six hours. At one time Ulloa remembers telling Haig not to allow the British to do anything rash that might break what he called (and what most parties now accepted) was a 'de facto truce'. Haig replied that he would do his best.

At midday General Galtieri told Belaúnde that he and his co-members of the junta accepted the seven points of the peace plan. The three of them, he said, would recommend the terms to the council of generals that was meeting at 5pm that afternoon. Success at the meeting, he said, was a formality; indeed, the feeling for peace in Buenos Aires at this stage was even stronger among the second-rank officers than it was in the junta itself.

The meeting, Galtieri supposed, would take about two hours and after that he could instruct his ambassador in

'We're on the brink of an agreement. The difference is about a single word'

Lima to initial a temporary treaty while he announced a cease fire.

Although many of the civil servants involved in Lima remained sceptical, feeling that Britain showed few signs of accepting *any* peace proposals, the Peruvian politicians themselves were confident of success. President Belaúnde calculated that a 'paving' peace treaty could be signed in his own palace at about 7pm Lima time (9pm Buenos Aires time). He ordered the preparation of the Peace Room, where peace between Honduras and San Salvador had been signed the previous year, and shortly before 5pm, a beaming Belaúnde, flanked by Ulloa and Arias Stella, threw a press conference in the presidential palace.

The language Belaúnde used in his opening statement showed just how sure he was that the proposals would bring peace: 'Before the journalists' first question about this proposal, may I say that it's an instrument by which there would be an immediate end to hostilities. The document is not a capitulation for either party, I think it has the merit of being a testament of victory for both sides . . . . The proposal which Peru has put forward with the firm support of the US government is to get peace very quickly, if possible tonight . . . '. Belaúnde's confidence in the peace proposal was shared both by Alexander Haig and the Argentinians. In Buenos Aires the politicians united with the generals in their hopes; at 1pm the Argentine Foreign Minister told reporters: 'We're on the brink of an agreement. The difference is about a single word.' Alexander Haig confirmed that a satisfactory treaty was near completion when he told *Panorama* on 16 April 1984: 'We had progressed rather well on the telephone. We were down to words, *single* words and specifically in two paragaphs . . . '

Early in the evening of 2 May the Argentine Military

GCHQ Unions banned for 'secrecy'?

On 12 January 1984, at a packed public meeting organised by Cunninghame North and Cunninghame South Constituency Labour Parties in Ardrossan, Ayrshire, MP Tam Dalyell made a startling and disturbing allegation about the sinking of the *General Belgrano*. He had heard from a reliable and informed source that the British chiefs of staff and the members of the War Cabinet had been well aware that the *Belgrano* was returning to port — therefore no threat to the Task Force — when the torpedoes struck. Dalyell's informant had told him that the orders to the Argentine surface group to withdraw had been picked up and decoded by the Government Communications Headquarters (GCHQ) at Cheltenham.

On 25 January 1984 — less than two weeks after Dalyell had made his accusation — Foreign Secretary Geoffrey Howe stood up in the Commons and made an announcement that astonished MPs on both sides of the House. Trades unions at GCHQ were to be banned. The government was taking this action because of a dispute at the intelligence unit that had obstructed the introduction of a polygraph — lie-detector — machine. GCHQ staff deal with highly classified information in

Above: Britain celebrates triumph with a Falklands Victory Parade in London in October 1982. Left: MP Tam Dalyell, one of the House of Commons' few Falklands 'dissidents'; his questions about Belgrano *raised many doubts about the government's veracity*

their work and the polygraph – which GCHQ director Mr Peter Marychurch was introducing on government orders – would monitor staff reliability and provide a safeguard against the leaking of secrets. Further industrial actions at GCHQ might be a danger to national security, the government argued. But the dispute that had prompted the decision to ban the unions had taken place three years before, so why had Howe's announcement come *now?* Tam Dalyell is convinced that the ban had little to do with events three years earlier but was a direct result of the leak to him of GCHQ's decoding of Argentine signals. Dalyell believes that on hearing his statement of 12 January, the government concluded that he had been tipped off about the Cheltenham decodification by a member of GCHQ staff – and they were gravely concerned that further information about the *Belgrano* affair might leak out. 'Did the government conclude,' asks Dalyell, 'that putting the fear of God into the employees at GCHQ by removing the psychological protection afforded by trade union membership was the best way to prevent employees coming forward on the *Belgrano?* No other more plausible explanation has been given for the astonishing actions of the government.'

Committee held a crucial meeting to discuss the treaty. Paragraph by paragraph the generals analysed the proposal and their mood was sympathetic. Then, shortly after 7pm, Admiral Anaya strode into the room with terrible news. The *General Belgrano*, a long way south of the exclusion zone and heading for home, had been torpedoed. She was sinking. There was heavy loss of life.

Suddenly there was pandemonium in the room. Many of the officers at the meeting had sons, brothers or other relations on the *Belgrano* and peace, now, was unthinkable. The terms of the treaty were rejected. The war was on. As Manuel Ulloa Elias put it to his Senate two days later: 'Argentine rejection of the Belaúnde peace proposals was due to the fact that Argentina had been attacked with the torpedoing of the *Belgrano* at the very moment that Peru was trying to find a dignified way out of the contest.'

Francis Pym heard the news of the sinking as he was sitting down to supper with the General Secretary of the United Nations, Perez de Cuellar, in New York. Pym was a member of the War Cabinet and yet, he claims, no one had consulted him about the decision to attack the *Belgrano.* (He would later undermine this claim by telling an interviewer that although the news of the *Belgrano* had come as a total surprise, he *had* been consulted about the change in the rules of engagement. Had he not asked the *reason* for wanting the rules changed?) His version of the events of 2 May is strikingly different to that given by Haig and the Peruvians. Haig says the discussions had come down to 'words, *single* words'; Pym says there was 'no actual text'. He insists that his discussions with Haig that day were vague

Below: on the first anniversary of the sinking of the General Belgrano, *relatives of the dead crew members, aboard the Argentine ship* Lago Lacar, *cast flowers onto the waters of the South Atlantic. The destruction of the* Belgrano *proved to be by far the bloodiest conflict of the short Falklands war. But if the cruiser had not been sunk, war might have been averted altogether — there might have been no losses on the British ships* Sheffield, Atlantic Conveyor, Ardent, Antelope *and* Coventry

and that nothing like a peace treaty had ever been suggested to him. 'If the Peruvians had prepared a treaty ready for signature on the evening of 2 May they certainly gave no indication of this in Lima,' he was to state. Yet at his press conference that afternoon, President Belaúnde had told journalists: 'In the palace we're in direct contact with Buenos Aires and Washington where Foreign Minister Pym has spent the whole day in the State Department.' But why, argues Pym, would he have left Washington for New York that evening if a peace treaty was so near at hand? One answer to this could be that the United Nations would clearly have played a crucial role in the settlement in setting up the four-country control group and monitoring the troop withdrawals. And the UN Secretary General Perez de Cuellar, with whom Pym was dining, is himself a Peruvian and perhaps the best person in all the United States to assess the proposals of his own country's political leaders.

Like Francis Pym, the British chiefs of staff and the members of the War Cabinet have all consistently denied any knowledge of the Peruvian peace moves prior to the sinking of the *Belgrano*. On 4 April 1984, in reply to a written question by MP Denzil Davies, Margaret Thatcher stated: 'The first indications of the possible Peruvian peace proposals reached London from Washington at 11.15pm London time and from Lima at 2am London time on 3 May.' The Peruvians, however, find this very surprising. 'We understood that Pym and Haig's contact was so close that whatever Haig accepted was all right with Pym,' Arias Stella was to say. 'That is, Pym passed it on at once to London, Pym spoke with the voice of London.' But London, according to Margaret Thatcher, received no word from Pym in Washington. He sent no messages about the peace proposals because he knew nothing about them. But even so, wouldn't London have heard about the peace plans from Lima itself? President Belaúnde, Manuel Ulloa and Arias Stella have all stated that they kept the British Ambassador in Lima, Charles Wallace, fully informed hour by hour and were certain that he was reporting back to London. And yet, according to Mrs Thatcher, he made no contact until 2am on 3 May.

It was not for six hours after the War Cabinet at Chequers had granted Lord Lewin's request for a change in the rules of engagement in order to sink the *Belgrano* that Commander Wreford-Brown received the order to attack. Why was the order not sent at once? During the six-hour delay, the old cruiser moved perhaps 70 miles (112 kilometres) further away from the Task Force and then suddenly, without warning, she was sunk. The result was to scupper the Peruvian peace plans and so bring on the Falklands War. Why did the War Cabinet not know of these plans? Was there really any justification for sinking the *Belgrano* — and, if so; what? The constantly changing official stories, the conflicting accounts and the air of secrecy can only add to doubts. Many questions remain unanswered 'in the interests of national security', many more have simply been avoided. The truth behind the attack on the *General Belgrano* has yet to be revealed. And for 368 Argentine sailors, the truth no longer matters.

DEATH OF A PLUTONIUM WORKER

In rural Oklahoma on the evening of 13 November 1974 28-year-old plutonium worker Karen Silkwood died when the car she was driving veered off the road and crashed into a concrete culvert. She was on her way to a meeting with a reporter from the *New York Times* to discuss safety issues at the plutonium plant where she worked as a laboratory analyst. Despite court cases and lengthy investigations, the cause of the crash has not yet been explained. In the last few months of her life Silkwood had become increasingly involved in union activities, complaining of health and safety risks at the plant. Only days before she died she had been seriously contaminated with plutonium and was worried about the consequences. How had she become contaminated? And why did her car crash? *IRENE MATTHEWS* presents the facts and theories and seeks some answers

AT 7pm on Wednesday 13 November 1974 Karen Silkwood left a union meeting at the Hub Cafe in Crescent, Oklahoma, to drive to the Holiday Inn in Oklahoma City – 30 miles (48 kilometres) away – for a rendezvous with a *New York Times* reporter to discuss safety at the Kerr-McGee plutonium plant where she worked as a laboratory analyst. It was a cold, dry evening with a light wind blowing; it was dark. Karen got into her white 1973 Honda Civic and drove along Highway 74 south towards Oklahoma City, across the Cimarron River and past the plant.

The road was virtually straight, passing through flat farmland. About 7 miles (11 kilometres) from the Hub Cafe, her car veered across the road and on to the grass verge on the left hand side. After travelling 80 yards (73 metres), it crashed into a concrete culvert running under the highway, hitting the wall at about 45mph. The car ended up on its left side. Truck driver James Mullins spotted the white Honda at about 7.30pm and stopped to investigate. He noticed some papers strewn on the ground by the car. In the driver's seat was a young woman, the blood on her face partly dried. She was dead. The previous day Silkwood had undergone tests for contamination and was found to have plutonium in her lungs. There are two major questions unanswered in the Karen Silkwood case: how did she become contaminated, and how did she die?

Karen Silkwood had never intended to become a martyr for the anti-nuclear cause. But evidence that emerged in the aftermath of her death has turned her case into a wide-reaching campaign. Various theories as to the cause of her death have been put forward, but the exact reasons for the fatal car crash remain a mystery.

Silkwood joined Kerr-McGee as a laboratory analyst in 1972 and worked at the company's plutonium plant on the Cimarron River in Oklahoma. Kerr-McGee manufactured fuel rods, containing plutonium pellets, to be used in fast-breeder reactors. Silkwood performed quality-control tests on the plutonium pellets and checked the fuel rods for flaws.

It seems that the dangers of handling plutonium were not at that time fully realised and the risk of contamination at the plant was high. Dr Donald Geesaman, a nuclear physicist who visited the plant, later commented: 'We had been led to believe that, somehow, in the nuclear age, accidents would be impossible because everything would be handled by a nuclear priesthood, who would be so absolute in their perfection that they would be able to handle this unforgiving fuel cycle. Then you go down to Oklahoma and what do you find? A bunch of high-school kids. . . . It's mind-boggling.' It has been said that teenagers were employed as cheap labour at the plant; training and information about health and safety were minimal; and workers were frequently found to be contaminated, or 'hot', having then to undergo brutal and painful 'scrubdown' treatment using harsh detergents.

Initially Silkwood was not particularly active in the union – the Oil, Chemical and Atomic Workers Union (OCAW) – which she joined soon after she started work at the plant. She had taken part in a small and ineffectual strike several months after she joined the company; the

Left: Karen Silkwood shortly before her death in 1974. Her friends said she was a carefree, fun-loving young woman and a loyal friend. Her detractors branded her as an emotionally unstable, drug-taking hippie. Her purse was found at the scene of her fatal car crash; it contained two marijuana cigarettes. Previous page: Silkwood supporters putting up a memorial sign at the scene of the fatal accident after the court case. Below: a publicity poster for the film Silkwood, *which starred Meryl Streep*

union was demanding higher wages, better training and improved health and safety programmes. But Karen later began to grow concerned about safety at the plant. In 1973 an accident with plutonium-contaminated waste caused seven workers to inhale 400 times the weekly limit of insoluble plutonium permitted by the Atomic Energy Commission (AEC). The laboratory in which Silkwood worked was considered a trouble spot by the company; there was talk of workers contaminating themselves, daring one another to 'get hot'. On one occasion the laboratory in which Silkwood worked had to be closed for three days after a

Below: the concrete culvert off Highway 74 in Oklahoma. After veering off the road, Karen Silkwood's car travelled along the grass verge and hurtled over the culvert, crashing into the concrete wall on the other side. The accident occurred less than two miles from the Cimarron plant where Karen worked as a laboratory analyst, checking plutonium pellets. Right: Karen's white 1973 Honda Civic after the fatal crash. The car had been fitted with special tyres for extra traction and a large white racing mirror. Her boyfriend Drew Stephens had taught her various road-handling techniques and she had taken part in women's car racing

contamination — this happened to be just before a holiday break. Silkwood herself was branded a trouble-maker — not only by her employers but by many of her fellow-workers, too. They feared she was rocking the boat and were worried about the possible loss of jobs if this resulted in the plant shutting down.

On another occasion Silkwood was found to be contaminated; the circumstances made the company suspicious. On 31 July 1974 she had been working a shift in the laboratory, checking plutonium pellets. After she had left, health physics technicians checked the air-sample filters for the three shifts that day and discovered that the filters used before and after Silkwood's shift were clean, while those used during it were highly contaminated. This puzzled them. Tests for radiation were carried out on Silkwood and the two other workers on that shift and only Silkwood proved to be contaminated. The source of the contamination was never discovered. It has been argued that Silkwood might have tampered with the filters herself.

A week later Silkwood was elected to the union bargaining committee; her concern was health and safety. The OCAW had fought hard for the health and safety of oil and chemical workers and now it decided to lodge complaints with the AEC about conditions at the plutonium plant. The AEC had been set up by Congress in 1946 with the dual role of stimulating uranium production and at the same time regulating the development of atomic energy. The union officials at the Cimarron plant were told to make studies and document incidents ready for a meeting with the AEC. Karen Silkwood took her role very seriously and began making notes on contamination incidents, asking questions of health technicians and interviewing workers. The meeting was arranged for September. In August, however, a drive began to decertify the OCAW as a representative body for the workers at the Kerr-McGee plant. There was to be a vote on the issue on 16 October. The union membership was at an all-time low at the plant, but without the union there would be no means of fighting for better conditions of work, argued the OCAW. It was necessary to canvass for votes.

The three-person union committee — Silkwood, Jack Tice and Jerry Brewer — left for Washington on 26 September. There they met top union officials, including Tony Mazzocchi and his assistant Steve Wodka, and took a catalogue of complaints to the AEC. The delegation accused Kerr-McGee of failing to keep levels of exposure to plutonium to a safe level, failing to monitor worker exposure and failing to educate and train workers adequately. It cited 39 cases to illustrate the allegations. The AEC decided to investigate.

There was talk of workers contaminating themselves, daring one another to 'get hot'

In a move to convince workers at the plant that the union was necessary to protect their safety, two experts were invited to a union meeting to talk about the dangers of plutonium and the health risks involved. The week before the vote, two nuclear scientists — Dean Abrahamson and Donald Geesaman — told the workers that plutonium was one of the deadliest substances in the world and caused cancer, and that the AEC 'safe' standards were inadequate. The union won its battle and contract negotiations began on 6 November. Meanwhile Karen Silkwood was preoccupied

Left: Karen Silkwood's graduation photograph, taken in 1964. Above: Karen with her three children – Beverly, Dawn and Michael

Small-town girl

Karen Gay Silkwood was born in Longview, Texas, on 19 February 1946 and grew up among the oil refineries of Texas. Her father, Bill, was a local paint contractor. She played the flute in the school band and received exceptionally good grades in science. She won a scholarship to study medical technology at Lamar College, Beaumont, graduating with honours in 1964. The following year she went to live with graduate Bill Meadows and had three children – Beverly, Michael and Dawn – during the next seven years.

Eventually Karen decided to leave Bill in 1972. He won custody of the children. After her death there were rumours that Silkwood had heartlessly abandoned her children, but friends said she suffered a great deal of heartache at having to give them up.

When Karen heard that the Kerr-McGee Corporation was opening a plutonium plant in Crescent, Oklahoma, she was excited by the prospect of working in the expanding new field of nuclear power. She started work as a laboratory analyst in August 1972 at the Cimarron plant. She formed a relationship with her fellow-worker Drew Stephens. His hobby was motor racing and Drew taught Karen many of the road-handling techniques he had learnt. She took part in women's races and won a trophy in one of them.

Drew helped her select a new car – a white Honda Civic – and had it fitted with special tyres for extra traction and a large white racing mirror. This was the car in which she had her fatal crash on her way to Oklahoma City in November 1974.

with a secret mission.

After the meeting with the AEC, she had told Mazzocchi that she suspected quality-controllers at the plant of touching up photographs of fuel rods to cover up flaws. She claimed that faults showing up on negatives were being painted out. Scientists disagree on what the consequences of a defective fuel rod in a reactor might be, but some say leaking fuel rods could cause a serious explosion. Mazzocchi realised the union could have a trump card in its hand with this one – but concrete evidence was needed before the story could be leaked to a national newspaper. Such publicity would give the union a strong bargaining position with Kerr-McGee. Silkwood was to provide evidence for a meeting with *New York Times* reporter David Burnham on 13 November. The story could then appear in the paper before the contract between the union and the management at the plant expired on 1 December.

The right sleeve and shoulder of her overalls showed a contamination level forty times higher than the AEC safe limit

Perhaps Silkwood did not fully realise the task she had taken on and the difficulties she faced in obtaining the relevant information. But the strain was showing in her – her fears about conditions at the plant, her worry over her own health, the resistance from her colleagues, and the pressure on her to supply the union with evidence to back up her claims. The more she investigated, the more anxious she became. She told a friend, former Cimarron worker James Noel, that she believed that 40 pounds (18 kilograms) of plutonium – enough to make three atomic bombs – had gone missing from the plant. In fact, 24 pounds (10·8 kilograms) of this was in 'hold-up' – the amount held in pipes at the plant. But the rest was unaccounted for. Silkwood lost weight, slept badly and made hysterical telephone calls to her family saying she was planning to quit her job as soon as her task was finished. She was taking sleeping pills prescribed by her doctor. He had given her Quaalude – a sleeping pill to be taken before bed. If used more than this, the user can build up a tolerance and the effect is therefore lessened. Silkwood had started taking Quaalude in May 1974 but by November she was using it as a tranquilliser, perhaps taking two pills a day.

Below: Meryl Streep as laboratory analyst Karen Silkwood in the 1983 film Silkwood. *The still shows Silkwood studying negatives of fuel rods at the plant to determine whether quality-controllers had been 'doctoring' the photographs to cover up flaws*

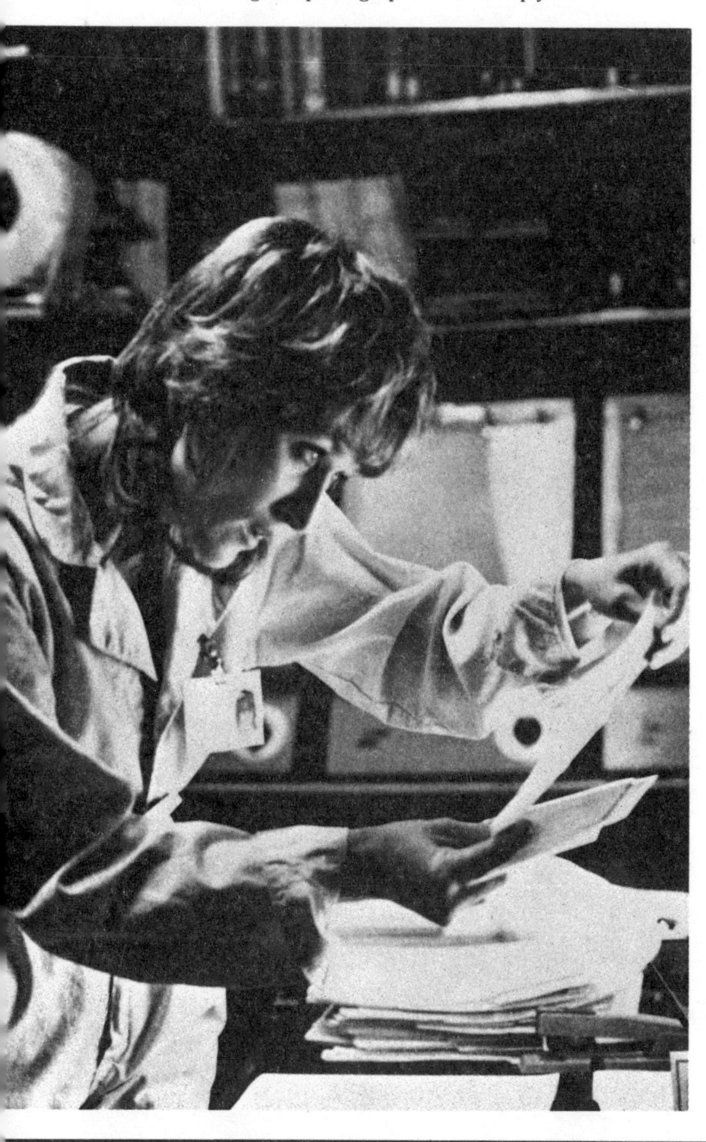

On 31 October Silkwood had a minor road accident. She swerved off the road and down an embankment, she said, to avoid hitting a cow. The right side of her front bumper was dented and the right rear lights smashed, but no damage to the *left* side of her car was recorded. Five days later Silkwood was again found to be contaminated. She had been checking plutonium pellets, handling them with thick protective gloves. When she left the laboratory the monitor began to click as she placed her hands over it. The right sleeve and shoulder of her overalls showed a contamination level forty times higher than the AEC safe limit. Her nasal smear showed a high level of contamination, too, yet the air in the laboratory did not. Karen was scrubbed down. Next day her right arm was contaminated and her nostrils showed an even higher level of contamination. The following day the levels were alarmingly high. The puzzled health physicists decided to check Silkwood's home and discovered high levels of contamination there. The explanation given for the cause of the contamination was that Silkwood's urine sample (which she was to submit for tests)

Far right: union official Steve Wodka. Silkwood worked with Wodka to gather information about conditions at Kerr-McGee's Cimarron plant. He arranged her meeting with New York Times *reporter David Burnham – but she died on the way there. Below: the tornado-proof headquarters of the Kerr-McGee Corporation in Oklahoma City. The organisation was one of the most powerful energy corporations in the US. Below right: self-starter Robert Kerr. He became a senator in 1948 and ran for the Presidency four years later. Bottom right: Kerr's business partner Dean McGee*

contained plutonium. It has been argued that Silkwood had spiked it herself to embarrass the company, but it has also been shown that the plutonium in question had come from a batch that workers had not been handling for several months.

Karen was terrified; she believed she had plutonium in her lungs and that she was going to get cancer and die. Kerr-McGee agreed to send Silkwood, her boyfriend Drew Stephens and flatmate Sherri Ellis for further examination at the AEC-owned Los Alamos Scientific Laboratory in New Mexico. After two days of tests, Stephens and Ellis were told their results were 'statistically insignificant'. Dr George Voelz informed Silkwood that her tests indicated that she had about eight nanocuries of plutonium in her lungs – half the maximum permissible lung burden stipulated by the AEC. The final results, however, would not be known for about two weeks and the count could, he said, be less than eight – or up to three times as high. Dr Voelz was

Dean McGee

reassuring, but many scientists have questioned whether the AEC safe limits were too lenient and have suggested that the acceptable level might vary depending on the individual. Silkwood was small and frail, asthmatic and a heavy smoker. After her death, scientists disagreed as to whether the amount of plutonium in Silkwood's body could eventually have led to her death.

Silkwood, Stephens and Ellis flew back to Oklahoma City on the evening of Tuesday 12 November. Karen was apparently in good spirits and ready for the important meeting with the *New York Times* reporter the following night.

Next day she attended a bargaining meeting between the union and management as part of the negotiations for a new contract. At 5.30pm she went to a union meeting at the Hub Cafe in the small town of Crescent, about 6 miles (9 kilometres) north of the Cimarron plant. The meeting ended at 7pm. Silkwood had made a brief report on the day's negotiations, but remained fairly subdued. Her colleague Jean Jung said Silkwood was clutching a large brown folder and a notebook. She set off on the familiar road she travelled to and from work nearly every day, through pastures and farmland. Less than 2 miles (3 kilometres) past the Kerr-McGee plant, her car left the road and hit the concrete culvert, and Karen was killed.

Truck driver James Mullins discovered the car at around 7.30 and his boss John Trindle went to a nearby gas station to call the police. Oklahoma Highway Patrol officer Rick Fagen and the Guthrie Fire Department ambulance were on the scene by about 8pm. Silkwood was cut out of the Honda and taken to Logan County Hospital where she was pronounced dead on arrival. Fagen picked up some papers strewn around the car and tossed them into the front seat. In her purse — lying near the car — were two marijuana cigarettes, a pill and half a tablet. Tests later showed that the pill was a sleeping pill and the half-tablet was too small to analyse. The wreck was hauled out of the culvert by garage owner Ted Sebring and one of his employees, Harold Smith. The car knocked against the wall as it was being recovered. Sebring, Smith and Fagen later gave conflicting reports as to whether the Honda was damaged further during the recovery. Such evidence was crucial to the theory that Silkwood's car was forced off the highway — as it left the question of how dents were caused to the left rear end of the car unanswered. Fagen did not find any skid marks on the road surface. With no more evidence than this, Fagen filed an accident report the following day. He concluded that Silkwood, under the influence of drugs and alcohol, had fallen asleep at the wheel.

To other people, this account of Silkwood's death was not satisfactory. The union decided to hire accident investigator Adolphus Pipkin, who examined the wreck — now in Drew Stephens' possession. Pipkin's report, released a month after Silkwood's death, noted that her car had gone off the left side of the road, whereas in other accidents where the driver had fallen asleep, the car had always drifted off to the right, because of the crown on the road surface. He also said the dents in the rear bumper of the Honda were made by something moving from the rear, rather than during

The power game

The powerful Kerr-McGee Corporation started off as a small business venture by an ambitious young self-starter from Oklahoma called Robert Samuel Kerr. Kerr made a bad start, however. At the age of 26, having lost a wife and three babies in childbirth and his grocery business in a fire, he made a fresh start; he married into an oil family and made his first million ten years later.

Kerr had borrowed heavily and taken calculated risks that paid off. In 1937 he brought in Dean A. McGee as a partner to run the Oklahoma wells while Kerr pursued a political career, becoming a senator in 1948. He died suddenly of a heart attack in 1963.

McGee had expanded the oil side of the company, and in 1952 made the shrewd decision to get in on the groundfloor of the nuclear industry. He bought a uranium-mining company, employing Navajo Indians. The uranium plant in Cresent, Oklahoma, opened in 1968. The warehouse-like building was built on a grassy knoll overlooking farmland and the Cimarron River. It manufactured uranium pellets for fuel rods to be supplied to nuclear reactors. The plant had no shortage of cheap labour in this rural area of Oklahoma. The plutonium plant in which Karen Silkwood worked was opened in 1970 on the same site.

By then Kerr-McGee had become one of the biggest energy corporations in the US with interests in gas, oil, coal and uranium. Its headquarters in Oklahoma City stood at 29 storeys — the tallest skyscraper in town.

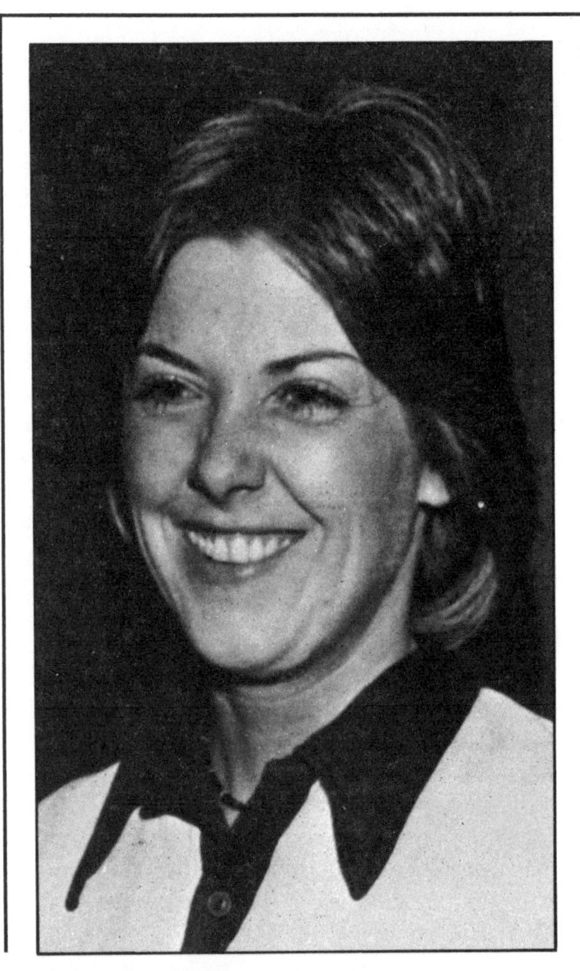

removal, because of the direction of the scratches.

Pipkin had also remarked that the steering wheel of the Honda had been bent forward at the *sides*, indicating that the driver was awake and gripping the wheel with both hands at the time of the accident. If she had been asleep her body would have fallen against the wheel on impact and the pressure would have bent the wheel at the *top* and *bottom* instead. ABC television conducted tests with a car like Silkwood's on the stretch of road where the accident occured. They concluded that if the driver had been asleep, the car would have come to a halt before hitting the concrete culvert. The autopsy on Silkwood concluded that her death was an

Above: a nuclear plant worker handling radioactive material in a sealed case through thick protective gloves. Right: how nuclear fuel rods are used to produce energy in a reactor

The doomsday industry

Nuclear energy is produced by the splitting of atoms, otherwise known as fission. When a certain amount of radioactive material is brought together – a 'critical mass' – the atoms will split in two, emitting an intense burst of heat. The process also emits atomic particles called neutrons, and when these hit another atom, that will split, too, establishing a chain reaction.

In an atomic bomb, this process is uncontrolled; in a reactor, it is harnessed to produce energy. The radioactive material is contained in rods inside the core of the reactor, and a cooling material is circulated around them. The coolant can be gas, as used in the Magnox and AGR (advanced gas-cooled) reactors in the UK, or water, as in the American PWRs (Pressurised Water Reactors). The coolant is heated to great temperatures by the fission taking place in the core of the reactor; it also becomes radioactive, so it is kept in a sealed circuit and used to heat water in another circuit. This drives a steam turbine, which is used to produce electrical energy.

The fuel used to produce the nuclear reactions was originally uranium. This radioactive element occurs naturally and is mined in Canada, the US, Namibia and Australia. Since only a small proportion of uranium atoms are suitable for producing nuclear fission, it

Left: Karen Silkwood's flatmate Sherri Ellis. She had to undergo tests for contamination after plutonium was found in the apartment she shared with Karen. The results were 'statistically insignificant'

accident and that she had a certain amount of methaqualone (sleeping pill) in her body. The union asked the Federal Bureau of Investigation (FBI) to look into the case and the AEC to investigate Silkwood's contamination and health and safety at the plutonium plant.

The FBI investigation concluded five months later that Silkwood's death was accidental and closed the file. The AEC report dealt with three issues: Silkwood's contamination; the OCAW's allegations of falsification of quality-control records at Kerr-McGee; and complaints made by Silkwood, Tice and Brewer about health and safety at the plant. The AEC concluded that Silkwood had been contaminated outside the Cimarron plant and that she had eaten and inhaled plutonium. The plutonium that had contaminated Silkwood's flat had come from pellet lot 29 which had been delivered to Washington in August 1974, apart from a sample kept in a vault at the Kerr-McGee plant. Silkwood had not worked directly with lot 29 nor had she had access to the vault. It was never reported whether any of the sample had gone missing.

On the question of quality-control, the AEC reported that laboratory analyst Scott Dotter had admitted touching up negatives of fuel rods with a felt-tipped pen. He said this was only to cover up flaws in the negatives, not the rods. He had done this without the knowledge or approval of his

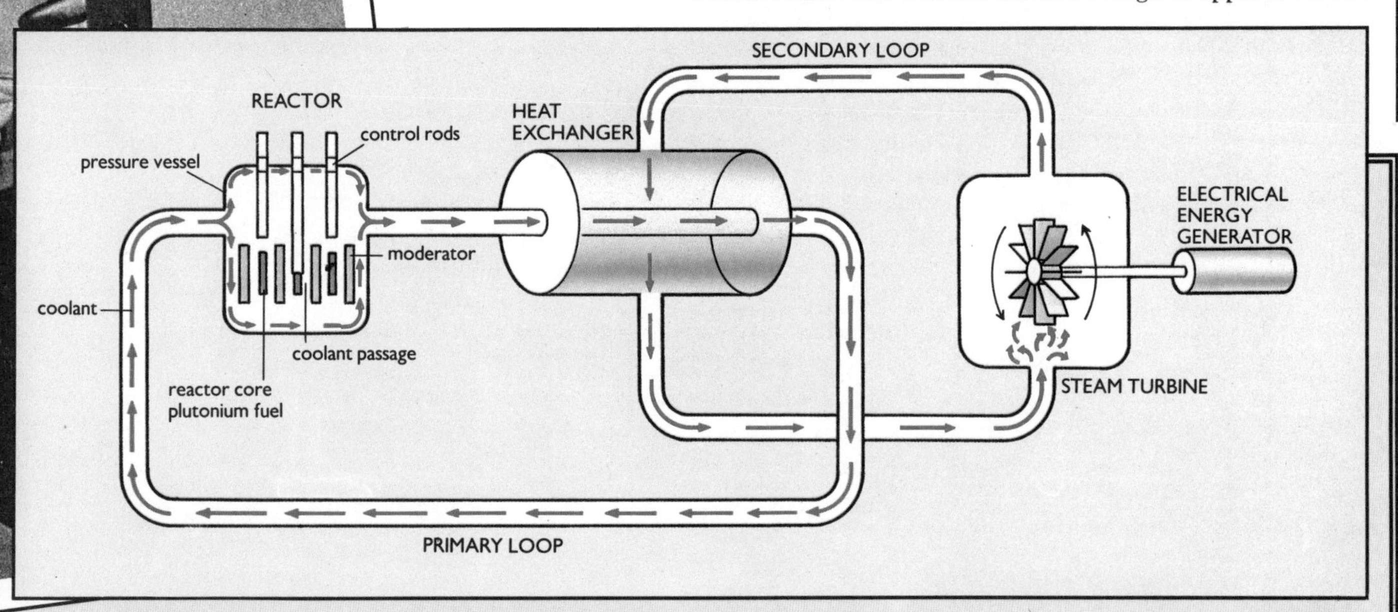

is often enriched first. The fission also produces radioactive waste; one of the elements in this waste is plutonium. Plutonium has long been used for making atom bombs; with the development of 'fast breeder' reactors, like the one at Three Mile Island, it could also be used as nuclear fuel. The waste it produces remains radioactive almost indefinitely and its storage poses immense problems and is the subject of great controversy.

The Cimarron plant where Karen Silkwood worked reprocessed plutonium nitrate from spent nuclear fuel into new fuel pellets. The plutonium nitrate was mixed with uranium; ammonium hydroxide was added, and the mixture was sent cascading down shelves. The radioactive liquid waste was drawn off and dumped underground, while the plutonium and uranium settled as a slimy green mixture. This was then baked dry and moulded into pellets, which were sealed into metal rods – 8 feet (2·4 metres) long and the thickness of a pencil. These fuel rods were then returned, under armed guard, to the reactor at Hanford, Washington.

Plutonium is deadly poisonous, even in minute particles. Once inhaled, it lodges in the bones, lungs, liver and lymph nodes. Plutonium emits alpha particles, which can hit a body cell and kill or damage it so that it begins to malfunction. When a number of cells start to malfunction, cancer can develop.

Below: the apartment Karen shared with her friend Sherri Ellis. Only days before her death health physicists from the plant discovered high levels of contamination at the apartment and removed all its contents in plastic bags. Right: Drew Stephens – Karen's boyfriend and fellow worker at the Cimarron plant. Stephens quit his job at the plant a few months before Karen's death. Below right: Karen's family outside the federal courthouse in Oklahoma City during their legal battle with Kerr-McGee. From left: her mother Merle, sisters Rosemary and Linda, and father Bill Silkwood

superiors. An AEC analysis of the negatives supported Dotter's explanation; it reported that, 'None of the markings was used to obscure weld defects themselves.' It was revealed that Kerr-McGee did sometimes produce flawed fuel rods but, the AEC found, these were all discovered and accounted for. Westinghouse, the buyer, received a total of 19,568 rods from Kerr-McGee. The initial rejection rate for rods was 3·5 per cent, but this eventually came down to 0·54 per cent which, officials said, was considered good. The AEC report did not find serious cause for concern over safety conditions at the plant. Although it substantiated twenty of the thirty-nine allegations put forward by Silkwood, Tice and Brewer, only three of these were found to be violations of the AEC rules, and these, the report said, did not threaten the health and safety of the workers. One of the violations was that Kerr-McGee placed more plutonium in a work area than was safe, given the high criticality of the element.

Kerr-McGee put much of the blame for poor conditions and safety at the plant on the workers themselves. The com-

pany claimed that many of the contaminations were self-inflicted and that there was a drug problem at the plant, with groups of workers smoking marijuana during their breaks. Later Karen Silkwood, in particular, was branded in some circles as a drug-taking, sexually promiscuous hippie who had abandoned her children and become obsessively involved with union activism and paranoid about nuclear hazards.

After Silkwood's death the Kerr-McGee company took vigorous security steps. It closed the plant for two weeks in December as AEC inspectors carried out their investigations. Kerr-McGee closed the Cimarron plant for good in January 1976 claiming that the plant had not been as profitable as the company had wished. The decision came shortly after the Nuclear Regulatory Commission (NRC) had recommended certain improvements be made at the plant.

When the Justice Department dropped the Silkwood case, the National Organisation of Women (NOW) took it up, on the instigation of Kitty Tucker and Sara Nelson. Its aim was to lobby congress to investigate the contamination and death of Silkwood. NOW made Silkwood an honorary member; candlelight parades took place and 13 November was declared Karen Silkwood Memorial Day. Tucker and Nelson formed the Supporters of Silkwood (SOS) organisation and, a year after Silkwood's death, they took a 7000-name petition to congressmen Senator Lee Metcalf and Senator Abraham Ribicoff, who agreed to hold an investigation. In charge of the case would be Win Turner, chief counsel to the Government Operations Subcommittee, John Dingell, the chairman of the House Subcommittee on Energy and Power, and congressional investigator Peter Stockton.

Stockton and Turner gained limited access to the FBI's

Right: Danny Sheehan — chief counsel for the Silkwood estate during the court case against Kerr-McGee — and Sara Nelson, who co-founded the Supporters of Silkwood (SOS) organisation to campaign for justice in the Silkwood case and raise funds for the fight. Bottom right: Karen's father, Bill Silkwood, with lawyer Gerry Spence (left), who took up the Silkwood case. Below: an anti-nuclear power demonstration in America in 1979 includes a banner which reads: 'Remember Karen Silkwood' — linking her death with the anti-nuclear cause

files on Silkwood, but many of their investigations were hampered by red tape. At this point a woman called Jacque Srouji came on to the scene. She said she was writing a book on nuclear power and wanted to include material on the Silkwood case. She claimed to have seen FBI files on Silkwood. The congressional hearings began in April 1976. Srouji's findings reinforced the theory that Silkwood was emotionally unstable and was under the influence of drugs at the time of her death. She suggested that Silkwood had undertaken an important mission when she was physically and mentally unfit to cope with it. Her death had provided a martyr for the union's cause.

The legal complications and political pressures effectively brought the congressional investigation to a halt by the beginning of 1977. But the groundwork had been done and the case had been brought into the limelight enough to keep it alive. The SOS was not going to give up now. The next step was to take the case into the law courts.

The SOS brought in civil rights lawyer Danny Sheehan and filed a civil suit against Kerr-McGee. There were three charges: 1) negligence by Kerr-McGee in the handling of plutonium that contaminated Silkwood; 2) conspiracy by 23 members of the Kerr-McGee Corporation to deprive Silkwood of her civil rights: for instance, trying to prevent Silkwood and others from improving conditions at the plant; punishing Silkwood, Tice and Brewer for complaining to

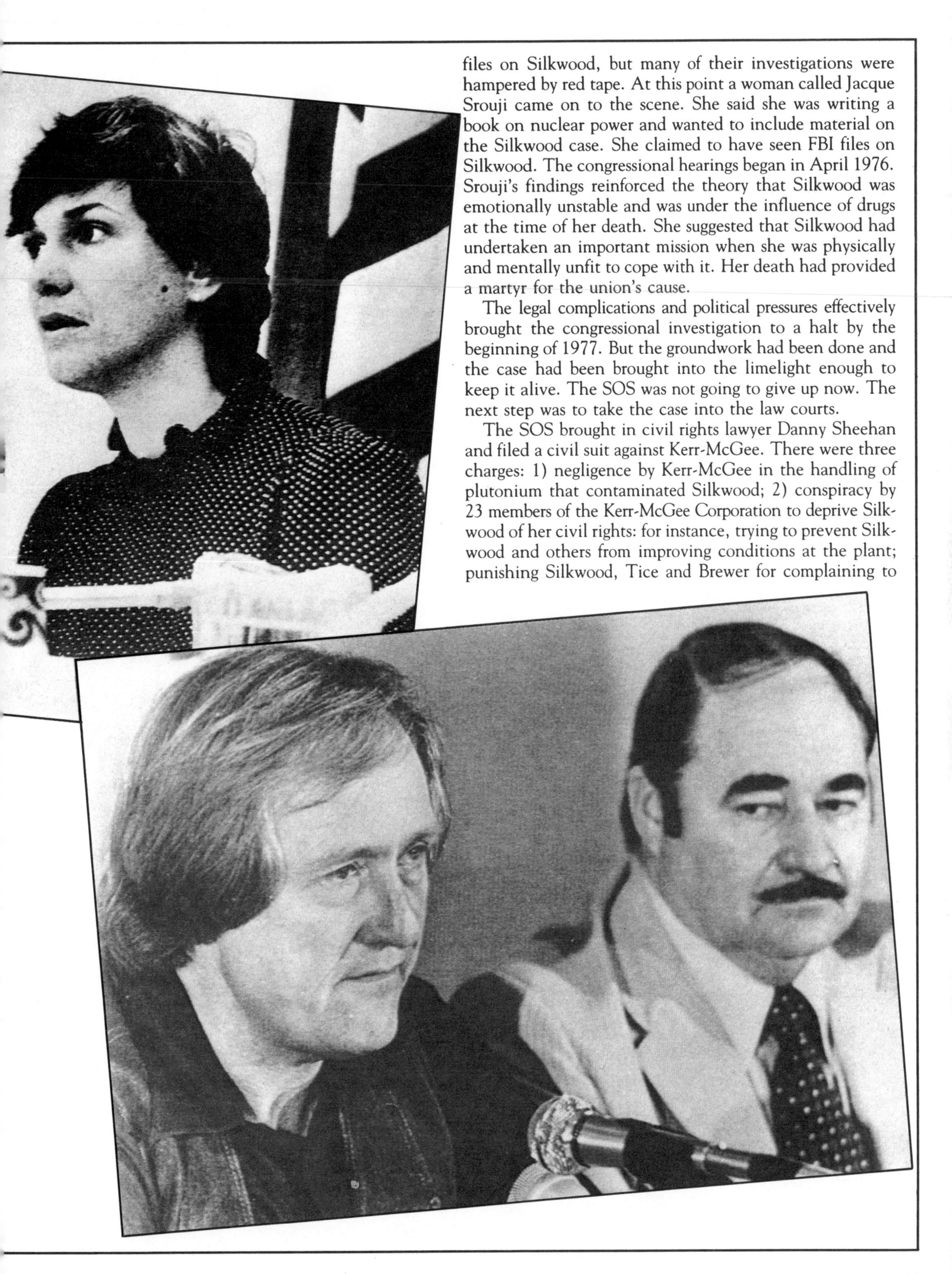

Nuclear power: the accident record

Below: radioactive steam escaping from the Ginna nuclear power plant near Rochester, New York State, after an accident in January 1982. Warning lights and bells indicated falling pressure in the reactor and rising radioactivity levels; the cause was probably a ruptured pipe in one of the steam generators – this resulted in safety valves opening and clouds of radioactive steam billowing out into the air. The plant was evacuated and roads from the plant were manned by police checking radiation levels. The situation was brought under control within 33 hours, but officials said it was one of the worst nuclear accidents in the USA since Three Mile Island

The Silkwood case was well under way when, on 28 March 1979, a reporter at the Oklahoma City Courtroom announced a startling piece of news. At the Three Mile Island nuclear plant in Pennsylvania an accident had released radioactivity into the air. The progress of this incident over the next five days assumed the status of a national drama. A hydrogen bubble was detected in the reactor's sealed core; unless it was removed carefully, it could expand and leave the top of the fuel rods out of the water that cooled them, causing them to melt. A 'meltdown' is one of the most serious possible nuclear accidents, in which the core of the reactor becomes a molten radioactive mass that breaks through the walls and buries itself in the earth – the 'China Syndrome'.

The incident was eventually brought under control, but not before a state of emergency had been declared and several thousand people had been evacuated. The radioactive material that escaped would remain in the environment of Pennsylvania for years to come.

The accident galvanised the American anti-nuclear movement – there were demonstrations in Washington, and many leading rock and movie stars lent their support

Right: a scene from the film Silkwood *shows one of Silkwood's colleagues being taken to be 'scrubbed down' after being contaminated by plutonium. The experience was particularly unpleasant and painful, the skin being scrubbed with detergent*

the AEC about conditions at the plant; and allowing surveillance and harassment of Silkwood and others; and 3) violation of Silkwood's civil rights as members of the FBI joined the conspiracy.

Sheehan engaged the help of private investigator Bill Taylor, who claimed to have learnt from an FBI 'mole' that a lot of evidence about the Silkwood case was being covered up and revealed that Silkwood had been under heavy surveillance for some time before her death; he claimed there were transcripts of taped conversations in the Silkwood file. Taylor spent time digging around for clues near the site of the accident, piecing together a picture of the events leading up to the crash. In a nearby disused barn he came across a to the growing campaign. Yet Three Mile Island was by no means the first nuclear accident in the US or elsewhere. In October 1957, at Windscale in Britain, the pile of one of the reactors there overheated during a secret military experiment. Although local reports of an explosion followed by a fire were denied by the UK Atomic Energy Authority, radioactive iodine was released into the air and distributed over an area of 200 square miles (520 square kilometres). The following day, the radio iodine content of milk produced in the area was six times the permissible level, and the police were called in to prevent its sale. The reactor was eventually junked and a secret report was sent to Prime Minister Harold MacMillan.

That same year, the world's worst nuclear accident occurred in the Soviet Union, near the town of Kyshtym in the Urals. A massive explosion – the exact cause of which is still the subject of controversy – filled local hospitals with thousands of casualties and contaminated a massive area, which still remains a 'forbidden zone'.

The Rocky Flats nuclear weapons factory in Colorado was the site of two fires in 1957 and 1969, which released plutonium dust into the air. The county health director marked on a map the areas where the wind blew the plutonium, and later found a marked correlation with cancer deaths. There was a near-meltdown at the Fermi reactor near Detroit in 1966, and in 1971 the Monticello reactor in Minnesota discharged 50,000 gallons (190,000 litres) of radioactive liquid into the public water supply. In the aftermath of the Three Mile Island accident, the *New York Times* published details of ten accidents that had occurred between 1975 and 1979 in the US, including the leak of radioactive waste at Hanford in Washington and a fire at Browns Ferry in Alabama.

Windscale in Cumbria continued to be the site of numerous accidents – more than 300 since 1950, in fact. In 1973 the General and Municipal Workers' Union went to court claiming compensation from British Nuclear Fuels Ltd on behalf of 36 contaminated workers. One was suffering from cancer of the bone marrow, another from cataracts on his eyes; both men died before the action came to court, and in September of that year a further 34 workers were contaminated in an accident. In court, contamination was admitted but liability not accepted. In the last quarter of 1978, no less than seventeen incidents were reported at British nuclear installations and in February 1979 there was a fire in Windscale's chemical separation complex.

Windscale, now renamed Sellafield, has been the target of a vigorous public campaign by environmental groups like Greenpeace against the plant's discharging of low-level waste into the Irish Sea, particularly after a Yorkshire Television programme revealed an unusually high level of leukaemia and cancer among local children.

The Silkwood trial itself contributed its own share of horror stories as former Kerr-McGee workers testified about safety levels at the Cimarron plant. In 1972 two maintenance men were sprayed with plutonium when a gasket burst. They had left the plant and eaten lunch at a local cafe before the contamination was discovered; the cafe was never visited or decontaminated. On at least two occasions, while workers with breathing equipment were deep inside storage vessels, their oxygen supply ran out, forcing them to inhale radioactive air. The general conditions at the Cimarron plant were summed up by a former Kerr-McGee health physicist who said in his testimony that 'the contamination was everywhere. . . it was just a battle that was lost'.

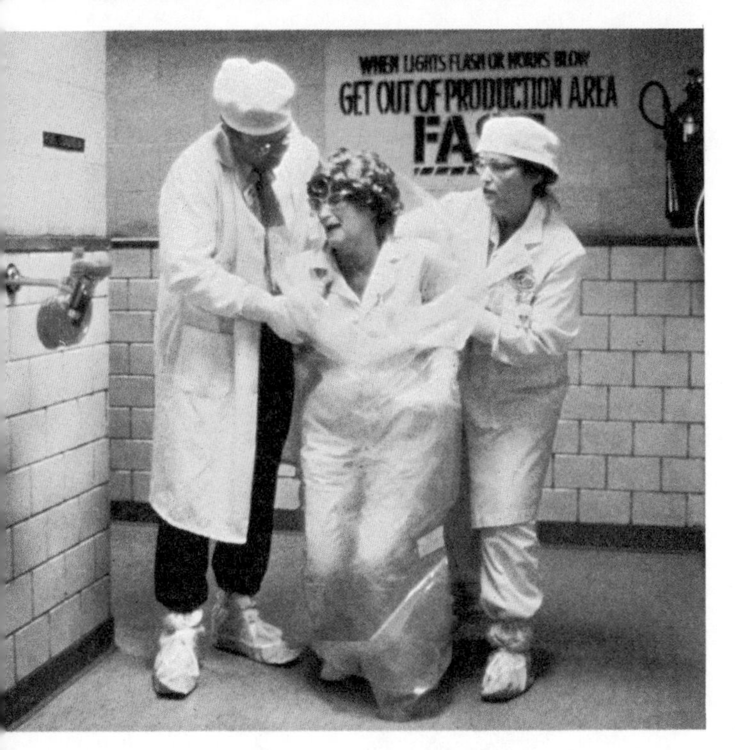

couple of envelopes tucked away on a dusty shelf. They were empty, but both of them bore a Kerr-McGee logo. Taylor suggested that Silkwood might have used the barn as a hiding place for documents she was smuggling out of the Cimarron plant.

Three different judges presided over the court proceedings. The first one – Judge Luther Eubanks – resigned from the case after Sheehan filed an application to have him removed because of remarks he had made in court that threw doubt on his impartiality. The second – Judge Luther Bohanon – was replaced by Judge Frank Theis after Bohanon's connection with Robert Kerr was discovered. Kerr had apparently been instrumental in securing Bohanon his judgeship.

In September 1978 Judge Theis dropped the conspiracy charges against Kerr-McGee and the FBI defendants. Even if, he argued, Sheehan had been able to prove the conspiracy and cover-up, there was no civil law under which the Silkwood estate could sue for damages. He also said that the Civil Rights Act of 1871 – on which Sheehan had based much of his case – only applied to blacks and other minorities. The Silkwood team now concentrated on the negligence charge. The SOS collected $452,000, through loans,

Right: the dent on the rear left side of Silkwood's car. Was this caused during the removal of the wrecked vehicle? Below: three scenes from the film Silkwood, *staring Meryl Streep*

benefits and contributions, to cover the cost of the investigations and trial, and brought in experts to testify about the dangers of plutonium. It decided to press the health and safety angle and steer away from anti-nuclear labels, aiming to hold Kerr-McGee up as a warning to other nuclear plants. Under the Oklahoma law of 'strict liability', the owner of a dangerous substance is liable for injury caused by it.

In order to win the case, the Silkwood team had to prove that:

1) Plutonium is 'ultrahazardous'
2) Silkwood had been contaminated with plutonium owned by Kerr-McGee
3) Silkwood did not contaminate herself
4) Contamination had led to personal injury of Silkwood between 5 and 13 November
5) Kerr-McGee was wantonly negligent in protecting its workers.

The claim was for \$1·5 million compensation for Silkwood's physical injury and emotional pain and \$10 million damages as punishment to Kerr-McGee. After expenses the money would go to Silkwood's three children. The trial – Oklahoma's longest – began in March 1979 and lasted ten weeks. Nuclear physicist and medical doctor John Gofman explained the link between plutonium and cancer and attacked the AEC and NCR safe limits. He was alarmed that Kerr-McGee had failed to inform staff at the plant of the dangers involved in working with plutonium, at the lack of training and the inadequate security there. Former health physics technician Kenneth Plowman said there was one contamination after another, pellets were thrown around and bags of waste hidden when the AEC inspectors visited the plant. Former Kerr-McGee worker Ron Hammock testified that faulty welds were ground down with sandpaper to make them look acceptable.

The Silkwood team won the case and the trial set certain precedents: Judge Theis defined plutonium as 'ultrahazardous' and defined injury in radiation cases ('injury' could be to cells, bone or tissue and may not be immediately visible or

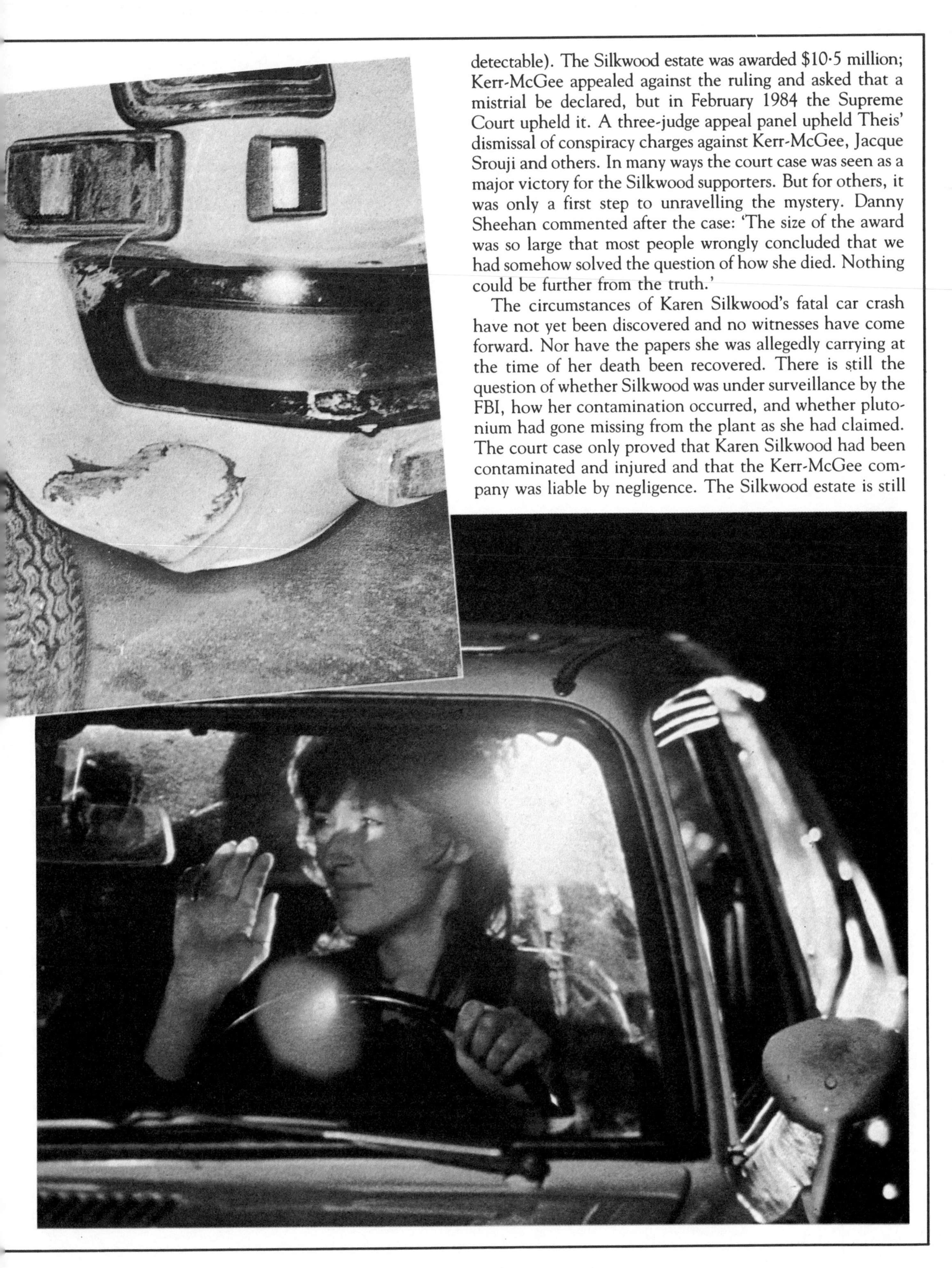

detectable). The Silkwood estate was awarded $10·5 million; Kerr-McGee appealed against the ruling and asked that a mistrial be declared, but in February 1984 the Supreme Court upheld it. A three-judge appeal panel upheld Theis' dismissal of conspiracy charges against Kerr-McGee, Jacque Srouji and others. In many ways the court case was seen as a major victory for the Silkwood supporters. But for others, it was only a first step to unravelling the mystery. Danny Sheehan commented after the case: 'The size of the award was so large that most people wrongly concluded that we had somehow solved the question of how she died. Nothing could be further from the truth.'

The circumstances of Karen Silkwood's fatal car crash have not yet been discovered and no witnesses have come forward. Nor have the papers she was allegedly carrying at the time of her death been recovered. There is still the question of whether Silkwood was under surveillance by the FBI, how her contamination occurred, and whether plutonium had gone missing from the plant as she had claimed. The court case only proved that Karen Silkwood had been contaminated and injured and that the Kerr-McGee company was liable by negligence. The Silkwood estate is still fighting to bring the conspiracy charges to court.

Bill Taylor for one was not satisfied that the case was closed. He has had no concrete evidence to go on, only theories and hunches. Taylor has continued his search to uncover fresh clues, often returning to the scene of Silkwood's death. One important lead strengthened his belief. He claimed that his source at the FBI had leaked information about the top secret Silkwood file. In it, he alleged, was an account of Silkwood's car crash. If such information were ever to come to light in detail, the investigation into the Silkwood case would have a fresh start and the truth about the tragic affair might eventually be revealed. But for now the events surrounding the death of plutonium worker Karen Silkwood remain a mystery.

Below: Bill Silkwood (centre), father of Karen Silkwood, faces a crowd of reporters outside the Supreme Court in Washington on 5 October 1983 as he arrives to continue the battle to win damages following his daughter's death. An award of $10·5 million was eventually made to the Silkwood estate and upheld by the Supreme Court, despite an appeal against the decision by Karen's employers, Kerr-McGee

THE ONE THAT GOT AWAY

This is the face of the fugitive Earl of Lucan, the gambling aristocrat whom friends knew as 'Lucky'. On the night of 7 November 1974 his children's nanny was beaten to death and his estranged wife brutally assaulted at the Lucans' elegant home in the heart of London's Belgravia. As the first police detectives arrived on the scene of the crimes, Lord Lucan disappeared – apparently into thin air. A coroner's jury found the earl guilty of murder, and his mysterious behaviour, both before and after the crime, points to his guilt. Yet the missing Lucan has never returned to face trial. Where is he now? Is he, even, still alive? *JOHN PENROSE* probes one of the most baffling murder mysteries of modern times

Above: the society wedding of Lord Richard John Bingham and Veronica Duncan on 28 November 1963. Initially the couple were happy, but it was a match of conflicting backgrounds. Lucan, born in 1934, came from a wealthy family of landowners and politicians, and in January 1964 inherited the Lucan title and the family fortune. Veronica, born in 1937, was a major's daughter who attended art college and did modelling. She was a person much more in tune with her time than her husband, who was an anachronistic figure, Edwardian in dress and manner. Below, far right: the innocent victim, Sandra Rivett, nanny to the Lucans' three children. She might not have died had she taken her usual Thursday night off. Above, far right: the United States mail bag in which her battered body was found

'Help me, help me . . . I've just escaped from a murderer . . . he's murdered the nanny'

IT was a cold, wet Thursday night in November when Lady Veronica Lucan ran from her Belgravia home to tell the assembled drinkers at The Plumbers' Arms of the murder she had just discovered. Wearing a rain-soaked dress, no shoes and with blood pouring from a deep wound above her face, she burst into the small pub lounge shouting: 'Help me, help me . . . I've just escaped from a murderer . . . my children, my children . . . he's in the house . . . he's murdered the nanny . . . .' Head barman Arthur Whitehouse helped her to a bench seat and laid her down while his wife brought damp towels to help stop the bleeding. The landlord telephoned for the police. They arrived within minutes and an ambulance took Lady Lucan to St George's Hospital at Hyde Park Corner. Two officers had meanwhile forced entry to the Lucan family home, an expensive five-storey Georgian house at 46 Lower Belgrave Street.

The lower half of the house was silent and in darkness. Police Sergeant Donald Baker shone his flashlight down the narrow hallway and discovered, at the far end by the stairs leading to the basement, what appeared to be bloodstains on the wallpaper. Cautiously, the two policemen made their way along the passage until they reached the top of the stairs, which led to a half-landing. There, beside a door leading to a breakfast room, they saw a pool of blood in which two or three footprints were evident. The officers began a search of the other floors. On the second floor they found the first light burning in the house, and in one of the bedrooms, on the pillow of a double bed, lay a bloodstained towel. On the top floor Baker found two children, a boy aged seven and a girl aged four, asleep in a nursery. He opened another door and saw ten-year-old Lady Frances Lucan, dressed in pyjamas and looking wide awake and bewildered. After comforting the child, he returned to the basement. There, on the floor, he discovered a large canvas mailbag. Inside it was the battered body of the children's dead nanny.

Baker had uncovered the victim of a murder that was to become one of the must curious mysteries in British criminal history. No one has stood trial for the nanny's murder and the seventh Earl of Lucan, Richard John Bingham, has not been seen since that night.

Thirty minutes after the alarm was raised, Detective Sergeant Graham Forsythe, who was eventually to become Lady Lucan's bodyguard, found the bloodstained murder weapon on the half-landing. It was a nine-inch (23-centimetre) piece of lead piping, weighing 2¼ pounds (1 kilogram) and wrapped in adhesive medical tape. The carpet, walls and ceiling at the head of the stairs were bloodstained, and down by the door leading to the kitchen lay some broken cups and saucers in a pool of blood, presumably dropped by the nanny as the attacker struck. Lying on a chair was an electric light bulb that appeared to have been removed from its socket in the ceiling.

Lady Frances, the eldest child, told Forsythe that she had been watching television with her mother in the main bedroom when their nanny, Sandra Rivett, offered to make a cup of tea. After about 20 minutes, Sandra having failed to return, Lady Lucan had gone down to the basement. Lady Frances had then heard a scream, but thought her mother had been scratched by Snooty, their cat. She continued to watch television until her mother, with blood on her face, returned to the bedroom accompanied by her father. She was told to turn off the television and go up to bed. She had not seen either of her parents since.

Forsythe reasoned that the body in the bag was that of Sandra Rivett, and with Lady Lucan lying semi-conscious in hospital he needed, above all, to talk to Lord Lucan. The peer owned a mews house at 5 Eaton Row, near the rear of the Lucan family home. Just after 11pm Forsythe checked the two-storey house, but found it empty. Then, he returned to Lower Belgrave Street. At the family house forensic scientists had begun their work. Lucan's mother, the Dowager Countess of Lucan, had arrived too. After Forsythe had explained the night's events to her, the Dowager Countess said that Lucan had just telephoned and asked her to go to the house.

She said that Lucan had told her that there had been a 'terrible catastrophe' at the house and that his wife Veronica was hurt and the nanny injured. He had asked her to collect the children. She told Forsythe that her son had said he was passing the house when he spotted someone attacking his wife. He had gone into the house, where his wife was screaming and shouting. Her son sounded shocked, said the Dowager Countess, and rang off without saying from where he was calling. The call came neither from a call-box nor through an operator.

Lucan's mother then gave police the first indication that there were problems in the relationship between her son and his wife. The couple, she told Forsythe, were separated and

Above right: Belgravia — the scene of events on the night of Sandra Rivett's murder. Above, far right: the Lucan family home where the nanny was killed. Above: Lady Lucan ran the thirty yards from the house to raise the alarm in this pub. Below: the Lucans' mews house in Eaton Row; a police search there revealed no trace of the missing earl. Below, far right: the men who followed Lucan's trail, Detective Chief Superintendent Roy Ranson (right) with Detective Chief Inspector David Gerring

her son did not live at the family house; the children had been made wards of court.

Next, Forsythe checked Lucan's flat at 72a Elizabeth Street, just 300 yards (250 metres) from the family home. Parked outside was the earl's two-year-old Mercedes. Inside, there were signs that Lucan had expected to return that evening. A suit was carefully laid out on the bed, and on a bedside table were his spectacles, the contents of his pockets, cheque book, small change and car keys. His passport was in a drawer.

Shortly after midnight Lucan again telephoned his mother; he asked about the children, and she told him they were safe. Then she said, 'Well, look, the police are here. Do you want to speak to them?' Lucan replied, 'I will ring them in the morning. And I will ring you.' But before the police officer standing next to the Dowager Countess could take the receiver from her hand, Lucan rang off.

Meanwhile, Detective Chief Superintendent Roy Ranson, head of A Division CID, which covers the Belgravia area, was contacted by his deputy, Detective Chief Inspector David Gerring, who informed him of the details of the nanny's death. Ranson had no reason, then, to suspect that Lord Lucan would not contact him. The suspicion that Lucan was the murderer had not yet formed in his mind. At this stage, the police were still treating seriously the story that Lucan had told his mother, that he had interrupted a fight. As a precaution, an alert was sent to ports and airports that Lucan should be stopped if he tried to leave the country.

But by Friday morning no call from Lucan had been received, although Lady Lucan had recovered sufficiently to give doctors and nurses a mumbled account of the events of the night. This gave Ranson his first firm indication that Lucan was his prime suspect.

Lady Lucan told police a similar story to that given by her daughter, Frances. The curious difference was that she said that everything had happened twenty minutes later than her daughter had estimated. Lady Frances could support her version of the events by the timing of the *Nine O'Clock News* on BBC television. If Lady Frances' story is correct, Lady Lucan could have spent up to forty minutes with her husband before raising the alarm.

Lady Lucan told the police that when she had gone to look for the nanny, she found the half-landing above the kitchen in darkness. She called out Sandra's name, but there was no reply. Then she heard a sound in the cloakroom behind her, and a man leapt out, striking her with a heavy weapon. She screamed and they fought, but her attacker tried to thrust gloved fingers down her throat and gouge out her eyes. After he had forced her to the ground, she grabbed him by the genitals and he let go. Her attacker, she said, was her husband. She had recognised his voice in the dark. According to Lady Lucan, he told her he had killed the nanny in mistake for her. Lady Lucan told detectives that she calmed her husband by offering to help him. They went upstairs to the bedroom where she lay on the bed and her husband went to soak some towels in the bathroom to bathe her wounds. When she heard the taps running she ran from the bedroom and out to the public house.

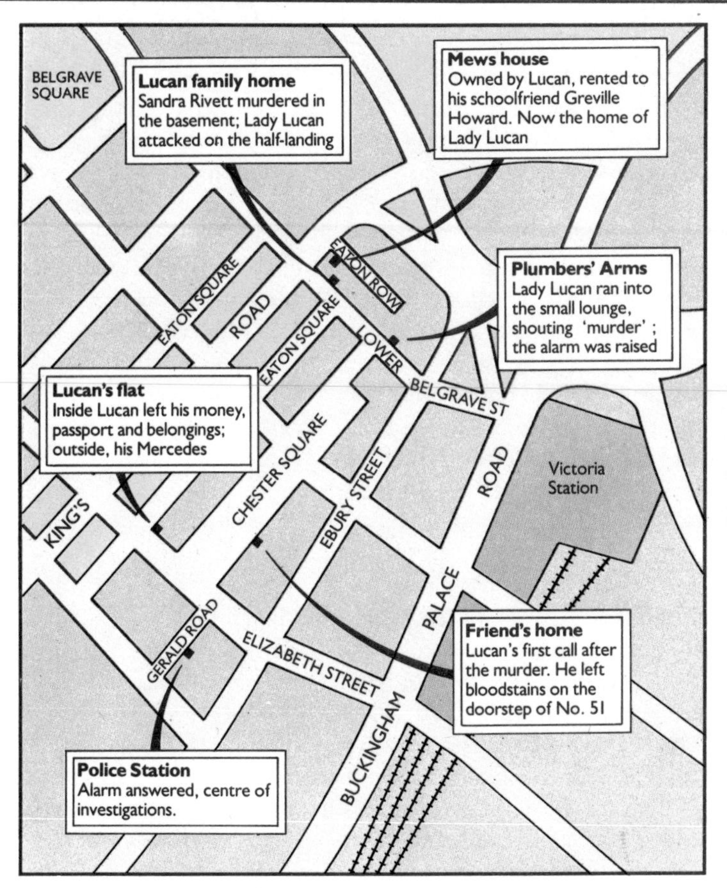

Ranson realised that without the testimony of the earl, the scientific evidence would be vital. The autopsy on Sandra Rivett, conducted by the distinguished pathologist Professor Keith Simpson, suggested that she had been attacked with considerable force by someone using a blunt instrument, almost certainly the lead pipe. She had died from bruising to the brain. Lady Lucan's injuries, he concluded, were probably caused by the same weapon.

In the meantime Ranson began gathering information about the victims and the possible killer. He discovered that Sandra Rivett came from a working-class background in Basingstoke, Hampshire. She was the 29-year-old mother of a small child and had separated from her husband, Roger, a security guard at Gatwick airport, in April the year before. Sandra was described by her family as a 'vivacious girl, always laughing', who had loved her job. She had worked for Lady Lucan for only five weeks, living in and being paid £25 a week to look after the three children. Ranson could discover no motive for her murder and wondered whether her death could have been a case of mistaken identity.

He learned that Sandra, although plumper, was the same height – 5 feet 2 inches (1·58 metres) – as Lady Lucan. More significantly, he discovered that she had a boyfriend, John Haskins, who was a relief barman at The Plumbers' Arms, where Lady Lucan had first sought help. Sandra's night off each week was usually Thursday, but that week she had taken Wednesday off instead to go out with Haskins. Perhaps, Ranson reasoned, Sandra's killer had gone to the house expecting only Lady Lucan to be there on a Thursday night. When he discovered that Lord Lucan had questioned

Above: Lucan in the army bobsleigh team at St Moritz. Lucan spent most of his leisure time in the company of men. One friend told how the earl sometimes became embarrassed when with women – 'He didn't really like women, or sex. I think he saw women as an inferior race.' Lucan was extreme in other views. He was devoutly right-wing and feared Britain was facing a class revolution. Below: on 8 June 1975 the Sunday Times *featured Lucan's aristocratic youth, his touring holidays and his sporting interests*

his daughter Camilla about the nanny's night off, the suspicion grew in Ranson's mind that Lucan was the killer.

Ranson found his suspect's background full of surprises. On the face of it the family was comfortably off, with a grand house in Belgravia, a second home, a live-in nanny, a Mercedes and all the other trappings of wealth. Gradually Ranson was to discover that Lord and Lady Lucan were far from happy, that they lived apart and that there had been an acrimonious court battle over the custody of the children, who had been made wards of court. The wealth was an illusion, too, as the house was owned by a family trust, Lucan's flat was rented and he was in arrears with the rent.

Ranson gathered his information slowly from the insular and deeply loyal circle who surrounded Lucan. However, he was experienced in dealing with the aristocracy. He had worked in Belgravia for many years and had dealt successfully with the kidnap attempt on Princess Anne earlier in 1974. Yet a reporter for *The Times* noted after the murder that the detectives 'had found themselves in a social milieu to which they were unaccustomed'.

One instance of this high-society life-style was the Lucans' courtship. Veronica Duncan first met Lucan when she was bridesmaid for her sister, Christina, at her wedding to Lucan's friend, the millionaire amateur jockey Bill Shand Kydd, at Holy Trinity, Brompton, London, in January 1963. In the spring of that year, Veronica stayed with her sister and new brother-in-law at their country estate in Bedfordshire. There Veronica again met the dashing Lord Lucan. A whirlwind courtship ensued that summer, and by autumn Lucan had bought a ring from Cartier's and announced their engagement in *The Times* of 14 October 1963.

The family circle An album of pictures covering the Lucan years from 1952 when he left Eton, via the tradition

Lucan (then Lord Bingham) with his Aston Martin at the Grand Canyon

Lucan at 18, boating in the Mediterranean soon after leaving Eton

On 28 November Veronica returned to Holy Trinity for her own wedding. In January 1964, Lucan's father died; he succeeded to the title and inherited a fortune, estimated at £250,000, which included family estates in Ireland, land in England and the family silver. Veronica became the Countess of Lucan. The couple bought 46 Lower Belgrave Street for £19,000 and moved in to begin a smart life of society parties and touring holidays. In October Veronica gave birth to their first daughter, Frances. Lord George Bingham was born in 1967, and three years later a second daughter, Camilla, was born.

At this stage, Lucan appeared to be financially secure. There was cash in a Rhodesian bank account, more in Berne in Switzerland and in Nassau in the Bahamas. It was a time of exchange control and these accounts abroad were used for holidays and gambling trips. His gaming skills were improving and one considerable win at chemmy earned him the nickname 'Lucky'. He would spend his afternoons and evenings at the Clermont Club in Berkeley Square, playing backgammon for high stakes; he might lose or win £5000 a day.

In the early years of his marriage Lucan was known as a perfectly charming English gentleman. His friends, however, noticed that, in the months leading up to the murder, he became increasingly depressed. Ranson realised that after Lucan had separated from his wife in January 1973, he had become obsessed with the welfare of his children. Two months after the separation, he had snatched two of them as they walked in a park with a nanny. He kept them at his Elizabeth Street flat while he fought and lost a case to gain custody.

The case cost him £40,000 and left him feeling bitter and angry about the legal system. He was already paying for the upkeep of the family home, a £40-a-week allowance to his wife, £25 a week – ordered by a High Court judge – to the nanny and the £50 a week rent and upkeep of his flat. At one stage it is estimated that Lucan was paying up to £400 a week on employing a private detective to watch his wife's home.

His debts were accumulating and his only income – fixed at £7000 a year – was from a family trust. The financial and emotional pressure affected his gambling and he started losing heavily and borrowing to live.

Lucan's decline became more rapid as he faced overdrafts at four banks, with debts running into five figures. He also began falling behind with his rent and payments on his Mercedes. The final ignominy came when he bounced a cheque to the Clermont for £10,000 and the club withdrew his credit facilities for a time.

Increasingly Lucan came to believe that his wife was responsible for all these problems. Secretly he began tape-recording conversations with her. He would play these tapes to his friends in an attempt to demonstrate that she was mentally unstable and unable to look after his children. He also tried to have Lady Lucan committed to a mental institution.

Further evidence of Lord Lucan's deteriorating state came shortly before the cataclysmic night of 7 November, when he confided to a friend, Greville Howard, cousin of the Earl of Suffolk, that he could see no way out of his difficulties. He did not want his son George to see him in court accused of bankruptcy, and the only answer, he said, was to get rid of

The house of Lucan

Above: Veronica Duncan joins the centuries-old heritage of the Lucan family – a portrait from 1964

The Bingham family have enjoyed wealth and privilege since the thirteenth century. All, save the missing earl, have provided valuable public service.

Lord Lucan's father, the sixth earl, and his wife surprised relatives and friends by becoming active supporters of the Labour party. Despite his parents' socialist convictions, however, Lord Lucan was educated in the traditional manner at Eton. After his National Service, he worked in the City for six years – but his passion was for highstakes gambling. In 1960 he became a professional gambler – and began to play to the full the part of the privileged aristocrat.

His wife Veronica's background is very different. She is the daughter of an Army major who died when she was two. Her mother remarried, and the family ran a small hotel at North Waltham in Hampshire.

With such discrepancy in their backgrounds, it is perhaps not surprising that the marriage should have been a stormy one. By the time of the murder, the Lucans were separated, and the children had been made wards of court.

Lord Lucan's heir, Lord George Bingham, is now sixteen years old, but he has not yet become the eighth Earl of Lucan. Lucan still holds the titles Earl of Lucan, Baron Lucan and Baron Bingham.

Perhaps Lucan did not know the nanny had been murdered? Perhaps he was not the killer?

his wife. Howard said it would be far worse for his son to see him in court accused of murder. Lucan said he wouldn't get caught.

By the evening of Friday 8 November, detectives had begun tracing Lucan's movements in the hours immediately before the killing. The night before, 6 November, they learned that he, and forty others, had had dinner with a friend, Selim Zilkha, chairman of the Mothercare chain of stores. On the morning of the murder, he bought a book on Greek shipping millionaires and then went to lunch with friends at the Clermont. After lunch he played some backgammon and then, at about 4pm, he visited a chemist, asking him to identify a pill belonging to his wife; he was told it was a tranquilliser. Later he met Michael Hicks Beach, a literary agent, to discuss a magazine article he was writing on gambling. He drove Hicks Beach home to his flat in Fulham and then, at 8.30pm, telephoned the Clermont.

Lucan spoke to the assistant manager, Andrew Demetrio, and booked a table for four people for dinner at 10.30 pm. About fifteen minutes later he arrived at the Clermont in person. He spoke to the doorman, Billy Edgson, for a few minutes, inquiring whether his friends had arrived, and then drove away. Edgson noticed Lucan was driving his Mercedes. The drive from the Clermont back to Lower Belgrave Street at that time of evening takes about ten minutes. The timing, Ranson reasoned, was perfect if Lucan had been trying to establish an alibi. When Greville Howard and three friends arrived at the Clermont at 10.45pm they told the assistant manager, Demetrio, that Lord Lucan was to be their host. A fifth chair was brought and another place laid for the host, who was never to arrive.

On the morning of Saturday 9 November police searched Belgravia and discovered that Lucan had called on a family friend, Mrs Madeleine Florman, in Chester Square. Her daughter attended the same school as the Lucan girls, and Lucan may have called to ask her to look after his children. She, however, had not answered the door to him. Forensic scientists later found blood on her doorstep. Later that morning, Ranson received a telephone call from Bill Shand Kydd, Lucan's friend, who said that two letters had arrived at his London home. Both of them were postmarked Uckfield, Sussex; Lucan's handwriting was on the envelopes. There was also what appeared to be blood on them. The first read as follows:

> Dear Bill, The most ghastly circumstances arose tonight, which I have described briefly to my mother, when I interrupted the fight at Lower Belgrave Street and the man left.
>
> V. [Veronica] accused me of having hired him. I took her upstairs and sent Frances to bed and tried to clean her up. She lay doggo for a bit. I went into the bathroom and she left the house.
>
> The circumstantial evidence against me is strong in that V. will say it was all my doing and I will lie doggo for a while, but I am only concerned about the children. If you can manage it I would like them to live with you.
>
> V. has demonstrated her hatred for me in the past and would do anything to see me accused.

Friends and relatives. Below: Bill Shand Kydd and his wife Christina, Lady Lucan's sister. The Shand Kydds' wedding was the occasion on which the future Lord and Lady Lucan first met. The runaway earl sent two of his last letters to Bill Shand Kydd, an old and trusted friend. Far right: Ian and Susan Maxwell Scott leaving their mansion home in Uckfield. Their friend Lord Lucan was last seen leaving this doorstep after speaking to Mrs Maxwell Scott on the night of the murder

The Pereira factor

Forensic evidence gathered by the Scotland Yard team convinced Detective Chief Superintendent Ranson that Lucan was the killer of Sandra Rivett.

The most important part of the investigation centred on the identification of the types of blood found in the house and in the Ford Corsair car that Lucan used to make his getaway. The vital work was carried out by Dr Margaret Pereira, principal scientific officer at the Yard's Metropolitan Police Laboratory. She and Dr Lewis Nickolls, a former director of the Yard's forensic science laboratory, made a worldwide breakthrough in blood typing during the early Sixties. They established that the two basic ingredients of blood, proteins and enzymes, had characteristics identifiable in individuals. Governed by genetic factors, these characteristics are present at birth and do not change during life.

Scientists discover most about blood-types when the blood is fresh; the older the bloodstain the less information they can gather. The Nickolls-Pereira test, by making more tests on the proteins and enzymes, enabled greater detail to be gathered from bloodstains than had previously been possible.

Using her methods Dr Pereira established that Sandra Rivett's blood type was of group B and Lady Lucan's was of group A. The blood in the basement of the Lucan house was primarily of group B, while bloodstains on the ground floor were of group A. The adhesive tape on the murder weapon was stained with both blood types. Lady Lucan had a smear of group B blood under a shoe. This could have been caused by the countess walking through the basement.

At the inquest Dr Pereira accepted that if Lord Lucan had run down the stairs and slipped in the blood his clothes would have been bloodstained. An innocent Lord Lucan could have transferred Sandra's blood to his wife's clothes and to the car. But Roy Ranson was convinced that the evidence disproved Lucan's story.

For George and Frances to go through life knowing their father had been in the dock accused of attempted murder would be too much for them.

When they are old enough to understand explain to them the dream of paranoia and look after them.' The letter was signed 'Lucky.'

The second letter was headed 'Financial matters' and again it began 'Dear Bill'. It went as follows:

There is going to be a sale at Christie's which will rectify the bank overdraft. Please agree reserves herein.

Lucan was referring to the sale of family silver; he then listed its estimated value, concluding: 'Proceeds to go to Lloyds, Coutts and National Westminster . . . and the other creditors can get lost for the time being.' This, too, was signed 'Lucky'.

This was the first indication Ranson had had of the seriousness of Lucan's financial debts. And the letters exposed the deep animosity between Lucan and his wife. But one line that particularly interested Ranson was Lucan's fear of his son seeing him in the dock accused of 'attempted murder' – not murder. Perhaps Lucan did not know the nanny had been murdered? Perhaps, after all, he was not the killer?

Ranson wondered if the letters were the work of a man about to become a fugitive or of a man intent on permanently disappearing. Above all Ranson wanted to know the significance of Uckfield. Shand Kydd told him Lucan's old friends Ian and Susan Maxwell Scott lived in the village, and Ranson was staggered to learn that Lucan had called at their house on Thursday night. He was furious that the police had not been contacted and he felt that the chances of finding Lucan had been halved as a result of the 36-hour delay.

Ian Maxwell Scott, a cousin of the late Duke of Norfolk, had helped John Aspinall establish the Clermont Club and he, like Lucan, whom he had known twenty years, was a compulsive gambler. His winnings had paid for their seven-bedroomed Victorian mansion, Grants Hill House, on the outskirts of the East Sussex village. The house had three

Above: Lady Lucan, after leaving hospital, prepares to join her children at a friend's house in the West Country. The countess had never managed to become part of her husband's social circle, and it certainly offered her no friendship after the tragic events of November 1974. One observer remarked that her perception was a little too sharp for the club coterie of male aristocrats who joined Lucan in the cloisters of the Clermont

acres of grounds, a croquet lawn, tennis court and swimming pool. Maxwell Scott's wife Susan, a trained barrister, was the daughter of Sir Andrew Clark, QC. The couple were devout Roman Catholics and had six children. In happier times the Lucans had been frequent weekend visitors to Grants Hill House.

When Ranson first interviewed Mrs Maxwell Scott he felt she had been particularly guarded about her answers. He knew, however, that she would be a vital witness in the case.

Mrs Maxwell Scott told Ranson that on the night of the murder her husband had telephoned at around 10pm to say he was staying in London. She had gone to bed at 11pm and was dozing a little later when the doorbell rang. She looked out of a window and saw Lucan standing below. After letting him in she gave him a scotch and water. Lucan, she said, had looked a little dishevelled and was wearing a light blue silk polo-neck shirt, brown sleeveless pullover and grey flannels with a dark patch on his trousers at the right hip. He told her he had been passing his home on his way to his flat to change for dinner, when he had looked through the venetian blinds of the kitchen window and seen a man attacking his wife. He had entered the house using his key, and as he went down to the basement he had slipped in a pool of blood. The man who had been attacking his wife ran off. Mrs Maxwell Scott said Lucan had said he had not chased the man but had gone to his wife, who was covered in blood and very hysterical.

Lady Lucan had cried out that someone had killed the nanny and then accused Lucan of having hired the man to kill her. Lord Lucan, according to Mrs Maxwell Scott, tried to calm his wife, persuading her to lie down upstairs while he got some towels to clean up the blood. While he was soaking the towels in the bathroom Lady Lucan ran out of the house. Lucan described the evening as an 'unbelievable nightmare experience'.

Mrs Maxwell Scott said she and Lucan had talked about the nanny in a roundabout way and Lucan said that no one would have wanted to kill her. He had seen the sack at Lower Belgrave Street but had not inspected it. During their conversation she thought Lucan was shocked, but not hysterical. He had mentioned telephoning his mother and he did so again from Uckfield. Then he wrote some letters and asked her to post them in the morning. Despite her appeals to him to stay the night, Lucan said he had to 'get back' to clear things up, although he did not mention London specifically. Mrs Maxwell Scott told police that Lucan drove away from her house at around 1.15am in a dark saloon car.

Ranson was stunned by this reply. He knew nothing of Lucan driving away in a car. And there were other questions. Why had the earl needed to write letters if he was intending to 'get back' in order to clear things up? Why had Mrs Maxwell Scott not contacted police, and where had Lucan vanished in this mysterious car? The answers were to bewilder the detective chief superintendent. The eventual discovery of the abandoned car, Lucan's strange reasons for borrowing it and the sudden emergence of a third, more desperate letter from the fugitive earl were all set to deepen the unsolved mystery of Sandra Rivett's murder.

At about 3pm on Sunday 10 November Ranson heard from police at Newhaven, on the East Sussex coast, that the escape car used by Lord Lucan had been traced to Norman Road, a quiet street away from the seafront and harbour. The car, a battered old Ford Corsair, had been borrowed by Lucan two weeks before from his friend Michael Stoop, a backgammon player and retired company director. Lucan had asked him for the use of a car; Stoop had offered him his Mercedes but Lucan had wanted his old Corsair. Stoop assumed Lucan needed an unnoticeable car to keep watch on his wife.

The abandoned Corsair had bloodstains on the inside of the driver's door, on the dashboard and on the steering wheel. Also inside was a full bottle of vodka, and in the boot was a length of lead pipe wrapped in adhesive medical tape, which seemed identical to the murder weapon. The car had been parked in the street on the morning of Friday 8 November, some time between 5am and 8am according to observant residents. The mystery facing Ranson was that if Lucan had left the Maxwell Scott house at 1.15am, where had he gone in the hours before the car was parked? The 16-mile (26-kilometre) drive from Uckfield to the coast could not have taken as long as 3¾ hours, let alone 7.

Two trawlermen told police that on the Friday morning they had spotted a distinguished-looking man walking along the jetty where their boats were moored. Perhaps Lucan had taken one of the many boats moored in the area or had boarded a cross-Channel ferry. One ferry had left Newhaven at 11am that day. It was also possible that Lucan, an accomplished boatman, had taken a boat out, although a force eight gale was blowing throughout the night of the murder. Detectives began the huge task of checking the thousands of boats moored at Newhaven, but none were found to be

Above: Lady Lucan with two of her children, Lady Frances Bingham and Lord George Bingham, at a friend's house in the West Country twelve days after the murder. Below: Detective Chief Superintendent Roy Ranson — haunted by the face of Lucan. Now head of investigations into breaches of security at the BBC, he keeps this Lucan gallery at his London office; he has speculated on how the earl may look now by drawing in false glasses and beards

Below: police used an auto-gyro to search for Lucan's body on the South Downs. It would have taken 1000 men weeks to cover the ten-mile (sixteen-kilometre) radius round the site where Lucan's abandoned car was found. The auto-gyro, which appeared in the James Bond film You Only Live Twice *(1967), was built and flown by former bomber pilot Wing Commander Kenneth Wallis. It was fitted with ultra-violet and infra-red cameras. Flying at 1000 feet (300 metres), its cameras could detect areas of recently disturbed ground and patches of abnormal heat that might indicate the presence of a decomposing body. But the search failed to reveal a corpse. Bottom: police frogmen searched Newhaven docks for Lucan's body after the car he had borrowed from a friend had been found in a quiet area of the town*

missing. Lucan, Ranson knew, had left his passport in London, but he could have obtained a 60-hour travel permit on the quayside at Newhaven, for which no proof of identity is required. But there was no record of this. Detectives travelled to Dieppe to check with immigration officials, but no one recalled anyone resembling Lucan. Boarding houses and hotels in the area were checked but produced nothing. Ranson drew up plans to search Beachy Head, the South Downs above Newhaven, and the waters in the harbour in case Lucan was hiding out or had committed suicide.

On Monday 11 November, police scientists reported that a fingerprint found on the rear-view mirror of the Corsair matched a print, probably Lucan's, found at the Elizabeth Street flat. There was no confirmation that the prints were Lucan's, as his were not on police files. The report said the murder weapon had been cut from the lead piping found in the car boot, and the blood in the car could be matched with blood from both Sandra Rivett and Lady Lucan. But, most significantly, tiny woollen fibres found on the murder weapon were also found in the car. They had also been found on the towel Lord Lucan had used to stop his wife's bleeding and in the wash-basin near where Lady Lucan was attacked. This, Ranson felt, was the first real evidence that might convince a jury that Lucan was the killer, as it linked him with the murder weapon and the car. Already, Lucan's story of what happened that night had been virtually disproved by a police reconstruction that showed that Lucan could have seen a man attacking his wife only by crouching down on the pavement outside the basement kitchen window of the family house. Ranson decided he now had enough evidence against Lucan to seek warrants alleging murder and attempted murder. He dictated a report to Sir Norman Skelhorne, Director of Public Prosecutions.

At 5pm on Monday 11 November, Ranson received a telephone call from Michael Stoop, the friend who had lent Lucan the Corsair. He told Ranson that he had just received a letter from Lord Lucan. Stoop, like Lucan a member of the St James's Club, said he had called there at 4.45 that afternoon and had been handed several letters by the doorman. The one from Lucan was in an unstamped, business-style envelope (the doorman had paid the excess postage) and was written on notepaper Stoop recognised as being from the glove compartment of the Corsair.

Police did not see this letter until 3am on Tuesday; and by then they had discovered that Stoop had thrown away a vital clue – the envelope with its revealing postmark. A police search of rubbish containers at the club failed to uncover the envelope. The letter read as follows:

> My dear Michael, I have had a traumatic night of unbelievable coincidence. However, I won't bore you with anything to involve you except to say that when you come across my children, which I hope you will, please tell them you knew me and that all I cared about was them. I gave Bill Shand Kydd an account of what actually happened, but judging by my last effort in court no one, let alone a 67-year-old judge, would believe me – and I no longer care, except that my children should be protected. Yours ever, John.

The hunters and the hunted

Above: former Lucan hunter Detective Inspector David Gerring in retirement

The two detectives who led the hunt for Lord Lucan have since both retired from the force, but the case still intrigues them.

Roy Ranson, who led the investigation, ended his career as a Detective Chief Superintendent dealing with complaints about the police force. He is a quiet, methodical man who would not seem out of place in a bank manager's office. He thinks that Lucan was guilty of the murder and that he killed himself. 'I believe Lord Lucan intended to kill his wife. He thought he had planned the perfect murder. Can you imagine his feelings when he realised he had killed the wrong woman?' said Ranson. 'When it all went wrong he committed suicide by throwing himself into the sea between Newhaven and Dieppe. I believe he probably caught the ferry from Newhaven on the Friday morning after the murder. There was a storm and he could easily have thrown himself overboard and vanished.'

If Lucan did indeed drown himself, his body has never been found. Ranson has an answer to this: 'I spoke to trawlermen down on the south coast. They told me that if they bring up a body in their nets – not an uncommon event – their entire catch is officially declared contaminated. It has been known, in such circumstances, for the body simply to be sent back down to the bottom by sticking a boat hook into its distended stomach. I believe that may have happened with Lucan.'

He also has a compelling reason for believing Lucan is dead: 'Lucan was a man who loved his children. I feel sure that, had he been alive, he would have made some attempt to make contact with them. There has been none. I don't believe Lucan was the kind of man who could survive alone.'

His deputy on the case, Detective Chief Inspector David Gerring, has always argued with Ranson over Lucan's fate. He, like his ex-boss, believes Lucan was the murderer, but is convinced that Lucan is alive and well. A much more outgoing character than Ranson, Gerring now runs a pub in Sevenoaks, Kent. He wanted to call it The Vanished Earl but the brewery refused the suggestion.

Gerring, known to his colleagues in the police force as Buster, said: 'You have to accept the fact that Lucan did not have an escape route. There was no need. He was going to commit a murder and only needed to dispose of the body. He did not need to make an escape. I believe he got away perhaps on the Channel ferry, adopted a new identity and started a new life, maybe in South Africa. He is probably living it up in some foreign casino.'

Ranson thought the tone of this letter was more desperate than that of the other two that had been received from Lucan since his disappearance, and judged that it might be a farewell letter. It was probably written by Lucan as he sat alone in the Corsair; if he had written it while with Mrs Maxwell Scott, he would surely have asked her to post it.

Later that Tuesday morning Bow Street magistrates' court issued two warrants for the arrest of Lord Lucan. One alleged he had killed Sandra Rivett, the other that he had attempted to kill his wife. It was the first time in 200 years that a peer of the realm had been a major murder suspect. The previous case was that of the sixth Lord Byron, accused and cleared of murder in April 1765.

Police began a more wide-ranging search for Lucan, allowing for the possibilities of his suicide or escape. Frogmen went into the waters around Newhaven, while police with dogs searched the South Downs. No clues emerged. The search was extended to cover large country estates, some owned by friends of Lucan, but nothing was uncovered.

On Wednesday 13 November, Lady Lucan was discharged

'When you come across my children please tell them that all I cared about was them'

Right: portrait painter Dominic Elwes, one of Lucan's closest friends from his schooldays at Eton, killed himself within a year of the earl's disappearance. His death stemmed indirectly from the events of the night of the murder of Sandra Rivett. Elwes was ostracised by many of his old friends after he produced a painting of a scene at the Clermont Club for a Sunday Times *article — published only a week before the inquest on the murder — that was unfavourable in its treatment of Lucan. Elwes, who was temperamental and an extrovert, had been depressed by this and by other personal difficulties when he took a barbiturate overdose on 15 September 1975. He is pictured with Tessa Kennedy, the girl with whom he eloped in 1957 and subsequently married*

from hospital, wearing a close-fitting turban to hide her shaved scalp and the scars on her forehead. She was driven by detectives to a High Court hearing on the future of her children, which had been scheduled several months earlier. After three hours in chambers, the judge made an order approving arrangments for them. However, details were not made public except for a statement which said that the children would be living with Lady Lucan.

After the murder, unfounded and exaggerated stories about Lady Lucan's mental state began to circulate, while other gossip suggested that friends of Lucan had not been forthcoming with police.

On Saturday 30 November in Johannesburg, South Africa, the first of many unconfirmed sightings of Lucan overseas was reported. The new year of 1975 brought hundreds of other sightings, none of them confirmed, and Ranson became convinced that the earl was dead. He hoped that, as spring came, Lucan's body might be found, perhaps by walkers on the South Downs. In early May, police launched another major search using an auto-gyro fitted with an infra-red camera, but again they found nothing.

The new year had also brought the first steps to declare Lucan bankrupt. Police had already sought a court order in November to open up the earl's bank accounts. But instead of finding, as they had hoped, information about withdrawals of cash that Lucan might have made since his disappearance, they discovered that, in addition to other debts, in four British accounts he owed a total of £14,477. To help pay these debts the Lucan family silver had been sold at Christie's for £17,410 on 27 November. Ranson had, however, discovered a deposit of 20,000 Rhodesian dollars (approximately £9000) in a bank in Bulawayo. But access to

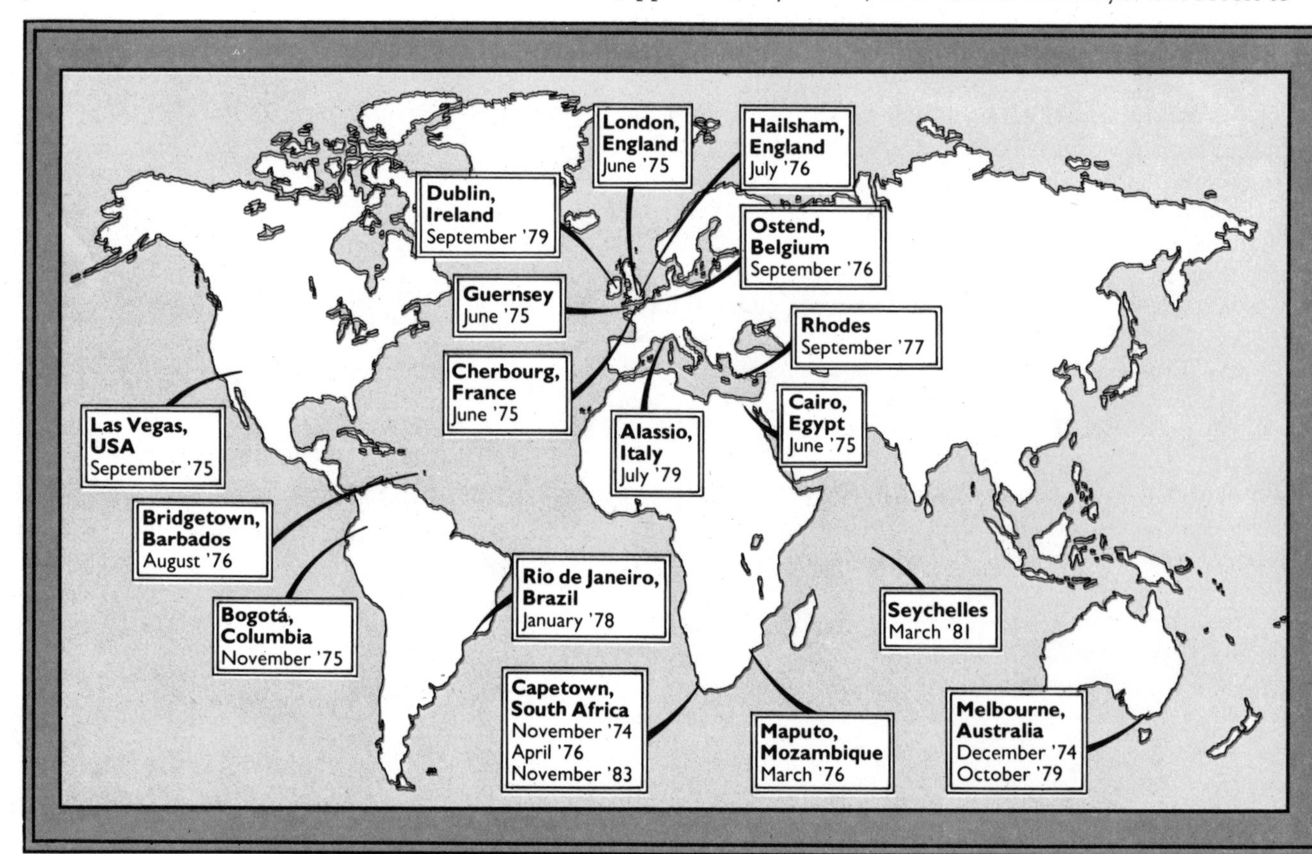

it was barred by the foreign exchange freeze imposed after Rhodesia's Unilateral Declaration of Independence in 1965.

By this time Lady Lucan, who had spent a quiet Christmas at home with her children, had come to agree with Ranson about the fate of her husband: 'My husband was always a very honourable man. So I am sure he would have thought the only honourable thing to do was not to go through the embarrassment of returning. . . . If he had access to a gun I think he might have used it on himself.'

The only conclusive act in the unsolved Lucan mystery was the long-delayed inquest into the death of Sandra Rivett, which opened at the coroner's court in Horseferry Road, Westminster, on 16 June 1975.

It was designed to investigate the nanny's death, but began to resemble a murder trial with the defendant, Lord Lucan, absent. In view of the legal difficulties relating to the naming of a killer not in custody, the Westminster coroner, Dr Gavin Thurston, decided that Lady Lucan should give evidence only 'in connection with part of the matters'.

On this tense note the inquest began. Lady Lucan gave the coroner a brief description of her deteriorating marriage with Lord Lucan. She told the court of the events on the night of 7 November. Her story was exactly the same as that given to police the day after the murder. But — for the first time in public — she claimed that the man who had attacked her on the night of the murder was her husband.

Then Michael Eastham, QC, counsel retained by the Dowager Countess of Lucan to keep a watching brief for her missing son, made the first defensive move of the inquest. Mr Eastham said he was aware that questions aimed at discrediting witnesses were not allowed at inquests, but he wanted to establish the type of relationship that had existed

'Sightings' of Lord Lucan

Since Lord Lucan disappeared, detectives have followed up hundreds of 'sightings' of the fugitive earl. Scotland Yard and police forces all over the world have checked out reports, some promising, some bizarre, that Lucan is alive and well. Bodies unearthed over the years have been checked. But none of the corpses dredged from the seas or found on lonely moors has proved to be the remains of the missing earl.

In the days immediately following the discovery of Sandra Rivett's body Scotland Yard received dozens of calls from people who thought they had seen Lucan (see map of major sightings, left). He had been spotted sunning himself on a Spanish beach, drug-running in South America, and even doing point duty as a policeman in Whitehall.

South Africa has been a favourite place for Lucan sightings. He had a great aunt in Rhodesia, a bank account in Bulawayo and one of his brothers, Hugh, went to live in South Africa shortly after the killing. Detectives reasoned that Lucan might easily be able to live inconspicuously in South Africa's structured, right-wing, white-dominated society. Other theories have suggested he is in South America, hiding under an assumed identity as have various Nazi war criminals.

One of the most surprising discoveries of the hunt for Lucan came in Australia on Christmas Eve 1974. Police in Melbourne, on the alert following the issue of Interpol warrants for Lucan's arrest, started to keep watch on a distinguished Englishman who had recently arrived in Australia. They eventually arrested him, believing him to be Lucan, but found that he was John Stonehouse, a former Labour government minister who, a month earlier, had faked his own drowning off the coast of Florida in an attempt to avoid impending business and financial ruin. He had entered Australia under a false identity.

Other leads had seemed promising, as when detectives had travelled to France to interview staff at a Cherbourg hotel in which Lucan was said to have stayed. But it was a fruitless trip.

Innocent people, Lucan look-alikes and victims of hoaxes have been stopped and questioned over the years. One, an unemployed boilermaker in Australia, was actually arrested and jailed until his fingerprints indicated he was not Lucan. All these sightings of Lucan, and the result of the inquiries made, are logged at Scotland Yard.

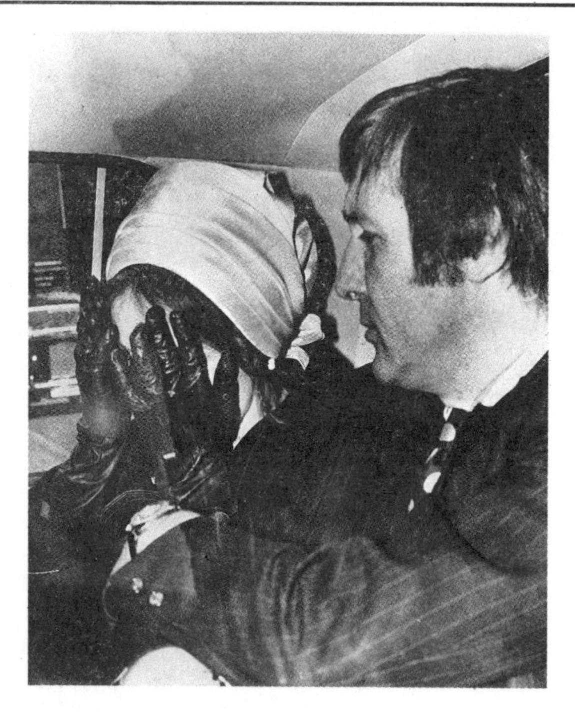

Above: Lady Lucan shows the strain as she is driven by detectives from Westminister Coroner's Court on 18 June 1975, day three of the inquest into the death of Sandra Rivett. Below: on 27 November 1974 auctioneers at Christie's sold Lucan's family silver, robes and even his watch and gambling chips to help pay his debts, which totalled £61,000. They were settled, with interest, after further funds were raised from Lucan's family trusts and the sale of furniture

between Lord and Lady Lucan. It would assist the jury when they came to consider what had happened on the night of 7 November. His instructions, he said, involved 'the inescapable and unpleasant duty of suggesting that what she is saying she knows to be untrue'.

Then Mr Eastham asked Lady Lucan: 'Even before the separation you entertained feelings of hatred against your husband, did you not?' Before she could reply, Lady Lucan's lawyer, Mr Bruce Coles, intervened. The coroner halted the inquest and ordered the jury from the room while a legal argument followed. When the jury returned after fifteen minutes, Mr Eastham offered no questions.

A graphic description of seeing her mother with blood on her face was given by Lady Frances Lucan in a statement read to the court by a woman police officer. In the statement she said she had not seen any blood on her father's clothes. After she had been sent up to her room she heard her father call out 'Veronica, where are you?' She got up and saw him coming from the bedroom on the floor below, then he went to the bathroom before going downstairs. 'That was the last I saw of him,' she said in the statement.

On the second day of the inquest the Dowager Countess of Lucan told the coroner that her son's feelings about his children were 'more like an obsession'. It was a great disappointment to him that he did not have custody of them.

The Dowager Countess said that during her telephone conversation with her son on the night of the murder, he had hesitated when she asked him if he wanted to speak to the police. She very much regretted not having pressed the point. Her son had used the words 'blood and mess' during the first phone call and had sounded highly shocked, expressing horror and disgust. During the second conversation he sounded much more 'on all fours'.

It was Mrs Susan Maxwell Scott who gave the most dramatic evidence of the day. After detailing Lucan's visit to her home on the night of the murder she went on to talk about Lucan's version of events. Lucan had told her that his wife had accused him of hiring a man to kill her. She said: 'This was something she frequently accused him of — a contract to kill. Lucan claimed it came from an American TV movie.'

On day three of the inquest Dr Margaret Pereira, a police scientific officer, gave evidence about her examination of the blood at the murder scene and in the car. Next, Michael Stoop told of receiving his letter from Lucan and again said that he had not noticed the postmark. As the inquest drew to a close, the jury wanted information from Lady Lucan about the nanny's murder, but the coroner told them that 'in law Lady Lucan was barred from giving evidence other than that concerning the assault.'

On Thursday 19 June Dr Thurston delivered his summing up: 'You know Lord and Lady Lucan are separated,' he said. 'They have been on either side of custody proceedings. It is fairly clear from Lord Lucan's letters that there is existing in the family animosity, tensions and matters, which if heard, could only be prejudicial. The airing of family tensions would not benefit this inquiry. You have heard Lady Lucan's evidence. You have heard her while she sat there for two hours and you saw the way she answered the questions. I ask you to consider the instinctive reaction of someone in Lady Lucan's position on the night of the attack. If, as Lord Lucan says, he was trying to help, would she have run to The Plumbers' Arms crying "murder"? Would Lord Lucan not have tried to telephone the police and an ambulance immediately?'

After speaking for ninety minutes Dr Thurston sent the three women and six men of the jury out of the court to consider their verdict. After 31 minutes they returned. Their verdict on the death of Sandra Rivett was murder by Lord Lucan.

The coroner said: 'It is very rare for a coroner's court that a person is named as you have done. It is my duty to commit that person to trial at the Central Criminal Court. In this case there is nobody I can commit for trial because we don't know where Lord Lucan is. There is no doubt that if he turns up he will be charged with the offence.'

Lucan's family, shocked by the verdict, vowed to take legal steps to try and clear his name. For Roy Ranson, the inquest was the culmination of a long, difficult inquiry, the most baffling in his career. He believes that Lucan is dead and will never stand trial for murder.

Scotland Yard's file on the case is still open and the mystery of Lucan's whereabouts remains. His actions on the night of 7 November 1974 cannot be easily rationalised whatever the motives. If, for instance, we believe that Lucan planned to murder his wife – a view that could be supported by his efforts to create an alibi, his borrowing of an 'old banger', his inquiries into the nanny's night off, his impending financial collapse, his hatred of his wife and his obsession with his children, made worse by the knowledge that the final court hearing over their custody was due later that month – then we might make three assumptions. First, that he would have wanted to avoid blame for the murder; second, he would have planned to avoid capture; and third, he would have tried to secure his children.

However, the events of that night, and accounts of them, seem to undermine all these hypotheses. If Lucan had wanted to avoid blame for the murder, why had he chosen such a clumsy murder method, or been foolish enough to leave the second half of the iron bar in the boot of his car, or been so careless as to book a table for four instead of five, and later send a bloodstained letter?

Perhaps whatever plans he had collapsed once he discovered he had murdered an innocent girl instead of the wife he hated. Or was he more calculating? Had he known and expected to be blamed for murder and decided to make his alibi attempts appear so desperate as to point only to suicide?

That leads us to the second assumption; his plans to escape. He might easily have prepared an escape route with the help of some of his rich and loyal aristocratic friends, perhaps via private boat or plane (the south coast has dozens of small, private airfields). There is still the mystery of the missing hours spent between Uckfield (1.15am) and abandoning the car at Newhaven (between 5 and 8am). Lucan had enough friends abroad, in South Africa for example, who could have helped him and could still be doing so.

Guilty without trial

Above: the Dowager Countess of Lucan, the earl's mother, appealed against the naming of Lucan as murderer in the inquest verdict

Lord Lucan was the last man in Britain to be branded a murderer by a coroner's jury. This created enormous controversy at the time and focused attention on the recommendations of an official inquiry into the powers of coroners, known as the Brodrick Committee on Death Certification and Coroners.

It filed its report in 1971, and suggested that coroners should no longer assess guilt or have the power to commit a person for trial. The inquiry felt that such features could seriously prejudice a named person's trial.

Lucan's family were particularly concerned that Lady Lucan was allowed to give as much evidence as she did given the absence of her husband at the inquest. Within weeks of the inquest verdict the government announced that the law would be changed to prevent any person being named as a killer by a coroner.

By 1977 the legislation to fulfil this promise had been introduced as Section 56 of the Criminal Law Act 1977. It stated that coroners could no longer charge a person with murder. Once this had become law, solicitors acting for Lucan's mother, the Dowager Countess of Lucan, petitioned the Director of Public Prosecutions to invoke retrospectively the new act and strike out his name, substituting 'murder by a person'. The petition was dismissed, and Lucan still stands accused of Sandra Rivett's murder.

Below centre: Lady Lucan at home in 1976; a portrait of Lord Lucan dominated her sitting room as his memory dominated her life. Although she recovered from her physical injuries, the mental scars remained. In December 1983 she was admitted to Banstead Mental Hospital after police found her wandering the Belgravia streets in a confused state. Until then, she had lived quietly on a small family trust income in a mews house just yards from the murder scene. Below: Lucan as he was in 1963. Bottom: an artist's impression of how Lord Lucan may look now

Moreover, although Lucan's British bank accounts were all in overdraft, it is still not known what was in his Swiss account or what happened to the £9000-worth of Rhodesian dollars in Bulawayo. Many of his friends have talked of how Lucan bought jewellery, knowing it to be easily portable, because he feared the possibility of socialist revolution in Britain.

Lucan may have changed his identity completely and, perhaps now clean-shaven and grey, may be living in an entirely different way from that to which he was accustomed. Yet his nature thrived on the gambling life of high society. Some of his friends have said he could never have lived abroad away from casinos, and his longstanding friend John Aspinall once described him as 'a warrior, a Roman. He was quite capable of falling on his sword, as it were.' If Lucan killed himself, it would have been from a boat, said Aspinall.

The argument for suicide is strongly linked with Lucan's attitude to his children. His letter to Stoop emphasises his concern for them, but its tone suggests that he thinks all is lost. It is possible that, if Lucan had hoped to snatch his children that night (as he had done once before) and was frustrated in the attempt, he might have felt that his last motivation had died and with it his reason for living.

It was probably Aspinall who best recognised the balance between the two possible fates that Lord Lucan could have met, when he said: 'As a gambler I would give even money on whether he is living or dead.' It is the frustrating absence of either a positive sighting or an identified corpse that keeps the punters guessing.

'SUICIDE' AT STAMMHEIM

In the early hours of Tuesday 18 October 1977, two members of West Germany's notorious Baader-Meinhof terrorist group were found dead in their cells at the top-security prison of Stammheim; a third was dying and a fourth was injured. The deaths followed two unsuccessful attempts to secure their release – through the kidnapping of German businessman Hans-Martin Schleyer and the five-day hijacking of an airliner. The official verdict was that Andreas Baader (above), Gudrun Ensslin and Jan-Carl Raspe had committed suicide and Irmgard Möller had tried to. Other theories, however, point to murder.

ANNETTE KENNERLEY examines the case

RAF

The only certainty was that the Baader-Meinhof terrorists had died as they had lived – secretly and bloodily

Left: the notorious terrorist group dubbed the Baader-Meinhof gang adopted the title of Red Army Faction in 1970. Their revolutionary symbol was a bright red star on which were superimposed a sub-machine gun and the initials RAF. Top left: Ulrike Meinhof in 1963 – the fashionable journalist and mother of twin girls. A year before she had written, 'One does not change the world by shooting. One accomplishes more by negotiating.' Centre left: Gudrun Ensslin in a pornographic film in 1965. Bottom left: a line-up of some of West Germany's most wanted terrorists in the early Seventies (from left) – Ulrike Meinhof, Andreas Baader, Gudrun Ensslin, Jan-Carl Raspe and Irmgard Möller

TUESDAY 18 October 1977 began as a routine day at Stammheim Prison in Stuttgart, West Germany. Two officials were taking breakfast – coffee, boiled eggs and rye bread – round the seventh-floor cells; at 7.41am they opened the door to cell 716 to find the terrorist Jan-Carl Raspe propped up on his bed and bleeding from a wound on the temple. The guards shut the door and alerted the prison hospital and governor. When the cell was reopened, a 9mm calibre pistol was found next to Raspe, who died in hospital three hours later. In cell 719 Andreas Baader was found dead in a pool of blood with a gun at his side, while across the corridor, in cell 720, Gudrun Ensslin was discovered hanging from a bar across her cell window. In cell 725, the fourth prisoner, Irmgard Möller, was found lying on her bed, badly injured with four stab wounds in her chest and a butter knife by her side; after emergency surgery, she survived.

At a press conference later that day, the Minister of Justice Traugott Bender gave the official verdict on the deaths as suicide, even though no evidence had yet been received from forensic scientists. Chancellor Helmut Schmidt called for a full investigation into the deaths in order to establish how the weapons had been smuggled into the jail, how they had remained hidden despite the highest security measures, and how the prisoners had managed to communicate with each other in order to plan a suicide pact – given that they were supposed to be kept in total isolation at that time. The only certainty was that the Baader-Meinhof terrorists had died as they had lived – secretly and bloodily.

The origins of the Baader-Meinhof group can be traced back to the student protests of the late Sixties when demonstrations were staged to oppose support for the war in Vietnam in particular, and capitalism in general. In 1968 an incident occurred that steered many pacifist demonstrators towards more violent forms of protest. During a large demonstration against the Shah of Iran's visit to Berlin, a young student named Benno Ohnesorg was shot dead by a policeman. It provoked a great outcry. Leftist journalist Ulrike Meinhof wrote that Ohnesorg was the 'victim of SS mentality and practice', and peace campaigner Gudrun Ensslin told the Socialist German Students Union (SDS) the day after the shooting that a 'fascist state' was emerging in West Germany that was 'out to kill us all', and that they could only answer this sort of violence with violence.

The tall, striking blonde with a thin, pale face and black eyeliner who addressed the SDS with her impassioned words was born in 1940 in a tiny village north of Stuttgart, the daughter of a free-thinking pastor. She had worked hard at school, helped her mother at home, taken Bible classes and trained to be a teacher. In 1965 she went to the Free University in Berlin, where she got involved in anti-Vietnam protests. In 1967 she met the swarthy, blue-eyed Baader and was dubbed 'his true revolutionary bride'. Andreas Baader was born in Munich in 1943, the son of a historian who was killed during the Second World War. Doted on by his mother, he was an obstinate child who was an academic failure at school and drifted to Berlin, where he dabbled in art and journalism and lived off a wealthy painter and his own good looks. He had a taste for glamour and flashy cars,

Right: the arrest of Holger Meins in 1972 after a shoot-out with police who raided the terrorists' hide-out in Frankfurt. Meins was the son of a businessman and had been recognised as a conscientious objector in 1961. After attending film school in Hamburg, Meins went to Berlin in the late Sixties where he undertook film and television studies and became involved in the Baader-Meinhof group. Below: a blood-spattered hostage emerges from the West German embassy in Stockholm after terrorists occupied the building in April 1975, killing two diplomats and detonating a number of bombs. The embassy was blown up as the police prepared to carry out a raid. The six terrorists responsible were members of the Socialist Patients' Collective (SPK) — former patients at the Neurological/Psychiatric Clinic of Heidelberg. The faction was nicknamed 'the crazy brigade'. They had demanded the release of 26 Baader-Meinhof prisoners

and was easily coerced by the strong-minded Ensslin into the world of the urban guerrilla.

Dressed in the revolutionary chic black sweaters and jeans, Baader and Ensslin entered a department store in Frankfurt in April 1968 and planted fire bombs — one of them in a piece of 'Old German' reproduction furniture. No one was injured but the couple were arrested and sentenced to three years' imprisonment. Ensslin declared: 'We don't care about burnt mattresses. We are worried about burnt children in Vietnam.' The prisoners were released in 1969 pending an appeal, and welcomed by the radical Left as heroes. When their appeal was rejected, Baader and Ensslin went underground and fled to Switzerland, remaining there until they considered it safe to return to Germany. In April 1970 Baader was arrested in a Berlin roadblock and sent to the Tegel Prison in Berlin.

In jail, Baader received visits from Ulrike Meinhof who had written in an article at the time of the Frankfurt arson

trial: 'It is better to burn a department store than to run one.' Meinhof was the daughter of an art historian and was born in 1934 in north Germany. She was orphaned as a young teenager and brought up by Renate Riemeck – a professor and co-founder of the German Peace Union. She was a studious, idealistic girl, interested in art and music; she was articulate, daring and liked to lead, though she also liked to belong to an elite. As a student she edited a pamphlet called *Das Argument*, working hard for the anti-bomb campaign. In the late Fifties, Meinhof met Klaus Rainer Röhl, editor of the radical newspaper *Konkret*, which she began writing for in 1959 and later worked for as foreign editor and editor-in-chief, making a name for herself as an outspoken political columnist. She also married Röhl.

By 1964 *Konkret* was in severe financial difficulties as the funding from East Germany dried up. To boost sales, Röhl turned it into a porn-with-politics paper that featured extracts from Swedish pornographic novels. It worked. The Röhls entered the fashionable society of the chic Left, materially secure and publicly successful; Meinhof, fashionably dressed and with her hair styled, appeared on television and radio, speaking out for the poor and underprivileged. When her marriage broke up in 1967 she moved to Berlin, leaving behind her fur coats and violin, and became a part-time lecturer at the Free University. Her writings showed increasing sympathy with the Left and her home became a meeting place for radicals. It was at this time that she met a quiet young man called Jan-Carl Raspe. He was the son of a chemical factory director, who had died when the child was young. Brought up by his mother, he became a sociologist and wrote a book on bringing up children. In Berlin, he became involved in the anti-bomb student protests, turning to more active political protest after the shooting of Benno Ohnesorg.

Meinhof's relationship with Baader and Ensslin, both of whom she had interviewed during the Frankfurt arson trial, was cemented too. And her movie-style rescue of Baader in 1970 was her initiation into the terrorist elite.

Shortly after Baader's re-arrest and imprisonment that year, Meinhof arranged to assist him with research for a book he claimed to be writing and for which he was allowed out of prison to study in a university library. As the two 'researchers' sat quietly talking at a table, two young women wearing wigs and carrying briefcases entered. Minutes later, a masked man with a gun rushed in and the two women produced pistols from their bags. In the gunfire that followed – although most of it was aimed at the floor – a librarian was badly wounded. Meinhof and Baader leapt dramatically from the library window and escaped in a silver-grey Alfa Romeo, driven by the young recruit Astrid Proll.

Along with the lawyer Horst Mahler, Baader, Meinhof and Ensslin chose to call their movement the Red Army Faction (Rote Armee Fraktion) after the Japanese Red Army, and flew to Jordan to be trained by the Popular Front for the Liberation of Palestine (PFLP). They made contacts for funding and weapons, and back home set up safe houses and communications networks to back up their operations. Their activities required stolen cars, false documents, disguises and electronic devices, as well as weapons. Bank raids were carried

As the Red Army Faction began to step up its campaign of terror in its attempt to secure the release of the Baader-Meinhof prisoners, more victims were added to their death list. In July 1977 banker Jürgen Ponto (below) was shot dead at his home near Frankfurt by terrorists who got past his bodyguard with the aid of his god-daughter Susanne Albrecht, 26 (above). She apparently told him over the security intercom: 'It's me, Susanne, let me in.' She and her two friends presented Ponto with flowers and then shot him. Far right: damage caused by a bomb planted at Hamburg University by terrorist sympathisers in April 1981

Astrid Proll's other life

One of the mysteries of the Baader-Meinhof case came to light in London in September 1978 when an instructress at a skill centre, off Finchley Road, Hampstead, was arrested by the anti-terrorist squad. She was Anna Puttick, a thirty-year-old German girl, dark, intense, handsome and a capable mechanic. It transpired that she was, in fact, Astrid Proll, sought by the West German police for over five years as a suspected terrorist in the Baader-Meinhof gang. After her arrest she fought for over twelve months against extradition.

Fascinating facts emerged during her legal struggle. She was indeed the Anna Puttick she claimed to be, having married a plumber, Robin Puttick, in 1975. The extradition rested upon whether she was a British citizen by marriage. She had arrived in England in 1974, travelling on false identity papers under the name of Senta Sauerbier. She had made no contact with any radical or revolutionary groups in England. She had built up a wide circle of friends and had attended the City and Guilds Institute and earned a certificate as a motor fitter.

She came from a rich, middle-class German family; her father was an architect in Frankfurt. At a time when European youth was seething with middle-class rebels, first in France, later in Germany, Astrid Proll and her brother Thorwald joined in rebelling against their comfortable middle-class environment and became involved with the Baader-Meinhof group. In May 1971 Astrid Proll was arrested and charged with taking part in a shooting battle in a Frankfurt street three months earlier. Her first trial began two years later, but she was declared unfit to take part because of a nervous complaint, apparently caused

out to finance the movement.

The Red Army Faction (RAF) began its real campaign in May 1972. In a protest against American intervention in Vietnam, the RAF planted bombs at the headquarters of the US Fifth Army Corps in Frankfurt, killing an American colonel and injuring thirteen others. Two weeks later bombs killed three and wounded five at an American Army base in Heidelberg. Other bomb attacks were launched at police stations and at the Axel Springer Press building in Hamburg.

In June 1972, after a tip off, Baader, Raspe and Holger Meins were arrested in a massive police raid and shoot-out at an arms hide-out in a Frankfurt garage, after the three drove up in a lilac Porsche. Baader was shot in the thigh. A week later, Gudrun Ensslin walked into a boutique in Hamburg and carelessly left her leather jacket on a sofa while she tried on some sweaters. An observant shop assistant picked up the coat and, noticing it was unusually heavy, felt in the pocket to find a pistol. Alerting the police, she delayed Ensslin until the police arrived. A second gun and newspaper cuttings on Baader's arrest were found in her bag. Before the month was out another tip off – this time by a Leftist who believed the terrorist gangs were harming

by solitary confinement and sensory deprivation. She was sent to a clinic in the Black Forest from which she escaped.

Her re-arrest was not, however, through international anti-terrorist intelligence. Proll walked into the West Hampstead police station one day to help out one of her students who was in trouble. The keen young desk policeman recognised her from a poster on the office door. The next day eight men from the anti-terrorist squad arrested Proll. She spent the next thirteen months in close custody in Brixton Prison. Eventually, Proll elected to return to Germany to face trial there. In October 1980 she was sentenced to five and a half years' imprisonment, which was waived and substituted by a small fine, as she had served two-thirds of her sentence awaiting trial. She is now studying photography in Hamburg. Nobody there cares who she was. She is not allowed back into Britain.

BILL DRISCOLL

Above left: Astrid Proll's interest in the revolutionary underground was kindled when she moved to Berlin to study graphic arts. It was here that she met Andreas Baader (reflected in the mirror of the café). Above: Proll in handcuffs at the beginning of her first trial in Frankfurt in 1973, after two years in prison

the Left – lead police to Ulrike Meinhof; in her luggage were found three pistols, one sub-machine gun, two hand grenades, a ten-pound bomb and a coded letter from Ensslin.

The authorities had succeeded in rounding up and imprisoning the main ringleaders of the Baader-Meinhof gang – they were later incarcerated in the specially built, top security Stammheim Prison at Stuttgart. Their trial did not begin until 1975; it took place in a special court house adjacent to Stammheim Prison, lasted nearly two years and was the focus of many legal wrangles. As the RAF began its bloody campaign to have its leaders released, other groups sprang up, sometimes working with them; one of these was The Second of June Movement, named after the date on which Benno Ohnesorg was shot. As terrorist raids became more widespread and murderous, a wave of alarm spread through Germany and the federal government began tightening up security. The necessity for this was further highlighted later in 1972 with the massacre of Israeli athletes at the Munich Olympics. The Munich terrorists' demands included the release of Baader and Meinhof. The demands were not met and, after a shoot-out with the police, all the hostages were killed. Subsequently, special anti-terrorist squads were set

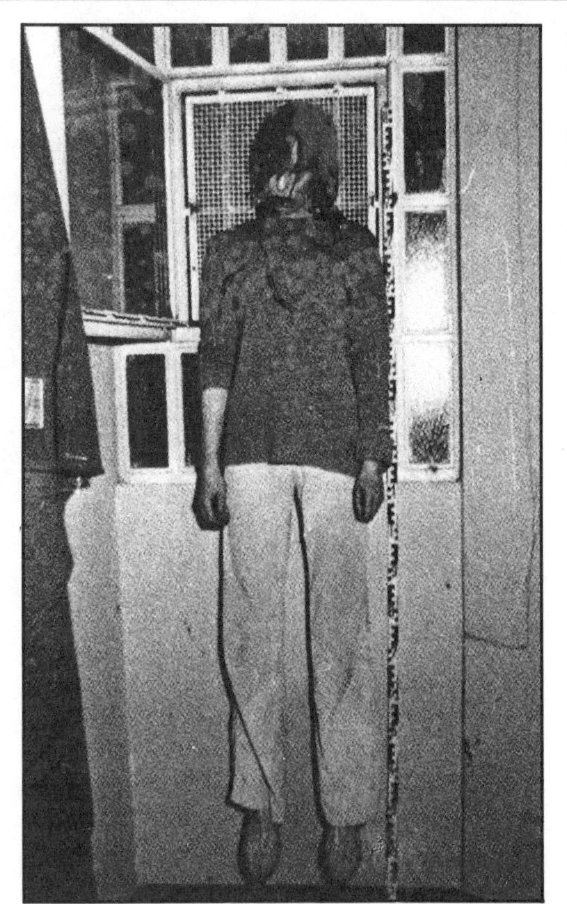

up, including the GSG-9 – a highly trained, mobile force that was to make its dramatic debut at Mogadishu in 1977.

In 1974 Holger Meins died in prison from a hunger strike and a number of arrests were made in the demonstrations that followed. A week later, the president of the West German Supreme Court, Günter von Drenkmann, was shot dead on his 64th birthday. In February 1975 The Second of June Movement kidnapped political leader Peter Lorenz and achieved its aim in exchanging their hostage for a number of prisoners – some of them Baader-Meinhof members.

In May 1976 violent riots broke out in several German cities after the death in Stammheim Prison of Ulrike Meinhof, who had been sentenced to eight years in prison for her part in Baader's rescue. Many factions refused to believe the official verdict that she had hanged herself and conflicting evidence that emerged fuelled the belief that she was murdered. Several days before the end of the Stammheim trial, a group of motorcycle-riding terrorists pulled up alongside the car of Siegfried Buback, West Germany's chief public prosecutor, and shot him dead. In April 1977, Baader, Ensslin and Raspe were given life sentences for the murders of four American soldiers in the army base bombings and 34 attempted murders, plus fifteen years for bombing two police stations, a publishing house, a judge's car and for the attempted murder of policemen during the shoot-out in which

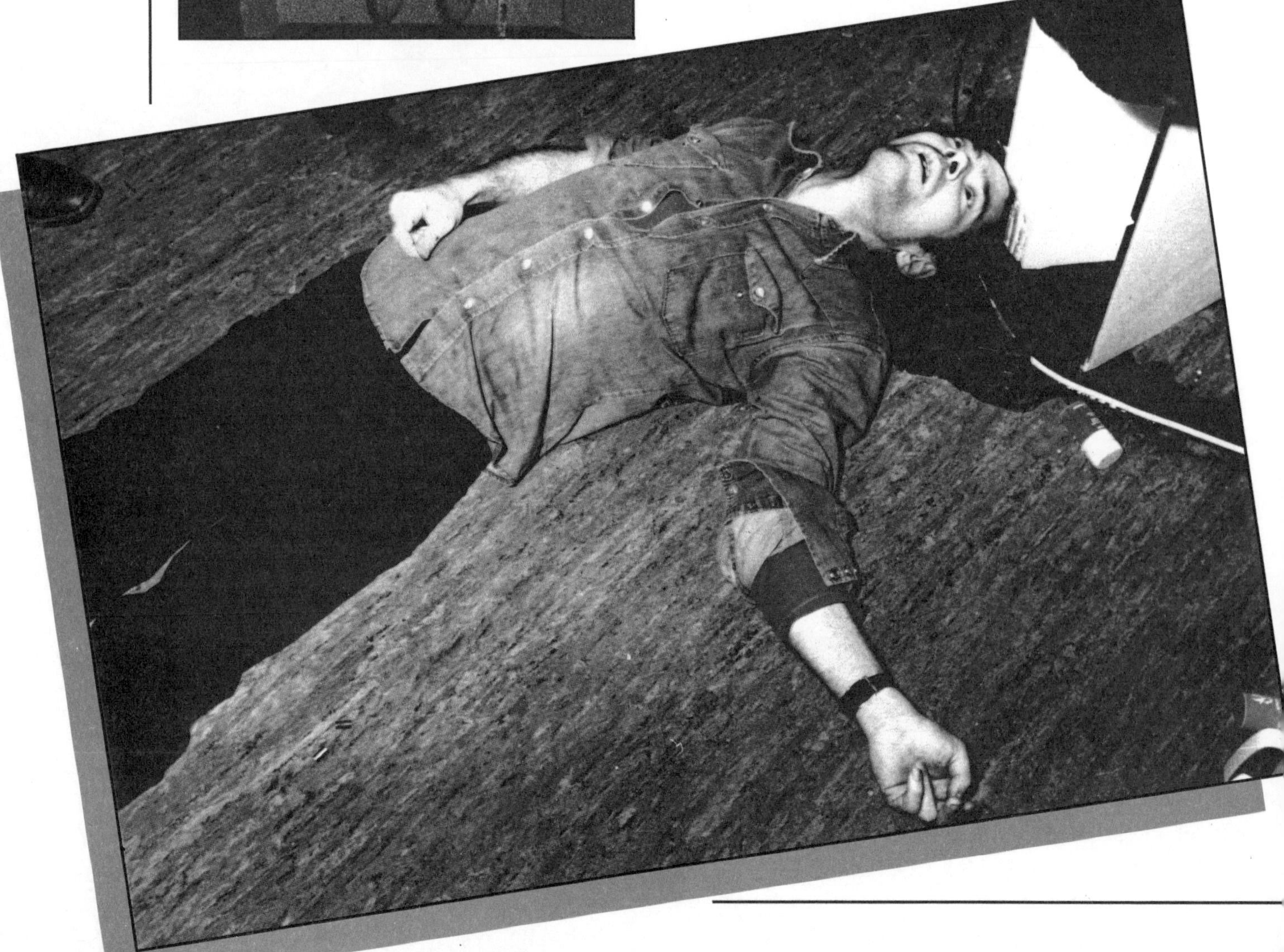

The nature of the prisoners' injuries raised doubts as to whether they could have been self-inflicted

The grim scene on the morning of 18 October. Left: Gudrun Ensslin was found hanging by a length of cable from a bar across her cell window. Ensslin was said to have cut the wire from the loudspeakers in her cell, but no tests were carried out to confirm this report. Below left: Andreas Baader was lying in a pool of blood with a bullet through his brain and a gun by his head when guards opened his cell door. Below: Irmgard Möller survived after being found with four stab wounds in her chest. Hamburg sexologist Professor Eberhard Schorsch has said: 'I have never come across a case of a woman trying to commit suicide by stabbing herself in the breast. There would be an inbuilt inhibition towards such an act.' Bottom: Jan-Carl Raspe died three hours after being found in his cell with a bullet wound in his head

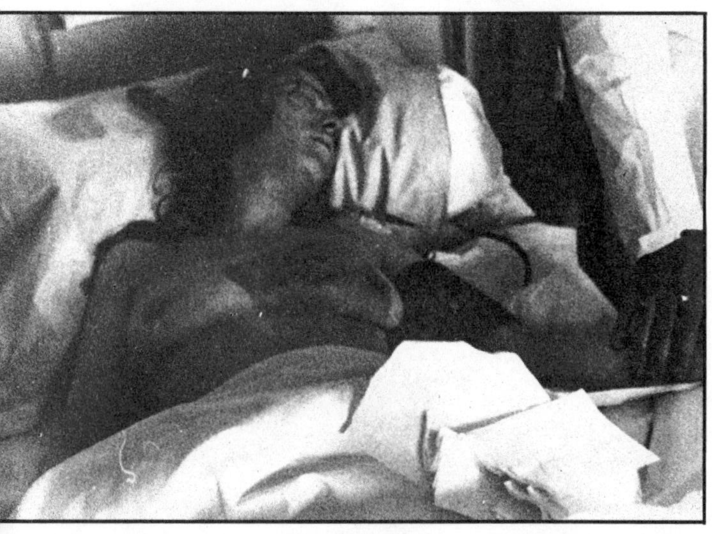

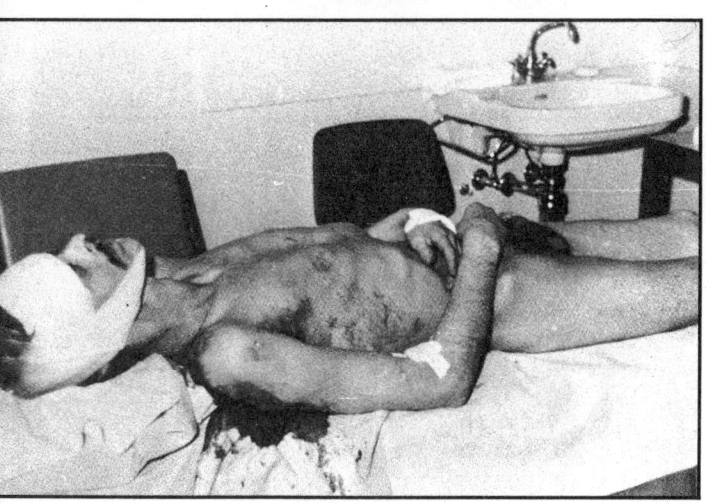

Baader and Raspe were arrested. In July terrorists killed Jürgen Ponto, head of a large German bank. The demand for the release of the imprisoned terrorists was repeated, along with threats of further violence.

No amount of security measures seemed to deter the Baader-Meinhof supporters and in Cologne on 5 September 1977 they kidnapped the powerful industrialist Hans-Martin Schleyer. Then, on 13 October, they hijacked a Boeing 737 airliner and flew it to Mogadishu, where the airplane and its 82 passengers were dramatically rescued by the GSG-9 anti-terrorist squad. This was a famous victory that produced a general feeling of relief that at last something was being done to combat terrorism. Hardly had the congratulations subsided when news of the Stammheim deaths on 18 October was released. Schleyer's fate was sealed: he was found dead the next day.

The official explanation for the events at Stammheim that night was that the terrorists' hopes of being released were dashed when the hijackers at Mogadishu were defeated – this, along with the government's refusal to give in to the demands made by Schleyer's kidnappers, compelled the four to carry out a suicide pact in their despair. Twelve hours before his death, Baader is reported to have requested a meeting with a government official at which he had seemed confident of his imminent release from jail, threatening that, if the Mogadishu hijacking failed, then Germany could expect an immediate 'major blow'. This could be taken as a reference to the suicide pact that would leave the government with the problem of explaining the terrorists' deaths. Government officials immediately claimed that the suicide pact had been deliberately made to look like murder.

As the facts about the Stammheim deaths began to emerge, the very nature of the prisoners' injuries raised doubts as to whether they could have been self-inflicted. As for a motive for their murder, it had become apparent by the summer of 1977 that as long as these particular terrorists were in jail, their supporters would have a motive for kidnapping and hijacking and increased violence in their bid to secure the prisoners' release. Much of the urban guerrilla activity during the ring-leaders' imprisonment had been geared towards this aim. The German government desperately needed to break the terrorist grip on the country; the killings of Drenkmann, Buback and Ponto, Schleyer's kidnap and murder and the Mogadishu hijacking strengthened their resolve. A convenient way of erasing the terrorists' motivation would have been to 'remove' their ringleaders.

Hundreds of police and criminal investigators were employed on the Stammheim case. Internationally recognised doctors gave expert opinions and a parliamentary committee from Baden-Württemberg conducted its own investigation. Six months later, in April 1978, the Stuttgart public prosecutor dismissed the preliminary proceedings, upholding the official verdict of suicide. This ignored contradictions in scientific and medical evidence and the fact that, despite allegations, the possibility of murder had never been investigated. The hearing was given the official title of 'Investigation into the suspected attempted and successful suicides'. Chief criminal lawyer Günter Textor, leading the Stamm-

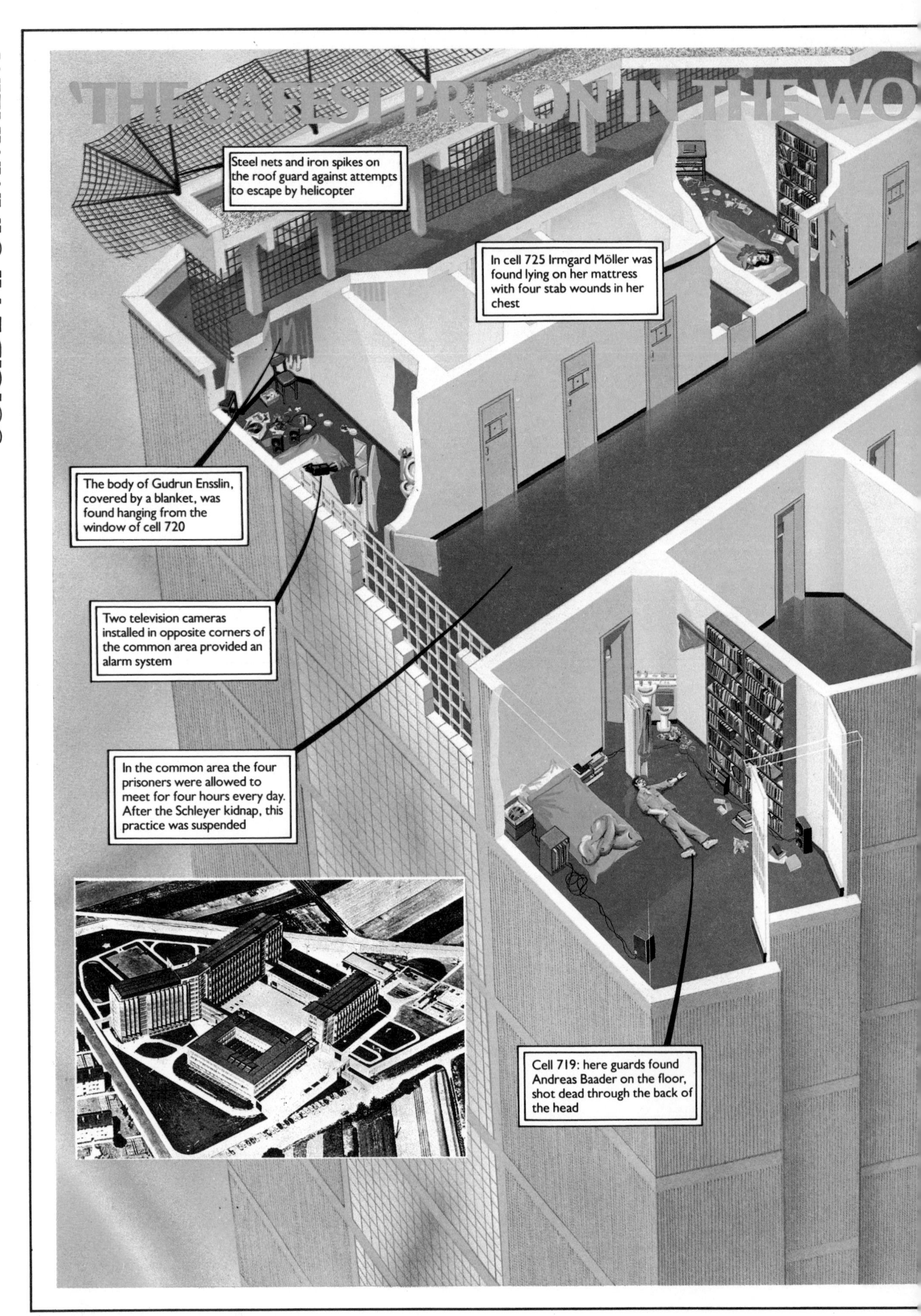
'THE SAFEST PRISON IN THE WO
Steel nets and iron spikes on the roof guard against attempts to escape by helicopter
In cell 725 Irmgard Möller was found lying on her mattress with four stab wounds in her chest
The body of Gudrun Ensslin, covered by a blanket, was found hanging from the window of cell 720
Two television cameras installed in opposite corners of the common area provided an alarm system
In the common area the four prisoners were allowed to meet for four hours every day. After the Schleyer kidnap, this practice was suspended
Cell 719: here guards found Andreas Baader on the floor, shot dead through the back of the head

'The safest prison in the world'. This was how the former Justice Minister of Baden Württemberg, Traugott Bender, praised the top security wing of Stammheim Prison at Stuttgart. For the trial of the Baader-Meinhof prisoners a special single-storey court house, with maximum security, was constructed adjacent to the main jail. Andreas Baader, Gudrun Ensslin, Jan-Carl Raspe and Irmgard Möller were all kept on the seventh floor. Inset: aerial view of Stammheim

heim special commission, said that 'violence by a third party was out of the question because, in such a secure institution as Stammheim, it would be simply impossible'.

Baader, Ensslin and Raspe had all been imprisoned on the seventh floor of the prison. They had been joined there in January 1977 by Irmgard Möller, who was charged with taking part in the Heidelberg bomb attack in 1972. Since the kidnapping of Schleyer, the four were supposed to have been kept in total isolation, according to a special law that had been passed. They were not supposed to receive any newspapers, letters, news bulletins on radio or television, were not allowed to communicate with one another, and their meetings with lawyers were conducted under the strictest security. A meticulous search of each cell was supposed to have taken place twice daily and the wires linking each cell to the prison radio service were supposed to have been disconnected, so that the gang would not be able to receive news of the Schleyer kidnap. An official report later claimed the prisoners re-connected their radio systems and communicated with each other, using the radio wiring. Raspe, it was claimed, communicated via his razor connection. He had been studying electronics in prison. The police also claimed that the terrorists had used their record player loudspeakers to make contact with each other in Morse code, but their record players were supposed to have been confiscated during the tightening-up procedures after the kidnapping. It was also claimed that Baader, Ensslin and Möller had concealed headphones in order to hear the prison radio broadcasts, but only Möller's were ever produced to substantiate these claims. Even the exact time of deaths was never accurately established. Pathologists had been unable to begin the autopsy until 4pm on 18 October because they had had to wait for the arrival of lawyers and representatives of the public prosecutor's office. The most accurate estimate was that Baader's death had occurred some time between 12.15am and 2.15am and Ensslin's between 1.15am and 1.25am, but when experts were asked whether the deaths could have occurred as late as 6am the answer was 'yes'.

Baader had been found lying on the floor, his eyes open, with his head – and a pistol – in a pool of blood. Near his knee were two spent cartridge cases. His was perhaps the most difficult of the deaths to explain. After a post mortem, experts arrived at the following conclusions: Baader was killed by a single shot that entered at the back of his neck (at the base of the skull) and exited on the other side of his skull, just above the hairline. They also said that the barrel of the gun must have been placed directly against the base of the skull. In addition, the forensic scientists found traces of blood on the palm and thumb of the right hand. These findings were reported at the hearing and it was accepted by the public prosecutor that Baader – who was left-handed – had held his pistol pointing upwards in his right hand, pressed it to the base of his skull and pulled the trigger with his left thumb. After the shot, blood had spattered onto his right hand. But the criminal police special commission had discovered that the cartridge case from the death bullet lay to the right of the corpse. Baader's weapon, a 7·65mm calibre pistol, is of a type that ejects the cartridges to the right.

Far right: the trial of the Baader-Meinhof terrorists took place in the special court-house adjacent to Stammheim Prison. Here Ulrike Meinhof (wearing glasses) and Gudrun Ensslin are escorted by guards to the courtroom

The criminal police therefore deduced that Baader had held the pistol pointing downwards and, directing the barrel at the base of his skull with his left hand, had pulled the trigger with his right hand. This is the only way that the position of the cartridge can be explained. This does not, however, explain why blood stains were found on his right hand and not on his left.

One important piece of evidence remained concealed from both the forensic scientists – German and foreign – and the parliamentary investigative committee, which concluded its work on 21 February with the verdict of suicide. On that day a ballistics report was filed with the Federal Criminal Office. Seven days later it arrived at the public prosecutor's office in Stuttgart. The ballistics expert Dr Roland Hoffmann had investigated the entrance hole of the bullet at the base of Baader's skull with gunpowder tests. Tests show,

The Schleyer kidnapping

The kidnapping of top German industrialist Hans-Martin Schleyer by the Red Army Faction on 5 September 1977 was one of the most spectacular of all terrorist acts. Three armed bodyguards and a chauffeur were shot dead while Schleyer was dragged to a waiting van and taken into hiding – an ordeal that lasted 43 days and ended with his death.

At that time Schleyer, 62, was considered number one on the high-risk list in West Germany. He was a director of Mercedes-Benz and president of the West German Confederation of Industry – an employers' association. Such credentials made him a prime target in the RAF's campaign against capitalism. At the funeral

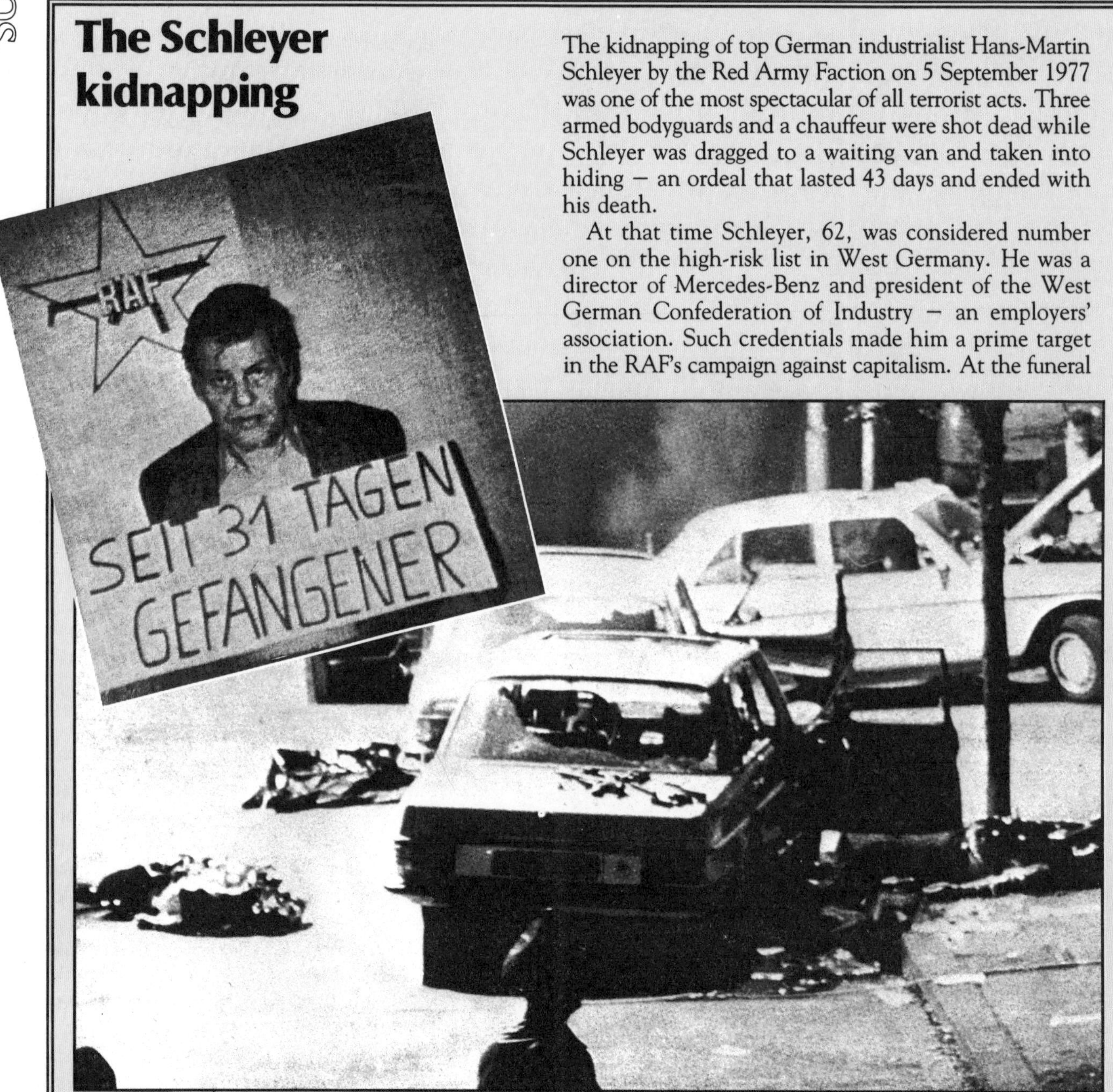

by deposits of lead and barium, the distance from which a shot has been fired: the more gunpowder deposits, the nearer the weapon was to its target. When tests were carried out using Baader's pistol and the ammunition used in Stammheim it was demonstrated that, on comparison, the deadly bullet must have been fired from a distance of between 12 and 16 inches (30 and 40 centimetres). Despite this discovery, the testimony of Dr Hoffmann was veiled in ambiguity. Even though he had uncovered all the signs of violence by a third party, Hoffmann testified that the powder deposits on Baader's skin must have evaporated. A shot with so few traces of gunpowder could be explained only by the presence of a silencer on the gun. No silencer was found in Baader's cell.

The distance from which the shot had been fired was ignored by the Stuttgart public prosecutor Rainer Christ on 18 April when he dismissed the preliminary hearing. And

gathering in August of the banker Jürgen Ponto — murdered by his god-daughter — Schleyer had prophetically remarked: 'The next victim is almost certainly standing in this room now.' Security was stepped up; Schleyer acquired three police bodyguards.

On a business trip to Cologne, Schleyer was being driven through the busy streets at about 5pm on the afternoon of 5 September. Close behind his Mercedes was an escort car carrying the three armed guards. As the convoy turned into a one-way street, a woman suddenly pushed a pram in front of Schleyer's car and a yellow Mercedes swerved across its path. Schleyer's driver braked hard, the escort car rammed into the back of it and a group of people standing on the pavement swung round and opened fire with sub-machine guns. It was thought that about a dozen terrorists were involved in the kidnap; over 200 shots were fired and the driver and three guards were killed within seconds. Schleyer was dragged from the back seat of his car and bundled into a white Volkswagen bus. The whole operation took about three minutes.

The next day a letter from the terrorists outlined their demands: the release of eleven terrorists, among them Baader, Ensslin, Raspe and Möller, flights to the country of their choice and £25,000 each. The German government was determined not to give in to the terrorists; it stalled for time as a massive search for Schleyer began. Six deadlines slipped by as the terrorists' hopes were encouraged by the news that government officials had been negotiating with other countries to seek asylum for the prisoners.

Schleyer's business partners tried to contact the kidnappers, offering a multi-million pound ransom, as did Schleyer's son with an £8 million offer. The latter was ruined by an advance publicity leak for which Schleyer's son later blamed the government. It was becoming apparent to many people that the government's delaying tactics were only prolonging Schleyer's ordeal. Even his notes began to acknowledge this fact; in one, he wrote: 'If Bonn is going to reject the demands they should do it soon.' and 'what you [the government] are imposing on me is senseless torture'. Schleyer's son even took legal action to try to force the German government to save his father's life, arguing that it was their obligation to protect every citizen of their country. The court ruled, however, that the government's obligation to the individual was overshadowed by its larger responsibility to the collective protection of all citizens, which meant taking deterrent steps and resisting blackmail.

As the days dragged by, fears grew that the frustrated terrorists would increase the pressure on the German government. On 13 October, it happened. A Lufthansa jet was hijacked and a five-day cat-and-mouse game between the hijackers and the government ensued. Again Chancellor Helmut Schmidt refused to concede defeat. The successful raid by the anti-terrorist squad on the aircraft at Mogadishu on the night of 17 October was also a blow to Schleyer's family. And the deaths of the Baader-Meinhof prisoners in Stammheim Prison hours later was the signature on Schleyer's death warrant. On 19 October the kidnappers issued the following statement: 'After 43 days we have ended Hans-Martin Schleyer's miserable and corrupt existence.' Schleyer's body was found in a car boot in France. He had been shot three times in the head at close range. Twelve hundred mourners attended his state funeral. Among them was Schmidt, who vowed to wipe out terrorism in West Germany. Hans-Martin Schleyer died in the battle to achieve this aim.

Top left: this photograph of kidnap victim Hans-Martin Schleyer was issued by the terrorists more than a month after he was ambushed in Cologne. Behind him is the RAF symbol. The banner in front of him reads: 'Held in captivity for 31 days'. Left: the scene of the ambush. The bodies of the three dead bodyguards lie beside Schleyer's escort car. In the background is the Mercedes used by the terrorists to block the path of Schleyer's car, which is pictured (centre) with the door wide open and the window shattered by bullets

Top: terrorist Yussef Akache — who called himself Captain Mahmoud during the five-day hijacking of the Lufthansa. He had posed for this poster in a gift shop in London's Soho as a joke. Below: Ulrich Wegener, leader of the specially trained anti-terrorist squad GSG-9, with some of his commandos

Christ did not clear up a further bone of contention between criminologists and forensic scientists — that three bullets had been found in Baader's cell. One was embedded in the mattress, one in the wall near the window, and the third — the one that had killed him — was to the right of the corpse, in front of the bed.

The police asserted that, in order to simulate a fight, Baader had first fired at his bed, then, from a sitting position on the floor, shot at the wall opposite him, before shooting himself. In a police report entitled 'Evaluation of the Evidence', the death shot was described thus: 'Having passed through the skull, the bullet lost speed and landed not far from the corpse.' The forensic scientists had discovered something else in Baader's cell. Near the bullet in the wall they found a trace of 'tissue or blood' and concluded that, after leaving Baader's skull, the bullet had ricocheted off the opposite wall and landed in the vicinity of the body, between it and the bed. But this evidence was not disclosed to the parliamentary investigative committee.

Nor was Raspe's death as clear-cut as it was made out to be. A bullet had entered his head at the right temple, and exited at the left. It then lodged in the bookshelves. In his summation, Christ claimed: 'Raspe must have fired the shot from the pistol that was found near him while in a sitting position, because of the way he was lying on his mattress when he was discovered. The pistol was lying near his right hand.' Two of the four prison officers, who found Raspe that morning bleeding to death in his cell, had clearly seen the weapon in his right hand, however.

Showdown at Mogadishu

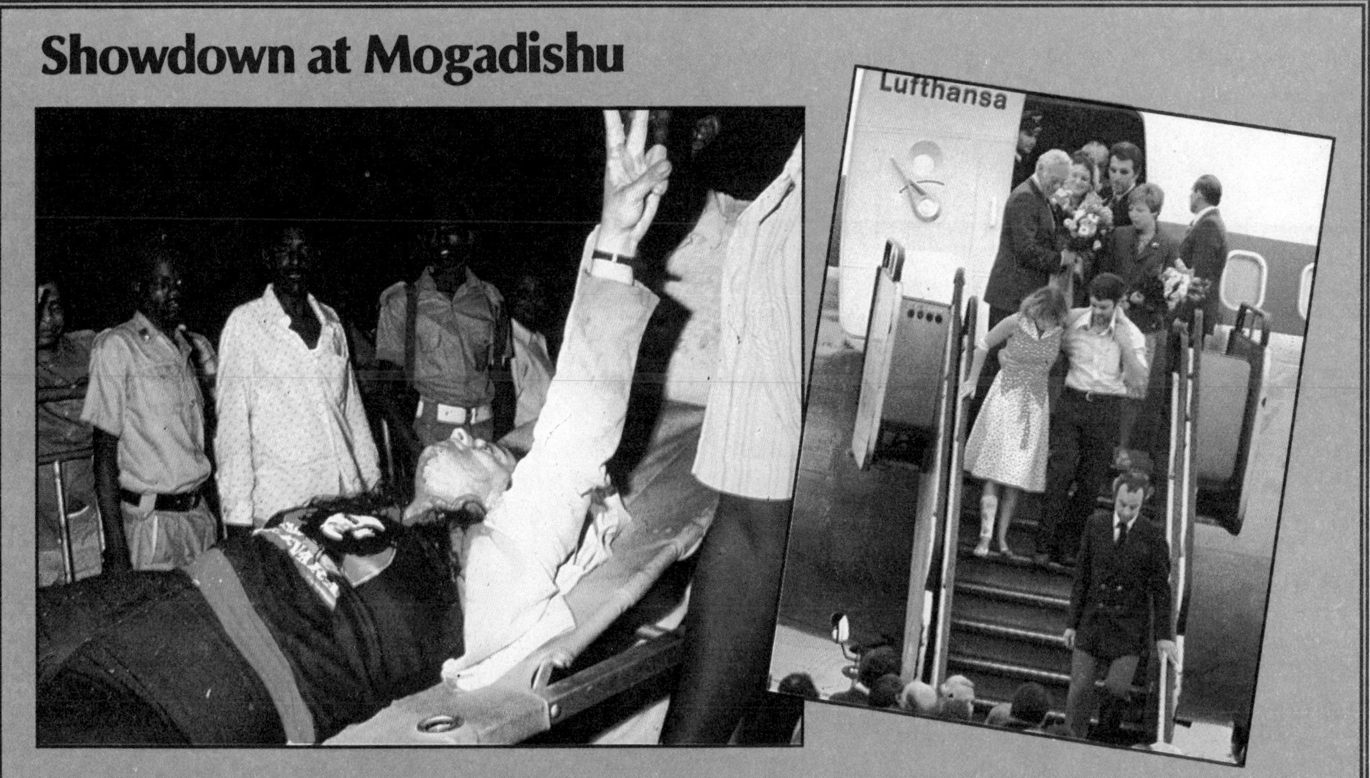

Top left: the surviving, but severely wounded, female hijacker gives a defiant victory sign and screams, 'Palestine, Palestine!' as she is carried from the aircraft. The terrorists were wearing Che Guevara T-shirts. Above: passengers arrive safely home after their five-day ordeal, which ended with the spectacular raid by the anti-terrorist squad as the aircraft stood on the runway at Mogadishu

On the morning of Thursday 13 October 1977 flight LH181 left Majorca with 86 passengers and five crew on board. It was bound for Frankfurt. An hour later two women drew guns and hand grenades out of their boots and two men burst into the cockpit and ordered the pilot Jürgen Schumann to divert to Rome. The leader of the terrorists called himself Captain Mahmoud.

The demands the hijackers made echoed those made by the kidnappers of Hans-Martin Schleyer and were written on the same typewriter. The pressure on the government to release the terrorists was being stepped up, but this only increased Chancellor Schmidt's resolve to combat terrorism. As the hijacked Boeing 737 left for Cyprus, the Grenzschützgruppe-9 (GSG-9) – the specially trained anti-terrorist squad – set off to launch a counter-attack on the hijackers. After five years of rigorous training, the time for action had come.

On the evening of Friday 14 October the hijacked aircraft landed at Dubai. By this time, there was little food or water left on board, the temperature was over 120 degrees Fahrenheit (56 degrees centigrade), the toilets were overflowing and the terrorists were keeping up the tension. Shots were fired at engineers approaching the jet to carry out maintenance. Shortly after this incident, however, Mahmoud allowed a cake and champagne to be delivered to the hijacked aircraft to celebrate the birthday of one of the air hostesses. On 16 October the jet flew to Arden. Schumann left the aircraft to inspect the damage to the landing gear and walked over to speak to airport security forces. When he returned to the cabin Mahmoud shot him through the head in front of the passengers.

The co-pilot then flew the aircraft to Mogadishu in Somalia, Africa, where it arrived on the morning of 17 October. The hijackers tied up the passengers, poured duty-free alcohol and perfume over them and taped explosives to the walls; their threat to blow up the aircraft was stalled by a false assurance from the German government that the Baader-Meinhof prisoners were about to be released and flown to Somalia. That evening the aircraft with thirty assault commandos on board landed at Mogadishu.

At 2.07am on 18 October the GSG-9 rolled an ignited oil drum in front of the aircraft to draw the hijackers to the cockpit. At the same time, the commandos placed stepladders up to the emergency doors and burst into the cabin. 'Stun' grenades were thrown into the cabin and the order to 'Get down!' was given. Two of the hijackers were shot dead, the other two were quickly overcome. All the passengers were safe; they were flown home to an ecstatic welcome in Cologne that afternoon and praise for the rescue operation flooded in from all over the world. The German government had won this stage of the battle, though not without criticism for the manner in which they had risked the lives of so many people. The implications for Schleyer, however, were grave; and the euphoria that surrounded the successful raid at Mogadishu was interrupted several hours later when the news of the prisoners' deaths at Stammheim Prison was received.

Prisoners of the state

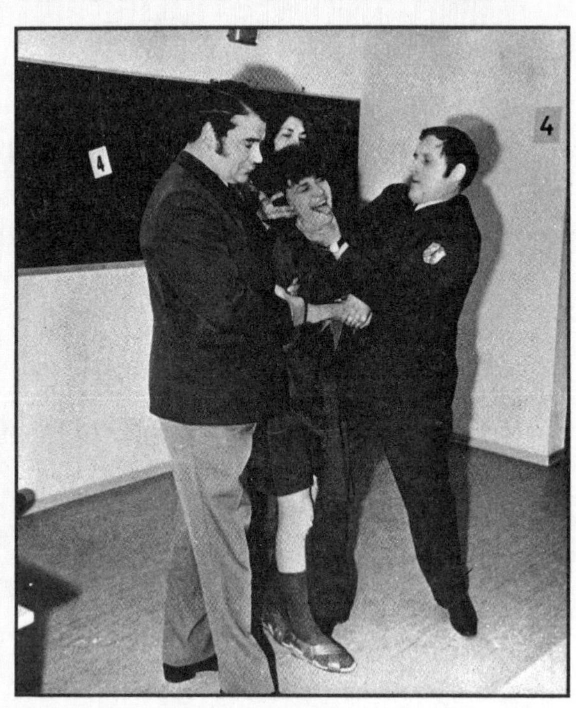

From the capture of the Red Army Faction's leaders in June 1972 until their deaths five and a half years later, controversy raged – at first over the conditions under which they were held, and later over the conduct of their trial. Three lawyers, headed by Klaus Croissant, began a campaign to protest against the 'isolation torture' of terrorists. The West German Ministry of Justice rebuffed the allegations and on 17 January 1973 the prisoners began a series of hunger strikes. The longest lasted 145 days during which time one of the RAF prisoners, Holger Meins, died following attempts to force-feed him.

On 26 November 1974 the Baader-Meinhof case had still not come to trial, but the authorities showed they were preparing for it by staging a raid on the offices of the RAF defence lawyers, seizing a number of defence documents. Three weeks later the parliament in Bonn passed a law – later dubbed the 'Baader-Meinhof law' – giving the courts powers to exclude defence lawyers who were suspected of supporting a criminal organisation or endangering state security, and also giving them power to continue a trial, even when the accused were incapable of appearing.

The trial had been delayed because no court-house in West Germany was considered secure enough. A new high-security court-house was built adjacent to the prison at Stammheim near Stuttgart. The court-house was made of concrete slabs bolted together and had a high metal ceiling. Inside and out, television cameras scanned every inch of the prison area. High metal railings, topped by

Above: Ulrike Meinhof being restrained by guards at Cologne Prison in 1974. Below: Holger Meins – one of the original members of the Baader-Meinhof gang. He died as a result of a prison hunger strike in 1974; the Holger Meins Commando was later named after him

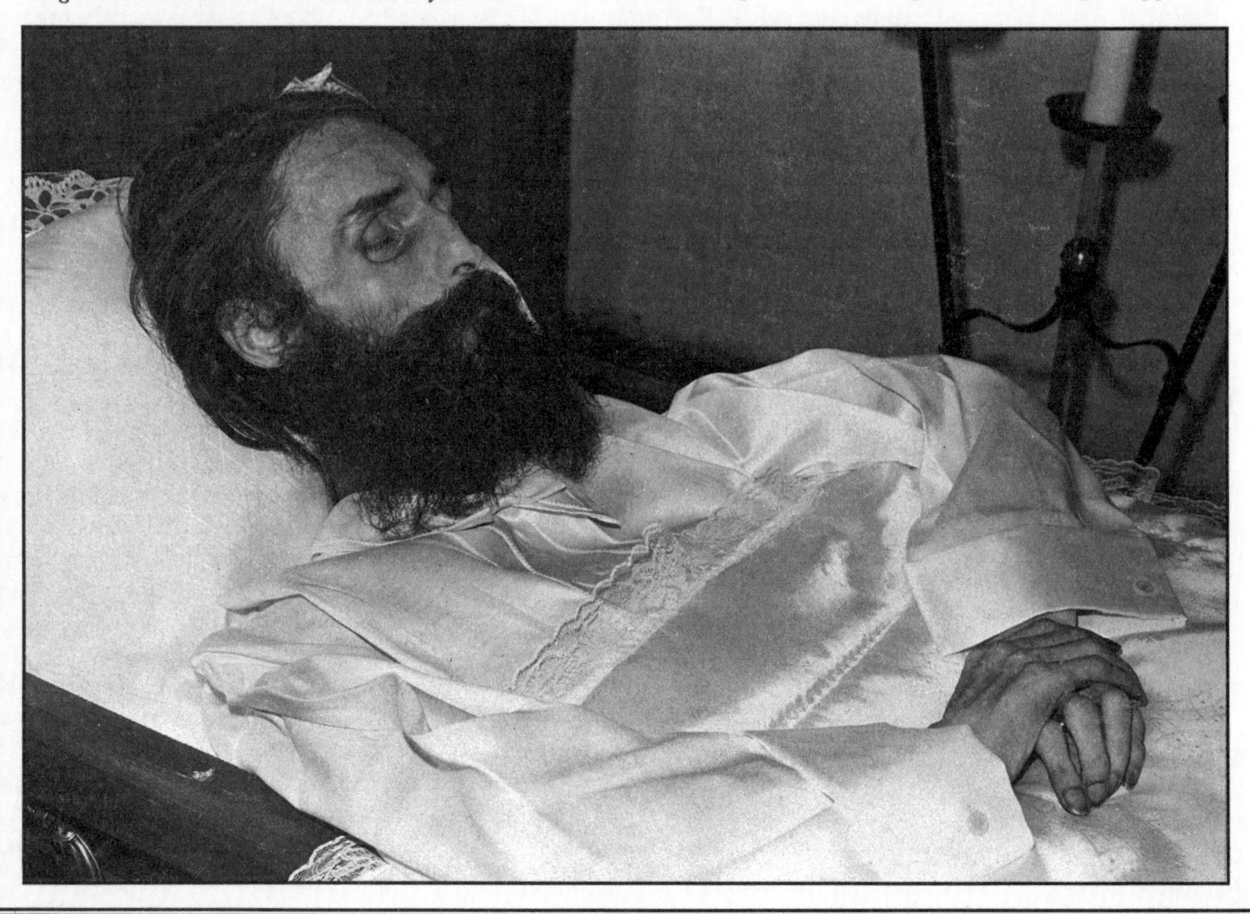

rolls of barbed wire, were separated from a second, outside wall by a deep trench of raked gravel. Armed guards, protected by bullet-proof windows, watched from towers.

On 21 May 1975 the trial began. Early in the proceedings Theodor Prinzing, the presiding judge, made use of the new law of 18 December by insisting that Klaus Croissant and the other lawyers be replaced. The four defendants – Baader, Meinhof, Ensslin and Raspe – tried to obstruct the trial but their long imprisonment had obviously weakened them. They appeared frail and haggard and had difficulty concentrating. At the end of September the defence claimed that the defendants were unfit to continue without receiving medical attention. The judge again made use of the 18 December law by ruling that the trial could continue in their absence.

On 9 May 1976 a prison warder found Ulrike Meinhof hanging from the cross-bar of the window in her cell; a noose had been made from strips of her sheet. A few hours later an official autopsy was carried out. When Meinhof's family were given access to her body, they handed it over to an independent pathologist, who found that parts of it had been cut away to such an extent that it was impossible to say exactly what had happened. The official report stated that the cause of death was suicide, but over the next few months details emerged that threw doubt on this verdict. Traces of semen had apparently been found on Meinhof's underwear; the report had described her as fully clothed when she died, but the pathologist had, in fact, found a saliva track 1⅜ inches (3 centimetres) wide running from her breast to her navel. Salivation is normal in death by hanging or strangulation, but the saliva on the skin suggested that Meinhof was not fully dressed at the time of her death. There were also bruises on the inside of her thighs. When all the available reports were eventually shown to an international group of medical experts by Meinhof's lawyer, it was agreed that throttling during a sexual attack could not be ruled out.

Early in 1977, as the trial entered its twentieth month, Judge Prinzing was dismissed at the request of his fellow judges who claimed he had been continually obstructing the defence lawyers. A month later, after repeated complaints, state authorities admitted having bugged talks between the accused and their lawyers. The lawyers then announced that they were boycotting the trial and for the final forty days the defendants had no legal representation. Finally, in April 1977, Baader, Ensslin and Raspe were each given life plus fifteen years' imprisonment.

The Stammheim prisoners now had little to hope for except a rescue attempt. On 5 September their supporters kidnapped Hans-Martin Schleyer as a bargaining point. The authorities responded by imposing even stricter conditions on the prisoners. They were now kept in complete isolation from each other and were not allowed to hear radio news or receive mail. This regime, which was known as *Kontaktsperrgesetz*, was legalised on 2 October and remained in force until the deaths of Baader, Ensslin and Raspe two weeks later.

Whether the weapon was *near* or *in* the victim's hand was a crucial point. Professor Sellier from Bonn has written in his book on pathology: 'If the weapon is still in the hand of the dead man it immediately indicates murder, because after the shot has been fired the victim loses consciousness and the weapon falls from his hand. In a case of suicide, the weapon always lies *near* the body.'

The most important witness on this point was Prison Inspector Erich Götz. On the morning of 18 October he entered the cell with two sanitary officers, picked up Raspe's pistol in a handkerchief, wrapped a tea towel round it and gave it to one of his colleagues for safe keeping.

A few hours later Götz made this statement to the police: 'His right hand, which grasped the butt of the pistol, lay next to his right thigh on the bed. The back of his hand was facing upwards.' Three other officials made similar statements. Prosecutor Christ accepted this testimony. For him it was confirmed by something else the forensic experts said before the parliamentary committee. Professor Hartmann reported: 'Anyone who had wanted to shoot Raspe while he was sitting on his bed would have had to stand behind the bed, between it and the wall. The gap between bed and wall is extremely narrow.' Professor Rauschke seconded him. Diagrams of Raspe's cell, however, suggest that there was plenty of room between the bed and the wall.

Much of the evidence in Gudrun Ensslin's cell was ignored, too. A simple test would have determined whether she died by her own hand or not: the so-called histamine test. The tissue hormone histamine always collects around the strangulation marks when a person commits suicide by hanging. If a person who is already dead is strung up to simulate suicide by hanging, the histamine will not be present. But this test was not carried out, nor was the chair supposedly used in the suicide ever properly examined.

When Ensslin's corpse was taken down from the window, something happened that was reported neither to the parliamentary committee nor by the public prosecutor in his summation: the noose broke. The public prosecutor maintains that it held while Ensslin, who weighed 7 stone 10 pounds (49 kilograms), jumped off the chair. Experts maintained that it held while the body was writhing in the throes of death. And yet it broke when there was least pressure upon it.

It was never discovered whether the wire was worn or, as Ensslin's sister Christiane suspects, 'perhaps only strong enough to support the weight of someone who was already unconscious, or dead'. It also remains unclear whether the chair was in the same position in which the forensic scientists found it on the afternoon of 18 October as at the time of Ensslin's death.

Irmgard Möller was the one survivor out of the four prisoners. The public prosecutor stated that 'the prisoner stabbed herself four times in the left breast with her breakfast knife. Two of the wounds were about 2 centimetres [¾ inch] deep, the others 4 centimetres [1½ inches] deep'. The deeper wounds 'were very nearly deep enough to penetrate the heart and cause fatal bleeding. Not much more pressure would have been needed to ensure death'. Prosecutor Christ explained Möller's wounds as an attempted suicide because

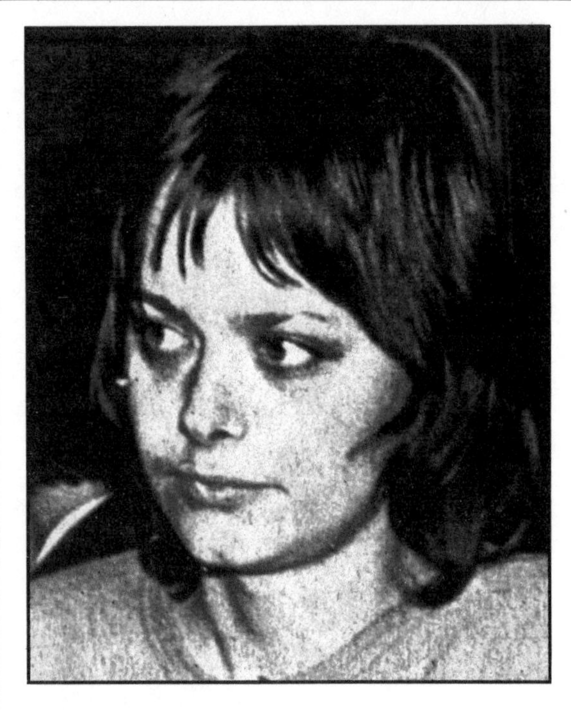

Above: Ingrid Schubert, 32, an original member of the Baader-Meinhof gang, was found hanged in her cell in Munich's Stadelheim Prison on 5 November 1977. A former medical assistant, she had been imprisoned in 1971 for her involvement in the rescue of Andreas Baader from jail in 1970 and in bank robberies. Explosives had been found in her cell at Stammheim Prison before her transfer to Munich. Her death, following so shortly after the deaths of Baader, Ensslin and Raspe, added further weight to the belief that there had been a plot to get rid of the imprisoned terrorists. Right: two books dealing with different aspects of the Baader-Meinhof gang. The German guerrilla: terror, reaction and resistance *(top) records an interview with West German guerrilla Hans Joachim Klein. Klein was wounded during the raid on the OPEC (Organisation of Petroleum Exporting Countries) building in Vienna in December 1975, an operation masterminded by the notorious Carlos; the cover shows Holger Meins' corpse.* Hitler's Children *(below), featuring Ulrike Meinhof on the cover, presents the story of the Baader-Meinhof gang*

Möller claimed to have heard a voice saying: 'Baader and Ensslin are already dead'

'a third party bent on murder would not have stopped short of penetrating her heart'.

However convincingly this argument reads, the prosecutor's version of events does not tie in with the evidence of Professor Hans-Eberhard Hoffmeister, who operated on the victim on 18 October 1977 in the University Hospital of Tübingen. Hoffmeister established that one of the wounds in Möller's chest penetrated 2¾ inches (7 centimetres). The knife blade itself was not much longer than this – it measured 3½ inches (9 centimetres). This deep wound induced blood to flow into the fatty tissue directly encasing the heart. The stab wound must have been delivered with considerable force, because a notch ¼ inch (5 millimetres) wide and ⅛ inch (3 millimetres) deep was found in the cartilaginous part of the fifth rib. The wounds would have been difficult to inflict, as the butter-knife had a rounded end and a serrated edge. Irmgard Möller later recalled that she woke up at about 5am on 18 October to hear 'two soft popping noises' and then a 'quiet squeaking sound'. She claimed to have heard a voice saying: 'Baader and Ensslin are already dead.' She recalled a 'whirling feeling' in her head and then waking up in hospital.

On 19 December 1977 Möller brought criminal charges 'against an unknown person for suspicion of attempted murder'. Testifying at a January hearing, she denied that there had been a suicide pact at Stammheim. 'We discussed suicide extensively after Ulrike Meinhof's death. We came to the conclusion that suicide was not part of the Red Army Faction's politics.' She also denied that the four had been able to communicate with one another during the hijacking period. She admitted that she had been able to listen to the prison broadcast on the night of 17 October, but that had come to an end at 11pm – an hour before the first reports of the rescue at Mogadishu were broadcast. Her ninety-minute appearance at the hearing ended with her being dragged out of the courtroom by two guards when she tried to confer with her two defence lawyers. On 18 April 1978 her investigation was lumped together with the hearing into the deaths of Baader, Ensslin and Raspe, though, in these cases, no mention of murder was ever made. In 1979 Möller was sentenced to detention for life.

Because the authorities had ruled out murder from the beginning, the question of whether a so-called 'killer commando' could have broken into 'the safest prison in the world' was not considered. On the seventh floor, with its extra security precautions, this was simply unthinkable. But the security system was not watertight. In particular, two video cameras trained on the communal area outside the RAF cells were found to be faulty.

One of the most intriguing theories connected with the Stammheim case concerns traces of sand allegedly discovered on Baader's shoes at the time of his death. This was taken to indicate that Baader had been flown to Mogadishu on 17 October to trick the Palestinian hijackers of the Boeing 737 into believing that the German government wanted to exchange the hostages on the aircraft and the kidnapped industrialist Hans-Martin Schleyer for the RAF prisoners. After the aircraft had been stormed and the crisis resolved,

Baader is said to have been flown back from the desert to Stammheim, where he was shot and dumped in his cell. There was no mention of sand in Christ's summing up.

Three weeks after Christ closed the Stammheim case, a report came from the laboratory in Wiesbaden, which described the investigation into 'substances adhering to the shoes of Andreas Baader'. When he first saw the corpse on 18 October 1977, Professor Holczabek had pointed out traces of sand on Baader's shoes. He was the only one to do so. He had inquired whether Baader had been allowed to go for a walk. In the cell the dirt on the floor near Baader's feet was removed with sticky tape. Three months later, on 26 January 1978, the Wiesbaden laboratory sent for samples from the exercise yard where seventh-floor prisoners were permitted to take a breath of fresh air.

The tests proved that Baader had got sand on his shoes: 'a mixture of fine, light and dark particles that had become stuck together. There were also minute pieces of gravel'. Where the sand came from, the investigators were unable to say.

The matter of how the terrorists came to possess their weapons was equally mysterious. The authorities alleged that the guns were smuggled into the prison, but could not say how. Nor is there any explanation for their remaining hidden despite the constant searches of the prison cells. The 7·65mm Heckler and Koch pistol by which Andreas Baader died can be stripped down into 44 pieces and easily reassembled using a nail file. But the same is not true of the 9mm calibre pistol found next to Jan-Carl Raspe. If, as the police suggested, the lawyers did try to smuggle in the weapons in parts or fully assembled, they would have had to face some formidable obstacles. Before each visit to their clients, the lawyers were searched with a metal detector. They had to deposit their bags outside the visitor's room and were not even allowed to take their dictaphones in with them.

The prison authorities complained later, however, that they were not allowed to strip-search the lawyers. The prisoners were stripped naked and received new clothes and underwear, both before and after the lawyers' visits. Defence lawyer Otto Schily explained that the contents of his briefcase were removed by prison warders, and all documents and files examined (even though they related to the court case and were therefore confidential). He was searched both bodily and with a metal detector; his shoes, which had metal clips on the soles, had to be removed before entering the visitors' room. Officials admitted that they bugged the visitors' room. After the kidnapping of Hans-Martin Schleyer, the lawyers were separated from their clients by thick glass.

Although it was unclear how the weapons could have been smuggled into the jail, the authorities stuck to their version of the events. And between 20 October and 6 December security specialists made an astonishing series of discoveries that seemed to corroborate the official line. In secret hiding places – such as behind skirting boards and electrical fittings – in and around the cells and rooms used by Baader, Ensslin, Raspe and Karl Croissant (the imprisoned Baader-Meinhof defence lawyer) were found a minute transistor radio, several caches of explosives, razor blades, a

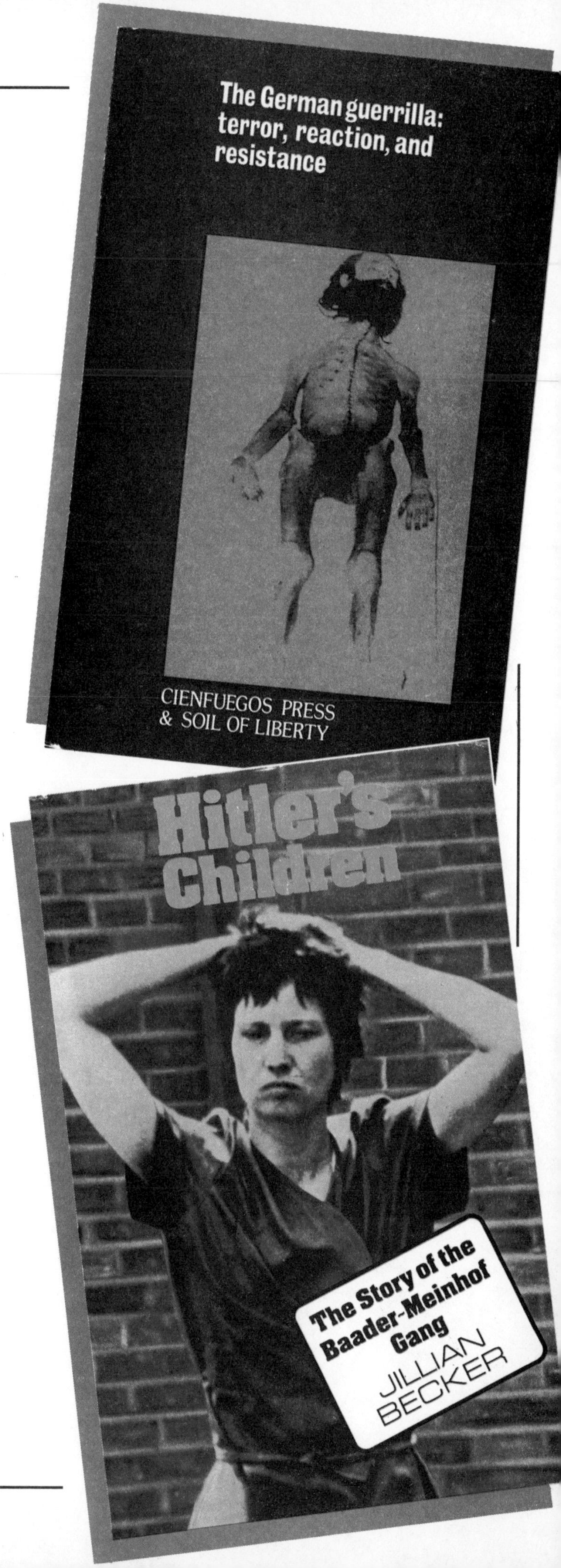

Below: 'Gudrun, Andreas and Jan were tortured and murdered at Stammheim Prison' — RAF sympathisers at the funeral of the Baader-Meinhof terrorists display a banner that gives their version of the events of 18 October. They hide their faces with scarfs. Baader, Ensslin and Raspe were buried at the Dornhalden Cemetery near Stuttgart on 27 January 1978. Many people objected to the idea of their being buried at the cemetery alongside war victims and politicians. But Ensslin's father, a Lutheran clergyman, persuaded the Mayor of Stuttgart, Manfred Rommel, to allow the burials to take place there. Rommel explained that Ensslin's father was determined to give himself some peace. The alternative, he pointed out, was that the preacher might take the issue to court which would have resulted in the funeral of the three terrorists dragging on for months and might have led to further waves of violent protest

stomach pump, a pistol, ammunition and a small loudspeaker that may have been used for sending and receiving Morse code. It was further revealed that on the seventh floor of Stammheim there was an 'extra' fire escape door that could be opened only from the outside — as well as a communications network between the terrorists' cells. No explanation was given, however, as to how this system had escaped detection until after the deaths. Indeed, the most significant conclusion that can be drawn from these findings is that security at Stammheim was poor, and that ample opportunity was given for the terrorists to kill themselves — or be killed — within the prison's supposedly impenetrable walls.

If the four terrorists at Stammheim did not commit suicide, then they can only have been murdered by the German government or by foreign agents with the government's permission. And how were the assassins able to enter and leave the building without involving so many witnesses that the whole operation would have become unmanageable?

The Stammheim investigation left many questions unanswered and had served only to throw up a wealth of conflicting evidence. Chancellor Schmidt's promise that 'the prisoners' deaths should be investigated and the facts established beyond doubt and published for all to see' had hardly been fulfilled. And the case for the official version of 'suicide and attempted suicide' is not a totally convincing conclusion to the story of some of the most notorious terrorists in history.

DEATH IN JEDDAH

In the early hours of Sunday 20 May 1979, Helen Smith, a 23-year-old English nurse, was killed only yards from the hospital where she worked in Jeddah, Saudi Arabia. She had been at an illegal drinks party thrown by an expatriate English surgeon and his wife in their sixth-floor flat. The initial Foreign Office statement '. . . that there was an accident, and Miss Smith fell from a building' was scarcely borne out by evidence later presented by top pathologists after a series of autopsies. But if Helen did not topple 70 feet to her death, how did she die? Her father, Ron Smith, has spent years in a remarkable quest to discover the truth – and in the process has come up against repeated obstructions, inconsistencies and contradictions. *PAUL FOOT* analyses the case in detail and offers some answers that the authorities may find difficult to swallow

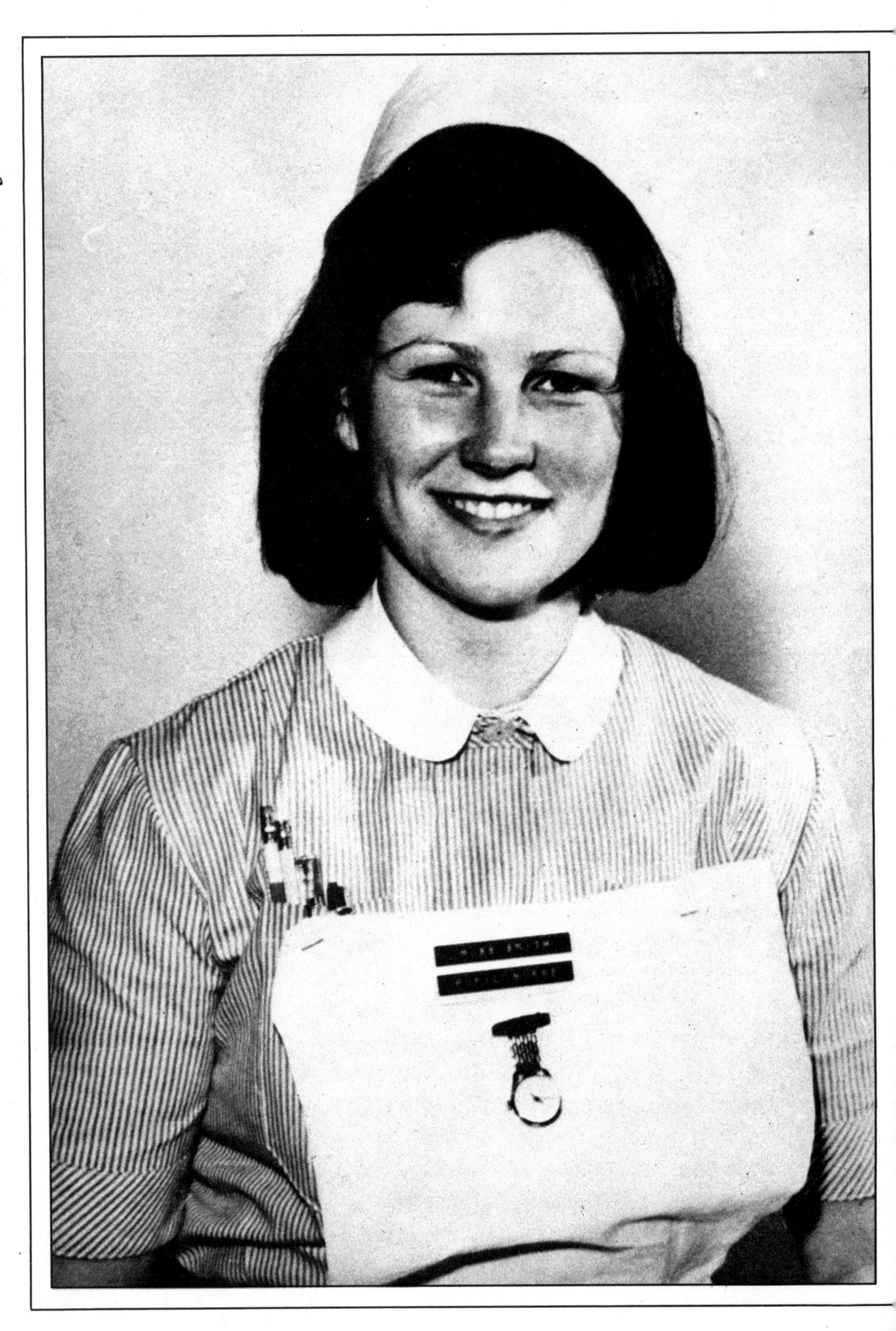

AT 2pm on Sunday 20 May 1979, Ron Smith, former company director and detective constable in the Leeds City Police, received a telephone call from his youngest daughter, Beverley. She told him that her elder sister Helen had died in Jeddah, Saudi Arabia. The police and the Foreign Office confirmed the terrible news. Apparently Helen had died 'after falling from the sixth floor of the Bakhsh Hospital', where she was employed as a nurse. Five days later Ron flew to Jeddah where the British consul, Francis Geere, took him to the jail in which Richard Arnot, the English senior surgeon at the Bakhsh Hospital, was being held. Arnot was in prison for holding the illegal drinks party at which Helen had died. His wife Penny and seven of the party guests had also been imprisoned for consuming alcohol. Arnot was able to offer Ron no explanation at all, only sympathy. Ron was growing increasingly suspicious that Helen had been the victim of foul play.

Geere had so far been evasive about the incident. When Ron insisted on seeing Helen's body, the consul protested, but to no avail. So, at 8pm on Saturday 26 May 1979, Ron was brought to the mortuary where Helen was lying. On seeing the face of his dead daughter, he was shocked to see a deep indentation in the middle of her forehead. 'What's this?' he asked aloud. Consul Geere hazarded a guess that Helen had fallen on a small stone. Ron immediately dismissed this as utter rubbish. If she had fallen on her head on a small stone from any height at all, he pointed out, let alone a height of 70 feet (20 metres) as had been suggested, her skull would have been smashed to pieces.

The consul's interjection, and the sight of Helen's face, which seemed strangely discoloured (as though 'she needed a wash', as Ron put it later), added to Ron's belief that Helen had died in strange circumstances. After arguments with the mortuary attendant, Subi Bakir, and with the consul, he got permission to inspect the rest of his daughter's body. To his amazement and consternation, it was largely free of injuries. There had been some internal bleeding on the right side, but the head, neck, legs and arms seemed in perfect condition. She looked as though she had just gone to sleep, said Ron.

From that moment, consistently and without ever doubting his first impression, Ron Smith refused to accept the version he had been given of his daughter's death – that she had fallen by accident from a balcony during Mr and Mrs Arnot's party. He has since devoted his life to disproving the proposition put forward in the official statement issued by the Foreign Office on the day after Helen's death: 'All we know is that there was an accident and Miss Smith fell from a building.' His daughter, he was convinced, had not fallen from the balcony. She had not fallen any distance at all. She had died by some other means, and Ron Smith was convinced that someone somewhere was trying to stop him finding out how and why it had happened.

Before long these suspicions received dramatic reinforcement. On Sunday 27 May Ron was taken for the second time to the Bakhsh Hospital where his daughter had worked as a nurse since its opening the previous January. Its proprietor, Dr Abdul Rahman Bakhsh, a powerful figure in Jeddah, as well as other hospital officials, was prepared to believe the

Left: Helen Linda Smith was born on 3 January 1956. She left Belmond-Birklands School, Harrogate, Yorkshire, in 1974, passed her nursing exams and became a state-enrolled nurse at St George's Hospital, Tooting, London. She joined the staff of St James's Hospital, Leeds, in 1977. In the autumn of 1978, her mother suggested she apply for a job at the new Bakhsh Hospital in Jeddah. She flew to Saudi Arabia on 5 December. On 20 May 1979 she was killed. Below: Ron Smith – 'I don't give a damn about the oil crisis, the Arab-Jew hostilities, or anything else of the kind. I want to know how my daughter died.' Ron's single-mindedness in his quest saw him through many battles with obstructive public officials in both Britain and Saudi Arabia

accident story. But as Ron left the hospital to walk to the Foreign Office Range Rover, which was standing just outside it, he was approached by two women in uniform. 'Mr Smith,' said one of them, 'your daughter Helen was a friend of ours, and we want to tell you how she was murdered.'

Leaving the consul behind him, Ron went into the hospital building with the two nursing sisters, who introduced themselves as Morag Keene and Joan Arundale. He spent that entire night talking to many members of the hospital staff. None of them admitted attending the party, but all of them urged him not to accept the official version of events. Something odd, they said, had gone on the previous Sunday night, and they doubted very much whether Helen, or the unknown Dutchman who died with her, had fallen accidentally from the balcony of the Arnots' flat as the authorities claimed.

This was unlikely, the hospital staff told Ron, for two reasons. First, some of them had seen Helen's body on the morning it was found at the bottom of the Arnots' block of flats. It did not look as though it had fallen that distance. Second, the British Embassy itself was in doubt about the official story. Fleming Aaen, catering manager at the hospital, told Ron that he and two other senior members of the staff had had a personal interview with Gordon Kirby, the British vice consul in Jeddah. Kirby said that he and his colleagues were not happy with the version of events that had been

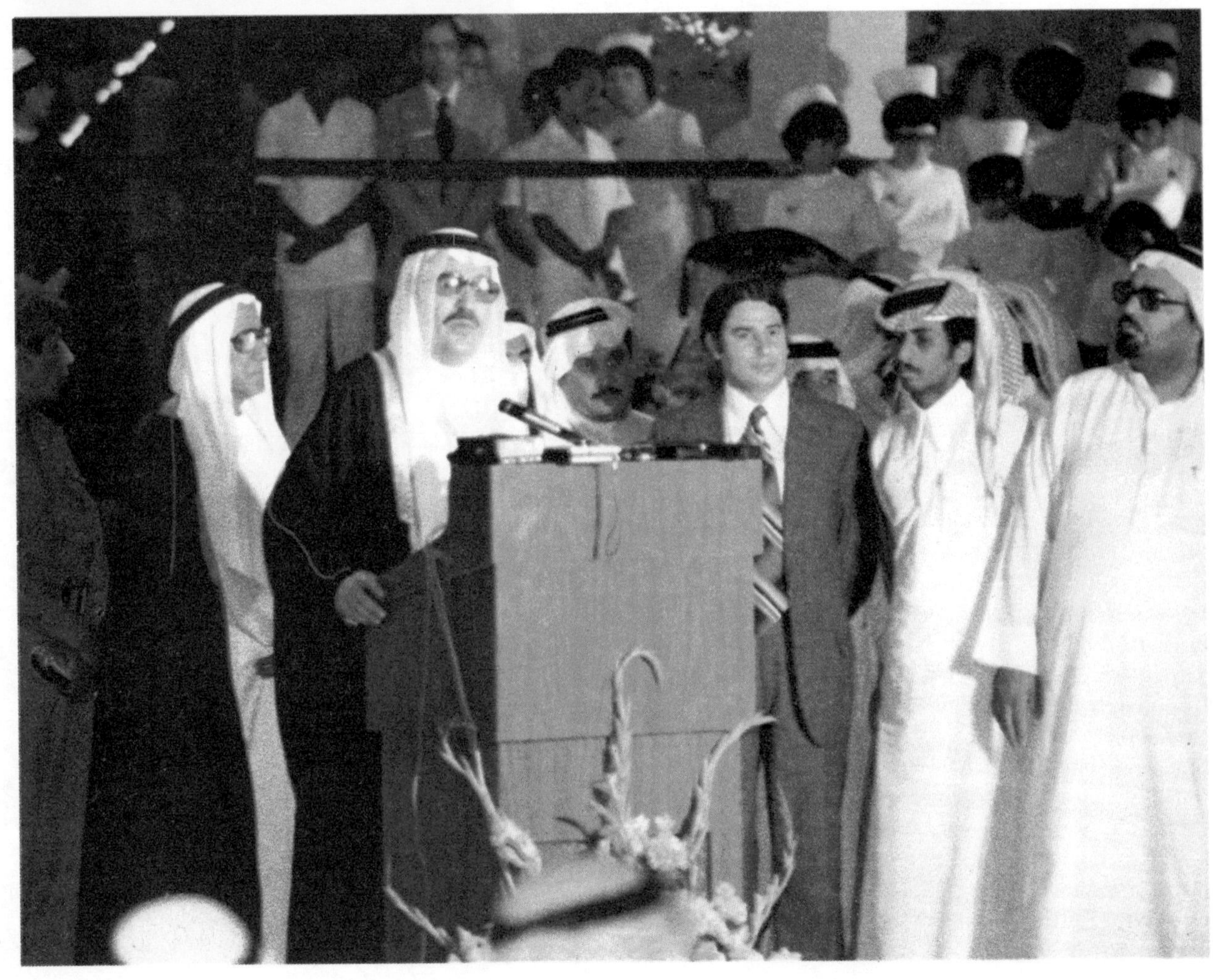

given them by Mrs Arnot on the morning the bodies were discovered.

Ron's anger and resentment were further inflamed when, returning to the Embassy, he asked to see the statement that Mrs Arnot had made to Kirby, and was refused. This refusal was confirmed by the British Foreign Office in London. What, Ron asked himself, were the Foreign Office trying to cover up? He comforted himself with the assurances he got from the Saudi police that they would not accept the doctor's story, but would pursue the matter as a murder inquiry. He also requested an autopsy on his daughter's body by a Saudi government pathologist, Dr Ali Kheir. This was conducted on 2 June. Dr Kheir found no evidence of fractures to the head, neck, shoulder blades or spine. He removed Helen's reproductive organs for further tests. Ron left Jeddah on 6 June without seeing the report of the autopsy, which first had to go to the police.

On his return to England, he was assured several times by an official at the Saudi Arabian Embassy in London that the Saudi police were pursuing a 'murder inquiry' into his daughter's death. With the Foreign Office insisting that the matter was closed, and that they were quite satisfied that his daughter had died by accident, Ron pinned his hopes on the Saudi police. Separated from his wife (who was soon to marry again), with no friends in high places or in newspapers, he pursued his lonely campaign to try to find out the truth. In December 1979, he noticed that, as the British Foreign Office had been, the Saudi Embassy was becoming evasive. He redoubled his enquiries.

In March 1980 the Arnots and their party guests were tried at the Serious Crimes Court in Jeddah. After spending

Far left: the official opening of the Bakhsh Hospital on 9 March 1979. Above, far left: Francis Geere, second secretary and consul at the British Embassy in Jeddah, whose position made him responsible for Ron Smith on his trips to Saudi Arabia to find out how Helen died. Cambridge educated, cool and courteous, Geere disapproved of Ron's aggressive tactics and described his conduct as 'unbecoming to an English gentleman'. In September 1980 he was transferred to the British Embassy in Berne, Switzerland. Above: the society wedding of Richard Arnot and Penelope Thornton on 25 July 1970. Top: the Arnots, who threw the party at which Helen died, and Tim Hayter, in Jeddah. Mr Arnot, senior surgeon at the Bakhsh Hospital, is the one with the knife in his mouth

five months in prison, all nine had been released on bail. Of the five Germans at the party, only two got any further sentence – 30 lashes each. The French guest, Jacques Texier, was acquitted. But the three other people who had been at the party got heavy punishments. Mr Arnot was sentenced to a year in prison, and 30 lashes; Mrs Arnot and Tim Hayter, the New Zealander, were each sentenced to 80 lashes, to be administered in front of a crowd. There was an immediate outcry in Britain, in protest that a British doctor's wife was to be flogged in public. Arnot was found guilty of consuming alcohol and allowing his wife to commit adultery, and Hayter and Mrs Arnot of adultery.

All this confirmed Ron Smith's feelings about the party his daughter had attended, but none of it satisfied him. He still wanted to know how his daughter had died, and still

Death of a Princess

In April 1980, as Penny Arnot awaited her public flogging for the offences she committed on the night Helen Smith died, a new incident compounded the worsening relations between Saudi Arabia and Britain. On 8 April the British commercial television channel networked a two-hour film entitled *Death of a Princess*. Directed by Anthony Thomas, it dealt with the execution in public of the Saudi Princess Misha in 1977 for adultery. She was shot and her boyfriend was beheaded.

The film was a dramatised documentary. It portrayed a real story by filming actors taking part in the supposed events. For instance, there was a sequence showing Saudi princesses picking out men in cars and contacting them to arrange assignations. This 'selection process' was filmed not in fact, but in fiction.

The film caused a tremendous outcry in Saudi Arabia. The ageing, traditionalist King Khaled had a special video of it flown to him in Paris. When he had seen it, he called an instant boycott of new commercial contracts with British firms. For a time, it looked as though the whole of British trade with the most expanding of overseas markets might be stopped. Foreign Office officials led by Lord Carrington, the Foreign Secretary, started a flow of grovelling apologies to the Saudis.

For a moment, the Helen Smith story became embroiled in high politics. It was believed in Britain that Penny and Richard Arnot (who also faced a flogging) might become victims of a new anti-British feeling in Saudi Arabia. As it turned out, diplomatic efforts succeeded in restoring good relations. The argument was patched up in late August 1980. Trade resumed and grew. The Arnots were released without their sentences being carried out.

Left: a scene from the television film Death of a Princess, *showing the public beheading of Princess Misha's lover. The film implied strong criticism of the moral standards of the Saudi royal family and almost provoked a major diplomatic row*

refused to accept that she had died by accident. In April 1980 he at last found out the identity of the 31-year-old Dutchman who had died with Helen. In Jeddah the previous year Ron had been told by officials at the British and Dutch Embassies that the man's name was 'Ottel'. He had combed the Amsterdam telephone directory for the name 'Ottel' and had even rung several people of that name, to no avail. Now, with the help of two Dutch journalists, Tine Van Houts and Bert Brevoord, he discovered that the man was Johannes Otten, a tugboat captain who had been hired by Harms Salvage, a big German dredging firm. Tim Hayter and the Germans who had attended the Arnots' party also worked for Harms.

Ron travelled to Holland to meet Johannes' parents, Mr and Mrs Klaas Otten of Elburg. They told him to his fury that on the advice of the Dutch Foreign Office they had had Johannes' body cremated without an autopsy being carried out. They had been told, like Ron, that Johannes had fallen accidentally from the balcony. Like Ron, they did not believe it. Through discussions with the Ottens and with Jonnike Schulte, Johannes' Belgian girlfriend, Ron established that Helen had not met the Dutchman prior to the party. The attitude of the Dutch Foreign Office towards Otten's death further convinced him that this could be an official cover-up of the circumstances in which the two young people died.

In June 1980 Ron travelled to Jeddah, again at his own expense, to bring his daughter's body home. This time he was shunned by the staff at the Bakhsh Hospital, who steadfastly refused to speak to him. What information he could get – from the police and from the Embassy interpreter Ayoub Quasim and the judge at the Arnots' trial – confirmed his view that the truth about what went on at the party had not yet come out. At the airport, as he prepared to return to London, he was apprehended by Saudi officials, forced to stay five more days in Jeddah, and to hand over all the photographs and plans he had made during that time (these were later returned to him).

As soon as he arrived back in Britain, he started a long battle with the coroner's office in Leeds, a battle that was to last for over two and a half years. He delivered Helen's body to the acting coroner in Leeds at the time, Mr Miles Coverdale, and asked for an inquest. To his amazement, the

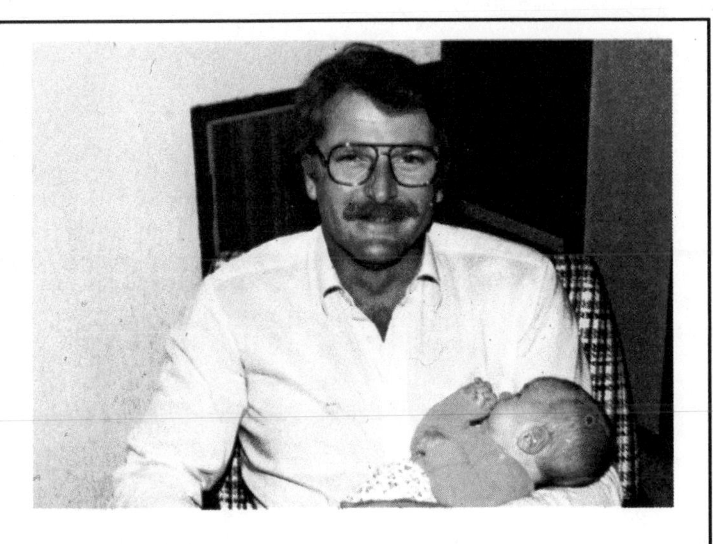

Above: Johannes Otten in Amsterdam, ten days before his death. The baby is his sister's. Otten worked as a pilot of boats in Dutch and Belgian waters until 1976, when he first found employment on marine projects in the Middle East. He went to Jeddah in 1978. Otten was the father of two children from the first of his two short-lived marriages

Ron Smith refused to accept that she had died by accident

No autopsy, no money

Why was the body of Johannes Otten, the Dutch sea captain who died with Helen Smith, not subjected to an autopsy? When it was returned to Holland from Saudi Arabia, his family had to decide whether to cremate it without opening the coffin, as the Dutch Foreign Office advised them to do, or whether to authorise an autopsy. After much argument and agonising, they went ahead with the cremation in the same coffin.

A few months later they were surprised to hear that the big Dutch insurance underwriters Roeloffs refused to pay out on the life insurance policies that Johannes, like all Harms workers abroad, had taken out with them. The reason, Roeloffs stated, was their 'information' that Johannes Otten's death was his own fault, the result of his own drunkenness.

This curious 'information' came from the insurance company's loss adjusters, Kiewit Howells, another firm of international repute. Yet at no time when seeking to establish the cause of death had Kiewit Howells suggested that an autopsy be carried out, or warned the Ottens that without an autopsy they might have to forfeit the insurance money if the cause of death was not a genuine accident. Frequently, in such cases, loss adjusters arrange for an autopsy to be carried out or try to persuade the family to arrange one. As usual, the case of Helen Smith and Johannes Otten was an exception.

A hard-working nurse, Helen Smith also enjoyed a busy social life in Jeddah, easily making friends within the hospital community. These photographs, from her own collection, show her and some of her colleagues at work and play. This page, above: a day out in the desert. Right: Dr Abdul Aziz Sarchal, the consultant paediatrician from Iraq with whom Helen had an affair in early 1979. Below right: Helen on duty at the Bakhsh Hospital. Opposite page, top left: Agnes Johnstone, matron at the hospital, dances at a Jeddah wedding reception. Top right: a party gathering on the roof above the Arnots' flat. Standing are Dr Sukhtian (left) and Dr Sarchal (centre), in front of them Sister Veronica Peters, Helen and young William Arnot. Centre: Helen sun-bathing. Below left: the mysterious Scot, Ron Low (left), possibly Helen's boyfriend at the time of her death. Below right: Helen scuba diving – probably in the company of the Arnots and Tim Hayter

The yellow Sun and the watching Eye

Above: a London news-stand shows the Sun *front page for 16 September 1980. Below:* Private Eye*'s first item on the Helen Smith affair*

Letter from Jeddah

Ronald Smith, a former Leeds policeman who now runs an electronics business in the city, has been here for several weeks: his daughter Helen was found half-naked and dead on May 20. The official version, strongly supported by the Foreign Office, is that Helen fell to her death while making love to a young Dutchman on a balcony. Ronald Smith is convinced that Helen was murdered, and her body placed on the ground as though she had fallen.

On arrival here, he went to the privately-owned Bakhsh hospital where his daughter worked, and studied the top-floor apartment next-door-but-one to that from whose balcony his daughter and the Dutchman were supposed to have fallen. The balcony was high enough to ensure that no one, however, drunk, could possibly have fallen from it.

Smith's doubts were reinforced by a short 10-minute interview he was allowed with Dr Richard Arnot, the British consulant, who works at the Bakhsh hospital, and at whose flat Helen attended a party on the night of her death. Dr Arnot and his wife Penelope are both held in custody by the Saudi Arabian police on ...ges related to alcohol, which, it is alleged, ... consumed on the night ... had

In the first 15 months of Ron Smith's campaign to find out what happened to his daughter, the newspapers took little or no interest. This changed dramatically when Richard and Penny Arnot returned to Britain in August 1980. In September thousands of column inches were devoted to the story, most of the coverage vacuous and sensational.

An example of the extremes resorted to by Fleet Street was the *Sun*'s front page story of 16 September. On that day the *Sun* led with an 'exclusive' under the banner headline GIRL WHO COULDN'T SAY NO. The story featured an anonymous former lover of Helen's, who gave some lurid accounts of her supposed sexual exploits.

The 'lover' – described by the *Sun* merely as an 'ex-soldier' – was quoted as saying that the 'the likeliest cause' of Helen's death was that she had fallen off the balcony. The *Sun* continued: 'He said: "Sex on the balcony would be just the thing to appeal to her".'

Not content with raising the alleged revelations of an anonymous lover and elevating these revelations to the status of evidence, the *Sun* went on to print on 29 September another front page 'proving' that Helen had been murdered by a Saudi lover and flung off the roof of the Arnots' block of flats. This story originated from a man whose wife's sister had looked after the Arnots' children in Jeddah. It was accepted by the *Sun* on a Sunday and published, without a word being checked, on the Monday morning. Subsequent inquiries by Ron Smith and various journalists showed there was not a word of truth in it.

One publication that avoided both lurid sensationalism and a complete lack of interest in the Helen Smith affair was *Private Eye*, the celebrated satirical magazine that comes out fortnightly in Britain. In June 1979 *Private Eye* printed a 'Letter From Jeddah' written by one of its more regular correspondents, Jack Lundin, who happened to be in that city working for the *Arab News*. Lundin met and befriended Ron Smith shortly before Ron flew back to London after his first visit to Jeddah.

The letter was followed fifteen months later by a remarkable article – also by Jack Lundin – alleging that Helen Smith had been beaten, raped and murdered, and that the Foreign Office was deliberately covering up the facts. In an extraordinary move, the Foreign Office issued a six-point denial. (Two of the points denied allegations *Private Eye* had not made.)

The denial had the effect of bringing the story to the attention of hitherto uninterested newspapers and the story flourished for six weeks. *Private Eye* continued with regular stories about the affair all the way through to the inquest in November and December 1982. Ron Smith came to regard the magazine as the only part of the media he could trust, and always passed his findings on to it first. Its constant flow of new facts helped to boost Ron's confidence in bringing the case to the Court of Appeal.

Above: Fleming and Lisa Aaen, who were dismissed from the Bakhsh in July 1979, two months after the tragedy. Fleming Aaen had been the hospital catering manager, Lisa a nursing sister in the gynaecological department. They were convinced that Helen had been murdered. Later they helped Ron's cause by putting him in contact with the pathologist Professor Dalgaard, a fellow Dane

coroner refused. This amazement turned to rage when the coroner even refused an official autopsy. Coverdale relented when it was pointed out to him that he was bound in law to order such an autopsy. It was duly carried out on 27 June 1980 by Dr Michael Green, a Home Office pathologist based at Leeds University.

On 16 July, Coverdale issued a press statement saying that he would not be holding an inquest into the death of Helen Smith. Dr Green's report, the statement said, made it clear that Helen's injuries were 'entirely consistent with a fall from a height'. The accident theory had therefore been vindicated and there was no need to look into the matter more closely. Ron Smith protested that this was nonsense. The injuries, after all, could be consistent with anything else, like furniture having fallen on Helen, for instance, or someone having kicked or hit her. How could theories other than accidental death from a fall be tested without an inquest? Ron was angered still further when he read the Green report, which was sent to him by the coroner.

The report referred to a 'sub-capital fracture of the right humerus', or upper arm bone, which could not have been sustained, wrote Green, unless the body had fallen from a height onto the right side. 'This fracture would account,' Green went on, 'for the bizarre position of the right arm described by the father and other witnesses at the scene of the incident.'

Ron could hardly believe it. It was not Helen's right arm that had been in a 'bizarre position', but her left arm. He and others had made this perfectly plain to Dr Green. If the pathologist could make a mistake like that, could he not make one even more crucial? Reading the small print in the Green report, Ron found references to 'bruises to the face' that were consistent with 'slaps or punches'. If Helen had been slapped and punched in the face before she died, did that not cast some doubt on the accident theory? 'Slaps or punches' suggested that Helen had been violently attacked.

If Helen had been slapped and punched in the face before she died, did that not cast some doubt on the accident theory?

Above: Ron Smith with Ayoub Quasim, interpreter at the British Embassy in Jeddah. In June 1980 Quasim risked his job by introducing Ron to His Honour Sheikh Al Amouri, the judge at the Arnots' trial, and generally assisted Ron in his inquiries. Right: Helen's body lies in its coffin in the Bab Sharafia Hospital

'If I was to say that Helen Smith's death was an accident, I would be a liar'

A month later, Dr Green himself gave public expression to his own doubts on the matter. In an interview with the *Sunday People* he said: 'If I was to say that Helen Smith's death was an accident, I would be a liar. My conscience would not allow me to say so.' He went on to say that the body had shown 'none' of the injuries he would have expected to see if Helen had fallen on her feet or on her head, and concluded: 'If someone had fallen from a block of flats this way in Britain there would have been a full-scale inquiry.'

This newspaper interview heralded a tidal wave of publicity over the Helen Smith affair. For the first time since his daughter had died 15 months previously, Ron Smith found himself at the centre of press and television interest in the case. Mr and Mrs Arnot, who had returned from Jeddah with their sentences commuted after direct intervention on their behalf by the Foreign Office, published their story in four articles in the *Daily Mail*, which paid them £10,000. But all

The coroner's powers

The office of coroner originated in England, probably in the tenth century. Then, the post of 'crowner' or 'coronator' (from the Latin *corona*, meaning crown) was subordinate only to the king, whose property it was his duty to protect. In modern times, the coroner's chief function is to inquire how, when and why deaths in his area of jurisdiction have taken place. A coroner asks for a pathologist's report only where a death is mysterious or where the cause is not obviously due to old age or illness. He need not be medically qualified himself: the Coroners Amendment Act of 1926 ruled that a coroner should be a barrister, solicitor or legally qualified medical practitioner of five years standing or more.

The coroner is appointed and paid by the relevant local authority, though he is not answerable to that authority and it cannot dismiss him. This can lead to difficulties. In the Helen Smith case the West Yorkshire County Council clashed bitterly with the coroner over the costs of the inquest. The coroner had promised the prosperous London solicitor Sir David Napley that his fees for representing Richard Arnot would be paid, but the local authority refused to pay without seeing the bill, which the coroner refused to reveal. This led to a great deal of public rancour on both sides.

The procedure in the coroner's court is 'inquisitorial', not 'adversarial'. This means that witnesses cannot be cross-examined or 'broken down' by lawyers respresenting the different parties. The lawyers cannot make closing speeches on behalf of their clients, even if their clients are the bereaved.

In controversial cases, a coroner is obliged to employ a jury, but *he alone* decides whether the case is controversial or not and often does so without a jury. Coroners' juries are not selected at random as ordinary criminal juries are, but from a special panel, operated and maintained entirely by the coroner. In the United States the coroner, either elected or appointed according to state laws, may have police power equal to that of the sheriff and be able to issue warrants for arrest in homicide cases.

Above: Philip Gill, who in 1981 became one of two coroners for West Yorkshire. His area of jurisdiction was Leeds and Wakefield – though not, according to him, Jeddah, despite the fact that the daughter of a Leeds ratepayer had died there in suspicious circumstances. Mr Gill eventually presided at the inquest into Helen Smith's death. Left: the late Miles Coverdale, solicitor, former mayor of Ripon and the deputy coroner for Leeds, whose decision not to grant an autopsy on Helen was set aside on 24 June 1980 after he had had a look at the Coroners Act

Professor Dalgaard's report appeared to confirm every one of Ron's suspicions

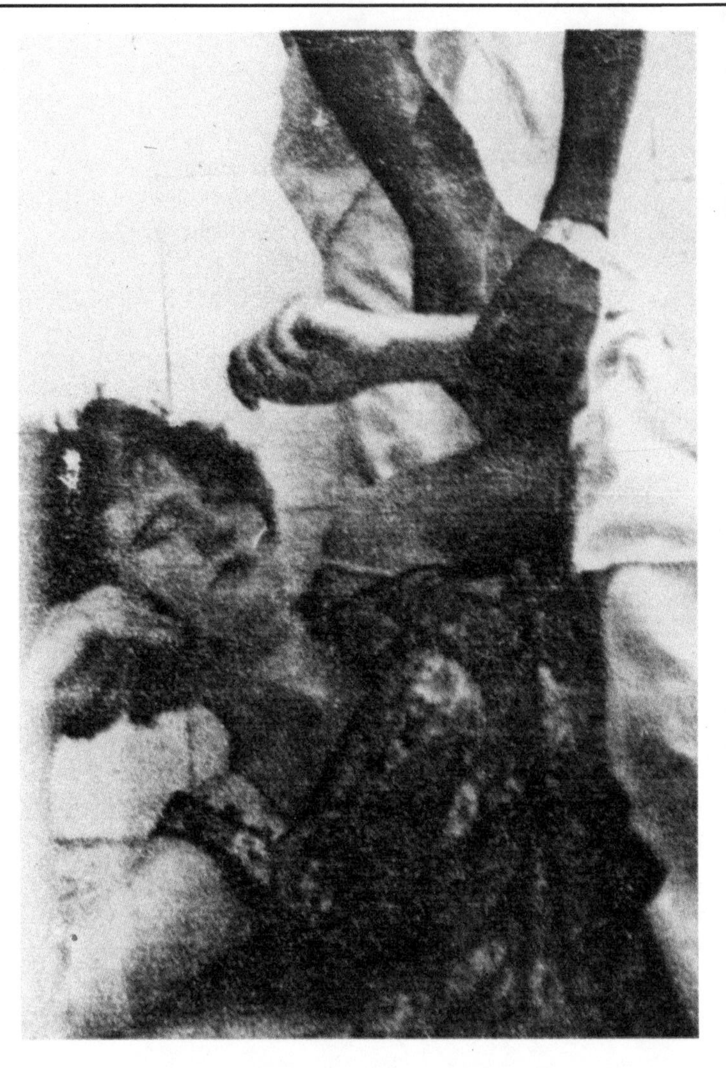

Right: taken on the morning of Helen Smith's death, this Saudi police photograph clearly shows the deep indentation in the centre of the dead girl's forehead. Below: based on Professor Alan Usher's original drawings of the injuries to Helen's head and face, this diagram shows the indentation (1) and the large 'lesion 13' on top of the skull. Far right: the block of flats where Helen Smith and Johannes Otten died, and behind it the back of the Bakhsh Hospital. The railings on which Otten was impaled have been removed, and the wall has been bricked in. The photograph was taken by Ron Smith less than a fortnight after the deaths. Inset: the positions in which the bodies were found. Helen lies on the marble floor with her head towards the building. Otten's body, pierced through the thighs, hangs on the railings

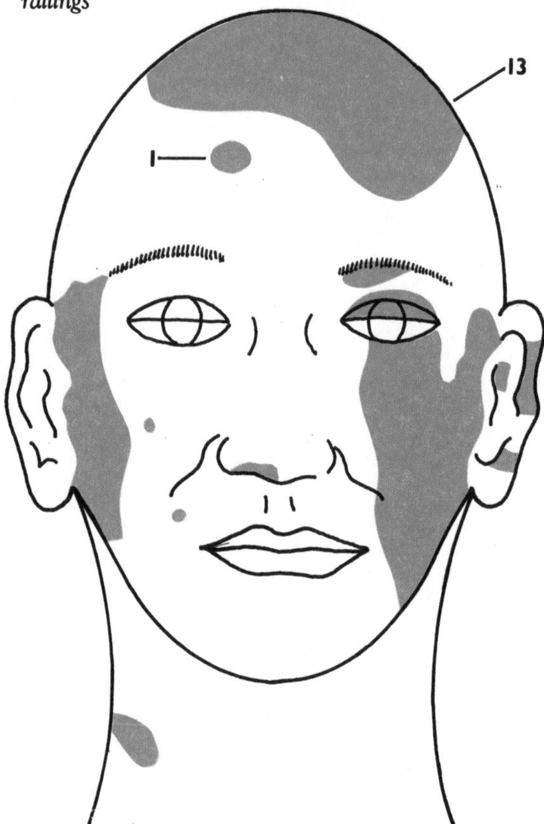

the press and television fever, which had started to die down by the end of September 1980, got Ron Smith nowhere. He realised that he would have to do something more himself.

He scraped together another £500 from his dwindling savings and approached a Danish professor of pathology, recommended to him by Fleming Aaen and his wife Lisa, who had been a sister in the gynaecological department of the Bakhsh Hospital. They had been dismissed by Bakhsh, for no apparent reason, and had returned to their native Denmark, where Ron visited them. They introduced him to Professor Jorgen Dalgaard, one of the most experienced pathologists in the country and a specialist in deaths from falls. The professor welcomed Ron into his house, where he stayed five days. After long deliberation the professor agreed that Ron had a case. He travelled to Britain and conducted his own detailed examination of Helen's body on 16 December 1980. With him was Dr Michael Green, who had carried out the second autopsy five months previously, and Professor Alan Usher, one of the Home Office's top pathologists. Professor Usher had been invited to attend by the deputy coroner, Miles Coverdale, because, as Professor Usher later explained, he wanted 'the home side to be represented'.

Ron got Professor Dalgaard's report on 1 March 1981. He read it with a mixture of relief and astonishment. Professor Dalgaard appeared to confirm every one of Ron's suspicions

Above: Detective Chief Superintendent Peter Smalley of the West Yorkshire Police, who conducted a secret investigation into Helen's death for the Leeds deputy coroner Miles Coverdale. With a colleague's assistance, Mr Smalley interviewed 46 people and flew to Jeddah during his inquiries, but at the inquest said, 'I wanted to come away from Saudi Arabia with something, but I didn't. I'm not a coward. . . but honestly I wasn't prepared to take the risk.' Below: Subi Bakir, the mortuary attendant at the Bab Sharafia Hospital, supervises the start of Helen's last journey back to England

over the last two years, although that so much revealing information about his daughter's injuries had been missed by the distinguished Dr Green the first time round was staggering.

Like Dr Green, Professor Dalgaard found that the injuries to Helen's face were consistent with punches or slaps. The whole of her left cheek from the top of her eyebrows to the jaw was covered in bruises. But then the professor discovered another wound that had apparently been completely missed by Dr Green. The presence of this wound struck him more forcibly than anything else about the body. It came to be known as 'lesion 13'. It was a wound measuring four by five inches (ten by thirteen centimetres) covering the whole of the left side of the scalp, spreading down as low as the temple. The blow had left underlying haemorrhages between the brain membranes. The professor concluded:

> A haemorrhage under the brain membrane usually causes rapid unconsciousness and may even cause death. The deceased has obviously survived the injury for a limited period, say at least several minutes, as the effusion of blood had reached the level mentioned, and no further.

Helen, in short, had been hit on the head and knocked out several minutes before she died. Indeed, the blow that knocked her out may well have killed her. Certainly she had been rendered unconscious.

How had this crucial 'lesion 13' escaped the notice of Dr Green and therefore not been known about by the deputy coroner Miles Coverdale when he made his decision whether or not to hold an inquest? The answer was astonishing. 'Dr Green,' reported the professor, 'suggested that the lesion might be a consequence of chemical irritation through hair-dyeing.' No, it could not, the professor had politely insisted.

Moreover, Dr Green had been mistaken in the vital

Science without certainty

It was long assumed that evidence given by forensic scientists was sacrosanct. While witnesses might differ as to what they saw, and make mistakes, forensic experts were dealing with science, and did not make mistakes.

In 1982, however, it was revealed that a Stoke-on-Trent lorry driver had been convicted in a murder trial on the evidence of a pathologist, Dr Clift, which subsequently proved totally unconvincing. The lorry driver was released after eight years in prison, and Dr Clift was suspended.

In the summer of 1983 a young man was acquitted after being charged for the murder of his girlfriend when a Home Office pathologist's evidence was found to be false. Dr Albert Goonetilleke had examined the body of the young woman and declared that she had been hit on the head with a blunt instrument. The defence pathologist could not agree with this and the woman's body was exhumed. It was seen at once that she had been shot. Dr Goonetilleke also appeared at the Helen Smith inquest and gave some controversial evidence on falls that fitted the official view.

Often, mistakes by pathologists and other forensic experts are due to simple human error and overwork. A busy British pathologist may be called upon to perform ten or more autopsies a day, and this number is at least tripled in some of the more violent cities of the United States. Professor Alan Usher, head of Sheffield University's Department of Forensic Medicine, who helped conduct the third autopsy on Helen Smith, recalls a Chicago medical examiner telling him that, so numerous were the shooting cases in that city, 'I just have time to count the holes in the front and the holes in the back.'

This may be a case of jocular exaggeration, but there is no doubt that it contains more than a germ of truth. In 1956 Dr Alan Moritz published his paper 'Classic Mistakes in Forensic Pathology', which has itself become something of a classic. In it he listed fourteen common errors, which included performing an incomplete autopsy, permitting the body to be embalmed before a medico-legal autopsy, regarding a mutilated or decomposed body as unsuitable for autopsy, failing to recognise or misinterpreting post mortem changes, failing to make an adequate examination and description of external abnormalities, not examining the body at the scene of the crime, not taking adequate photographs, and 'talking too much, too soon, or to the wrong people'.

Between the Saudi and British medical examiners, all these mistakes seem to have been made in one form or another in the case of Helen Smith. An error of another kind, Dr Kheir's assumption that there would be no further examinations of Helen's body, and his removal of her internal organs, made later autopsies ineffective.

Above: Dr Michael Green, the Home Office pathologist who conducted the first English autopsy on Helen Smith and delivered a controversial report on it

matter of the right humerus or upper arm bone, which had not been fractured, as Dr Green had claimed. A tiny part of the bone on the joint that joins the right arm to the shoulder had flaked off, by way of a minor abrasion such as may happen when a body is dragged along the floor by the right arm. It was definitely not a fracture. So, if Helen had fallen from 70 feet (20 metres) onto her right side, she had managed to do so without breaking her shoulder bone. From these and other findings, Professor Dalgaard drew exactly the same conclusions as Ron had done when he had gazed at his daughter's body two years before. Dalgaard wrote: 'A fall from a sixth-floor balcony can thus be excluded.'

'A fall from a sixth-floor balcony can be excluded'

The professor reached this conclusion after close consultation with the other two pathologists who had inspected the

'. . . these injuries suggest that some violent activity had occurred, probably against this girl's will'

body with him. Dalgaard, Usher and Green met in Sheffield for two days in February to discuss their findings. All the tissues they had taken from the body had been divided in triplicate so that all three men could examine them separately. It was probably the most meticulous autopsy in all history. The three men agreed on the basic findings. Dr Green, for instance, though he remained publicly silent on the matter, conceded that 'lesion 13' could not have been caused by hair dye.

Professor Usher, who submitted a detailed report nine days after Dalgaard, agreed that the injuries suggested that Helen had not fallen from the Arnots' balcony. She could not have fallen, he wrote, from more than 30 feet (9 metres) – half the height of the balcony. He thought that she had fallen, and that the fall had caused her death. But in an interesting passage, he reported:

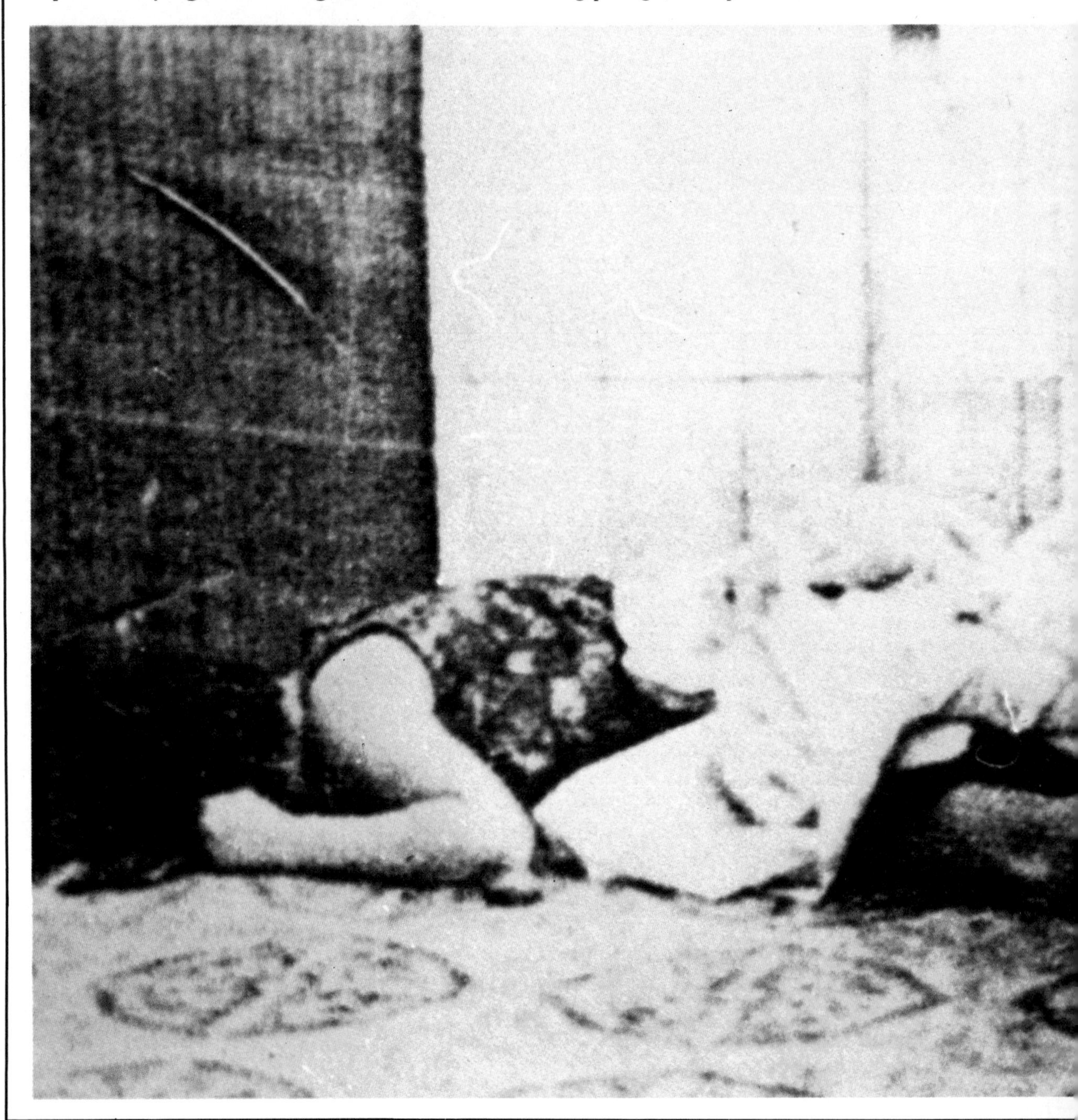

> It has to be admitted, however, that the bleeding around the fractures of the arm, ribs and pelvis was very slight, so that were it possible to account for the extensive bruising in the right loin and thigh by some other trauma unrelated to a fall, then the possibility that this girl was already dead when her body fell into the courtyard would exist.

Professor Usher also turned his mind to the injuries in the body's genital regions, and noted:

> It is difficult to account for such lesions by the mechanism commonly encountered in a fall death, but I have often seen similarly sited lesions in both living and dead female victims of sexual assault and rape. They arise when the victim's thighs are prised apart by an assailant's knee or knees. Taken together with the bruising of the vulva . . . these injuries suggest that some violent activity had occurred, most probably against this girl's will.

Below: Saudi police photograph of Helen Smith's body as it was found in the courtyard of the Arnots' block of flats. Her feet point towards the railings on which the body of Johannes Otten is impaled. Helen's body lies in the recess caused by the setting back of the first-floor balcony and beneath the lip of the second floor balcony. It is hard to see how it could have fallen directly into that position from higher up

Ron Smith, who had been believed by nobody at the time, and generally dismissed as an obsessive and a crank, now had in his hand reports from two of the most authoritative and respected pathologists in Europe. They cast grave doubts on whether Helen Smith fell from anywhere. If she did fall, both reports agreed she could not have fallen from as high as the Arnots' balcony. More crucially, all the evidence pointed away from an accident. Helen had been beaten several times in the face. She had sustained a savage and possibly fatal blow to her head. She was probably unconscious when she fell. And she had been sexually assaulted, perhaps raped.

The press statement made by the deputy coroner, Miles Coverdale, the previous July – in which he had claimed that there was no need for an inquest because the nurse had clearly fallen from a great height – had been made to seem nonsense. Ron Smith waited a few days, hoping that the deputy coroner would order an inquest.

Then came the bitterest blow in the whole of his long battle. On 4 August 1981, six days after Parliament had gone into recess and Ron had completed a series of articles on the case in Malaysia, he was woken by a telephone call from the Leeds coroner's office. Shortly afterwards a letter was pushed into his hand by a couple of policemen who had come to his door.

The letter was signed by Philip S. Gill who had, on 1 July, become coroner for the whole of the eastern district of West Yorkshire, including Leeds. Ron was surprised by this. He had never spoken or communicated with Mr Gill before. But his surprise turned to anger as he read Gill's letter concerning Helen: 'As her death occurred outside the jurisdiction of the English courts,' it read, 'I am satisfied that this case does not fall within my jurisdiction for the holding of an inquest. Accordingly, I am not able to take any further action in the matter. . . .'

Ron Smith could not believe any of this. Not once during the previous year, not once since he had brought his daughter's body back from Jeddah, had anyone in authority, any lawyer, any coroner or policeman, ever suggested to him that there was no jurisdiction to hold an inquest into his daughter's death. Inquests on deaths abroad were, he knew from his police experience and from observation, quite common. The pre-

Above: Richard and Penny Arnot with their children William and Lucy. They returned to England from Saudi Arabia on 8 August 1980. They were divorced a year later – Mr Arnot blaming the Helen Smith affair for the collapse of his marriage. Mrs Arnot remarried and left for the United States a few days before the inquest started in November 1982. Richard Arnot has subsequently settled in Australia where he, too, has remarried

vious acting coroner, Coverdale, had never once doubted this jurisdiction. Yet now the new coroner, Gill, was seeking to close the matter once and for all.

With a heavy heart, Ron Smith prepared himself for battle once more. He consulted his lawyers. They told him the law was in doubt. He spent days leafing through old copies of Yorkshire newspapers. He discovered to his outrage that Mr Gill himself had held at least two inquests into the deaths of people who had died abroad. Ron applied to the Divisional Court for a writ to set aside the decision of Gill and to order him to hold an inquest. The case came up before Lord Justice Ormerod and Mr Justice Forbes on 25 March 1982. On 2 April they gave their judgement. There was, in their view, no jurisdiction to hold inquests on deaths abroad, so all such inquests that had been held up to then were null and void in law. Ron Smith was still unbowed. He next tried the Court of Appeal. The court heard the case on 28 July and gave judgement the following day. From the outset, the presiding Lord Chief Justice, Lord Lane, supported by Sir John Donaldson, Master of the Rolls, showed little patience with the case for the coroner. As Sir John Donaldson said, 'If you have bodies lying about, as it were, you have to enquire why those bodies are there, don't you?' People could be prosecuted for the murders of British citizens abroad, so why should not coroners investigate the deaths of people who died there? The Coroners Act of 1887 quite specifically did not absolve coroners from responsibility to hold inquests on mysterious deaths abroad. Lord Lane ruled against the Divisional Court and called for an inquest. At last there would be a public hearing into the circumstances of Helen's death.

A few days later, on 3 August 1982, Penny Arnot, who had been living in the United States since her divorce from her husband the previous year, announced that she had married an American journalist called John Close. She had met Close in Jeddah when he was working for the *Arab News*, an English-language newspaper there. Close had strong links with Saudi Arabia. His father, Raymond H. Close, had been head of the Central Intelligence Agency (CIA) in the Middle East for many years.

Ron thought that this was one of the more remarkable coincidences of the case. Immediately after it had been decided that an inquest would be held into the death of his daughter, and that the Coroner had powers to instruct people to attend from anywhere in Britain, the hostess of the party at which Helen had died suddenly announced her marriage to an American citizen, thus ensuring that her stay in America was certain to be prolonged. This meant that she would be entirely free from the coroner's subpoena.

'If you have bodies lying about, as it were, you have to enquire why those bodies are there, don't you?'

The inquest was opened and adjourned at once. Then it was adjourned again. It finally started on 18 November 1982, in Leeds, before a packed press gallery, which seated 96. The proceedings were expensive. Witnesses, including Mr Arnot, who had come from Australia, were flown in from all over the world. The ratepayers of West Yorkshire were paying. The leader of their council, Mr John Gunnell, told the press that no expense would be spared to ensure a fair hearing for the Smith family. 'It is,' he said, 'the inquest of the century.'

Mr Arnot was woken with the news that 'something terrible' had happened

Below: Helen Smith on an evening out in Jeddah, probably in January 1979. Helen had adjusted well to both work and the social life that was centred around the Bakhsh Hospital. In February she wrote home to a friend: 'I have got the job I was always wanting. I am the senior member of staff to the sister. So I have a lot of responsibility, and I really enjoy my job here very much. . . . I feel different, a new person altogether.' By the end of May she was dead — but it took her father three years and a month to win an inquest into the circumstances of her death; it finally began in November 1982

Until the inquest, the chief characters in the grim story that had ended in his daughter's death had not been personally known to Ron Smith. He had met Richard Arnot for 20 minutes in the prison yard in Jeddah in 1979. But most of the other witnesses were just names. In particular, he had tried in vain to speak to the German workers from Harms Salvage who had gone to the Arnots' party. Four of the five who were there gave evidence at the inquest. The other had made a statement to police, which was read out in court.

Each of the Harms workers told his story of what had happened in the Arnots' flat that night. None of them varied much in the details. The party, they said, had been arranged at fairly short notice to say goodbye to one of their number, the New Zealand diver Tim Hayter. Tim had become friendly with the Arnots while teaching them scuba diving. He had taken Mrs Arnot and the children to see the floating crane from which Harms operated in Jeddah harbour, and Mrs Arnot had invited the workers to the party. Martin Fleischer, a university student who was working with Harms while on a trainee course, had travelled to the party in a separate car. So had Harry Gutzeit, the manager of the Harms salvage team, who had his own flat in the city. Four other Harms workers, Manfred Schlaeffer, Klaus Ritter, Dieter Chapuis and the Dutchman Johannes Otten, had gone together in one of the company cars.

Martin Fleischer, who gave evidence first and proved the most articulate of the Harms workers, said that he had arrived slightly later than his four colleagues. Hayter and Mrs Arnot arrived later still, bringing soft drinks, crisps and nuts. Helen Smith, who often baby-sat for the Arnots, and whom Fleischer had met at a children's party at the flat a few days earlier, came on a bit later. So did Mr Arnot. There were one or two other people there including a Malay called Jimmy, who had driven Tim to the party. Later still, the Frenchman Jacques Texier arrived.

There was plenty of whisky available, Fleischer said. Open bottles were left about, and the guests filled their own glasses. Helen had started the evening chatting to everyone, but had eventually got attached to Johannes Otten. Mr Arnot went to bed at about 2am. When Fleischer left, bored and a bit drunk, at 2.30, Johannes and Helen were dancing close in one of the rooms that had been set aside for dancing. That room adjoined the other main room. The sliding doors connecting the two rooms were open. There was a door out onto the balcony from each of the rooms, but Fleischer had not seen them open, nor anyone going through them.

He had gone back to his digs on the accommodation barge in Jeddah harbour, where all the Harms workers except

Above: Professor Jorgen Dalgaard, the distinguished Danish pathologist, at a press conference on the Helen Smith case. Firm and authoritative, speaking fluently in English, Professor Dalgaard was convincing in his presentation of evidence at the inquest. An expert on deaths from falls, he persuasively argued that Helen could not have fallen from any great distance onto her right side since neither her head nor her right arm (which might have protected the skull) were fractured. His opinion was backed up in court by Dr Joseph Deguara, chief pathologist at the Bakhsh hospital at the time of Helen's death. Dr Deguara said that he had seen the body a few days after death and 'was struck by the lack of massive injury which I would have associated with a fall from a height.' He had even called for a Home Office autopsy but had been ignored

Mr Arnot slept soundly until his wife woke him with the news that 'something terrible had happened'

Harry Gutzeit lived. Early in the morning Fleischer was woken by a frenzied Tim Hayter, who told him that Helen Smith was dead. She had, he said, 'fallen off the balcony', while 'screwing' with Johannes. Hayter then ordered Fleischer to take his car and fetch Harry Gutzeit from his flat in town, and bring him back to the barge for an urgent meeting. Instead, Fleischer said, he went back to the Arnots' flat, imagining that Gutzeit was still there. When he got there, he saw the body of Helen Smith under a sheet at the foot of the building and that of Johannes Otten impaled on the street railings. Fleischer was arrested, and with Mr Arnot, compiled a list of all party guests, and led the police back to the port. There the Harms workers were all arrested. Together with the Arnots and Texier, they would spend the next five months living in the most appalling conditions in a Saudi prison.

At the inquest the other Harms workers agreed with every detail of Martin Fleischer's description of the early part of the evening. They could carry the story a bit further in time. At about 3.30am, an hour after Fleischer left, they said, they had all decided to go home. They had looked round for their colleague Johannes, who had come with them. He was not there. Nor was Helen Smith. None of the Harms men had seen them going anywhere – neither out onto the balcony nor towards the main door of the flat. They did not hunt the flat for their colleague. Klaus Ritter said he had called out 'John, we are going home,' or something like that. When there was no reply, they all assumed that Johannes and Helen had gone off somewhere for sex.

At any rate, the Harms men said they left the party at about 3.15 or 3.30am and drove back to the port. Dieter Chapuis said they had got lost on their way and were held up for an hour. They heard nothing until about 6.30 in the morning, when Tim Hayter alerted them that Helen was dead. Before long, they were being taken to the police station.

All five Harms workers insisted that the party had been extremely quiet and friendly. There had been, they said, no arguments or hints of violence. They all agreed that Mr Arnot went to bed at about 2am and that Tim Hayter, Jacques Texier and Mrs Arnot were the only people left in the flat when they left for home. They also all testified that Johannes Otten had been wearing a pair of jeans plus a white shirt and sandals. None of them could offer any explanation at all as to how Helen and Johannes met their deaths.

Mr Arnot knew even less. He arrived at the party at about 9pm and then left at about midnight for a tour of the hospital where he had patients under surgery, returned and finally went to bed at about 2am. He had noticed that Helen and Johannes were 'getting close' and had bidden them goodnight while they were dancing. He had slept soundly until his wife woke him about 5.30am with the news that 'something terrible had happened'. Helen and Johannes seemed to have fallen off the balcony, she told him. Arnot said he dressed quickly and ran down the stairs. There he found that both Helen and Johannes were dead. He had not seen any marks of violence on Helen's face, nor was there any blood on her. Later, wandering into the street, he had found a passport and some papers belonging to Johannes. He had put them back under the body. He had noticed that Otten's penis was erect. 'I concluded from that,' he said, 'that he was in a state of some sexual excitement when he fell.' Asked about Otten's trousers, which were not on the body, Arnot replied that they must have been pulled off his legs by a passer-by, and stolen.

Mr Arnot said he could only assume that, while he himself was asleep, Helen and Johannes had gone out on the balcony for sex, and had fallen over by accident. He had no explanation for the marks on her face, head and thighs. He said he thought that his wife and Hayter had had sex after he had gone to bed, and that the Germans had left. Asked why he had told the *Daily Mail* in 1980 that he was sure his wife and Hayter had not had sex, he could only reply that he was, at that time, trying to protect Penny.

During the inquest, statements were read out from two senior consultants at the Bakhsh Hospital who had discovered the bodies that hot, grim Sunday morning. Dr Hag Faad Abdel Rachman, a gynaecologist, had been woken by a Sudanese porter at 5.30 with the news that there were two bodies below. His statement went on: 'The man was hanged upside down on an iron bar at the left side of the building. . . . The girl on the ground, face to earth, wearing blue dress without underwear, no blood or violence indications.'

Dr Rachman said that he had knocked on the Arnots' door soon after this discovery, and it was opened at once by the surgeon: 'He started saying: "If you mean that event down the building, I know about that, leave it to me and I will deal with it." I saw behind Dr Arnot a white, short man with a beard. I heard a lot of noise from within the flat.'

Dr Walid Sukhtian, an orthopaedic surgeon, had been woken up at about the same time by the same porter. He, too, had rushed downstairs. He saw that the body on the railings was wearing only underpants and a watch. The watch had stopped at exactly 3.10. Helen was 'lying on her stomach, with the head resting on the right side of her face. . . . There was no bleeding from Helen's body.' Both consultants, backed by Dr Bakhsh himself, testified that Helen's face was very close to the wall of the block itself – that is, underneath the lip of the balconies above it.

There was only one person at the inquest who could give evidence about what was going on in the Arnots' flat at this time. He was Jacques Texier, a middle-aged, itinerant marine biologist, who had dived with Tim Hayter and knew him well. Texier had been invited to the party by Hayter and arrived about 11pm. At about 2am, he said, he (alone of all the people who had been at the party) had seen Helen and Otten on the balcony. In his first statement, taken by Leeds police, Texier said he had seen them from the kitchen window while making a sandwich. When it was pointed out to him that the kitchen window looked out on a quite different balcony than the one from which Helen and Otten are supposed to have fallen, he changed his evidence, saying he had seen them from another window.

At about 3am, Texier had asked Mrs Arnot if he could stay the night in the flat. He explained that he was staying with a friend, an official at the French Embassy, who lived

Four men who attended both the party at which Helen Smith died and the inquest into her death. Above left: Jacques Texier, a French marine biologist. He came to the inquest to clear his name. Top left: Manfred Schlaeffer, captain of the Harms floating crane in Jeddah harbour. Top right: Klaus Ritter, cook on the Harms workers' accommodation barge. Above right: Martin Fleischer, a student who was working as buyer for the Harms salvage operation. Texier's evidence, corroborating Penny Arnot's vital statement about Helen and Johannes Otten going out on the balcony and about the morning after, contradicted the original statements that he had made. The evidence of the Harms men, though some of it varied from their original statements, presented a united front to the court

Above: Gordon Kirby, the British vice-consul in Jeddah. It was he who had taken Penny Arnot's statement on the morning of Helen Smith's death – and had doubted its truth. Mr Kirby's involvement in the affair led him to sue Private Eye. *When Ron Smith was contacted about Kirby's writ he incidentally learned that – through an order of* mandamus *(whereby a court can be ordered to perform a duty by a superior court) – he could apply to the High Court to overrule the coroner Philip Gill's decision not to hold an inquest into Helen's death; this he successfully did. Above, far right: Dr Ali Kheir, the pathologist from Jeddah University who carried out the first autopsy on Helen. He confirmed at the inquest this belief that she and Otten had fallen over the balcony and that Helen had not been sexually assaulted*

not far away, but he did not want to wake his host. Mrs Arnot consented and, as soon as the Harms workers left, Texier stretched out on the sofa and went to sleep. At about 5am he was woken by the unmistakable noise of Penny Arnot and Tim Hayter making love behind him. 'It was,' he said cheerfully, 'the moment of orgasm.' Then he, Hayter and Mrs Arnot had all gone into the kitchen, made coffee, and strolled out on to the balcony to discover the dead bodies lying down below. Mrs Arnot woke her husband and they all immediately started to clear the flat of alcohol.

As soon as the flat was clear, Texier and Hayter left. Texier went to his friend's house, and then on to his boat nearby where he was arrested.

Tim Hayter and Penelope Arnot did not come to the inquest to give evidence. Both had been interviewed previously. Mrs Arnot had talked to the British vice-consul in Jeddah, Gordon Kirby, on the morning the bodies were found. She had told him that after the Germans had left the party, Texier and Hayter had gone to sleep in the main room and she had wandered round the flat, clearing up, listening to music and drinking coffee.

In his minute about this version, which he had written for the Foreign Office at the time, Gordon Kirby was extremely sceptical:

> There are several items in this story that puzzle me.
> (a) Apart from Mrs Arnot, Helen Smith was the only other female present at the party. With a good party and several single men in the offing at the home of the hospital's senior British doctor, why didn't some of the other British nurses attend, or did they?
> (b) Mrs Arnot is a working mother with two, small, energetic children. I find it hard to believe that she chose to sit alone, drinking coffee and listening to music after cleaning the debris of a hectic party. At 2am she would probably have been awake since 6.30 the previous morning and she alleges that she then stayed awake until the discovery of the bodies at 5.30am.

No wonder the Embassy had been so reluctant to pass this statement on to Ron Smith when he first asked for it way back in May 1979. Mr Kirby's doubts had been compounded soon afterwards when Mrs Arnot suddenly confessed to her interrogators in prison that she had had sex with Hayter that night. This statement was hurriedly withdrawn after Foreign Office officials pointed out to an hysterical Mrs Arnot that the penalty for adultery was the same as it was for murder. It was no good her answering a charge of murder with the 'alibi' that she was making love to Tim Hayter at the time. She could be executed for that as well.

Accordingly, in September 1979, Mrs Arnot changed her 'confession' and denied adultery. In the *Daily Mail* version of the events, written and signed by her and her husband, she strenuously denied having had sex with Hayter, even though by that time she was well clear of the Saudi police and Saudi law. No, she insisted, what she had said to Kirby had been right from the start. She had been listening to music and drinking coffee all the time.

This was reversed again at the inquest, though not by Mrs Arnot, who refused the coroner's twice-repeated invitation to attend, even though all expenses would be paid. The jury saw a television interview with Tim Hayter, who also refused to go to the inquest in person. In that interview, Hayter repeated what he had told the *News of the World* for a substantial fee, namely, that he and Mrs Arnot had been locked in love during the crucial hours after the Germans' departure. 'We made love together for a short time,' he said. 'I'd say it lasted about an hour.'

Richard Arnot strongly supported this version of events, though he had not witnessed them himself; according to his own testimony, and that of his wife and party guests, he had been asleep at the time. He told the inquest he was sure that his wife and Hayter had had sex that night, even though he had told the *Daily Mail* only two years earlier that he was sure they had not.

The official version of events which all this evidence seemed to fit, was that Helen and Otten had got gradually drunk at the party, had slipped onto the balcony unnoticed, had toppled over the wall – which was about 3 feet 6 inches (1 metre) high – and plunged to their deaths. Even without the medical details, there were a number of questions thrown up by the evidence to which no satisfactory answer has yet been given:

In Helen's words

Avril 1979 | April 1979
Vendredi | Friday
13 | 13
17 Jumâda I 1399 | 17 Jumâda I 1399

Very very bad day
Everything went wrong
Had a quarrel with DR Nayle.
Went to China Rose with Tim, Susan
+ Bosses. Nearly killed-
Just not my day.
Also finished with Sarchal.
HOW?

TIM
NEARLY KILLED

WHO IS SUSAN?

SARCHAL

Helen Smith left behind several diaries of the few months she spent in Jeddah. They are often concerned with the friendships she had with different young men. Her boyfriend at the start was Robert W. Gurusamy, or 'Guru', a Malaysian on the hospital staff. Before long she had struck up a relationship with a consultant paediatrician called Dr Sarchal. He had a wife and children in his native Iraq and flew home to visit them regularly. When Helen found this out she was angry and broke off the relationship. But Sarchal persisted.

In March Helen recorded in her diary an operation for appendicitis. None of the pathologists who examined her body could find any trace of an appendix scar.

Helen had continued to see Guru, but on 17 April he was sacked for no apparent reason, along with four other employees of the Bakhsh Hospital. Helen was furious and decided to leave. She gave in her notice at the hospital and exchanged her return ticket to England for a one-way ticket to Malaysia, where she planned to join Guru.

Shortly before her death she started going out with a Scotsman called Ron Low. Mr Low has never been contacted by any of the people making inquiries into Helen's death, but he reputedly attended the party at which she died.

Helen's diaries give a vivid picture of the frantic social life of the English community in Jeddah. They sketch in some of the people who may know more about her death. They also indicate that she was a busy working nurse who enjoyed life, and whose friendly, lively disposition made the manner of her passing all the more tragic.

Left: a page from one of Helen Smith's Jeddah diaries, with notes added by her father

Below: *Professor Alan Usher, Professor of Forensic Pathology at Sheffield University, who conducted the English autopsy on Helen Smith with Professor Dalgaard and Dr Green. This eminent Home Office pathologist had originally reported that he thought it 'improbable' that 'lesion 13' had been caused by 'a glancing blow against a flat surface'; at the inquest he thought it 'possible'. He had also reconsidered the injuries to Helen's thighs and suggested that these may have been caused by them slapping into each other during a fall, not necessarily by a sexual attack. 'I have had the opportunity to think about it since and I think a bit differently now,' he said*

1. *What was heard?* No one in the Arnots' flat apparently heard anything to suggest that the couple had fallen. Mrs Keith, who lived in the flat below, heard a 'very, very loud noise'. But the Germans heard no such thing. Perhaps they had gone by that time. Mrs Arnot, Texier and Hayter heard nothing either. Texier said: 'I am sure I would have heard a scream.' But he did not. Nor did anyone else.
2. *What happened to Otten's trousers?* Otten's body was found naked except for a pair of black shorts and a watch. His shoes, Arnot said, were found in the flat. So were his spectacles. But his trousers were never found. Arnot surmised that a robber had taken them off him as Johannes lay spread-eagled over the railings. But how then to explain the documents – identity card, passport and so on – that were found in the middle of the road? Had the thief, as Arnot seriously suggested, gone through the trousers then and there to rid himself of any incriminating documents?
3. *What was the exact position of Helen's body?* Several witnesses said that Helen's body was underneath the lip of the balconies. How then could she have fallen backwards? The only conceivable answer – if she had fallen – was that she had fallen on top of Otten on the railings and then bounced off under the balconies. But this would have been a very long 'bounce' – about seven or eight feet (2 to 2.5 metres).
4. *Why was the body of Johannes Otten abandoned?* Klaus Ritter said in evidence that it would be extremely dangerous for a foreigner to try to get back into the closely guarded Jeddah harbour if he was drunk and on foot, or even in a taxi. The authorities were very tough on such lone arrivals. Yet the friends of Johannes Otten, who had travelled to the drinks party with him, apparently left the party without even looking for him in the flat or on the balcony, and without even asking the other guests at the party or their hostess about him.
5. *Why did Martin Fleischer go back to the Arnots' flat?* Fleischer had already been alerted by Hayter of Otten's death when he returned to the flat. What was his motive in going back? Was he rushing to help or was he merely curious? He claims that Hayter had told him to go and collect Harry Gutzeit at *his* apartment, but he had mistakenly gone to the Arnots' flat instead.
6. *Who was the mystery man?* It is still not known who was the short, white man with a beard seen by Dr Rachman in the Arnots' flat immediately after the bodies had been found. The only men in the flat, according to the official story were Arnot, Hayter and Texier – none of them short or bearded.
7. *Did Arnot check the bodies?* Did Mr Arnot, as he claimed in evidence, rush down the stairs to check that Helen and Otten were dead, after he had been woken up by his wife with the terrible news? Jacques Texier, in evidence (under tough questioning by Arnot's lawyer), and Tim Hayter in his television interview, denied that any such check took place. 'I was the first to leave the flat,' said Texier. If Arnot did not check the bodies, why not? Did he know that the two young people were dead already?
8. *Why are there no photographs?* Helen Smith took a camera to the Arnots' party. She carried her camera everywhere and took pictures everywhere. She would hardly have taken a camera to

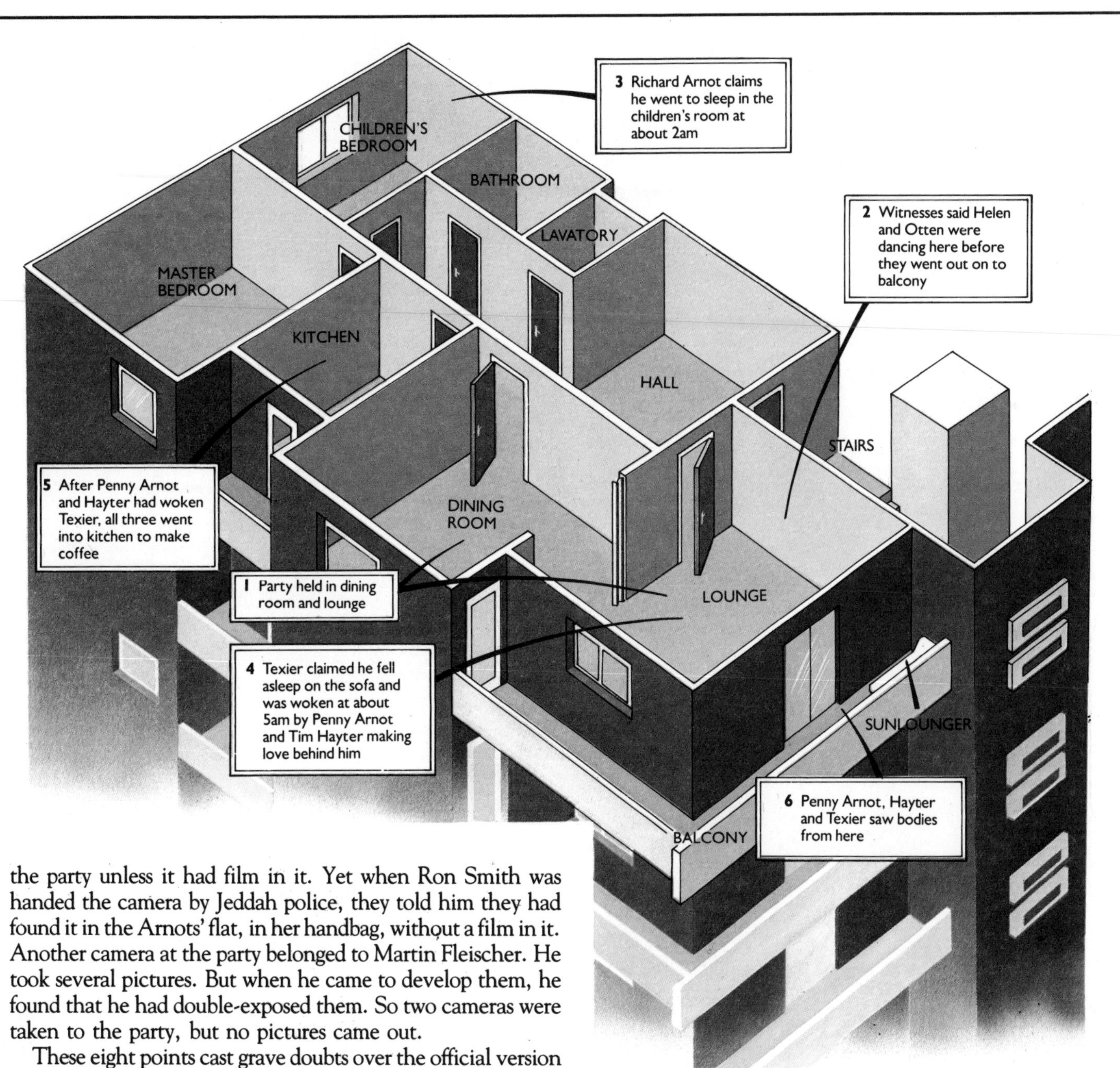

Above: diagram of the layout of the Arnots' Jeddah flat, showing where various witnesses said they were at different times during and after the party in the early hours of 20 May 1979

the party unless it had film in it. Yet when Ron Smith was handed the camera by Jeddah police, they told him they had found it in the Arnots' flat, in her handbag, without a film in it. Another camera at the party belonged to Martin Fleischer. He took several pictures. But when he came to develop them, he found that he had double-exposed them. So two cameras were taken to the party, but no pictures came out.

These eight points cast grave doubts over the official version of how Helen Smith died. Four pathologists gave evidence at the inquest. Only one, Dr Ali Kheir, supported the view that Helen's death was an accident. He agreed that he had taken no tissue from the face or body. He thought that the internal injuries to her lower abdomen proved she had fallen from a height, as he had been told by the police. He saw nothing suspicious or surprising about any of the evidence he had seen.

This was contradicted in almost every detail by the three European pathologists, Green, Dalgaard and Usher. Dr Green started his evidence with the startling revelation that he had withheld evidence about the marks on Helen's thighs and genital regions on the instructions of Deputy Coroner Miles Coverdale (who had since died). He agreed that the marks in those regions, and to the face and head, were clear evidence of violence to Helen's body before she died. But he thought, as did Professor Usher (who went back on his report of March 1981), that she might have fallen from the Arnot flat.

Professor Dalgaard would have none of it. He emphatically

Why did Martin Fleischer go back to the Arnots' flat?

Above: the impaled body of Johannes Otten as it was discovered – and photographed by Saudi police – on the morning after the party. It faces towards the courtyard of the block of flats. A sheet has been placed over the lower half of the corpse

excluded any such fall, and insisted that if Helen had fallen at all, it was for only a very short distance – 10 feet (3 metres) or less. He said (directly to the jury):

> The arm is important. If it was up [and here he held his right arm up against his head] it must have fractured. If it was here [and he held his arm down along his side] the head must have been fractured. Yet there was no fracture of the arm or head. If the arm is not protecting the neck, no human being can fall that distance and keep their neck stiff. Their head will break. I should expect, therefore, a very great fracture of the skull, at least a lesion of the brain, a fracture of the neck and probably of the spine. Yet none of these things happened here.

Turning to the sinister 'lesion 13', the Professor said that it must have been caused by a 'fairly extensive blow' from something that curved with the surface of the head. He thought a blow with the open hand was by far the most likely explanation. Such a blow would certainly have knocked Helen unconscious, and might have directly killed her.

Professor Usher, though more cautious than he had been in his own report the previous year, introduced a new element of mystery. Helen's sternum, or chest bone, he said, had been fractured. A likely explanation for that, he added, might be a vigorous attempt to resuscitate Helen by someone who feared she had suffered a cardiac arrest.

The overwhelming impression from the medical evidence was that some awful violence had been done to Helen before she died: violence that was obviously related to her death. Even if she did topple over the balcony in the course of that violence, then the proper verdict was unlawful killing. If Helen fell while being beaten or sexually assaulted, then her assailants were murderers every bit as much as if they had shot her down. Indeed, if the most impressive and consistent of the medical witnesses, Professor Dalgaard, were to be believed, she had fallen hardly any distance at all, perhaps not at all, but had been battered to death and slung into the courtyard where she was found. And here is the nub of the Helen Smith mystery. Battering, violence, blows and sexual assault were clearly to be deduced from the medical evidence, yet there was not a word of any of this from the people at the party, or from the staff of the Bakhsh Hospital or from the Foreign Office officials who came to give evidence. The clash between the scientific evidence and the statements of the witnesses at the scene of death dominated the whole inquest from start to finish.

The jury left the box at 11.15am on 9 December 1982. It took them eight hours to reach a decision. Helen, they concluded, had fallen from the sixth-floor balcony. But how and why? They could not answer. They brought in what, in the circumstances, was the only possible conclusion: an open verdict.

In March 1983, three months after the verdict, more information came to light that deepened the mystery and flung more doubt on the one definite conclusion of the inquest jury. On Christmas Day 1982, the Saudi authorities, who had largely refused to co-operate with the inquest, and had sent two senior Yorkshire policemen back from Jeddah without a single photograph or interview, suddenly delivered to those same policemen the photographs that had been taken by the Jeddah police photographer on the morning of the deaths. There was no explanation or apology about the extraordinary delay. The coroner held the photographs and their accompanying documents for two and a half months before releasing them to Ron Smith.

Two crucial photographs of Helen's dead body vindicated what Ron Smith had been saying ever since first seeing his daughter's body. The first showed her flat on her stomach right up against the wall of the building, with her feet pointing directly towards the courtyard railing on which Otten was impaled. Almost the whole of her body lay behind the edge of the balcony from which she is alleged to have fallen, and directly in front of a small gate which led into the courtyard, and which was flung open. The position of her body suggested immediately that it had been thrown from the gate. The photograph showed that Helen's body was much closer to the wall than any of the witnesses had suggested, and, if available at the inquest, would have cast serious doubts on the jury's conclusion that Helen fell from the balcony.

A second picture of Helen being lifted by a policeman shows, unmistakably, the clear mark of indentation on her

Battering, blows and sexual assault were clearly to be deduced from the medical evidence

A father's story

The Foreign Office picked a tough adversary in Ron Smith. Ron was born in 1927, the son of a Huddersfield policeman, and he served an articled apprenticeship as an electronics engineer and did three and a half years in the Royal Electrical and Mechanical Engineers in Britain and Palestine.

After leaving the army in 1948, he went to the Wireless College in Manchester and later joined one of the pioneering teams in colour television in Cambridge. He joined the Leeds police in 1950. He proved a competent detective but, five years later, fed up with the 'antiquated' attitudes of the police to the new electronics that interested him, he left and started a television repair firm. That same year, 1955, he married Jeryl Boothroyd. On 3 January 1956 their first daughter Helen was born. Before long there were three more children, Graham, David and Beverley, all of whom were educated privately. By the late Seventies Ron Smith was the prototype of the successful self-made businessman.

Ron Smith was proud of his abilities in the wide world outside his business and his home, and fiercely protective of what he saw as his by right. He was, and is, an unusually hard man, not used to giving ground. The break-up of his marriage in 1977 was a terrible blow to him. The children sided instinctively with their mother. The business was sold. When the news of Helen's death reached him nearly two years later Ron was living alone in the big family house in Guiseley. His hurt pride, his stubbornness and his sheer downright cussedness were admirably suited to the task he set himself when he stood over his daughter's dead body. 'Her flesh was my flesh,' he has often said.

Ron's fervour and tenacity have overpowered, infuriated and depressed many observers and journalists he has met. But he tempers such qualities with a rare and unquenchable sense of humour. His smile and his satire break out at the most unlikely times.

Top people in Britain are always trumpeting the values of individual initiative and 'fighting for one's own'. In Ron Smith they found rather more of these qualities than they could stomach. In short, he was a match for the lot of them.

Left: father and daughter in happier days

Above: Helen Smith, somewhere outside the city of Jeddah, in typically cheerful mood.
Below: Ron Smith, in the front room of his home in Guiseley, in contemplative mood. His struggle to find out how his daughter died continues. However, the Helen Smith affair has come to represent much more than one man's quest for truth. It has become a battlefield for legal and financial wrangles, such as West Yorkshire County Council's dispute with the unpaid inquest lawyers, which stemmed from the coroner's reluctance to produce the bills. Characteristically, Ron sticks to his guns. 'Honesty and justice will prevail,' he said, in November 1983, and added stoically, 'Everything will be resolved in God's good time'

forehead that Ron had described so graphically from his first sight of the body. There was no way such an indentation could have been collected in any process connected with a fall. It gave further confirmation to the pattern of violence that appears to have been inflicted on Helen's body before her death.

Finally, the pictures of Otten show that he was not jack-knifed on the railings as had been suggested at the inquest. He was spiked on the upper legs, with his legs pushed out straight and upwards behind him. This position made it even more unlikely that any trousers could have fallen off him in any fall, or that a passing thief had picked them off his body.

How and why did Helen Smith and Johannes Otten die? On the evidence provided by the most consistent and authoritative of the pathologists, Professor Dalgaard, it seems certain that Helen did not fall from a great height, if she fell from any height at all. It seems much more likely that the wounds to her body were inflicted directly by aggressive blows, and that her body was dumped in the courtyard to get it out of the way, or to suggest that it had fallen accidentally from above. Those guilty of the assault, or witnesses to it, may have been attempting to get Helen to the hospital at the time she died. The broken sternum suggests that there was an attempt to resuscitate her after she had been beaten unconscious. It seems certain, however, that Johannes Otten was killed by falling from a great height; he was so deeply skewered on the railings that it is clear that he, at least, fell the full 70 feet (20 metres) to his death.

Only by rejecting the medical evidence can we conclude that Helen and Johannes *both* fell the full distance, maybe one being pulled over trying to save the other. But the medical evidence will not go away. For example, if 'lesion 13', which almost certainly rendered Helen unconscious before she fell, is to be taken into account, how could Helen then have got up and tripped over the balcony?

No one giving evidence suggested that there had been any atmosphere of violence during the party or after it broke up – how then did these two people die so inconspicuously, without anyone else at the party apparently realising what was going on? Was there a conspiracy of silence? Some of the evidence is suspect, some of it *has* to be false. For example, Penny Arnot and Tim Hayter, neither of whom attended the inquest, told different stories at different times about what they were doing when the Germans left the party. Which is to be believed?

We do not know where Helen Smith was attacked. It could have been on the balcony, on the roof area to which the Arnots' parties often spread, in the flat or, if she was escaping from it, on the stairs. She could have even received her fatal blows in the courtyard itself. There is an endless number of permutations of place and attacker. How Helen Smith died, and why, is still a mystery.

It is possible that more evidence will emerge as the indefatigable Ron Smith pursues his relentless search for the truth. What is certain is that every fresh piece of evidence that has emerged has cast doubt on the conclusion that the Foreign Office trumpeted to the world the day after Helen Smith died.

'BUSTER' CRABB'S LAST DIVE

Against the strictest orders of the prime minister, British Naval Intelligence sent a frogman to spy on the cruiser that arrived in Portsmouth Harbour in April 1956 with the Soviet leaders Khrushchev and Bulganin aboard. But no information was gathered by the British – for the spy, Commander Lionel 'Buster' Crabb, never returned from his dive. The result was acute political embarrassment for Britain when the mission was revealed – and a mystery that has never been solved. What became of Crabb? Did he drown, or was he captured by the Soviets and either executed or 'turned'?

CHAPMAN PINCHER examines this extraordinary case

'BUSTER' CRABB'S LAST DIVE

OF all the mysteries that have captured the newspaper headlines none has caused such embarrassment to the government of the day as the disappearance of the naval frogman Commander Lionel Kenneth Philip Crabb, OBE, GM, RNVR, in the waters of Portsmouth Harbour, Hampshire, on 19 April 1956. Crabb was carrying out an act of espionage that was so common as to be almost routine, but on that particular day the circumstances were so peculiar that the enterprise was fraught with the gravest political consequences should it go wrong – as it did, catastrophically.

The joint leaders of the Soviet Union, Nikolai Bulganin and Nikita Khrushchev, were visiting Britain on a goodwill mission by which the British government, under the premiership of Sir Anthony Eden, set great store for the improvement of east-west relations and the thawing of the Cold War. They had chosen to arrive by sea in the cruiser *Ordzhonikidze*, with a destroyer escort, and the ships lay moored at Portsmouth Harbour while the Soviet leaders and their entourage travelled to London by train. The proposed spying operation looked simple enough.

In the previous year British Naval Intelligence, which was then under Admiralty control, had made full use of a visit by the *Ordzhonikidze*'s sister ship, *Sverdlov*, to examine the new technology being incorporated in the new generation of Soviet warships. As the *Sverdlov* had passed Dover, radar

Left: 18 April 1956 — the Ordzhonikidze, *with the Soviet leaders Nikita Khrushchev and Nikolai Bulganin aboard, sails up the English Channel towards Portsmouth. On arrival the Soviet ship received a thirteen-gun salute from the British naval destroyer* Vigo. *She was then escorted to Nab Tower and finally to the South Railway Jetty at Portsmouth Harbour, where Commander Crabb attempted to spy on her. Below: the British prime minister, Sir Anthony Eden, greets Bulganin and Khrushchev (right) at Victoria Station in London. This optimistic start to the ten-day diplomatic visit was soon to be overtaken by events*

equipment that had been set up invisibly in galleries in the white cliffs there recorded the cruiser's 'radar image', while a submerged submarine took sound, pressure and echo recordings and high-flying planes of the Royal Air Force took hundreds of photographs. The most intimate examination was made by Crabb, who had been selected for the task because he was easily the most experienced operator available. He was also a freelance, having been retired from the navy a few months previously, and if anything went wrong he could be disowned — the usual fate of a freelance spy.

Crabb's main task was to examine the submerged hull to see if the ship was fitted with a device code-named 'Agouti'. This device reduced the effect of 'cavitation', which is responsible for much of the noise made by a ship's screws and increases the chance of long-range detection by sonar (the system of finding objects underwater by reflected or emitted sound). He was also required to measure the pitch of the screws and other details providing information about the cruiser's likely performance in battle. Because of the depth and turbidity of the water Crabb had to make his assessments by feel, but he had become experienced at doing that through his work in removing limpet mines placed by enemy frogmen on the hulls of British ships during the Second World War.

The *Sverdlov* operation was regarded as routine because whenever a British warship visited Leningrad the harbour swarmed with frogmen blatantly performing the same jobs. Full authority had therefore been given for the project and the Admiralty hoped that the same attitude would be taken with the *Ordzhonikidze*. Before the latter arrived, however, intelligence operations of any kind against her were expressly forbidden by Eden because, with the Soviet leaders aboard, it was a highly sensitive political situation. Unfortunately for Crabb — and for others — the order, which was interpreted by the Admiralty as coming from a 'wet' prime minister, was widely disobeyed.

The radar equipment was set up again in the Dover cliffs, though on a smaller scale, and a submarine lay on the bottom of the English Channel as before. While the RAF refrained from making reconnaissance flights, photographs were taken by American CIA agents from a civil airliner. And Crabb was again employed to make an underwater examination.

While everyone was to lie later about Crabb's involvement, there is no doubt that it originated with a letter from Naval Intelligence in the Admiralty to the Secret Intelligence Service (MI6), where a copy is still on file.

The request had gone from Rear Admiral John Inglis, the Director of Naval Intelligence, to the London station of MI6, where it was accepted by the head there, Nicholas Elliott. As the Admiralty particularly did not want official involvement Crabb was an obvious choice and he accepted with alacrity, being short of work. It was appreciated that, at 46, he was rather old for the task and was not really fit, being overly addicted to cigarettes and alcohol, but he had proved his effectiveness only a few months previously with the *Sverdlov* mission.

Though nothing can detract from Crabb's courage and enthusiasm, the endeavour was foolhardy for a particular reason: extreme security precautions had been taken by the

The British security authorities knew that Serov was aboard the ship and this should have made them specially watchful for any local security problem

Soviets themselves to protect their leaders wherever they might be, and the penalty for any failure would be especially severe. The leaders were staying at Claridge's Hotel in London and a team of Soviet electronic engineers had been sent over to 'sweep' the suites for eavesdropping 'bugs', which had, in fact, been planted by the British Security Service (MI5), and which they failed to detect. The whole Soviet operation was under the personal control of the chief of the KGB himself, Ivan Serov. He had visited London by air the month before to inspect the accommodation at Claridge's and discuss the British security arrangements. But he had received such a rough reception from the press and public because of his blood-stained record that he did not leave the *Ordzhonikidze* when he returned with the Soviet leaders. The British security authorities knew that he was aboard the ship and this should have alerted them to the fact that the crew would be specially watchful for any local security problem.

The Crabb operation was kept as secret as possible and very few people are supposed to have been aware of it in advance. On the afternoon of 17 April Crabb travelled by train to Portsmouth with his fiancée Mrs Patricia Rose, who went purely to keep him company. On the way he told her what he intended to do and said that the Admiralty was employing him, though indirectly so that it would not seem to be concerned if problems ensued. Pat Rose tried to talk him out of the project, believing it to be too dangerous, but Crabb, whom she called 'Crabbie', insisted that, having accepted the contract, he would have to keep his word. He told her that he was to be paid £50, a modest sum for such a task even in those days, but an MI6 informant has assured the author that no fee had been fixed. Presumably £50 was

Crabb the frogman — being helped on with his diving gear (below) while investigating a suspicious object in the sea off Hastings, Sussex, in 1953; a mission completed (right). The Commander's last dive was made in the vicinity of the South Railway Jetty at Portsmouth Harbour (below right)

the figure that Crabb had in mind.

Crabb left Pat Rose at Portsmouth station and she returned to London while he went into the town to meet an MI6 'minder' who had been detailed to assist him. The two then booked in at the Sally Port Hotel in Old Portsmouth High Street, which was handy for HMS *Vernon*, a shore-based establishment near where the Soviet ships were berthed that housed the naval diving school. Crabb signed his real name in the hotel register but, in the usual 'cloak-and-dagger' way, the MI6 man booked in under a pseudonym — 'Bernard Smith'. Incredibly, he gave his address as 'Attached Foreign Office', which is the standard jargon for an MI6 officer (used, for example, in entries in *Who's Who*).

On the following morning, 18 April, the two men went to the dockyard to make a reconnaissance, presumably having passes to do so or acquiring them by some subterfuge. Having considered the times of the tides Crabb decided to make his foray at about 7am next day. It is believed that Crabb visited HMS *Vernon* in the afternoon and managed to acquire some oxygen cylinders. If so, the storeman, and possibly others, may have realised what he was proposing to do.

On the morning of the dive, 'Smith', who in reality was a local MI6 officer called Teddy Davies, suffered a minor heart attack but insisted on carrying on with the operation. Again they must have had passes to enter the enclosed area, especially in view of the presence of the Soviet ships, so more people must have become aware of the arrival of Crabb, who was well known by sight as a 'character', and they must have divined his purpose.

The selected point of entry was about 300 yards (275 metres) from the Soviet warships and Crabb changed into

Loyal and fearless

Below: Crabb holds forth to an audience of schoolboys on holiday in Tobermory, on the Isle of Mull, in 1950. Crabb had tried his hand at various jobs after the war, including selling furniture, but he had taken the first opportunity to return to diving and one of his first missions was to explore wrecks of Spanish ships sunk off the Isle of Mull in 1588. The navy had then asked him to test new diving equipment and finally conspired with MI6 to send him on his tragic mission

Lionel 'Buster' Crabb, born in 1909, tried his hand at various jobs with little success before the Second World War. When war broke out he became a gunner on a tanker while trying to join the navy, which he succeeded in doing, being commissioned at the end of 1941. Unable to do regular service at sea because of an eye weakness, he joined the navy's mine and bomb disposal service and went to Gibraltar in that dangerous capacity at the end of 1942. He was badly needed there because Italian frogmen, using advanced equipment, were sinking ships by swimming from an Italian tanker berthed in a nearby neutral Spanish port. Small depth charges were being exploded at irregular intervals to deter the Italians, but with only modest success – so the main defence had to be regular searches of the Allied ships' hulls by divers to locate and remove Italian limpet mines.

Crabb, then aged 32, could hardly swim, but he operated so effectively and so courageously, diving night and day in all weather, clad only in swimming trunks, that he was awarded the George Medal. He and his equally brave colleagues not only removed the mines and the heads of man-guided torpedoes but dragged them ashore and stripped them to discover how they worked. Being deprived of equipment through general war shortages, they also rigged up their own counter-devices. Day after day while convoys of merchant ships and their naval escorts were examined and de-mined, Crabb accumulated unrivalled expertise as well as a reputation for being fearless. He had found his forte in life.

When Italy – and its frogmen – were forced out of the war in 1943 Crabb moved there and cleared mines left in the ports of Leghorn and Venice, dangerous work for which he received the OBE. He was demobilised in 1948 with diving as his only profession. He worked for fishing companies, on an enterprise to explore the wreck of a Spanish galleon, and investigated the bed of the Thames to find a suitable discharge site for a pipe from the atomic weapons station at Aldermaston. When recalled to the navy to assist in an attempted rescue of men trapped in a submarine, he was promoted to commander. To his distress he was required to leave the navy on age grounds in March 1955, and until his disappearance the following year he worked as a freelance frogman.

Crabb's friends and colleagues described him as intensely patriotic and the last person who would have wanted to help the Soviets; but he was bitterly disappointed at being pushed out of the navy when he believed – perhaps wrongly – that he could continue diving for a further five years at least. If the alternative to diving service with the Red Navy was imprisonment in a labour camp or liquidation, it is not impossible that he could have chosen to continue his diving career, for the Soviet Union was not openly at war with the west. Crabb's reaction to the Italian frogmen who had been his deadly enemies in Gibraltar was one of high respect for their courage and he bore them no grudge. He could possibly have taken a similar view about Soviet naval frogmen if, in fact, the opportunity to work with them ever occurred.

his frogman suit and flippers and donned his oxygen closed-circuit breathing apparatus, his 'minder' assisting and looking after his discarded civilian clothing. It has been suggested that because Crabb was a freelance his equipment was poor, but the author has been assured that it was in first-class order, though the closed-circuit breathing system had inherent dangers. Crabb then headed for the *Ordzhonikidze* but returned after a few minutes for an extra pound (0·5 kilograms) of lead ballast to decrease his buoyancy. He is then said to have swum off and never to have been seen again by his colleagues.

At 7.30am, according to a later Soviet statement, Crabb was seen by Soviet sailors swimming at the surface near one of the *Ordzhonikidze*'s destroyers. Whether this was before or after he had returned for the extra ballast is unknown. If it was before, then Crabb could not have known that he had been observed – if, in fact, he really was.

What happened to the gallant commander? MI6 is totally convinced that he died as a result of an accident, either through damage to his oxygen supply or through drowning, perhaps because he dived too deeply under the cruiser's keel. There are, however, other definite possibilities. Crabb could have drowned or been deliberately killed in an underwater battle with Red Navy frogmen, who were either on routine protection duty or knew that a British frogman was going to appear. Those who knew Crabb believe he would have tried to defend himself and escape. He knew that the *Ordzhonikidze* had a 'wet compartment' – a chamber below the waterline from which defensive frogmen could operate unseen. The ship could also have been fitted with submerged 'jackstays' – wires along each side to which frogmen could hold while awaiting any frogman spy.

He could have been captured by Soviet frogmen and taken aboard the *Ordzhonikidze* for questioning. In that event he might have been taken to the Soviet Union as a captive. He might even have been summarily executed as a spy or – according to one account – might have died from exhaustion or a heart attack aboard the ship.

When Crabb failed to return from the dive 'Smith' took his clothes and unused parts of his equipment and returned to the Sally Port Hotel, where he paid the joint bill and removed Crabb's possessions that were still there. He then returned to his MI6 station and alerted London MI6, where there was immediate consternation, as there was at Admiralty headquarters in Whitehall. Crabb was supposed to have returned to London after the dive to report his findings to MI6 and then to see his fiancée in the evening. When he failed to appear, and did not telephone, Pat Rose assumed that he was missing and told friends so.

The Admiralty and MI6 decided to seek the help of MI5 in an attempt to cover up the disaster. In the hope that a complete cover-up might be successful, ministers were told nothing. At that stage the Admiralty and MI6 officials had no knowledge that the Soviets were aware of Crabb's mission and they were very anxious to avoid the wrath of the prime minister, who had forbidden any such operation. Confident that the cover-up would succeed, the Admiralty sat tight but, unfortunately, the commander of the Soviet flotilla,

Below: Colonel-General Ivan Serov, head of Soviet state security, at the Soviet embassy in London on 26 March 1956. The purpose of his visit was to discuss security arrangements for the April visit of Khrushchev and Bulganin. Behind him stands Superintendent Grant of Scotland Yard. Appropriately, Serov – who was not welcomed back by the British – was on board the Ordzhonikidze *when Commander Crabb made his disastrous attempt to break through the security net in Portsmouth Harbour*

Rear Admiral V. F. Kotov, reported to the chief of staff of the Portsmouth base, Rear Admiral Philip Burnett, that: 'At 7.30am on 19 April sailors aboard the *Ordzhonikidze* had observed a frogman floating between the Soviet destroyers. The frogman was seen on the surface for a short time and he had then dived alongside the destroyer *Smotriashchin.*' Burnett, who knew nothing of the operation and was aware that there was a ban on any frogman activities, rejected the complaint, believing that it was a deliberate provocation or that the sailors had been mistaken. Whatever Burnett told his superiors, ministers remained in the dark and might have continued in ignorance but for an event that had taken place on the evening of the 19 April.

James Thomas, the First Lord of the Admiralty, was dining with some of the Soviet visitors and was asked: 'What was that frogman doing off our bows this morning?' The following morning inquiries were put in train and ministers were shocked and angered when they were told, grudgingly, what had happened. Eden, of course, was enraged at the way a major political and psychological advantage had been handed to the Soviets. It was still hoped, however, that the Soviet leaders would avoid making public political capital out of the episode and these hopes were fortified by Admiralty assurances that what Crabb had attempted was meted out as routine treatment to British warships visiting the Soviet Union.

Throughout 20 April, which was a Friday, there were many secret meetings in Whitehall about the continuation of a cover-up. The one possibility to which no thought whatever was given was the issue of an official statement admitting the fault and apologising to the Soviet leaders. Instead, all thought was concentrated on preventing any clue to the

Pat Rose's theory

Commander Crabb's fiancée, Mrs Pat Rose, was the last of his close friends or relatives to see him alive. Two days before the fatal dive they took the train together from Victoria Station in London and parted for the last time at the station in Portsmouth. There Crabb left Mrs Rose in a distressed state, explaining that he had to carry out his duty. Mrs Rose, who now lives in Sussex, remains convinced that he was transported to the Soviet Union, and that he may still be alive, though she has never heard from him directly. In a recent conversation with the author she confirmed that she had been approached on several occasions in the past by people who were quite unknown to her but had clearly sought her out to give her assurances that Crabb was alive and well. She is satisfied that the assurances originated from the Soviet Union; but if they did, this could have been part of a Soviet disinformation exercise.

Because of her belief that the torso clad in a frogman's suit that was washed ashore at Chichester Harbour in June 1957 was not Crabb, she avoided visiting the grave where the torso was buried and that bears a headstone inscribed with his name. Recently, however, attending

Above: Pat Rose, who insists: 'Crabbie is still alive'

Above: the Sally Port Hotel in 1984. Crabb stayed here on the eve of his disappearance

embarrassing gaffe reaching the British public or Parliament where inquiries by Labour Opposition MPs might have enforced a government statement, encouraging the Kremlin to take full advantage of Britain's obvious treachery. On MI5's advice – which proved to be counter-productive to say the least – the head of the Portsmouth CID, Detective Superintendent Stanley Lampert, was asked to visit the hotel on Saturday 21 April and remove all evidence of Crabb's stay there. He saw the hotel manager, Edward Richman, and on the basis of his identity card tore four pages from the visitors' book. Why he thought the removal of four pages was necessary has never been explained. Perhaps the names went on to two pages and MI5 had required the removal of the names of all other guests who might have seen Crabb so that they could not be traced and questioned by journalists if the news became public. When the manager objected Lampert threatened him with the Official Secrets Act if he told anybody what had happened. As was to be made clear in Parliament later, this was both irregular and unwarranted and the removal of the pages was illegal.

The Soviets stayed their hand concerning any official complaint to the Foreign Office, or any leak to the media, and might have continued to do so but for an unfortunate political incident that occurred at a dinner at Claridge's on the evening of 23 April. Bulganin and Khrushchev were the guests of honour at a dinner given by the Labour Party Executive Committee and the two Labour leaders, Hugh Gaitskell and George Brown, were present. Brown (now Lord George-Brown) took the opportunity to make a plea for human rights in the Soviet Union and when Khrushchev brushed the request aside Brown cried, 'May God forgive you!' Khrushchev immediately asked for the remark to be translated and became extremely angry, regarding the criticism as a personal insult.

By the time the Soviets departed with their warships the goodwill mission had been an all-round disaster, but while the row at Claridge's was widely publicised the public remained ignorant of the Crabb affair. The British authorities would dearly have liked to have kept it that way but Crabb's friends and relatives had to be told of his disappearance. On Saturday 28 April, nine days after the commander was last seen, a naval officer from the Admiralty called on Pat Rose and, as she was out, left a message saying that he was missing. On the following day the Admiralty announced that Crabb was missing, presumed dead, having failed to return from 'a test-dive in connection with trials of certain underwater apparatus in Stokes Bay'. Stokes Bay was three miles (five kilometres) from Portsmouth and Crabb could not possibly have swum to the Soviet ships from there.

The statement was, of course, a deliberate lie manufactured to give the impression that Crabb's dive had had nothing whatever to do with the Soviet warships, should this possibility be raised by the press. In those days the Admiralty was a law unto itself and Naval Intelligence thought the lie justified 'in the national interest'. It showed that, at that stage, the navy chiefs were confident that the whole episode could be satisfactorily suppressed.

As could be expected, the statement was not believed by

a hospital close by, she did go to see it and felt totally unmoved by any possibility that it contains the remains of her lover.

Minor mysteries continue to worry her. Crabb did not go out in civilian clothes without taking his gold-headed cane, which was in fact a swordstick, and Mrs Rose is confident that he had it with him at the Sally Port Hotel prior to his dive. The swordstick, which should have been sent to her or to Crabb's mother, seems to have disappeared. The author Bernard Hutton claimed that it had somehow fallen into Soviet hands and been passed on to Crabb.

Mrs Rose confirmed that Hutton had shown her the dossier on Crabb and other documents which, he claimed, had been smuggled to him from behind the Iron Curtain. These documents offer the information that Crabb was taken to the Soviet Union and joined the Red Navy as 'Korablov'. Hutton's analysis of the dossier on Crabb presents the frogman spy as a hero who bravely resisted Soviet interrogation.

'I know you can dismiss it as only a feeling in my bones but Crabbie and I were very close and I am absolutely certain that he is still alive – in Russia,' she insists to this day.

Below: Portsmouth Harbour, showing the South Railway Jetty, where the Soviet ships were berthed, in relation to HMS Vernon, where Crabb based his operation. Below centre: the coastline from Portsmouth to Chichester. Stokes Bay was the location the authorities ascribed to the mission they invented for Crabb. Far right: Crabb (left) on a rescue operation in the Thames Estuary in 1950. Below, far right: main gate of HMS Vernon. Bottom: HMS Vernon from the sea

many journalists, who speculated that Crabb had been spying on the Soviet warships, and drew attention to the extraordinary fact that no attempt at all had been made to find the body. It emerged that one of Crabb's wartime colleagues, Sidney Knowles, had wanted to look for the body but was dissuaded by a naval officer who seemed convinced that he would be wasting his time – a response that was later to seem to have sinister significance.

When inquiries revealed the removal of the pages from the Sally Port Hotel register and what had been in them, it

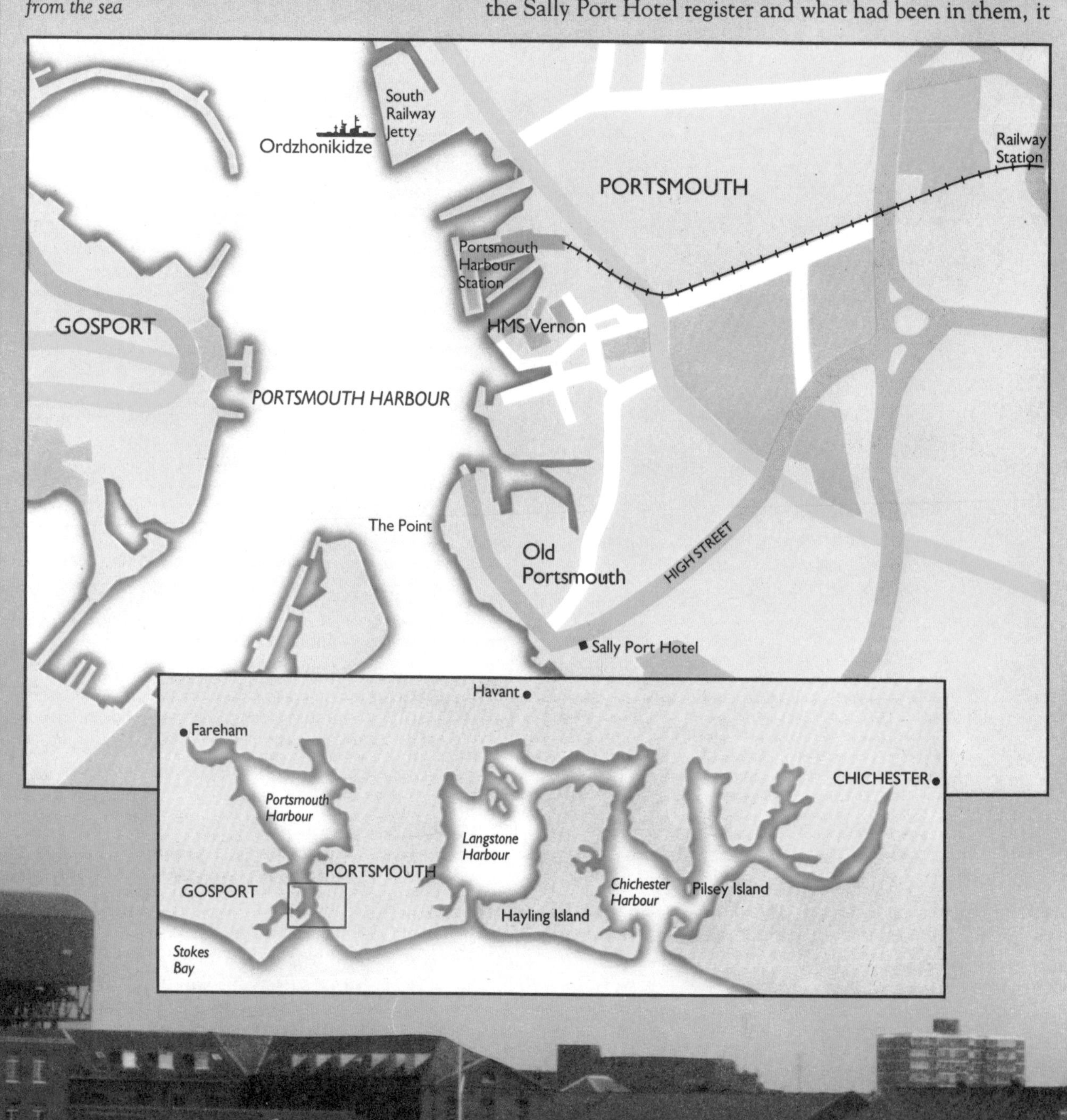

quickly became clear to Parliament and the public alike that they had been the victims of an Admiralty and MI6 'disinformation' cover-up, and that lies had been told to spare embarrassment in Whitehall and Westminster.

After deliberations with Kremlin colleagues, the Soviet leaders decided to make what political capital they could out of the situation and the Soviet embassy in London sent a note to the Foreign Office claiming that Soviet sailors had seen a frogman and that when Rear Admiral Kotov had drawn the attention of Rear Admiral Burnett to the incident he had categorically rejected the possibility. Referring to British newspaper reports that secret underwater tests had resulted in the death of a British frogman, the note asked for an explanation – 'attaching great importance to such an unusual fact as the carrying out of secret frogman tests alongside Soviet ships on a friendly visit in the British naval base of Portsmouth'.

The Whitehall authorities still hoped to keep the note secret but Soviet embassy officials, clearly acting on instructions from Moscow, leaked the fact that Soviet sailors had seen a frogman and that there could be little doubt that it was Crabb.

This immediately led to a flurry of newspaper speculation about what might have happened. One theory claimed that Crabb had been captured and taken to the Soviet Union, another that he had been killed by the Soviets in the water and even that his body had been found by the British navy and secretly buried at midnight in a local cemetery, 'with full naval honours'. Realising that it had already made a monumental blunder by issuing its Stokes Bay statement, the Admiralty declined to confirm or deny any of the theories, though trusted journalists were privately assured that Crabb must have drowned, his body having been swept out to sea where, presumably, it would surface one day.

The most exciting theory, and the one offering the biggest bonuses to the KGB, was that Crabb had been captured by Soviet frogmen, ever alert to any danger threatening a Soviet ship, and had been taken back to the Soviet Union for questioning. As will be seen, this theory, which made the British navy and intelligence services look incompetent, not only in the eyes of the British public but to Britain's allies, was to be developed with a mass of detail that even cast doubt on Crabb's loyalty.

Meanwhile, the Foreign Office had secretly replied to the Soviet note admitting that Commander Crabb had carried out frogman tests and had, presumably, lost his life while performing them. It then went on to admit that: 'The frog-

man who, as reported in the Soviet note, was discovered from the Soviet ships swimming between the Soviet destroyers, was in all appearances Commander Crabb. His presence in the vicinity of the destroyers occurred without any permission whatever, and Her Majesty's Government express their regret for the incident.' This statement was false in respect of no permission having been given, and it seems that the Foreign Office hoped that the Soviets would believe that he had operated entirely independently, which was untrue, as both the Admiralty and MI6 had been intimately involved. The Foreign Office and the other Whitehall departments involved in the fiasco were hoping that the diplomatic exchanges would remain secret but, as more realistic advice might have counselled, the Kremlin released the text of both notes, thereby making the matter more embarrassing for the British which, of course, was the objective.

As always happens, whatever the party in office, the opposition took advantage of the government's chagrin to make its own political capital. The publication of the notes forced the prime minister, Eden, to make a statement to Parliament on 9 May admitting that Crabb had been the frogman and

Below: the First Lord of the Admiralty the Right Honourable J. P. L. Thomas MP tests a Gannet anti-submarine aircraft attached to the Ark Royal *in the Mediterranean Fleet in January 1956. Only hours after Crabb had disappeared, Thomas was asked by the Soviets to explain, 'What was that frogman doing off our bows this morning?'*

had been near the Soviet warships. He insisted that the operation had been 'without authority' or the knowledge of ministers and said that 'appropriate disciplinary steps' were being taken. Otherwise he refused to be drawn, pleading the traditional respect for secrecy in such matters.

Eden had, in fact, ordered a secret inquiry by a group headed by Sir Edward Bridges, a very senior civil servant. Various officials who gave evidence were admonished and some were transferred. The chief punishment was reserved for the chief of MI6, Major General Sir John 'Sinbad' Sinclair, who was retired early and replaced by the man who was serving as director general of MI5, Sir Dick White. MI6 had always regarded itself to be superior to MI5 and White's appointment was considered by MI6, and Whitehall in general, to be the severest punishment that could have been inflicted.

Like the Admiralty and the rest of the Whitehall establishment, Eden hoped that the matter would then be laid to rest, but the Labour opposition forced a short debate on 14 May in the hope of pressing the government into further damaging admissions. All the known facts were aired and MI6, the Admiralty and the government were rightly accused of 'a very grave lack of control' – but Eden refused to be moved.

The issue seemed to be dying away when, on Sunday 9 June 1957, fourteen months after Crabb's disappearance, a fisherman called John Randall saw a headless body in a frogman suit floating off Pilsey Island, a sandbank at the mouth of Chichester Harbour, Sussex, around ten miles (sixteen kilometres) from where the Soviet ships had berthed. He and another fisherman hauled the body aboard and it was handed over to the police. As the hands were also missing, the pathologists were unable to identify it with any certainty. Crabb's former wife Margaret inspected the body but could not positively identify it either. However, what remained of the suit on the body seemed to be identical with that which had been supplied to Crabb by a manufacturer and no other frogman had been reported missing in the area.

An inquest was held on 11 June and it was revealed that there were signs of a scar on the body's left knee. Crabb's former colleague, Sidney Knowles, testified that the missing frogman had had such a scar, the result of an accident with barbed wire Crabb had suffered when they were diving together. The coroner recorded an open verdict but said he was satisfied that the remains were those of Crabb, who had died gallantly in the service of his country. This view received support from a newspaper report that the body of a frogman with the head attached had certainly been dredged up by a lone fisherman a few months previously. The fisherman was said to have told the local police that he had grabbed the head to haul the body aboard and it had come away in his hands, as it might well have done after so long in the water. Being quite horrified he had dropped the head into the water and rowed away. The police apparently recorded the incident but took no further action.

The convenient absence of the head and hands quickly gave rise to speculation that the body was not really Crabb's but that of another person from which the main identification

One dive or two?

It is certain that Commander Crabb entered the water not far from the Soviet warships shortly after 7am on 19 April 1956. It is also certain that he returned after only a brief interval to pick up an extra pound (0·5 kilograms) of lead weight because his buoyancy was too great, and then swam off again. According to the statement made by the chief of the Soviet flotilla, Rear Admiral Kotov, his sailors saw a frogman swimming at the surface at about 7.30. Yet several witnesses and friends of Crabb testified that they saw him alive later that day.

One possible explanation is that, after returning for the extra ballast weight, Crabb, who was not very fit, decided to return and rest before his next attempt to explore the cruiser's hull, changed back into his ordinary clothes and went back into Portsmouth. A friend in London claimed to have received a telephone call from him at 9.30am, while another said he saw him in a pub at about 2pm. If that evidence is correct he must have returned to the dockside in the late afternoon, changed back into his frogman suit and re-entered the water.

MI6 sources, however, insist that the dive on which he disappeared occurred in the early morning and that Crabb never returned to Portsmouth. Nothing from the security authorities concerning the Crabb affair is necessarily to be believed, however, because of the overriding need for cover-up.

Above: Rear Admiral V. F. Kotov of the Red Navy

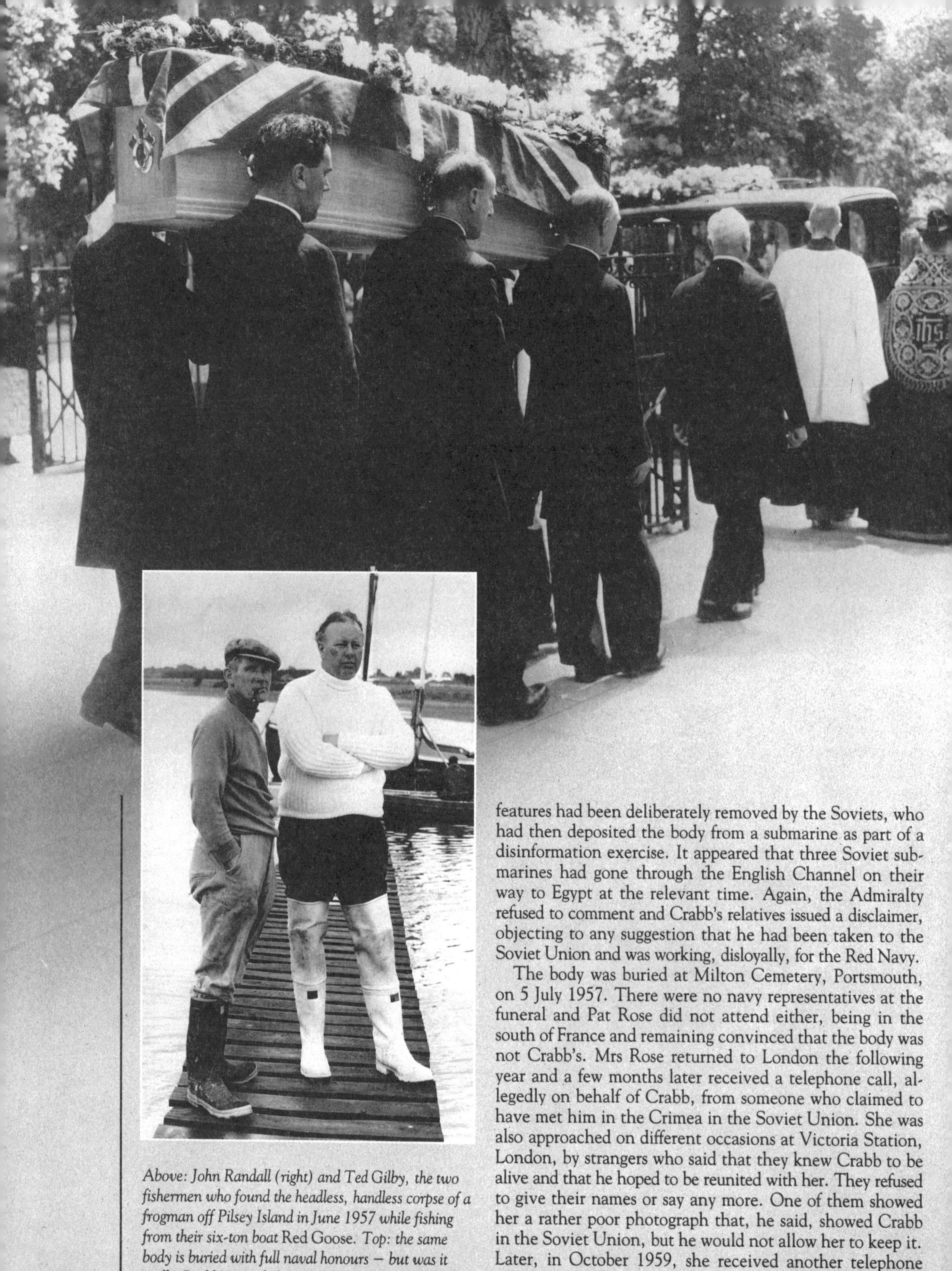

Above: John Randall (right) and Ted Gilby, the two fishermen who found the headless, handless corpse of a frogman off Pilsey Island in June 1957 while fishing from their six-ton boat Red Goose. Top: the same body is buried with full naval honours – but was it really Crabb's? And if not, whose was it?

features had been deliberately removed by the Soviets, who had then deposited the body from a submarine as part of a disinformation exercise. It appeared that three Soviet submarines had gone through the English Channel on their way to Egypt at the relevant time. Again, the Admiralty refused to comment and Crabb's relatives issued a disclaimer, objecting to any suggestion that he had been taken to the Soviet Union and was working, disloyally, for the Red Navy.

The body was buried at Milton Cemetery, Portsmouth, on 5 July 1957. There were no navy representatives at the funeral and Pat Rose did not attend either, being in the south of France and remaining convinced that the body was not Crabb's. Mrs Rose returned to London the following year and a few months later received a telephone call, allegedly on behalf of Crabb, from someone who claimed to have met him in the Crimea in the Soviet Union. She was also approached on different occasions at Victoria Station, London, by strangers who said that they knew Crabb to be alive and that he hoped to be reunited with her. They refused to give their names or say any more. One of them showed her a rather poor photograph that, he said, showed Crabb in the Soviet Union, but he would not allow her to keep it. Later, in October 1959, she received another telephone call from an anonymous person who said that Crabb was

Was Crabb betrayed?

When the KGB defector Anatoli Golitsin was interrogated in 1963 he admitted that Soviet naval intelligence knew in advance that a British frogman would attempt to spy on the Soviet cruiser *Ordzhonikidze*. He also said that he had been told, in Moscow, that the frogman had been captured. He said he was so sure of his facts that he believed them to be further evidence that a Soviet agent was operating in the Admiralty, MI6 or MI5.

As Golitsin proved to be reliable about so many other factual matters, the possibility that Crabb was doomed – through an espionage betrayal before he entered the water – must be seriously considered. Among spies known to have been in the Admiralty, such as the clerk John Vassall and the Soviet agent at Portland, Harry Houghton, none was aware of the project, so far as can be ascertained. Several people in MI6 knew of it but no suspicion had ever attached to them. (One German account names Kim Philby as the betrayer but he had been expelled from MI6 in 1951 and it is most unlikely that he would have heard any whisper about the operation.) Of those officials in MI5 who knew of it, Sir Roger Hollis, who was the Deputy Director General, was later to come under serious suspicion. Though Hollis was declared innocent in Parliament in 1981, he remains the likeliest source of any leakage from the secret services.

According to Bernard Hutton, who claimed to have received a stolen KGB dossier proving that Crabb had been captured, the man who signed the Portsmouth hotel register as 'Bernard Smith' was Matthew Smith, an American; this man, who apparently told Crabb he would be working for the CIA, was supposedly a Soviet agent and betrayed the frogman to the Soviets. There is no doubt, however, that 'Smith' was really an MI6 officer called Ted Davies.

Of course, it may be that the Soviets had learned that Crabb had carried out an underwater survey of the previous Red Navy cruiser to visit Portsmouth, the *Sverdlov*, and had then taken routine precautions. In that case Crabb would have delivered himself, literally, into Soviet hands.

Below: the Sverdlov *– did Crabb's spying mission against her seal his fate a year later?*

alive in Vladivostok. Some of these occurrences could have been hoaxes, but they would also have been in keeping with the KGB's tactics.

The possibility that Crabb had been captured and was alive in the Soviet Union was developed and embellished by a middle European who wrote books under the name of J. Bernard Hutton. He claimed to have received a 'dossier' in November 1959 via the 'anti-communist' underground; it contained information said to prove that Crabb had been taken alive, drugged aboard the *Ordzhonikidze* and flown into the Soviet Union by a helicopter that alighted on the cruiser when it was homeward-bound in the Skaggerak on 29 April 1956. The master of a Danish destroyer was said to have witnessed the lift-off operation through binoculars and to have seen three men, one of whom was being led, climb aboard the helicopter, which then flew towards a military airfield.

The 'dossier' was packed with names. Crabb's case officer was given as Colonel Zhabotin, and Crabb was supposed to have been questioned at the 'Khimsky Naval Intelligence Centre' by an 'Investigation Judge' called 'Colonel Aleksei Feofilovich Myaskov'. During relatively brief interrogations Crabb was said to have been shown a body with similar measurements to his own and to have been told that, if he agreed to co-operate, it would be dumped near Portsmouth after a suitable interval of decomposition in sea water. If he declined to co-operate then the body that would be dumped would be his own and, to rub in the hopelessness of his position, he was told that the British authorities had already presumed him dead. Under the circumstances Crabb is said to have agreed to co-operate, which meant joining the Red Navy, to which he would devote his services as a diver and instructor. After 'rehabilitation' at the KGB centre at Selskoye, Crabb was supposed to have been given a crash course in Russian (at which it is likely he would have been extremely bad) and told that for the ensuing ten years he would be in the Red Navy under a new name — Lev Lvovich Korablov. He was told that if he misbehaved he would be shot.

As promised, so the 'dossier' claimed, the false body was towed behind a submarine in a canister and released near Portsmouth shortly before the time that it was washed up and discovered by the fisherman.

Information about Hutton's 'dossier' and his forthcoming book began to leak to the newspapers and CRABB IS ALIVE headlines appeared in the British newspapers in February 1960, being, of course, denied in Moscow which, however, took the opportunity of recalling Britain's perfidy. British security and intelligence authorities declined to comment but they privately dismissed the information as having no foundation in fact and that is still their opinion, or alleged opinion. They were careful, however, not to deny the existence of the 'dossier'.

Left: The Silent Enemy *was a 1958 film about Crabb's exploits starring Laurence Harvey (right) and Michael Craig as Crabb's fellow diver Sidney Knowles. Below left: Crabb's former wife Margaret at the premiere of the film. Below: the British government avoided telling the truth — but could not prevent the Soviets making political capital out of the issue. As a result, heads rolled*

FINAL NIGHT EXTRA

CLOSING CITY PRICES

COGNAC
BISQUIT DUBOUCHÉ
A Rare Compliment to your Palate

Evening Standard

41,029 WEDNESDAY, MAY 9, 1956 Twopence

LES PARFUMS WORTH Je Reviens

HOW DID CRABB DIE? EDEN WILL NOT SAY

'Not in the public interest to tell'

'WE DID NOT KNOW ABOUT IT'

Disciplinary action being taken

Evening Standard Parliamentary Reporter

Sir Anthony Eden told the House of Commons today that "it would not be in the public interest" to disclose the circumstances in which Commander Lionel Crabb is presumed to have met his death.

"While it is the practice for Ministers to accept

MYSTERY

In 1961 Hutton had a windfall in the form of a statement by Sir Percy Sillitoe, the former director general of MI5. He had been retired for eight years and had no contact with security affairs, but his name carried weight with the public when he claimed that a similar dossier had been obtained by British intelligence agents. He agreed with Hutton that the body buried in the Portsmouth cemetery was not Crabb's. Hutton also secured the support of a naval officer who had been much in the public eye, Commander J. S. Kerans, formerly of the warship *Amethyst*, which had run the gauntlet of a Chinese bombardment and escaped from the Yangtse

river. Kerans, who had become an MP, said in writing that he was confident that Crabb had been taken to the Soviet Union. He also raised questions in Parliament about him but with no result.

It remains possible, though only remotely in the author's opinion, that the 'dossier' was genuine and contained the truth. On the other hand, it could have been a fabrication and, in that case, the interest centres on the fabricators. It could have been a journalistic enterprise but the view among several professional intelligence officers is that it originated in the KGB's disinformation 'factory'. This belief was fortified by the arrival in Hutton's hands of a photograph allegedly smuggled out of the Soviet Union and purporting to be 'Korablov' – that is, Crabb – in Soviet uniform aboard a Red Navy warship. Hutton immediately claimed that the photograph showed Crabb and was genuine, but some naval officers rejected it. Understandably, by that time, people who wanted to believe that Crabb was alive, like his former wife and Pat Rose, believed that the sailor was Crabb; while there was some facial resemblance, the man in the photograph, said to be a first lieutenant, looked younger than Crabb. If the 'dossier' had been produced by the KGB then the supply of the photograph would have been a further subterfuge guaranteed to resurrect the speculation.

Pat Rose, in some desperation, wrote to Khrushchev for information but received no reply. Little more was heard until 1964 when the late Colonel Marcus Lipton, a Labour MP who specialised in such causes (especially if they were likely to get his name in the newspapers), attempted to reopen the case in Parliament. He got small change from the prime minister, Harold Wilson who, like Eden before him, took the view that the Soviets had made more than enough political capital out of the episode. Indeed, Wilson may well have been advised by the security authorities that the Soviets were behind this new attempt to sow contentious disinformation. Though it may be coincidental, from the time of the Crabb affair the KGB had changed its general policy, deciding to concentrate more effort and resources on the use of disinformation as a way of confusing and discrediting Cold War adversaries such as Britain. The Crabb débâcle had certainly presented the KGB with a ready-made opportunity, and it is the view of MI6 officers that it was taken and pursued with much success.

Another MP, Bernard Floud, Labour member for Acton, was a friend of Hutton who satisfied him that the 'dossier' was genuine. Floud agreed to try to reopen the case and, according to Hutton, he claimed that, through some friend in MI6, he had established that the Secret Intelligence Service had secured its own copy of the 'dossier', which differed from the one in Hutton's possession only in minor details. According to Hutton, in his book *Commander Crabb Is Alive*, Floud told him that he had established that two naval officers from HMS *Vernon* had witnessed the capture of Crabb by Soviet divers, had submitted reports and had been ordered to remain silent. Floud also claimed to have discovered that coded Soviet secret service messages deciphered by Government Communications Headquarters had mentioned the capture of a frogman in Portsmouth Harbour, and he provided other evidence supporting Hutton's case.

This would seem to be virtual proof of Hutton's account, but in 1967 Floud was exposed as a Soviet agent, having been recruited by the KGB while at Oxford University, the recruiter being the communist James Klugmann. Floud's treachery was revealed during the interrogation of Anthony Blunt, after the latter confessed to having spied for the Soviets thoughout the Second World War while he had been serving in MI5. Though still an MP, Floud was questioned in 1967 by MI5 officers who believed that he was still in touch with KGB agents in London and, after a series of interrogations, he returned home and committed suicide. Floud may have concocted his information believing it to be in the Soviet interest, but it is more likely that it was provided for him by the KGB because agents are actively discouraged by

Far left: Bernard Floud MP, who tried to reopen the Crabb case in support of Bernard Hutton's account. Eventually, though, Floud was exposed as a Soviet spy. Below, far left: Lieutenant-Commander J. S. Kerans, when commander of the Amethyst. *As an MP Kerans later expressed his belief that Crabb had been taken to the Soviet Union*

The 'Roman' conspiracy

A remarkable account of the fate of Commander Crabb was given by the convicted Soviet spy, Harry Houghton, who at the time was working at the Underwater Weapons Establishment at Portland. After serving a fifteen-year sentence for his part in betraying naval secrets to the KGB in what became known as the Portland Spy Ring, Houghton wrote his memoirs, *Operation Portland*, in which he claimed to have been told the truth about the Crabb affair by his Soviet controller, whom he knew as 'Roman'. He alleged that 'Roman' had been alerted to Crabb's dive following a remark that he overheard in a Dorset pub, while he and Houghton were having a drink there. A woman from the Portland establishment was at a nearby table with one of the navy's shallow water divers, who said that he had been training for something special, which had been called off. Houghton claimed that 'Roman' then made inquiries, and that as a result Soviet frogmen were stationed along the hull of the *Ordzhonikdze* in case a British diver appeared.

According to the details that 'Roman' gave Houghton, the Soviet frogmen interfered with Crabb's oxygen supply long enough for him to become unconscious and then took him through the cruiser's wet compartment. He recovered consciousness and was able to answer questions but suddenly collapsed and died. To Houghton's astonishment 'Roman' said that he himself had been aboard the vessel and had seen Crabb die.

'Roman' said that Crabb told the Soviets that his purpose had been to attach a magnetic device that would transmit impulses when the cruiser was on its way back down the Channel, and that these would tell the British scientists what they needed to know.

The Soviets were said to have been embarrassed by Crabb's death as they had hoped to be in the position to hand him over and so cause maximum dismay to their British hosts. Shortly after the ships left their berths Crabb's body was returned to the water.

Houghton certainly knew more than he told his interrogators — because MI5 rejected his offer to turn 'Queen's Evidence' in return for a full confession. There is no doubt, however, that he fabricated much of the material in his book to improve its saleability, and his Crabb story may be part of that. On the other had, since there is no doubt that Houghton was in close contact with a number of KGB officers during his seven years of active and very damaging espionage, 'Roman' may indeed have given him the information. But it would still be impossible to tell if the KGB fed him false information.

Below: Harry Houghton with fellow Portland spy Ethel Gee after their release from jail in 1970

Below: Crabb in action, on this occasion returning from a diving mission. Did the sea finally claim him or did he go to the Soviet Union as a prisoner on board the Ordzhonikidze, there to be coerced into diving for the Red Navy? Or was he executed? Bottom: the tombstone at Milton Cemetery, Portsmouth is strong evidence of the official view that the body found in Chichester Harbour was Crabb's and that it was duly laid to rest. But the body had not been identified for sure and the grave could contain the skeleton of a 'switched' body dumped by Soviet disinformation agents

Moscow from taking any initiative without first securing professional agreement. If that occurred it would be hard evidence to support the belief that the 'dossier' was part of a KGB disinformation operation.

According to Hutton, he continued to receive news from the Soviet Union about Crabb's career in the Red Navy, indicating that he had been promoted to commander and was enjoying life there so much that he had extended his ten-year contract. These titbits, which may have been deliberately fed by the KGB to keep the story going, were supported by others appearing in European papers indicating that Crabb was still alive.

Crabb's much prophecied reappearance on this side of the Iron Curtain has never materialised. It was always a forlorn hope. Had he ever served as a diver in the Red Navy he would have known too many secrets to be permitted to reveal them to the west.

The Crabb case, therefore, seems destined to remain unsolved for all time, with even those who accept the evidence that he was accidentally drowned being prepared to concede that they are not entirely sure. The only certainty is that to this day Whitehall, and the secret services in particular, remain extremely sensitive about the Crabb affair. Officials with inside knowledge of the case have been expressly forbidden to make any mention of it in their memoirs. This ban may simply be due to the desire to bury for good a deplorable and deeply embarrassing episode — or it might indicate that there are super-sensitive details that have still not been revealed.

MURDER AT MANILA AIRPORT

Benigno 'Ninoy' Aquino, charismatic leader of the opposition in the Philippines, stepped off his aircraft at Manila airport at midday on 21 August 1983. Despite massive security and a military escort, within minutes he was lying dead on the ground, victim of a single bullet to the head. Beside him on the tarmac lay the body of a second man; this, claimed the government of Ferdinand Marcos, was Rolando Galman, Aquino's assassin. Galman was allegedly a hit-man hired by the communists, but at the commission of inquiry very different stories about him emerged. *PHILIP JACOBSON* tells the story and asks: what really happened at Manila airport that Sunday?

AVSECOM

Left: the bloodstained body of Rolando Galman lies on the tarmac at Manila airport. Galman, disguised as an airport maintenance worker, had allegedly got into the airport compound despite massive security. He had hidden beneath the service steps to Aquino's aircraft, then leapt out and shot him the minute he reached the ground. Armed guards from the airport security organisation, Avsecom, had promptly shot him dead. But this official account of events has serious flaws. Below: the scene at the airport a few minutes later, when the body of the dead senator was being lifted into an Avsecom van. The security officers menaced the journalists who were still taking photographs from inside the aeroplane

As China Airlines (CAL) Flight 811 began its descent to the international airport at Manila, capital of the Philippines, a round-faced, bespectacled passenger disappeared into the lavatory. When he came out, he was wearing a lightweight bullet-proof vest beneath the jacket of his white safari suit. 'Of course, if they hit me in the head, I'm a goner anyway,' he joked to his companions. Just before the aircraft landed, he bowed his head briefly in prayer, then sat back, calm and composed.

It was approximately 1pm on 21 August 1983, and Benigno 'Ninoy' Aquino was coming home from three years of self-imposed political exile in the United States to lead the growing opposition to the government of President Ferdinand Marcos. Aquino was anything but a welcome guest to Marcos, who had once kept him in prison for more than five years. The Philippines government had refused to issue him with a passport to re-enter his own country; more seriously, it had warned that his safety could not be guaranteed if he did come back. Aquino was travelling under an assumed name yet, at the stopover in Taipeh before the final leg of his trip, he had received alarming news when he had telephoned his wife Corazon in the United States. His face white with shock, Aquino had told one of his party: 'They're going to get me at the airport, then kill the guy who did it.'

Aquino's arrival in Manila was expected with rapture by his many supporters. The capital was festooned with yellow ribbons, symbol of his party, and some 20,000 excited Filipinos had gathered at the airport to welcome him, among them the politician's 75-year-old mother. And the government had prepared its own greeting – a massive security operation at the airport designed to seal off the entire passenger arrival area and the tarmac in the vicinity of Aquino's aeroplane. Even so, on the short flight from Taipeh, Aquino's aides made no secret of their concern for his safety. He was uncharacteristically subdued, but still defiant: 'I can't allow myself to be petrified by the fear of assassination and spend my life in the corner.'

The aides were proved correct in all their fears. Less than one minute after leaving the aircraft, Benigno Aquino lay on the tarmac, blood gushing from a massive wound at the back of his skull. A few feet away from him lay the body of another man, dressed in blue trousers and a white shirt. There was pandemonium around the aeroplane as heavily-armed Filipino troops and security men screamed into their walkie-talkies, mingling with airline officials and the shocked passengers from Flight 811. Outside the terminal, rumours that something dreadful had happened spread swiftly through the vast crowd, who were waving banners that proclaimed: 'Ninoy, you are not alone!'

A number of foreign journalists and television crews had been travelling with Aquino and, although security men tried to prevent them from sending out their dramatic stories, their accounts were soon making headline news around the world. All were broadly agreed on the sequence of events after the aircraft had parked at gate 8. First onto the airbridge 'tube' after it was connected were three or four uniformed soldiers who approached Aquino and began to lead him along

Above: Salvador Laurel, one of the leaders of the Philippines opposition party Unido, attempts to calm the excited crowds waiting for Aquino outside the airport. The thousands of supporters discovered that Aquino had been shot only when the other passengers on the same flight were eventually allowed to disembark and leave. They relayed the news to Laurel, who then had the task of informing the crowd. Perhaps surprisingly, people quietly began to disperse and go home – the protests came later. Right: Aquino's mother, who had been at the airport to meet him, grieves at the news of her son's death

the tube towards the main door. As they left, other guards in plain clothes prevented journalists from following, and finally closed the main door at the end of the tube.

The last time any of the journalists saw Aquino alive, he was being escorted by at least five uniformed men onto the platform of the steps that led down the tube service door to the tarmac below. A few seconds later, a single shot rang out then, after a brief pause, two or three more. Inside the aircraft people rushed to the windows to find out what was going on, and saw Aquino face down in his own blood. There was no sign of the uniformed troops who had been with him in the tube just a few seconds earlier but, as the journalists watched in horror, several members of the airport security unit, Aviation Security Command (Avsecom), fired at the prone body of the second man. One, in particular, placed his automatic rifle on the man's body and coldly pumped bullet after bullet into his stomach. Other Avsecom

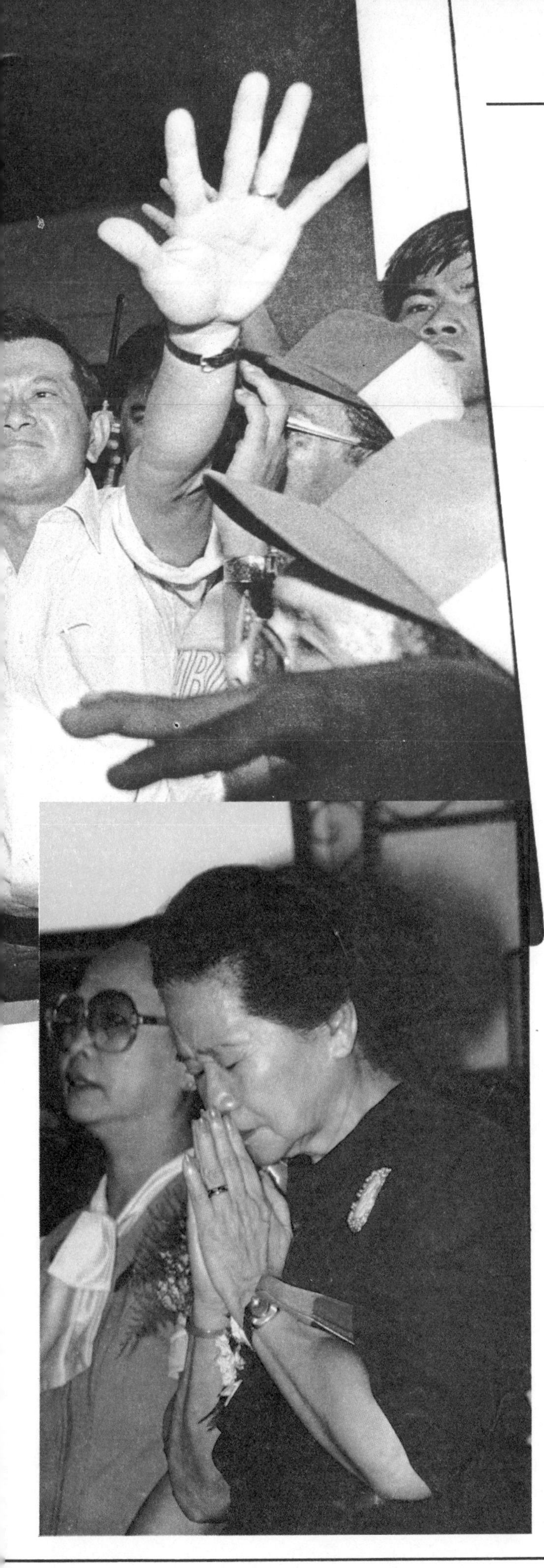

men menaced the people watching from the CAL aeroplane by firing shots into the air. As they ducked below the windows, the journalists just had time to see Aquino's white-suited body being bundled into an Avsecom van and driven off at high speed.

When the passengers from Flight 811 finally disembarked, they passed their shocking account on to the frantic well-wishers outside the passenger terminal. Salvador Laurel, the leader of the opposition party, Unido, took a loudhailer to announce: 'Our beloved Ninoy has returned, but you may not be able to see him. Eyewitnesses say that he has been shot.' The stunned crowd began to disperse, and Aquino's family arrived home in time to hear an announcement on the radio that doctors at Fort Bonifacio – Aquino's old prison camp – had pronounced him dead on arrival.

It was five hours before the Filipino authorities allowed the story that already horrified the world to be reported within the country, and a whole rumour-filled day before President Marcos publicly presented the official version of events at Manila airport. Looking frail and ill, Marcos asserted that he had 'almost begged' Aquino not to return. His killer, Marcos said, had clearly been a professional, firing a single shot from a ·357 Magnum – one of the most powerful handguns in the world – into Aquino's head from a range of 18 inches (46 centimetres). Aquino's security men were not armed, the president insisted, but they had tried to shield him with their own bodies.

Official briefings later provided the press with more information. The alleged assassin was 5 feet 6 inches (1·67 metres) tall, weighed about 12½ stone (79·4 kilograms), and was between 30 and 35 years old. The only clue to his identity was the word 'Rolly' embroidered on the waistband of his underpants and an 'R' engraved inside his gold wedding ring. Yet even without a name to go on, the Marcos regime had no hesitation in attributing the killing to a communist plot, deliberately designed to blacken the Philippines government with its allies abroad, above all in the United States – President Reagan was due to visit Marcos in a few months' time. According to officials, Aquino's killer had disguised himself in the uniform of an airport maintenance worker in order to penetrate the intensive security. When Aquino arrived on the tarmac from the service steps, he had rushed out from his hiding-place beneath the CAL aircraft, shoved past the escort and fired the fatal shot. Avsecom troops had then shot him dead.

Two days after Aquino's death, as his widow Corazon and their children arrived in Manila for his funeral, President Marcos announced the formation of an official commission under the Chief Justice of the Supreme Court to undertake 'a free, unlimited and exhaustive' investigation into the murder. It was swiftly rejected by the Aquino family, the opposition party and the influential Catholic Church, all of whom accused the government of choosing 'Marcos mouthpieces' to carry out a cover-up. The president subsequently made a somewhat extraordinary offer of £30,000 reward for information leading to 'the arrest of the killer or killers' – and this was also ridiculed. Had not Marcos himself already assured the nation that the assassin was the man in the blue trousers,

Above: ten days after his assassination, Benigno Aquino was given a state funeral. More than two million people were estimated to have followed his funeral procession. His coffin, festooned with flowers, was driven slowly through the Manila streets on the back of an open lorry, while a supporter on the roof of the cab held aloft the Philippines flag. The funeral marked the end of a period of stunned disbelief and grief; from then on, the protests against the Marcos regime – suspected by many of being involved at the highest level in the killing of Aquino – became more and more violent

Why was the alleged killer riddled with bullets instead of being captured for questioning?

in the pay of the communists, whom the troops had shot?

There was, in addition, mounting disbelief that the security authorities still could not identify the alleged killer, despite having his fingerprints and other physical leads. Surely, opposition leaders insisted, a professional hitman would already be known to the police? 'Anyone out there know Rolly?' asked one newspaper headline sarcastically. And other equally uncomfortable questions were being raised about the Marcos version of events. As the opposition leader, Salvador Laurel, pointed out, how could a lone assassin have penetrated the tight security cordon of some 2000 troops without inside assistance? How could he have known exactly where to lie in wait for Aquino, who came down the service steps instead of disembarking normally? Who were the soldiers with Aquino just before he died, and where were they now? Why was the alleged killer riddled with bullets instead of being captured for questioning?

As pressure on the authorities mounted, a name for the dead man in the blue trousers was finally released, nine days after the assassination. He was Rolando Galman, officially described as 'a notorious killer and gun for hire'. Government sources reported that Galman was known to have links with left-wing subversive groups. But any hope that this would reduce pressure from the opposition for a truly unfettered investigation was quickly shattered. Rumours travel like lightning around the close-knit Filipino society, and soon remarkable stories about Galman began to circulate. According to his family, he had been taken from his home by armed men four days *before* the death of Aquino. And two days *after* the assassination, more armed men had picked up Galman's common-law wife Lina and held her for some days – the first of a number of mysterious summonses.

Another sensation followed. Philippines air force officers, it was established, had picked up Galman's mother and sister after the killing and held them incommunicado for four days before the corpse was publicly identified. All this fuelled the anger of the vast crowds of Filipinos – peasants and bankers, students and office workers – who had taken to the streets to protest against the regime's handling of the Aquino affair. Placards openly accused the government of having directly organised the elimination of the most effective and popular opposition leader. Underground newspapers were naming members of the escort party in whose company Aquino had passed his last few seconds alive: one particular sergeant was even singled out as the probable trigger-man.

Early in September 1983, the government's commission of inquiry opened its hearings. It was boycotted by Aquino's family and the opposition. One of the first witnesses was a government pathologist, Dr Benvenido Munoz. In sworn testimony, Dr Munoz asserted that the shot that killed Aquino came from a weapon pointed upwards at the back of his head. The bullet had then been deflected downwards to exit through his jaw. It was highly controversial evidence. Aquino's family had already announced that examination of his corpse (before it was laid in state for mourners to pay their respects) had established clearly that he was killed by a bullet in the skull just below his left ear, fired from behind

The boy wonder

Nobody understood the hazards of politics, Philippines-style, better than the late Benigno Aquino. Highly intelligent, humorous and likeable, he was also ruthless in his personal ambition. He was quite prepared for – indeed, almost welcomed – the accompanying risk of making dangerous enemies in the intensely personal school of Filipino power-broking, where family ties and obligations are always more important than issues, and where feuds are never forgotten.

Benigno Aquino was born in the province of Tarlac, near the capital, in 1933; like his greatest adversary Ferdinand Marcos, he came from a family of great wealth and influence. As preparation for politics, Aquino had a fling in journalism, covering the Korean War at the age of nineteen. The family machine then started to propel him through the ranks towards high office: he was, successively, the country's youngest ever deputy mayor, mayor, provincial governor and national senator. By 1970, aided by the usual blend of bribery and intimidation, 'the boy wonder from Tarlac' was clearly on course for the presidency. Aquino knew Marcos well enough to understand that the latter would not step down meekly. 'We both know that when the time comes, it's going to be curtains for one of us,' Aquino told friends.

As street violence increased along with political tension, Aquino stayed safely in his palatial headquarters in Quezon City, just outside Manila. Marriage into the family of the nation's leading 'sugar barons' had helped make him a wealthy man. Never travelling without armed bodyguards in his bullet-proof limousines, he deliberately intensified his attacks on corruption and favouritism within the Marcos circle, concentrating his most bitter personal attacks on the president's wife, Imelda.

Aquino expected trouble, and he got it. One of the first politicians to be locked up when Marcos declared martial law, he was tried in 1975 on trumped-up charges of murder, rape and subversion – and sentenced to death. The sentence was not carried out, but it was never officially commuted. Aquino spent the next five years in Fort Bonifacio military jail and, as the Marcos regime grew steadily more unpopular, he became an increasingly potent opposition figure. In 1978, campaigning from his cell, he almost beat Imelda Marcos in an election for the national assembly.

In 1980, under pressure from President Carter's US administration, Marcos allowed Aquino, who suffered from a heart complaint, to go to the United States for medical treatment. His wife Corazon and their five children accompanied him, but Aquino never lost touch with the political opposition back home. As the economic and social problems of the Philippines intensified, he became convinced that the Marcos regime was tottering. Fearing that events would pass him by in the USA, Aquino made up his mind to come back, whatever the risks: 'If fate falls that I should be killed, so be it.'

Below: the body of Aquino lies in state two days after his death; thousands of mourners came to pay their last respects. Aquino's mother made the decision to leave his body exactly as it was after the killing, to show the world 'what they have done to my son'. The hole where the bullet exited through the chin is clearly visible

Above: the five members of the second commission of inquiry were headed by Mrs Corazon Agrava, a retired judge (centre); the public nicknamed them the 'Agravators'. Below: the short-lived first commission hears testimony from Dr Benvenido Munoz, a government pathologist. Holding up a demonstration skull, he showed how Aquino was killed by a bullet shot upwards into his head, which was then deflected downwards to exit through his chin

and slightly above him, which had travelled on a sharp downward trajectory to exit just below the mouth. These findings were later confirmed by an independent forensic expert in the United States.

The alleged assassin, Galman, was certainly no taller than Aquino. To fire such a shot when, as the government insisted, Aquino was already on the tarmac, Galman would have had to be holding the pistol aloft at the moment of pulling the trigger. Highly unlikely, the opposition claimed, pointing out that Dr Munoz's experience of forensic examination in gunshot cases was severely limited. As it happened, his findings were soon forgotten. On 10 October 1983, under severe pressure, all five members of the board appointed by Marcos resigned, to make way for 'a more credible investigation'. That very day, they had been due to hear testimony from the five soldiers who were escorting Aquino when he was killed.

Sources close to the investigation said that damaging evidence against the members of the escort was going to be presented. This, it turned out, was the result of 'paraffin tests' carried out the day after the assassination on four of the five escorts – all supposedly unarmed at the time – to discover if any of them might have fired a gun. The National Bureau of Investigations had established that traces of nitrate, a component of gunpowder, were present on two of the soldiers – a strong indication, though not proof positive, that they may indeed have fired a shot during the previous 72 hours. One of them, the underground press reported, was the sergeant already singled out as the most likely killer.

Clearly shaken by the size and ugly mood of the huge

demonstrations raging around his Malacanang Palace, President Marcos moved swiftly to conciliate the opposition. He announced the formation of a new commission of investigation, headed by a widely respected retired judge, Mrs Corazon Agrava, and invited critics to nominate four other acceptable members for the new board. The Agrava Commission began work in November and soon showed that it meant business.

Most Filipinos would agree that the Agrava hearings in the hot, stuffy Magsaysay auditorium provided the nearest thing to a thorough examination of the Aquino affair that was possible in the circumstances. Sessions were normally open to the public – only top-security evidence was heard behind closed doors – and the talkative crowds that frequently attended exercised the right to pass down questions of their own for witnesses. They also enjoyed heckling uncooperative witnesses, especially unpopular soldiers and policemen.

The Marcos administration never budged from its original version that the assassination was a communist-inspired plot carried out by Rolando Galman. The regime's key appearance at the Agrava hearings came from General Fabian Ver, Chief of Staff of the armed forces and a man many Filipinos consider the most powerful in the land. In some fourteen hours of testimony, General Ver politely and urbanely took the commission through the military's story from the time in early 1983 when it became clear that Aquino was thinking seriously about returning to the Philippines.

Not long afterwards, Ver said, military intelligence began looking into reports of a plot to kill Aquino. The original source of this information, he admitted, was 'hazy' – a conversation overheard in a public restaurant – but it appeared to raise the possibility of an assassination being carried out in such a way as to put the blame on the Marcos regime. As a result of this, in about July 1983, Ver initiated 'Project Four Flowers', designed to collect, collate and evaluate all information concerning the possible threat to Aquino, and to take 'appropriate action'. One threat that was examined, according to Ver, was a planned operation by the New People's Army of communist guerrillas, but it had not been possible to acquire solid information about this from agents in the field.

Ver told the commission that another theory examined by 'Project Four Flowers' was whether any of Aquino's numerous political enemies – perhaps even including some of the present opposition to Marcos – might want him dead. Such a possibility certainly could not be ruled out, Ver testified, noting that President Marcos himself considered that certain Filipinos had 'valid reasons' to kill Aquino. But early in August 1983, with Aquino's return virtually inevitable, military intelligence had lost contact with 'Agent Baby', an undercover man who had been providing valuable information about the assassination threat. That agent, Ver said, had surfaced again only after the killing at the airport. For some reason, the commission did not pursue this mysterious affair further, not even suggesting that 'Baby' appear before them in private.

Ver told the commission that military intelligence had made a last desperate effort to establish whether an organised

Above: President Marcos (right) and armed forces Chief of Staff Fabian Ver arrive at a press conference on 23 August, two days after Aquino was killed. This was the first time Marcos was seen in public after the assassination, and the first occasion on which he made a statement on the matter. The body of Rolando Galman had still not been officially identified, and the government made a number of appeals to the public to help them to do so. But evidence later brought to the Agrava Commission revealed that the military must have known all along who Galman was, since he had just spent almost a year in detention under their close observation. Why had Ver pretended ignorance? General Ver was described by Aquino before his death as the man he had most cause to fear in the Philippines. And Galman's children claim that their mother Lina was arrested on his personal orders

In October 1983 all five members of the board appointed by Marcos resigned, to make way for 'a more credible investigation'

Below right: Ferdinand Marcos, bedecked with a garland from well-wishers, speaks at a political rally. The ruler of the Philippines since 1964, Marcos imposed martial law in 1972 after two terms of office, in order to stay in control. Martial law was lifted in 1981, but the killing of Aquino united the opposition and Marcos' rule is now sufficiently threatened to make re-imposition of martial law a distinct possibility. Right: a protestor at an anti-Marcos rally gives a vivid demonstration of life for the opponents of the president's regime. The poster behind him shows a soldier in riot gear and the flag of the USA. Marcos, who was due to receive President Reagan on an official visit shortly after Aquino was killed, claimed that his rival was murdered by the communists in order to embarrass the government and jeopardise its relations with the US

assassination plot existed, and that President Marcos had been kept informed of 'Project Four Flowers' from the beginning. Ver testified that after considering all the intelligence data, he had recommended to Marcos that Aquino should be prevented from coming home for at least another month. Then he had received information from opposition leader Salvador Laurel that Aquino intended to return on 21 August, probably aboard a Japan Airlines flight. From that moment, Ver said, the priority was to protect him against any attack.

The head of the air force, General Luther Custodio, was fully briefed on the danger of an attempted assassination and a new file, 'Operation Plan Homecomer (*Balikbayan*)', was opened, giving General Custodio total authority over the airport security, Avsecom. Two options were under consideration, according to Ver: either send Aquino away on the aircraft he arrived in if he lacked proper travel papers; or allow him to land, then whisk him away to his old cell in Fort Bonifacio prison under the original warrant for his arrest, since the order of 1977 affirming his death sentence had never been rescinded.

The government's last hope that warnings about the danger to his life might persuade Aquino to stay away disappeared

Winner at all costs

At least half of the fifty million inhabitants of the Philippines today have never known anything but the regime of Ferdinand Marcos. It is almost twenty years since the slender, snub-nosed Marcos came to power, and he has held on through chaos in the streets, military rule, economic crisis and political turmoil with such superb understanding of his sprawling nation – consisting of some 7000 islands – that many Filipinos can hardly conceive of life without him. Seriously ill with a kidney complaint, worn down by his intensely personal style of government, the 66-year-old president seemed to be on his last legs at the time of the Aquino assassination. Yet he rallied with such vigour and determination that the opposition, gleefully exploiting the killing, was caught off balance.

Ferdinand Marcos was born in 1918 in the remote, mountainous province of Ilocos Norte, often called 'the Scotland of the Philippines'. Son of a prominent local politician, he excelled at school and as an athlete, then became an outstanding law student. At 21 he was in jail, charged with murdering a political opponent of his father: found guilty and sentenced to death, he secured his freedom on appeal after a brilliant performance in his own defence. He was destined for politics, but his career was interrupted by the Japanese invasion of the Philippines in 1942. The Japanese executed his father and put a price on Marcos' head. Not all Filipinos today accept the glowing official version of the guerrilla exploits of their president, but few dispute that he did fight valiantly for his country.

After the war, Marcos moved smoothly ahead in politics, deserting his own party in 1964 the moment he saw an opportunity to run for president with the other main political party. Surviving a violence-ridden first term, he was re-elected in 1968 after an exceptionally dirty campaign. By law, Marcos could not stand a third time, but in 1972 he imposed martial law in the name of 'peace and order' and continued to rule by personal decree alone until 1981. And among the first of his political opponents whom Marcos jailed without proper trial was Benigno Aquino.

After lifting martial law in 1981 Marcos relied on intimidation, corruption and his huge skill as a political manipulator to maintain immense personal power. The Filipino military, who benefitted greatly during martial law, are considered loyal to him – Chief of Staff General Ver is a distant relative – and his lavishly financed New Society Movement (KBL) controls much of everyday life for ordinary citizens.

Yet the explosion of anger and frustration that followed the Aquino killing shook Marcos badly, raising the question of whether the family dynasty can survive after him. A complex man who believes deeply in astrology, lucky charms and lines of destiny, he knows that the KBL's poor showing in the elections of May 1984 reflects a huge desire for change among ordinary Filipinos, especially the young. The opposition party, Unido, claimed that only massive vote-rigging prevented the government from doing even worse. Few doubt that Marcos is ruthless enough to have ordered the assassination of his rival, but most people find it hard to believe that he would have sanctioned an operation that was so dangerous and – above all – so clumsy.

when information from Philippines missions abroad made it clear that he was on his way. Japan Airlines had been warned that it would lose all future landing rights if it flew Aquino in, but Ver insisted that when the decision to arrest Aquino on arrival was taken, nobody knew exactly what flight he might come on. Indeed, Ver testified that he went back to his quarters in Manila at 11am on 21 August still not knowing that Aquino was on China Airlines Flight 811. At about 1.30pm he learned that Aquino had flown in and that 'somebody had been shot'. Half an hour later General Custodio telephoned him with the news that Aquino was dead. Ver said he broke the news personally to a shocked and disbelieving President Marcos.

The Agrava Commission pressed Ver hard about the tragic failure of 'Op. Plan Homecomer'. Ver cited the killing of Egyptian leader Anwar Sadat and the assassination attempt on President Reagan in 1981 as examples of the failure of intense security measures. Mrs Agrava was not impressed: 'With Sadat and Reagan, it was known where the assassins came from. In this particular happening, we're finding it very difficult to determine where the alleged assassin came from – despite the fact that ten, twenty, thirty persons could have seen it.' In addition, it is highly significant that the plan to take Aquino off the aeroplane by the normal passenger exit was only changed ten minutes before the aircraft was due to land. At this point, normal security guards were ordered out of the critical area and Avsecom men took over. Even if Galman had penetrated the security cordon as the government claimed, how could he have known about such a last-minute change of plan? The place where he allegedly hid in order to fire the fatal shot required prior knowledge of how the senator would be leaving the aircraft.

Ver was also asked about reports that one of Aquino's army escort, Sergeant Arnulfo de Mesa, had since become a lieutenant. It was true that de Mesa had been recommended for promotion since the assassination, explained Ver, but he had passed the qualifying examinations long before the killing. 'He has not', stated Ver firmly, 'been rewarded for anything.'

During General Ver's testimony, members of the late Rolando Galman's family were parading outside with posters declaring: 'Father is dead. Is Mother dead too?' Galman's two children, 16-year-old Roberta and 11-year-old Reynaldo, testified to the commission. Their mother had been taken

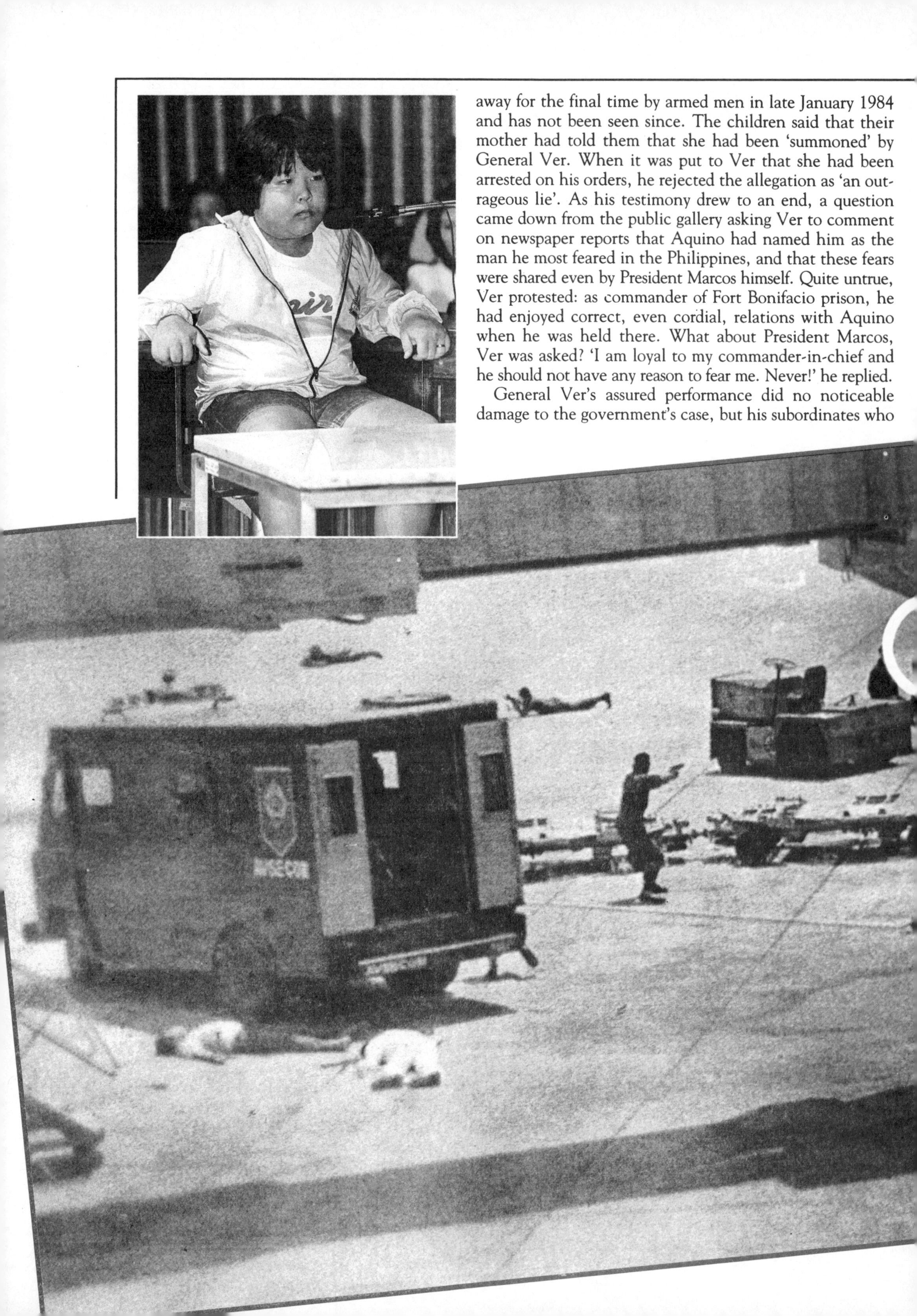

away for the final time by armed men in late January 1984 and has not been seen since. The children said that their mother had told them that she had been 'summoned' by General Ver. When it was put to Ver that she had been arrested on his orders, he rejected the allegation as 'an outrageous lie'. As his testimony drew to an end, a question came down from the public gallery asking Ver to comment on newspaper reports that Aquino had named him as the man he most feared in the Philippines, and that these fears were shared even by President Marcos himself. Quite untrue, Ver protested: as commander of Fort Bonifacio prison, he had enjoyed correct, even cordial, relations with Aquino when he was held there. What about President Marcos, Ver was asked? 'I am loyal to my commander-in-chief and he should not have any reason to fear me. Never!' he replied.

General Ver's assured performance did no noticeable damage to the government's case, but his subordinates who

Above left: Galman's young son, Reynaldo, testifies to the Agrava Commission. Both he and his sister claimed that their father had been arrested and taken away several days before Aquino was killed. Left: one of the photographs that provided evidence about the movements of the various security officers and members of Aquino's escort in the critical seconds after the killing. The figure on the far right, ringed in white, is clearly running away from the scene, gun in hand. Under questioning, Captain Llewellyn Kavinta, an Air Force officer and member of Avsecom, admitted that he was the man marked. When asked why he was running away, he could give no satisfactory reply. Below: the members of Aquino's security escort, nicknamed 'the five wise monkeys' by Aquino's supporters when they each insisted that they had seen nothing of the killing, despite being right next to Aquino at the time he was shot. From the left they are: Rogelio Moreno, Mario Lazaga, Arnulfo de Mesa, Claro Lat, Castro Jesus. Above: General Luther Custodio, head of the Air Force, testifies to the commission. Under the security plan for Aquino's return, he had complete control over Avsecom

went before the commission were far less impressive. The picture that emerged from hours of testimony from officers and other ranks actively involved in 'Op. Plan Homecomer' was one of worried men clinging hard to stories that often started to break down under scrutiny.

Sergeant Armando de la Cruz was a good example. Assigned to an Avsecom back-up security team on 21 August, de la Cruz was in the airbridge tube when Aquino was escorted from the aircraft, his elbows held on either side by uniformed soldiers. When he first testified, de la Cruz claimed that he was still inside the tube when the shooting started and therefore saw nothing. At a subsequent hearing, however, a videotape film shot by one of the foreign television crews on Aquino's aeroplane clearly showed Sergeant de la Cruz on the platform of the service steps, looking downwards *after* Aquino and his escorts had started to descend. Under severe pressure, de la Cruz admitted that he had originally lied to the commission, but still stuck to his story that he had seen nothing. 'What was in the shoulder bag the video shows you were carrying?' he was asked. 'Lunch and a T-shirt,' de la Cruz replied, 'I carried my gun on my waist.' 'Where was Aquino when you saw him last?' 'On the fifth step of the staircase going down towards the tarmac.' 'Are you willing to swear to your changed testimony?' 'Yes.' Sergeant de la Cruz then became the first Agrava witness to be warned that he could face charges of perjury.

Sergeant Reynaldo Pelias was in the same security team as de la Cruz, standing inside the tube as Aquino was led towards the service door. He had helped push back the journalists who were trying to follow, Pelias testified, and had not been in any position to see the shooting. Mrs Agrava then showed him a photograph, taken by a journalist on the China Airlines aeroplane, showing Aquino being escorted towards the door of the service steps. Pelias was visible in the photograph, but claimed, astonishingly, that he could not identify Aquino. 'You were supposed to provide Aquino's security, you were *there*, you saw this man *in front* of you and you mean to tell us now that you can't identify him?' Agrava asked incredulously. She summoned the commission official who habitually played the part of Aquino in recreations of the positions of witnesses in the moments before the shooting. As the man crouched down, almost touching Sergeant Pelias, Mrs Agrava asked, 'Just this close to you, right? The man you are supposed to be protecting, right?' There was a long pause, then Pelias replied, 'Yes.'

Another man who had been very close to Aquino actually inside the CAL aeroplane was Sergeant Clemente Casta, attached to the Presidential Security Commission and assigned that day to collecting the list of passengers (called the manifest) from Flight 811. Casta testifed that when he reached the door of the aircraft, an Avsecom officer had told him to lend a hand inside. Cross-examination established that it was highly unusual for anyone to enter arriving aeroplanes ahead of customs officers, and that Casta had been carrying a bag, about 12 inches (30·5 centimetres) in length, which he normally used for storing the manifests. Casta told the commission that he had waited inside the aircraft until Aquino was escorted towards the exit, only then following

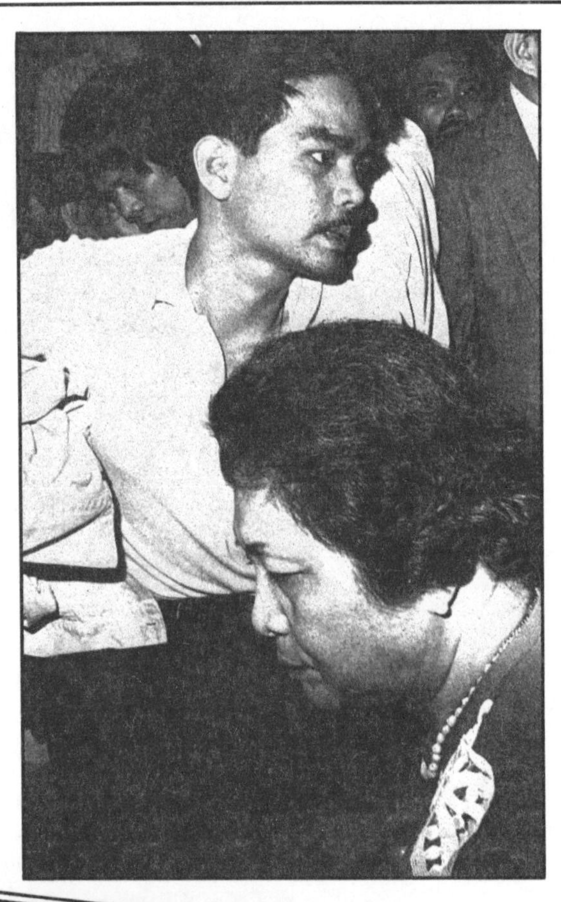

himself. But once again the video film showed a different story. Casta had, in fact, been standing in the tube when Aquino was led past him. And on the film, he appeared to have passed something to the last soldier in the escort.

But the most extraordinary military testimony came from what wags were quick to nickname 'the five wise monkeys' – the team of five men that had escorted Aquino from his aeroplane and down the service steps. 'Saw nothing, heard nothing, said nothing,' was the repeated theme of their evidence; the obvious incredulity of the Agrava board and the hostility of the public gallery could not budge them as, one after another, they each insisted that despite being within a few feet – even a few inches – from Aquino they had nothing to contribute about the moment of his death.

Seargeant Claro Lat was actually holding Aquino's right arm when the fatal shot was fired. 'I heard a big bang,' he testified, then Aquino had gone limp and he could not hold him up. Lat fell on top of the dying man, then got up and ran for cover. Surely he must have seen something of the killing, the board asked. 'No, everything happened so fast that I failed to witness it.' Private Rogelio Moreno was a few feet behind Aquino, ideally placed to see if an assassin had shot him from behind. 'Unfortunately,' Moreno testified, 'I was looking somewhere else at that moment.' All he saw was Aquino falling and a man in blue trousers with a gun in his hand. Paraffin tests on Moreno two days after the assassination found several specks of nitrate on both hands. Moreno claimed, however, that this was because he had been on the shooting range the day before Aquino's arrival.

Sergeant Filomeno Miranda testified that he was the last of the escort party descending the service stairs; he heard a shot, glanced up and saw Aquino and Sergeant Lat falling. Moreno had immediately taken cover nearby. In the face of the board members' obvious disbelief, Miranda insisted that he had seen nobody else at all on the tarmac – not his colleagues in the escort team, not Galman, not even the Avsecom troopers blazing away at the alleged killer's body.

The most intense interest centred on the testimony, lasting eight hours, of Sergeant Arnulfo de Mesa, a baby-faced mountain of a man, at 24 the youngest of the escort. A skilled marksman and karate expert, de Mesa had been one step behind and above Aquino on the service stairs, with both hands on Aquino's left arm. De Mesa insisted that the escort group was already on the tarmac, heading for the waiting Avsecom troop carrier, when he suddenly felt a hand holding a gun nudge his right shoulder. There was a shot, de Mesa said, then he turned and felled the gunman with a karate chop, forcing him to drop the Magnum ·357 pistol he was holding. De Mesa said he had picked up the weapon, then run for cover.

Paraffin tests carried out on de Mesa two days later had proved positive on both hands: he, too, maintained that he had been on target practice the day before the assassination (though Private Moreno could not recall having seen him on the range). De Mesa's performance was less than convincing in the face of the considerable evidence that he had been perfectly placed to fire the fatal shot behind Aquino's left ear. A Manila magazine featured him on its cover, asking, 'Why is he everybody's favourite suspect?'

At the end of the escorts' evidence, a frustrated Mrs Agrava gave them a piece of her mind. 'Only two possibilities can be surmised from your testimonies,' she snapped. 'One is that Galman could not have been on the tarmac when Aquino was shot. . . because it is difficult to believe that none of you saw him shoot Aquino. The other possibility is that all of you are not telling the whole truth, you are trying to hide something from the board.'

An Avsecom officer, Captain Llewellyn Kavinta, was on tarmac security duty when Aquino's aircraft arrived at gate 8. Kavinta was shown a photograph, taken from inside the CAL aircraft, of a man sprinting across the tarmac, gun in hand. He agreed that the figure was himself. 'This was before the shooting, when we were already going to deploy, going to the staging area,' he asserted. But in one corner of the photograph two bodies were partially but clearly visible. Surely, then, it must have been taken *after* Aquino was shot, Kavinta was asked? He agreed nervously that he must have been mistaken – 'There was much confusion on the tarmac.' So why had he been running *away* from the scene of the killing, gun in hand, after the assassination? To loud barracking from the public gallery, Kavinta said unconvincingly, 'I can't remember.'

All the military witnesses who had been in the vicinity of Aquino just before and after he died were instructed to perform one final, macabre task before the commission allowed them to step down. They had to read aloud, often at different speeds and with varying inflections, passages from

Filipino guns

The sign outside a Manila discotheque says: 'Please deposit your deadly weapons and firearms at the counter.' A police officer and an army colonel get into an argument over a beauty queen, reach for their guns and shoot it out in a crowded street – the policeman is killed. English peer Lord Moynihan, now living in the Philippines, quietens some talkative guests during a singer's performance and suddenly feels the cold steel of a cocked revolver in his ear.

The violence that erupts so frequently in Manila is not characteristic of the nation as a whole, and it is rarely directed at foreigners. But the threat is always there – embedded, it seems, in the volatile character of the Filipinos and their bloodstained history of ferocious colonisation by the Spanish and cruel wartime occupation by the Japanese. Guns are everywhere: in the glove compartments of cars, tucked into trouser waistbands under the long Filipino shirts, hanging on nails inside front doors. When tempers rise, shooting all too often follows. During President Marcos' first term in the mid Sixties, it was estimated that there was a killing every minute, and the murder rate remains very high today.

Much of the violence is political in origin. Left-wing guerrillas operate freely in large areas of the Philippines and there is a constant and nasty little 'dirty war' of assassination and counter-assassination between them and the security forces. The corruption of everyday politics also invites intimidation and extortion. Nemesio Yabut, go-getting mayor of Makati, Manila's smart financial district, was leaving a racecourse a few years ago when his car was riddled with automatic gunfire. Yabut survived serious wounds, but today he never travels without two heavily-armed bodyguards.

The rich in Manila live in elegant 'villages', surrounded by high walls and patrolled by gun-toting security guards. The poor live in squalor, coping as best they can until the pressures become too much and someone 'runs amok'. In one incident, a young man who had lost his job and his house on the same day walked off and killed three strangers, using an ice-pick on one, before police shot him dead. The miracle is that in the midst of such violence, poverty, corruption and exploitation, ordinary Filipinos remain such charming and hospitable people.

Left: Sergeant Roland de Guzman of the Philippines Air Force, a member of Avsecom's Special Weapon Attack Team, demonstrates to the commission how he fired at Rolando Galman. Above left: Ramon Balang, a ground engineer at Manila airport, with Mrs Corazon Agrava. Well before Aquino's aircraft had landed, Balang claimed, he had seen Galman smiling and chatting with the security escort and the Avsecom officers

Above: Imelda Marcos arrives at Heathrow with her 12-year-old son, Ferdinand, who was coming to start his first term at school in Crawley, Sussex. During her stay in Britain, Mrs Marcos was a guest of the British Government and was formally received by the Queen

the transcript of a tape-recording made inside the CAL aeroplane by several journalists, including Sandra Burton, a *Time* magazine correspondent. Burton had been close behind Aquino as he left the aircraft and had kept her recorder running when the pushing and shoving began in the airbridge tube as security men obstructed the journalists. On her tape, and on others made by television crews, different male voices can be heard saying in Tagalog, the Filipino language, what sounds like: 'Here he comes. . . I'll do it. . . Them, let them do it. . . Go on! Shoot! Shoot!' Burton testified that, as she was being forced back into the aircraft, she recorded a single voice saying, 'I'll do it.' A shot is then heard on the tape, then voices wailing, 'What's happened?' Three more shots ring out, the confusion increases and a man shouts, 'He's dead, he's dead.' A flurry of shots follows.

Played over and over again before the commission, the tapes never lost their dramatic impact on listeners. Lawyers for the armed forces accepted their authenticity, but challenged the validity of accepting the recordings as legal evidence on the grounds that what was being said on them was not completely clear. A Japanese expert in 'voice printing' had prepared an analysis of the different voices they contained, but this was not admissible, the military's lawyers argued, because they had not been given the chance to question the expert on his qualifications and technique.

Some of the testimony most damaging to the government came from the civilian witnesses who appeared before the commission. A lawyer, José Espinosa, exposed the government's lies in claiming that it took a long time to identify the dead man in the blue trousers as Rolando Galman. Espinosa had once acted for Galman, and his evidence made

'The Iron Butterfly'

The official title of Imelda Romualdez Marcos is First Lady of the Philippines. But friends and enemies alike also call her, respectfully, 'The Iron Butterfly', a nickname that reflects her ruthless determination. Born in 1929, Imelda Marcos has helped construct a dynasty that has turned government in the Philippines and control of the country's richest businesses into the personal preserve of the Marcos clan. One of the world's richest women herself, Imelda also holds enormous powers of patronage as Governor of Metro Manila and Minister of Human Resources.

There are several versions of Imelda's origins, not all of them flattering. The most common is that she came from the poorer, provincial branch of a fairly prosperous family. Moving to Manila in her early twenties, Imelda worked as a salesgirl. She was clearly a beauty – Rose of Tacloban and runner-up to Miss Manila – and soon caught the eye of up-and-coming politician Ferdinand Marcos. They were married in 1954 after a whirlwind eleven-day courtship – each, perhaps, sensing in the other an equally fierce determination to succeed.

As First Lady, Imelda says she is 'a soldier for beauty, both slave and star'. Her public duties do not prevent her from making frequent trips to the jet-set corners of the world (her closest friend is Christina Ford, formerly married to the head of the motor empire, and immensely wealthy), usually in the company of adoring hangers-on and a vast collection of luggage. She is also renowned for putting up elegant, enormously expensive buildings in Manila, such as a £20-million movie palace for her much-ridiculed international film festivals. Ordinary Filipinos may once have tolerated her costly excesses but now, with the economy in ruins and real hunger in the slums, there is great bitterness about Imelda's 'magic circle', and sharp personal hatred of the lady herself.

Impulsive and emotional, Imelda Marcos does not lack courage – her hands carry the scars of a knife attack, and she has survived other attempted assassinations – but few observers consider she is politically adept enough to gain power personally after Ferdinand Marcos goes. But her son and two daughters, all educated in Britain, have been carefully groomed for power, and Imelda will certainly fight hard for her dynasty.

Right: anti-Marcos demonstrators burn a picture of Imelda Marcos in a rally in the financial centre of Manila

it clear that — far from being an anonymous corpse — he was known to the security authorities long before the assassination, and may even have had close contacts with senior officials involved in 'Op. Plan Homecomer'.

According to Espinosa, Rolando Galman had been arrested early in 1982, charged with robbery, car theft and possession of an unlicensed gun. But, instead of facing an ordinary criminal court as an offender with a previous record, Galman was sent to a military detention centre, Camp Olivas, under a special order introduced by President Marcos under martial law for use mainly against political offenders. Espinosa had got to know Galman towards the end of 1982, and in January 1983 Galman's wife Lina had retained him to work for her husband's release.

Espinosa revealed that he had asked a high-ranking air force intelligence officer, Colonel Arturo Custodio, for advice on securing Galman's release: on one occasion, he told the commission, Colonel Custodio had accompanied him to Camp Olivas for a meeting with his client. Late in February 1983 Galman was released because the Philippines Defence Ministry had said there was no case pending against him. 'He wasn't released because of my efforts,' Espinosa testified, but he had advised Galman to stay out of trouble and avoid associating with 'shadowy characters'.

A day or two after the assassination, Espinosa had asked Colonel Custodio what he knew about the killing. Custodio, he believed, was close to Avsecom. According to Espinosa, the colonel had replied with something like, 'They're crazy, that guy was already dead when they dumped him on the tarmac.' At that point, Espinosa had no idea that 'that guy' was his former client Rolando Galman. Whom did he think

Above: Imelda Marcos testifies on 2 July 1984, her 55th birthday. She had met Aquino in a New York hotel, she explained, and begged him not to return until the government was sure his life was no longer in danger. She denied Aquino's version of the meeting in which he claimed that she had bribed him not to return, and had threatened that he would be killed if he did

Above: Aquino's mother (right) attends a political rally in the company of Galman's mother (left). The public association of the two families and the support they have given each other since the killings serve to highlight the belief of both groups that Rolando Galman did not assassinate Aquino as the government described, but was himself a victim

On reaching the tarmac, the escorts let Aquino's body fall to the ground. Blood was clearly visible on the back of his white jacket

Custodio meant, asked Mrs Agrava? 'As far as I can recall,' replied Espinosa, 'I think what Colonel Custodio told me was that it may have been the military escort who shot the late senator.' Custodio denied that, along with the claim by Galman's children that he had been with the men who removed their father from his home four days before Aquino was killed. But his role in the Aquino affair greatly intrigued the Agrava Commission. There had been persistent rumours in the Philippines that Custodio was linked in some way to the organisation of the 'salvage' teams that have murdered hundreds of people considered by the authorities to be subversives or communist sympathisers. Common criminals are sometimes used to carry out these killings. Custodio conceded that he had known Galman since 1979 and that Aquino's alleged murderer had visited his home on several occasions.

A few more days after the assassination, the newspapers carried the first pictures of Aquino's alleged assassin, still officially unidentified. The commission wanted to know why Espinosa had not come forward then to provide identification of his former client. 'Because I believed that the military would be the first to know, because Rolando Galman was under their detention for almost a year. They should know that it was Galman who was there at the airport.' Had anybody from the government subsequently asked Espinosa about the Aquino killing and his late client, he was asked? 'No, sir!' he replied with a chuckle, 'I think they found it hard to find me.'

Several airport workers on duty when Aquino arrived also significantly undermined the government's case. Fred Viesca, a cargo handler, testified that he was no more than 20 yards (18·3 metres) from the rear of the China Airlines aeroplane at gate 8 when he heard a single shot. He looked up to see a man in a white suit fall from the mid section of the service door steps. Viesca panicked and ran off, hearing more gunfire behind him, but he was adamant that Aquino had not yet reached the tarmac when he was killed, as the official version maintains.

A Philippines Airlines (PAL) ground engineer, Raymondo Balang, bravely come out of hiding to give the commission his story. He said that he had been on the tarmac near CAL 811 when it landed and had seen the man he later discovered to be Rolando Galman among the soldiers and security men gathered there. 'He was just standing there, smiling with them,' Balang testified, explaining to the commission that he had gone into hiding when he learned that military intelligence was looking for him. Balang's story was supported by an account given to a US television network by Ruben Regelado, another PAL ground technician on duty when Aquino was shot. Regelado said that he fled to Japan for his own safety after the assassination. He claimed that a third PAL employee working with them had told him of seeing a man on the service stairs shoot down Aquino.

Efren Ranas offered perhaps the most dramatic – and for the government, the most damaging – eyewitness testimony. A private security guard on tarmac duty about 15 yards (13·7 metres) away from the service steps to gate 8, he described how he had heard a single shot when Aquino was still descending and was about four steps above the ground. After the shot, Aquino's head seemed to be hanging to one side, and it appeared that he was being supported bodily by two of the escort. On reaching the tarmac, they let Aquino's body fall to the ground. Blood was clearly visible on the back of his white jacket.

Accounts by two Japanese journalists who were aboard CAL 811 with Aquino go some way towards strengthening the evidence of these airport ground workers. A special session of the commission was held in Japan to take their testimony. Kyoshi Wakamiya, a freelance writer, said that he had been right behind Aquino when the soldiers led him out of the aircraft. At the door to the service steps, security men barred the way and stopped journalists from taking pictures. Wakamiya said he then lost sight of Aquino, but watched four soldiers going down the service steps towards the tarmac. They were about half-way down the steps when there was a shot. Then:

> I saw Aquino falling face down. . . I could see blood coming out of his head. At that time, as I was staring at Aquino, a man wearing blue clothes appeared. . . staggering as if he was pushed out by someone. . . Soon three or four men wearing caps like berets appeared, all of them aimed their guns at the man in blue clothes, fired several shots and disappeared. The man in blue fell backwards face down.

It is important to point out that Wakamiya changed his story to the commission considerably from an account he had given at a press conference a couple of days after the assassination. On that occasion, he had claimed that he had actually seen two of the soldiers on the steps with Aquino pull out pistols. One had then fired into Aquino's head, Wakamiya had insisted. But, according to other journalists on the CAL flight, Wakamiya – a personal friend of Aquino – was in a highly emotional state after the shooting, and some of his colleagues doubted that he could have been in a position to see everything he had described.

The last category of evidence examined by the Agrava Commission concerned the possible timing of the final moments before the assassination. Analysis of the various tape-recordings and videotapes made available established that the shot that killed Aquino was fired 11 seconds after a US television crew, filming inside the CAL aircraft, lost sight of him when he was led into the airbridge tube. On the videotape made by a Japanese crew, the first shot is heard 9·2 seconds after Aquino and his escorts began to descend the nineteen service steps towards the tarmac. Sergeant de la Cruz, the soldier faced with perjury charges after changing his testimony, finally agreed that the fatal shot came approximately 6 seconds after Aquino had begun to descend, when he was on about the fifth step down.

The official military view is that Aquino could have covered the distance between the top of the steps and the spot where his body fell to the tarmac in just 11 seconds 'at a fast pace'. The members of the Agrava Commission made several visits to gate 8 to recreate the scene: they found that it took them between 13 and 15 seconds to descend the steps to the tarmac at a normal pace. The difference of a

Hit-man or fall guy?

Above left: Rolando Galman's mother, called in by the military to identify her son, weeps over his body. Above right: two women shared Galman's life and the fate of both is unknown. Lina Lazaro (top), who was his common-law wife, and Anna Oliva (bottom), a girlfriend, both disappeared after Galman's death

Rolando Galman, Aquino's alleged assassin, grew up in a farming town called Zaragoza, slipped into crime in his teens, and killed two men in a family feud before he turned twenty. The rest of his life remains an almost total blank. His police record shows a string of arrests for serious crimes, including murder, robbery and kidnapping, yet his common-law wife Lina found him a quiet and amiable man, fond of the children. Galman kept a girlfriend or two on the side, to whom he would occasionally boast that he was involved in secret work for very important people, but he had no steady job and was usually broke.

It remains a mystery why a small-time criminal like Galman should ever have been detained under regulations normally reserved for prominent political opponents of the Marcos regime – Benigno Aquino, for instance. Some speculate he may have been recruited while in detention to handle occasional assignments for the security forces. In the last few weeks of his violent and aimless life, Galman was certainly nervous and despondent about something. He told an army officer he knew that he had been given 'an important mission for my group'. Was that what led the stout, swarthy man in blue uniform trousers to sudden death on the tarmac?

On the balance of evidence, it would not be difficult to conclude that Galman did not pull the trigger

few seconds in these estimates is anything but trivial – according to Sandra Burton's tape-recording, the whole bloody business, from the first to the last shot, took barely 17 seconds.

It is clear that the Agrava Commission believed that the careful timing of its reconstructions held the key to understanding what had really happened at gate 8. They spent many hours there, often in blazing sunshine, experimenting with different recreations of Aquino's final moments. Significantly, they were particularly concerned with discovering whether, within the known time-frames, it was possible for the military escorts accompanying Aquino down the service steps to have passed a concealed handgun to one of their group, shot the victim, then smuggled the gun away from the scene in the chaos that followed the assassination.

Somewhere in the thousands of pages and millions of words of evidence presented to the commission, the truth about who killed Aquino, and on whose orders, lies buried – possibly for ever. Few Filipinos believe that Mrs Agrava and her colleagues, for all their stubborn and courageous efforts to peel away the many layers of uncertainty and conjecture, will be prepared to name anyone other than Galman as the assassin. Even so, on the balance of the evidence, it would not be difficult to conclude that Galman did not pull the trigger. For the vast majority of people in the Philippines this would be confirmation that the military was implicated at the very highest level, and that it is barely conceivable that the regime of President Marcos did not know about it.

Below: an anti-government rally in Manila; since the murder of Benigno Aquino, such demonstrations have increased in frequency – and in violence. Supporters of the opposition party have had their case boosted by unexplained inconsistencies in the government's account of the assassination and the military's doubtful role in the so-called protection of Aquino when he left his aircraft. Ferdinand Marcos has been severely discredited and attenders at anti-government rallies never lose the opportunity to remind him of their dead 'Ninoy'

WHO KILLED JANIE SHEPHERD?

One Friday evening in February 1977 a young Australian woman, living and working in London, set off in her car to visit her boyfriend. She stopped on the way to buy some groceries at a late-night supermarket in Queensway in central London — and then, apparently, vanished into thin air. Her distraught boyfriend and the cousins with whom she lived reported her missing to the police in the early hours of Saturday morning. On Tuesday her Mini was found, covered in mud and scratches and cut on the inside with knife-slashes. Almost eleven weeks later, the body of Janie Shepherd was found, miles away in Hertfordshire. She had been strangled. How did Janie Shepherd disappear, and who killed her? *SANDY FAWKES* tells the story of one of the most appalling murder mysteries of recent years

Above: Janie Shepherd's dark blue Mini where it was found by police on Tuesday 8 February 1977, four days after she had disappeared. Badly parked on a yellow line, it had two parking tickets on the windscreen and was covered with mud and scratches

ON the evening of Friday 4 February 1977, Janie Shepherd, a 24-year-old Australian living and working in London, left the luxury flat in St John's Wood where she lived with her cousin Camilla and Camilla's husband Alistair Sampson. She ran down the steps calling, 'I must dash, I'm frightfully late,' climbed into her dark blue Mini – and vanished.

Janie was heading for a quiet weekend with her boyfriend Roddy Kinkead-Weekes. It was 8.40pm and Roddy was expecting her by 9pm. On the way to his flat – just 3·5 miles (5·6 kilometres) away in Lennox Gardens, Knightsbridge – Janie was intending to call at a late-night supermarket to pick up groceries for their supper. When she had not arrived by 9.30pm, Roddy rang the Sampsons' flat to see if she had left on time or whether she was going to be late. Camilla and Alistair had gone to the cinema, but their maid informed him that Janie had left fifty minutes earlier.

When there was still no sign of Janie at 10pm, Roddy rang her home again, and then regularly at half-hour intervals. By the time the Sampsons returned home around midnight, all three felt real cause for alarm about Janie's whereabouts. Telephone calls to the main London hospitals produced no information and finally, at 3.15am on Saturday 5 February, Alistair Sampson officially reported Janie Shepherd missing at St John's Wood Police Station. Roddy Kinkead-Weekes went to Chelsea Police Station on the same mission.

Her description and the details of her car were circulated immediately, and the car was checked on the police computer to see if it had been stopped or seen anywhere. The

Fears grow for lost Janie

THE mystery of missing beauty Janie Shepherd deepened yesterday.

It was revealed that an intruder had slashed open the sun roof of her Mini.

Police also disclosed that her handbag was found in the car—but about £40 in cash had disappeared.

They now believe that the 24-year-old blonde Australian may have been murdered.

A spokesman said: "In view of all the circumstances, we fear that foul play is involved.

Concern

"We have grave concern for the girl's safety."

Janie vanished last Friday night after leaving the house where she was staying at St. John's Wood, London.

She planned to have a meal with her boyfriend, MCC cricketer Roderick Kinkead-Weekes, at his Chelsea flat. But she never turned up.

By JACK McEACHRAN

When she left St. John's Wood, her dark blue car was spotless. It had been cleaned the previous day.

But when it was found on Sunday in Paddington it was spattered with mud inside and out.

The Mini had been locked, and the keys were missing.

Two slashes in the canvas sun roof would have made it possible for an attacker to reach inside and assault the driver.

Janie's jewellery—including gold rings, a heavy bangle, a watch and gold chain necklace—was not found in or near the car.

House-to-house inquiries by a special CID squad led by Detective-Chief Superintendent Henry Mooney, of Scotland Yard's Murder Squad, have established that the car was parked in Elgin Crescent on Sunday.

But police are not sure exactly when it was left there.

● Heartbreak Trail—See Page Three.

MISSING: Blonde beauty Janie Shepherd. She vanished a week ago.

Above: an article that appeared in the Daily Mirror *on Friday 11 February. By this time the police were seriously doubting whether Janie Shepherd was still alive. Public appeals and house-to-house inquiries produced a few results in the early days, but once investigators had pieced together Janie's last known movements, there was nothing further for them to go on*

police quickly established that Janie was not the sort of girl to drop into a pub or club on her own, and that if her car had broken down or if she had unexpectedly met friends she would have telephoned Roddy. A stable, happy girl, Janie would not have disappeared of her own volition. But she was the heiress to a considerable fortune (her stepfather was chairman of British Petroleum in Sydney) and the possibility that she had been kidnapped occurred immediately to her family and the police alike. Through a long, anxious weekend they waited for a ransom demand; it never came.

Right: Janie relaxes with her boyfriend Roddy Kinkead-Weekes. They had been going out together for almost a year. Below: Janie's mother and stepfather, Angela and John Darling, in London after Janie was reported missing. They flew from Tehran, where John Darling had been on business, and spent weeks conducting their own search for their daughter

The frustration that was to dominate the whole case made itself felt to the police in the very first days, even hours, of Janie's disappearance. She seemed to have vanished literally without trace, despite the clues that enabled the police to piece together her last known movements. At 6.15pm she had left the Caelt Art Gallery in Westbourne Grove where she worked as an assistant and driven 0·75 miles (1.2 kilometres) to her home only to discover that she had left her keys at the gallery. She had to ring the bell, and when her cousin Camilla let her in she apologised for having brought her to the door. Refusing the offer of a cup of tea, she went straight upstairs to pack for the weekend. At 7pm her boyfriend Roddy rang and suggested that they had a quiet supper together at his flat. Over the telephone they planned a simple meal of smoked trout, celery and cheese: Janie said she would buy the food on her way over and would arrive at about 9pm.

When she left the flat – at 103 Clifton Hill – at 8.40pm, she was wearing jeans tucked into Cossack boots, a man's check shirt over a thin, fawn polo-necked sweater, and a thick, white cardigan with a reindeer motif. Into her big red satchel bag she had put £40, some clean underwear, and a black sweater with a vivid red polo-neck and bright green cuffs. She also added a tapestry she was working on, along with some balls of coloured wool.

Detective Inspector Roger Lewis of St John's Wood CID was put in charge of investigating Janie's disappearance. By Monday he was already in serious doubt that she would ever be seen alive again. And the following day, Tuesday 8 February, there was a breakthrough in the case that seemed to confirm his worst fears. Janie's dark blue Mini was found in Elgin Crescent, Notting Hill. It was parked on a yellow line and there were two parking tickets on the windscreen, one dated Monday 7 February at 11.45am, the other Tuesday 8 February at 12 noon.

When Janie had left home on the Friday night, her car had been clean and shiny. A week earlier she had decided to sell it and had cleaned and polished it ready for potential buyers. She had placed an advertisement in the London *Evening Standard* for four consecutive days, and had put a large 'For Sale' notice in the rear window. But when it was found, the car was so covered in mud that several witnesses remembered seeing it as early as 1.10am on Saturday, barely five hours after Janie had disappeared. The 'For Sale' notice was still clearly displayed in the rear window.

Inside the car were Janie's Cossack boots and her red shoulder bag; the £40 in cash and her National Westminster cheque card were missing, as were her change of clothing, the tapestry and the balls of wool. In her red bag was a supermarket receipt and a receipt for £2.40 for petrol she had bought on Friday, an important clue for the police. This showed that she had topped up the 7·5 gallon (34-litre) petrol tank with 3 gallons (13·6 litres) of four-star petrol at a self-service garage in Bayswater, and enabled the police to make a rough assessment of how far the car could have been driven. Given the amount of petrol left in the tank, it looked as though the Mini could have travelled about 75 miles (120 kilometres).

Above: a police poster appealing for help from any witnesses who may have seen and remembered Janie on the night she disappeared. Part of the publicity about the case that was put out in west London, it reflects the police's lack of any real leads and their enormous reliance on public help

On Tuesday 8 February there was a breakthrough in the case that seemed to confirm Detective Inspector Roger Lewis' worst fears

Janie's life

Above and above right: holiday snapshots of Janie, looking happy and relaxed. She was above average height for a woman, with striking looks. Detective Chief Superintendent Ronald Harvey of Hertfordshire CID said of her: 'This was an outstandingly beautiful girl. Someone must have noticed her'

Janie Shepherd was born in 1953 in Sydney, Australia, into a prosperous middle-class family. Her father, Tony Shepherd, died of a massive heart attack in 1964 when Janie was eleven, and her mother Angela later married John Darling, a merchant banker and Chairman of British Petroleum in Sydney, whose job took them frequently to Europe. Janie stayed at school in Australia, but spent summer holidays with her parents in Italy or Yugoslavia, and went ski-ing with them in the winter.

An outgoing, attractive girl, she first visited London in 1971 when she was eighteen. She quickly made many friends, and they provided her with casual work – she kept the books for boutiques and cooked in a restaurant in Regent's Park. She kept in constant touch with her parents through long letters and telephone calls, but they missed her enough to persuade her to return to

Sydney in 1974. There they set her up in a boutique selling Persian carpets and paraphernalia from the Middle East – a job she enjoyed since it enabled her to travel occasionally to Tehran.

But Janie hankered after London and she returned in March 1975. Six months later she was introduced by friends to Roderick Kinkead-Weekes, a solicitor and keen amateur cricketer. They were immediately attracted to each other, but their friendship was delayed by Roddy's departure on a six-month trip to South Africa. After he returned, they spent a lot of time in each other's company, enjoying visits to the theatre, the cinema, the occasional nightclub and auction sales. And during the summer of 1976 Janie spent many happy hours at Lords Cricket Ground, watching Roddy play for Middlesex. They had known each other for almost a year when Janie disappeared on her way to Roddy's flat.

Chief Superintendent Henry Mooney of Scotland Yard's Murder Squad was called in to oversee the investigation. One look at the interior of the car and he knew that 'something outlandish', as he put it, had happened. There were two parallel slash marks in the sun-roof and further forensic analysis revealed that a tremendous struggle had taken place inside the car. It had been driven deep into the country, since the mud splashed on the bodywork and embedded in the tyres showed traces of chalk and flint, also of oak and beech leaves. Further investigation of the tyres suggested that the car had actually been stuck in mud at some time, and fibres found in the tyres indicated that Janie's tapestry might have been propped under the wheels to give leverage. When analysis of the soil on the car showed it could have been driven to Oxfordshire, Hertfordshire, Wiltshire or Surrey, police from all those counties were alerted. The supermarket receipt was traced to Europa Foods in Queensway, where the till operator remembered Janie because 'she looked like a film star or model'. And a search in the vicinity of Queensway revealed the food that matched the receipt (smoked trout, yoghurt, tomatoes and chicory at a cost of £3.05) scattered around various back gardens.

Chief Superintendent Mooney also launched a direct appeal to the public. A full description of the clothes and jewellery Janie was last seen wearing was issued – her jewellery included a gold 'Woodstock' charm, a present from Roddy that she wore on a chain given to her by her mother; a Gucci digital watch on a grey leather wristband; a heavy gold bangle, and a traditional three-part gold Russian wedding ring.

On Wednesday 9 February Janie's distraught mother, Angela Darling, and her husband John, arrived in London from Tehran where John had been working. Chief Superintendent Mooney warned them to expect the worst; he was certain from the evidence of the car's interior that an attack of considerable violence had taken place.

On 11 February the police used helicopters to search the gardens of derelict houses between St John's Wood and Notting Hill, the banks of the Grand Canal and wastelands in the north London area. The 'Case of the Missing Heiress', as it was described in the newspapers, roused considerable public interest, and there were daily reports of the police searching in helicopters equipped with infra-red cameras over a 70-mile (110-kilometre) radius from Notting Hill Gate, over the areas with soil similar to the samples found on the abandoned car. Body-sniffing dogs, trained in ways similar to drug-sniffing dogs, were used for the first time in a British murder investigation. Police lines, moving slowly across suspect areas, were also used in the search for Janie Shepherd's body. But the weeks passed by with no clue as to Janie's fate.

Soil samples were examined by mineralogists from ICI, micro-palaeontologists from London University and other experts in an attempt to discover the exact spot where Janie might be found. Meanwhile, routine murder inquiries included interviews with all known sex offenders in the west London area. These inquiries resulted in many of what Detective Inspector Roger Lewis described as 'spin-off arrests':

Chief Superintendent Henry Mooney of Scotland Yard's Murder Squad was certain from the evidence of the car's interior that an attack of considerable violence had taken place

Below: on Friday 11 February 1977, a week after Janie Shepherd's disappearance, the Daily Mirror *devoted a front page article and a whole inside page to the case. At this stage her stepfather still believed that she may have been kidnapped, but as the days passed with no demand for a ransom, hopes that she might still be alive rapidly faded*

Mirror seeks clues to fate of lost Janie

DAILY MIRROR, Friday, February 11, 1977 PAGE

HAPPINESS: A smiling Janie on holiday last year

TOGETHERNESS: Janie with Roddy Kinkead-Weekes

CHEERFULNESS: Another snap from the holiday album

HEARTBREAK TRAIL OF THE MISSING BEAUTY

By JOHN JACKSON

WEALTHY John Darling yesterday followed the route taken by his missing stepdaughter on her last known journey . . . and told of his fears about her fate.

Australian-born Janie Shepherd, a 24-year-old blonde, vanished a week ago.

Mr. Darling, a merchant banker and boss of British Petroleum (Australia), believes she may have been kidnapped in Hyde Park.

As the Daily Mirror took him on a drive past the Serpentine, he said: "This could be where the answers lie.

"Anyone could jump out and stop a car.

"Look at this section, where the mud has been churned up.

"Who knows what goes on here at night?"

Janie has not been seen since 8 p.m. last Friday, when she left the house where she was staying at Clifton Hill, St. John's Wood.

She was planning to have a meal with her boyfriend, Old Etonian and Middlesex cricketer Roddy Kinkead-Weekes, 25.

But she never arrived at his flat in Lennox Gardens, Chelsea.

Her mud-spattered car was found abandoned three days later in Paddington.

Receipts found under the dashboard have given police two vital clues about her movements on Friday evening.

Alarm

They showed that she bought three gallons of petrol at an all-night garage in Bayswater Road and that she shopped at the Europa food store in Queensway.

The shop bill was timed 9 p.m.

Janie had arranged to cook at her boyfriend's home.

When she failed to turn up he raised the alarm.

Mr. Darling—aide de camp to the Queen on her first Australian tour in 1954—flew to London from Teheran.

When I told him yesterday that I was about to drive along the route which Janie would probably have followed to Roddy's flat, he asked: "Could I come with you?

Look

"I feel I must get out and have a look for myself."

With his 18-year-old daughter, Camilla, we drove from Clifton Hill via Carlton Vale, Randolph Lane, Warrington Crescent, Warwick Avenue, Bishops Bridge Road, Westbourne Grove, Queensway, Bayswater Road, Hyde Park and Exhibition Road to Lennox Gardens.

For several days Janie had had a "for sale" notice in the back window of her car . . . and this was another factor which police believe might have led to tragedy.

Prostitutes use similar signs to signal that they have sex for sale.

Janie was anxious to sell the car quickly and she let any prospective buyer test-drive it.

Hurry

Antique dealer Alistair Sampson, husband of the cousin Janie was staying with, said: "She had promised to buy a friend's Renault for £900.

"She was asking £1,250 for her P-registration Mini, so that she could also knock £300 from her overdraft.

"The friend became impatient, and Janie was in a desperate hurry to sell."

SEARCHERS: Mr. Darling with his daughter. Picture: CHARLES LEY.

HOME: The St. John's Wood house where the lost blonde was staying with her cousin.

GARAGE: The filling station where Janie bought three gallons of petrol for her Mini.

HUNT: John Darling at the spot in Paddington where his stepdaughter's car was found.

Foot rejects debate on Haines

By DAVID THOMPSON

COMMONS leader Michael Foot last night turned down a call for a debate next week on the Joe Haines revelations in the Mirror.

The call was made in the Commons by Tory MP Nicholas Fairbairn.

He asked: "In view of recent revelations, some of which MPs regard as trivial, will you have a debate on the proper method of preparing the Honours List and the conduct of central government at the highest level?"

Mr. Foot replied: "We are NOT going to have a debate on that next week."

In a jibe over Mr. Fairbairn's Silver Jubilee poem, he added: "And we are not ever going to write a poem about it."

● Terence Lancaster—Page Two.

CHEERS! THE PRICE OF BEER IS TO BE PROBED

By PETER PRENDERGAST

DRINKERS who complain that they pay too much for a pint of bitter got some cheering news yesterday.

The Price Commission is to investigate the cost of beer and the profits made by brewers and publicans.

Prices Secretary Roy Hattersley ordered the inquiry after a barrage of complaints from beer drinkers throughout Britain about recent price increases.

Several MPs have criticised the size of brewers' profits.

The inquiry represents a victory for Mr. Hattersley over Agriculture Minister John Silkin, who felt that any interference with beer prices might affect jobs and investment in breweries.

altogether, eighteen people were detained in connection with other offences as a result of the Janie Shepherd investigations.

There were many false trails; the caretaker of a local block of flats reported having seen a dark-coloured Mini with a blonde girl and a man of Arabic appearance in it parked nearby. He had noticed them because they had the car radio on very loud and he had told them that they were parked on private property. A month later, on 11 March, the police confiscated a blue cashmere coat covered with mud that had been deposited at a dry-cleaner's in Notting Hill Gate. It had been handed in by a dark-complexioned man, but had never been claimed.

Meanwhile, Angela and John Darling, armed with Ordnance Survey maps of the areas pinpointed by forensic experts as possible sites where their daughter might be found, drove out into the country daily from their rented flat in St James's Street to search. For 65 days they explored copses, commonlands and beauty spots, but all to no avail. They returned home to Australia on 12 April 1977.

Then, on Monday 18 April, there was another breakthrough. Two boys, schoolfriends and next-door neighbours, eleven-year-old Dean James and ten-year-old Neil Gardner

The soil and leaves found on Janie's abandoned Mini widened the police search from London to the Home Counties. Various police forces made use of highly sophisticated equipment in their search. Below: police searching near Beaconsfield along the route of the A40 out of London are briefed by officers in charge of the case. Below right: a police officer communicates by radio-telephone with one of the specially-equipped helicopters used in the search. Right: a helicopter with infra-red cameras which, by detecting temperature changes in the ground, can indicate the presence of a hidden body or a shallow grave. The helicopter crews carried out systematic low-level flights, radioing their finds to the men on the ground to assist them in their search

of Queen's Crescent, Marshalwick, St Albans, Hertfordshire, were out cycling during their Easter holidays on Nomansland Common when they spotted what they thought was a pile of rags half-hidden among gorse and hawthorn bushes. Curiosity soon gave way to fright, and the boys dropped their bikes and ran. Then, persuading themselves that what they had seen was probably only a dummy, they crept back to retrieve their precious bikes – and Dean saw what he thought looked like blonde hair. They raced home, too frightened to tell any passers-by what they had seen. It was dusk by the time Dean James finally blurted out to his father, Peter James, that he thought he had seen a real body on the common. Peter James immediately contacted the police who came round to interview the boys.

Accompanied by their fathers, the boys led the police to the place; it was quickly established that they had indeed found a body. It was in a slight dip, a mere 25 yards (22·8 metres) from the B651 road from St Albans to Wheathampstead, in an area used extensively by motor-cyclists and model aircraft enthusiasts, known locally as Devil's Dyke. The Hertfordshire police were called in and the area cordoned off. An official call was put out to Professor James Cameron, a leading pathologist from the London Hospital, Whitechapel, and his colleague Bernard Sims, a forensic dentist. By now it was dark and raining quite heavily. After preliminary tests and the filming of the body on the spot, the corpse was removed to St Albans' mortuary.

The body was fully clothed in jeans, striped socks and a

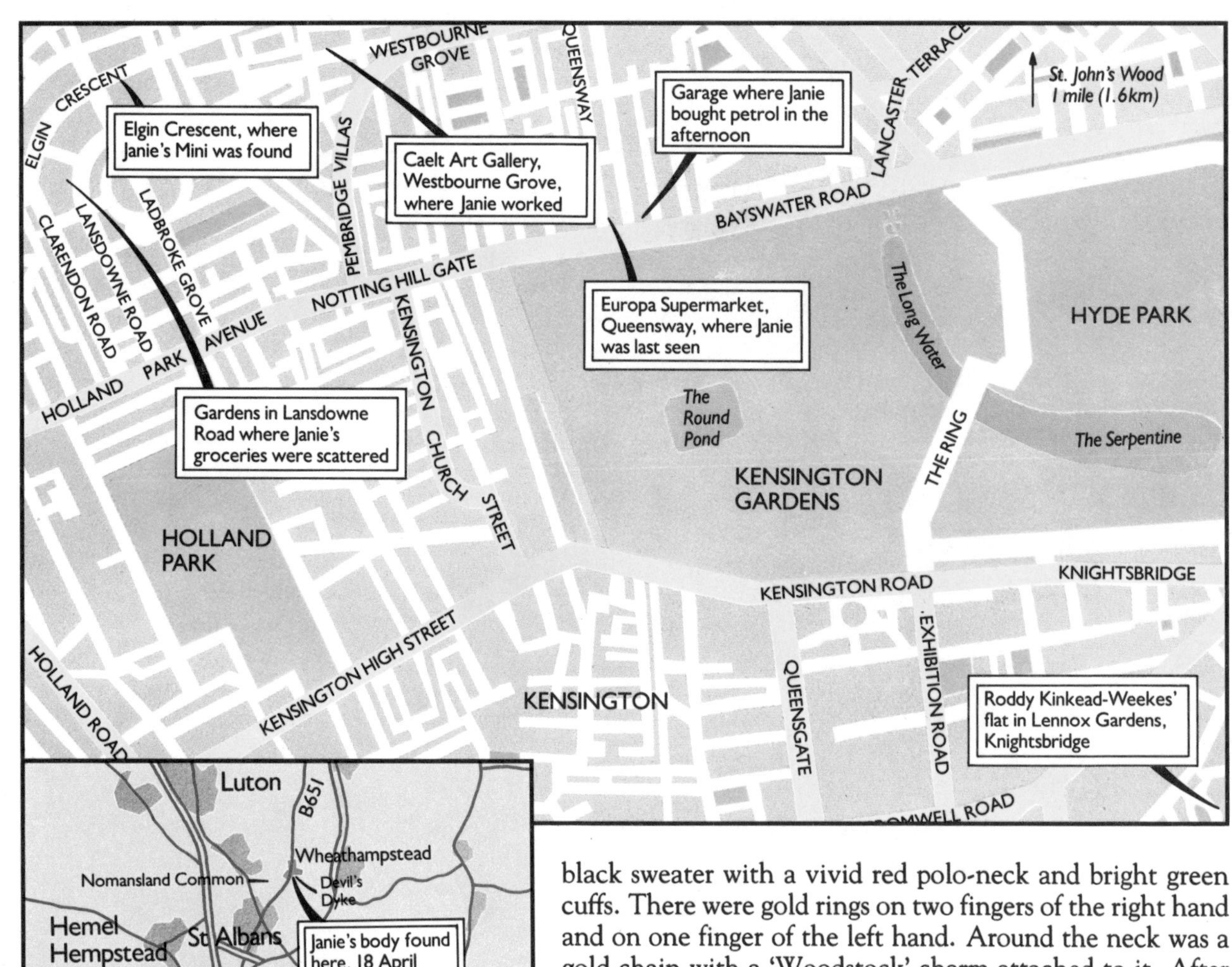

Top: map of the area in west and central London where Janie was last seen. Above: map showing the part of Hertfordshire where her body was found, more than 20 miles (32 kilometres) from London. Hertfordshire police consider it likely that the route taken out of London was up the M1, then through St Albans and out towards Wheathampstead on the B651. Above right: a police aerial photograph of Nomansland Common, showing the spot where Janie's body was found only a few steps from the road. Right: police investigated the site for clues, digging gently into the surface of the earth, but they found very little to help them

black sweater with a vivid red polo-neck and bright green cuffs. There were gold rings on two fingers of the right hand and on one finger of the left hand. Around the neck was a gold chain with a 'Woodstock' charm attached to it. After ten weeks and six days, Janie Shepherd's body had been found.

It was 11.15pm by the time Professor Cameron and Bernard Sims began the post mortem examination, and it took four hours to complete. Cameron noted ligatures on the outside left ankle above the socks, indicating that the feet had been bound before death with the right leg placed in front. There were also ligatures on the upper arms, extensive bruising on the upper arms and chest and, possibly, fingernail marks on the breasts, along with additional bruising on the back of the left foot, the right shin, the right thigh and the left temple. There was no indication of fracture to the skull, but the lung and heart surface revealed elements of asphyxia. By 3.15am Sims had definitely identified Janie Shepherd's body by her dental charts, and Cameron had concluded that she died from compression of the neck. Death had apparently occurred about ten weeks previously.

At 8am Sydney time, on 19 April, Angela and John Darling were informed that Janie's body had been found. The distraught parents had been within 3 miles (4·8 kilometres) of the spot only weeks before, while searching for their daughter.

Usually the finding of the body sheds some light on a mystery, but in Janie Shepherd's case it only confused the situation. When Janie had left the Sampsons' flat in Clifton Hill on 4 February she had been wearing a check shirt over a thin sweater, a thick white cardigan, jeans and boots. When her body was found it was clothed in the jeans, unzipped but buttoned at the waist, but in her other sweater, with the red neck and green cuffs, that she had been carrying in her bag. The pants Janie was wearing were the clean ones she had put in her bag. But her other clothes and her bra were missing. How, when and where had this change of clothes taken place, and where were the missing items?

The post mortem disclosed that Janie had been sitting upright before her death, but the degree of decomposition of the body made it impossible for the police to state whether or not she had been raped or indecently assaulted. The mystery deepened further when it was discovered that the soil in the area where the body was discovered did not match that on the tyres of the Mini. One explanation for this could be that Janie was abducted and attacked in her own car, but at some later time transferred to another car and driven to Hertfordshire, where her body was dumped. If that was the case, then where was the Mini driven to for it to become so splashed with mud? The police became convinced that if they could only find the place with soil that matched the soil on the car, then they might also find Janie's missing clothes and tapestry, and possibly other evidence as well. But no witnesses have ever come forward to say that they saw the Mini anywhere except in Elgin Crescent.

Detective Chief Superintendent Ronald Harvey of the

Are Janie's clothes still half-buried somewhere in the countryside around London? Or did Janie's killer destroy them?

Hertfordshire CID took over the investigation on 18 April but was unable to find any trace of the missing clothes, or the tapestry, in the area around Nomansland Common. To this day, they have never turned up. Are they still half-buried somewhere in the countryside around London? Or did Janie's killer destroy them? The police – who had hoped and even hinted that the finding of the body would lead them to one man – were confounded.

The Mini had revealed frustratingly few clues – and none that led the police to any particular suspect. There were some traces of semen, but semen is a bio-destruct enzyme that disintegrates very quickly: after four days it is difficult to learn anything conclusive from it, not even whether it has come from one man or several different men. There

Below: Neil Gardner (left) and Dean James, who found Janie's decomposed body while out on their bicycles on Monday 18 April during their Easter holidays. After their parents had informed the police, they went back with officers to the spot where their gruesome find was confirmed. Janie Shepherd's corpse was identifiable immediately by her clothes and jewellery. Below right: after careful investigation of the site, police officers remove Janie's body. Right: Detective Chief Superintendent Henry Mooney of Scotland Yard (left) and Detective Chief Superintendent Ronald Harvey, head of Hertfordshire CID, discuss their find at Nomansland Common

were no fingerprints inside the car either from Janie or her attacker or attackers, since only certain types of surface attract and retain fingerprints. The forensic experts found no identifiable pubic hairs or clothes fibres.

The Hertfordshire police believed that the killer may have driven, or forced Janie to drive, out of London on the M1 from Hendon, left the motorway at junction six, then gone via the A405 to St Albans and turned on to the B651 to Wheathampstead. But this was not necessarily in the Mini – it could have been in another car, perhaps the killer's. Or Janie and her killer could have driven in convoy – but that would presuppose that she knew her attacker and went willingly with him, without telephoning Roddy to let him know, and there has never been any evidence to support

such a theory. And it is also a distinct possibility that Janie was raped and killed far from St Albans – maybe even in London – and that her body was kept hidden for several days before the killer eventually felt safe enough to drive out to Hertfordshire and dump it. The police were still unable to estimate or examine the number of places where the killer may have stopped, and no witnesses have come forward to help.

The inquest on Janie Shepherd was opened on 22 April 1977 at the Coroner's Court, St Albans, where the coroner, Dr Arnold Mendoza, heard formal identification from Bernard Sims and Ronald Harvey that the body found on Nomansland Common was indeed that of Janie Shepherd. The inquest was then adjourned for further forensic tests. John and Angela Darling and Roddy Kinkead-Weekes, who was in Tehran on business, had volunteered to travel to London to identify Janie, but the police had sufficient evidence to spare them the ordeal.

The hunt for Janie Shepherd's murderer continued and on 24 October 1977 the inquest was re-opened before a jury. Professor James Cameron told the jury that Janie

Below: the incident room at St Albans Police Station where the Janie Shepherd inquiry was co-ordinated. Detective Chief Inspector Power is shown holding some of the clothes found on Janie's body. The noticeboard behind him shows the Metropolitan Police poster appealing for witnesses and various police photographs taken of the abandoned Mini

Impressions of a psychic detective

Robert Cracknell is a psychic detective who has been involved in a number of baffling investigations. Primarily a fraud investigator, he gave assistance to the police in their search for the missing Devon schoolgirl, Genette Tate, in 1978; and he also had a fleeting connection with the Janie Shepherd investigation, which he relates here.

'My involvement in the Janie Shepherd murder case began with a telephone call from a freelance journalist who wished to interview me for *Prediction* magazine about my involvement in various crimes and mysteries as a psychic detective. This was during the summer of 1977. At the interview we naturally discussed current mysteries and in the course of the conversation the journalist asked me what I felt about the Janie Shepherd murder. I had an immediate psychic reaction, and told him that I could see the Mini. I then described the state of the interior, and the journalist promised that he would communicate with the police press information department to see if my feelings matched up with anything they had found.

The result was that a couple of days later two detectives from the Murder Squad arrived to question me. Obviously, they wanted to know where I had got my information from. They spent two hours with me and for the first five minutes or so it was fairly clear that I was on their list of suspects. But when I confirmed what the reporter had already told them – that my information had come from a sudden psychic impression that had flashed into my mind during a telephone conversation – and when I sketched out my psychic involvement in

Shepherd had died of compression of the neck, but he was unable to say whether the compression was manual or caused by some hard object being pressed against the neck. He added that she had been bound hand and foot and that extensive bruising on her body suggested either that she had struggled desperately or that she had been beaten up.

Her cousin Camilla's husband, Alistair Sampson, gave evidence of her good health and high spirits when he saw her last, and confirmed her plans for the evening of 4 February. Roddy Kinkead-Weekes told the court how she had failed to arrive at his flat for supper. The jury then heard that despite taking 825 statements the police had still failed to identify her killer. An inch-by-inch examination of the area surrounding the spot where the body was found had failed to produce the garments Janie was last seen wearing, or the tapestry or wool she had with her. The jury returned a verdict of murder by a person or persons unknown. Later that day, Janie Shepherd's remains were cremated at Garston Crematorium near Watford; the service was attended by Angela Darling, who had not been able to face the court hearing, her husband John, Roddy Kinkead-Weekes and a

Janie had been bound hand and foot and extensive bruising on her body suggested either that she had struggled desperately or that she had been beaten up

Above: psychic detective Robert Cracknell's autobiography, published in 1981, contains an account of his involvement in the Janie Shepherd murder case

other criminal cases, it was obvious that they believed me. After talking with them, I was able to describe certain physical characteristics of the man whom I believe to be Janie Shepherd's killer. It turned out that this man was, in fact, already high on their list of suspects. He is now serving a long jail sentence for another rape and attempted murder.

Before they left, they asked me if I would be willing to sit in Janie's Mini, which was still in police custody, and try to pick up further impressions. Naturally I agreed, and they asked me to ring them the following day to make arrangements. But when I rang, they had changed their minds. This time they thanked me for my help, but said that they did not feel that I could be of any further assistance with their inquiries. Evidently their superiors – who would have had to give permission for the experiment – were not convinced of the usefulness of psychic detection.

Members of the public have very little opportunity to keep their concentration on a murder that took place more than seven years ago, however well publicised it was at the time. And it is well known that the police, when seeking for public support in solving a crime, are understandably reluctant to release all the facts known to them – the recent case of the Yorkshire Ripper is a good example. But even when the police have a suspect, there is very little they can do without one essential thing – free access to him or her. There is not a police officer in the country who can demand to see a prisoner serving a sentence if he does not wish to be interviewed. And though there is no limit to the period of time within which a person may be brought to justice for a serious crime such as murder, in practice it is not very common for the police to charge someone immediately he is released from a long prison sentence for a previous offence.'

David Lashley

The lack of obvious clues in the Janie Shepherd case, despite the finding of the car and eventually the body, left the police with a very difficult and frustrating job. But certain patterns emerged about the crime that they were able to compare with other known crimes to see if any points in common might emerge. This approach led the police in the direction of a possible suspect, now serving a jail sentence for rape and attempted murder.

On 12 February 1977, eight days after Janie's disappearance and four days after the Mini was found, police went to the home of David Lashley in Southall, Middlesex. Lashley, a 38-year-old boxer from Barbados who was earning his living as a car-sprayer, had been granted parole in 1976 from a twelve-year sentence for rape, indecent assault and robbery. In four of the five cases with which he was charged, he had assaulted and robbed the women in their own cars. Despite being dubbed 'The Beast of Shepherd's Bush' by the press for his savage crimes, Lashley had been released after serving only half his sentence, partly as a consequence of having gone to the aid of a warder in a prison riot.

Lashley denied all knowledge of Janie's fate. On 4 February, he stated, he had gone to the north of England with a girlfriend and had returned to London in the early evening. From 5.30pm to 7pm he had been at work. From 7pm he was at home, watching television, until he went to bed at 9.30pm. The witnesses he gave all corroborated his alibi.

But less than a week after police questioned him, he was picked out at an identity parade by a 24-year-old student who had been abducted and raped at knife-point in her own car in west London in June 1976 – only a month after Lashley had been freed. Lashley was remanded in custody in Brixton Prison, and came to trial at the Old Bailey in November 1977. Michael Corkery,

Above: David Lashley's former wife Jean and his daughter Sandra. Below: Lashley and a Daily Mail *article about his conviction in 1977, in which his name is linked with the disappearance of Janie Shepherd*

Daily Mail, Wednesday, December 14, 1977

PAGE 10

18 years' jail for the rapist who hates white women

THE rape and murder of beautiful heiress Janie Shepherd remained unsolved yesterday as one of the worst rapists the Old Bailey has ever known went to prison for 18 years.

David Lashley, 38 — once questioned about Janie — was sentenced for the rape and attempted murder of another blonde, 'Miss A,' while on parole from jail.

After raping her Lashley, a West Indian, slashed her with a knife and said he hated whites.

Slashed

Lashley, a large, powerful man, of Beaconsfield Road, Southall, Middlesex, was described as 'the Beast of Shepherd's Bush' in 1970 when he was jailed for 12 years for a series of rapes and assaults on five women.

After serving six years he was released on parole as a reward for going to the aid of a warder in a prison riot.

Only a few weeks later, in June last year, Miss A became another of his victims.

Then in February he was questioned about Janie, whose body was found at St Albans, Hertfordshire, ten weeks after she vanished in North London.

Janie Shepherd . . . heiress

Lashley always denied knowing anything about her death.

Mr Michael Corkery, prosecuting, said that the facts in the case of Miss A made an appalling story.

On the evening of June 9, 1976 she was with a boyfriend until 11 p.m. and then drove back to her flat in Chesterton Road, Kensington.

When she arrived she was in a horrifying state, covered in blood.

She banged on a neighbour's window and screamed: 'I have been raped, help me'. One of her wrists had been slashed with a knife and fluid was oozing from her neck.

She said that she was parking her car outside her flat when Lashley opened her car door, pushed her over and got into the driver's seat.

He then threatened her with a knife. Miss A was driven to a back street where she was held captive for two hours. During that time she was raped twice, and forced to take part in oral sex.

Lashley told her: 'I was wondering about killing you.'

After saying he wanted to kiss her he put his hands round Miss A's throat and squeezed. She was convinced she was going to die.

Then he slashed one of her wrists with his knife after saying he hated whites because of the way he had been treated.

Miss A pleaded with him to let her go, promising not to complain to the police. Blood on the girl was of the same group as Lashley's.

'As her attacker drove past a woman with a young child he said to Miss A: 'If you cry out I will knife you and then I will knife the woman and the little girl.'

Ordeal

By that time Miss A was convinced that her last hour had come.

But at last her ordeal was over when her assailant suddenly jumped out of her car and ran away.

Somehow she managed to drive home one-handed, holding her other in the air to try to stem the bleeding from her wrist.

Mr Corkery said that Miss A made an Identikit picture which was shown on the Police Five TV programme of a man wanted for a brutal rape and attempted murder.

The picture was recognised by a woman friend of Lashley's and when she told him she had recognised his face and his spectacles on the Police Five programme Lashley ceased to wear his glasses for two weeks and then bought another pair of frames.

When placed on an identification parade Miss A picked out Lashley without hesitation.

Lashley was found guilty of eight charges of raping, indecently assaulting, wounding and attempting to murder Miss A.

He was arrested by chance. The fact that he was questioned by police at all was a 'spin-off' from their extensive inquiries into the Janie Shepherd kidnapping.

Detective - Chief - Inspector Roger Lewis said after yesterday's case: 'In an inquiry as wide as Janie Shepherd's you look at as many people as you can . . . all the past cases and unsolved matters.

'In the course of such an inquiry you always get other "spin-off" arrests.

'In our Janie Shepherd inquiries we had something like 18 other arrests of people brought in for questioning on assorted matters.'

Chief - Inspector Lewis thought the Janie Shepherd inquiry would go on for ever.

Treatment

When Lashley was jailed for 12 years in 1970, Judge Mervyn Griffith-Jones told him: 'I don't suppose in the whole history of this court that there has ever been such a dreadful series of rapes.

'You behaved like an animal with no thought for the harm and the damage you were doing to the women you attacked.'

Yesterday Judge Bernard Gillis, QC, said: 'Some of the circumstances of those crimes seven years ago were unfortunately repeated in the case of Miss A.'

Lashley was said to have told the police: 'I know there is something wrong with me. I am not afraid of going to prison but I don't want to come out and do the same thing again.

'I want treatment. I want to be cured.'

Fear that broke the part-time firemen

PART-TIME firemen thrust into the violent front line of the firemen's strike revealed a catalogue of intimidation last night.

The retained firemen at Epping, Essex, are too frightened to carry on after a week of trouble.

They finally closed the doors of their station when a mob of 200 pickets hurled a brick through the windscreen of their fire-tender on Monday night.

But the intimidation had been building up—a smoke-bomb hurled into the cab of the fire-engine last week was a signal that the strikers were determined to shut down the one-tender station.

The part-timers — paid £1·50 to answer a call—say they have even been followed to fires and jeered at by strikers.

They say they have had the tyres of their cars deflated, and have been told they might end up inside a blazing building when they turn out with full-time colleagues after the dispute.

Crew leader Jim Warren, a 55-year-old gardener, said: 'I could never face those picket lines again. I feel like a broken man.

Essex's deputy chief fire officer Mr Duncan McCallum alleged that the confrontation had been 'stage managed' by the strikers.

Police are studying a tape recording of the hoax call and have also interviewed Mr Warren about the trouble outside the station on Monday night after two pickets claimed they were hit by his car.

Hopes of ending the strike before Christmas were crushed yesterday by the overwhelming weight of votes against the pay offer made to the men.

It is now virtually certain that the Fire Brigades Union executive council will today spurn the offer

QC, prosecuting counsel, told the court that on the evening of 9 June 1976 the victim had been with her boyfriend until 11pm and had then driven back to her flat in Chesterton Road, Kensington. As she was parking the car outside, Lashley opened the driver's door, pushed her over into the passenger's seat, and got into the driver's seat. Threatening her with a knife, he drove her to a railway arch in a back street where he held her captive for two hours, raping and sexually assaulting her. At one point, when a woman walked by pushing a sleeping child in a pram, Lashley told the girl, 'If you make a sound I'll kill you and then I'll knife the woman and the child.' He also put his hands round her neck, telling her she was about to die, and slashed one of her wrists, saying that he hated white women. Eventually he jumped out of the car and ran away into the darkness.

The victim, with blood pouring from one hand, managed to drive herself home, where she collapsed in the arms of a neighbour, who immediately called the police. During her four-day stay in hospital, she made an Identikit picture of her assailant that was shown on the television programme *Police Five*. The court heard that one of Lashley's women friends had seen the programme, and warned him to change his appearance or he would be arrested. He stopped wearing his usual spectacles and two weeks later bought a different pair. He was actually arrested by chance, while being questioned — along with all other known sex offenders in the area — about the disappearance of Janie Shepherd. Police officers on the case recognised him from the Identikit picture and in due course his victim identified him unhesitatingly, helped by a distinctive scar that he had on one cheek.

On 13 December 1977, after a four-hour deliberation, the jury of ten men and two women found Lashley guilty on two counts of rape, two of indecent assault, one of attempted murder, one of wounding and one of possession of a knife as an offensive weapon. Sentencing Lashley to eighteen years' imprisonment, Mr Justice Gillis said that the case was a 'carbon copy' of his previous crimes, adding, 'It is clear to this court, not only because of the outrageous character of this crime, but in the interest and for the safety of the public, that a heavy sentence must follow.' It was alleged that Lashley had said to the police, 'I know there is something wrong with me. I am not afraid of going to prison but I don't want to come out and do the same thing again. I want treatment. I want to be cured.' Seven years earlier Mr Justice Griffith-Jones had remarked, 'I don't suppose in the whole history of this court there has ever been such a dreadful series of rapes.'

David Lashley became eligible for consideration for parole in December 1983, having served a third of his sentence. But with new restrictions on parole for prisoners serving more than five years for serious offences, it is unlikely that Lashley will be released until he has served most of his term; with full remission for good conduct, his sentence will be twelve years.

few close friends.

By the end of the year, the police admitted they were still no nearer to finding the killer of Janie Shepherd. Detective Inspector Lewis said that he thought the Janie Shepherd inquiry would go on forever.

The file on Janie Shepherd remains open — and many questions about the events of the night on which she died remain unanswered. How did Janie meet her killer? She was last seen alive in the crowded Europa Foods supermarket in Queensway. Tall, blonde and beautiful, she would stand out in any crowd — and she was alone and concentrating on her shopping. Did her killer spot her in the supermarket and follow her, in the expectation that she lived nearby? Or did he act on impulse, using the 'For Sale' sign so prominently displayed in the rear window of her Mini as an excuse to strike up a conversation? Janie was anxious to sell the car in order to buy a new one: could she have accepted an on-the-spot offer and invited her killer in for a run around the block? Janie was an independent girl who had travelled the world alone — perhaps the very idea of danger from someone, even a stranger, in the middle of London simply never occurred to her.

For three consecutive Fridays after her appearance the police staged a repeat-action operation at the supermarket, on the principle that most people are creatures of habit and that many of the shoppers who were in the area on 4 February would regularly be there on Friday nights. Some 6000 people — all potential witnesses — were questioned, but apart from the caretaker who had told a couple in a dark Mini to move on nobody had seen anything unusual happen.

Perhaps, when the killer entered the car, murder was not on his mind; it is possible that he intended only to drive Janie to some darkened back street in order to rape or assault her. Then he may have noticed the full petrol-gauge and decided on a safer area, such as a little-used country lane. There is no evidence to show who drove the Mini that night, only enough to prove the killer possessed a knife.

But exactly where Janie was attacked and murdered remains a mystery. The spot with soil exactly matching the mud and debris found on the car and tyres has never been identified. The night of 4 February was rainy and many of the mud-splashes adhering to the bodywork of the car could have come from the banks or puddles of narrow country lanes. The problem is made more difficult because of modern farming methods. With scientific fertilising to balance the structure of the soil, it is almost impossible to pinpoint an area where the soil analysis might be crucially different between one side of a hedge and the other. The only thing that is known for certain is that the soil in the place where the body was found did not match the soil on the car.

Did the killer change Janie's top clothes — if so, was it before or after her death? Of the likelihood that rape took place inside the car the police are in little doubt, and it is probable that Janie's clothes were ripped during the struggle. Perhaps her attacker then persuaded Janie to change her clothes herself with the promise of letting her go in exchange for her guaranteeing not to report him to the police.

The changing of Janie's pants could mean one of two

The law on parole

One man who was at one time high on the police's list of suspects for the murder of Janie Shepherd is an offender currently in jail for another crime. At the time of Janie's death, he was out on parole, having been jailed several years earlier for crimes of violence.

The parole system for fixed-sentence prisoners was introduced in the United Kingdom by the Criminal Justice Act of 1967. The act provided for the home secretary to appoint a parole board, which must include at least one judge, probation officers, psychiatrists and criminologists. Currently there are approximately fifty members of the board. The act also provides for the home secretary to appoint a local review committee at each prison. The total size of these committees depends on the case-load to be reviewed, but each panel must consist of the prison governor, one member of the prison's board of visitors, a probation officer and two independent members.

Parole-eligible prisoners are automatically considered before the earliest date on which they may be released but if parole is refused, each case must then be reviewed

Below: Janie's cousin Camilla Sampson and her boyfriend Roddy Kinkead-Weekes arrive at the Coroner's Court in St Albans for the inquest on 24 October 1977. Below right: Professor James Cameron, the pathologist who performed the post mortem on Janie's body and gave evidence at the inquest that she had died from compression of the neck

annually. A dossier is compiled of all the relevant facts, together with reports by prison officials and probation officers. The committee then meet to consider the case and decide whether the prisoner is suitable for a parole recommendation. The dossier and the opinion of the committee are then sent to the parole board, which exercises its own discretion. A favourable recommendation by the board is normally accepted by the home secretary, though in 1983 there were twenty cases in which he declined to grant parole. He cannot, however, grant parole in cases where the board has not recommended it. In 1982 66 per cent of all applications for parole were successful.

In the autumn of 1983, at the Conservative Party conference, the home secretary announced plans to toughen the rules concerning the release on parole of serious offenders, to be operative from July 1984. Prisoners serving sentences of more than five years for offences of drug-trafficking or of violence are to be granted parole only in cases where their release under supervision for the last few months of their term can actually be shown to *reduce* the long-term risk to the public, or in circumstances that are genuinely exceptional. Previously, the offender's conduct in prison and his home circumstances were automatically taken into account by the parole board when considering each case; in future, they may no longer be.

The effect of the new recommendation will certainly be to make release on parole for violent offenders much less widespread, since original sentences should now stand in all but a very few cases. However, it must also be remembered that remission for good conduct, which takes a third off a sentence, is earned automatically as an entitlement. Only if a prisoner is punished by losing part or all of his remission, or if the judge at the trial has actually recommended a minimum period in prison, does he serve more than two thirds of the sentence that was passed. Under the new guidelines, offenders sentenced to life imprisonment – such as the killers of policemen, sexual or sadistic murderers (especially of children) and those who kill in the course of armed robbery – will henceforth be expected to serve a minimum of twenty years in jail. Unless the climate of opinion and of government change again in future years, the circumstances that allowed multiple rapist David Lashley to be released after serving only six years of a twelve-year sentence in 1976 should never recur in this country.

things. If she had simply been raped, and not murdered by her rapist, he may have been knowledgeable enough about semen tests to demand that she change her pants – a woman reporting rape would be examined immediately by a police doctor for traces of semen because it is known to disintegrate quickly. It could be possible that she was then murdered by someone else. But equally, her killer may have changed her pants after death to suggest this very idea – that the man who had raped her had not killed her. He could not have been sure that the body would remain undetected for so long, and was obviously taking no chances.

That the killer was cunning is certainly in no doubt. Janie's gold jewellery was worth several hundred pounds, but the selling of it openly would eventually have been traced. Most of it was left on her body – but her £40 in cash was stolen. It is difficult to tell whether the killer knew the area where Janie's body was found for, although the spot he chose on Nomansland Common was in a slight dip and he covered the body with branches and leaves, it was an area frequently used by local people. That the body was not discovered for ten weeks, when it was only a few paces from a major road, can only be put down to chance.

It is perhaps useless to hope that any further information will come to the surface to throw light on the mysteries surrounding the disappearance and death of Janie Shepherd. Roddy Kinkead-Weekes, now married with a family of his own, summed up everyone's feelings when he said: 'You cannot forget the past but I believe the future is more important. Of course I sometimes think of Janie. It took me a long time to adjust to life. The months following Janie's murder were without doubt the worst in my life. . . Even now it is worrying that her killer has not been charged.'

Taking leniency too far

Above: women demonstrating in July 1977 in central London against rape and sexual assault

It is generally acknowledged, by the police and judges as well as the public, that the crime of rape goes widely unreported. Support centres such as the Rape Crisis Centre in London estimate that as many as 75 to 80 per cent of rapes are not reported to the police through the victim's shame or fear of the police or court procedures. Of sexual assaults reported by women to support centres, about two-thirds involve relatives or friends – that is, men known to the victims – and the remainder involve total strangers. Of rapes reported to the police, it is likely that a far higher proportion concern strangers; sexual assault within families is more likely to be hushed up.

Home Office figures for the year 1980 show the number of rapes recorded by the police in England and Wales as 1225: 'recorded' means cases that the police investigated. Of these, about half went to magistrates' courts and half to crown courts; they resulted in 421 verdicts of guilty, and 339 sentences of immediate imprisonment.

But the sentences handed down vary enormously, depending on the nature of the crime and, more arbitrarily, on the views of the judge. In a notorious case at Ipswich Crown Court in January 1982, a businessman was found guilty of raping a 17-year-old hitch-hiker who had missed the last bus home. Passing sentence, the judge, Mr Bertrand Richards, commented: 'I am not saying that a girl hitching home late at night should not be protected by the law, but she was guilty of contributory negligence.' The offender, John Allen, was fined a mere £2000, and walked from the court a free man. The judge even commented that the case was 'a tragedy' for the man – who had a wife and children – and said that it was the first time he had ever not imposed a custodial sentence on a rapist.

Public opinion was outraged and the controversy became a subject for nationwide discussion. A former High Court judge, Sir Justice Melford Stevenson, remarked that girls who hitch-hiked alone at night were 'asking for it'. But the Lord Chancellor, Lord Hailsham, was sufficiently disturbed to write to Mr Justice Richards requesting an explanation of his sentencing, because it was certainly not in line with the general level of sentencing for rape. In particular, it was made clear that the concept of 'contributory negligence' has no validity in cases of rape, which should always attract custodial sentences.

But despite the Lord Chancellor's guidelines, lenient sentencing and acquittals continue. In December 1982 a man charged with dragging a woman into a flat and raping her was acquitted. Mr Justice David Wild said in his summing-up: 'It is not just a question of saying "no". It is a question of how she says it. If she does not want it, she has only to keep her legs shut. . . ' And lenient sentencing is, surprisingly, not confined to cases where there is doubt as to whether the woman consented, or whether the offender *believed* she consented. In a highly disturbing case also reported in December 1982, a man who admitted two charges of raping a six-year-old girl was given only a 12-month sentence, part of which was suspended; taking into account the remission he earned for good conduct and the time he had already been held on remand, he was released after spending only 25 days in jail.

In July 1984 a crime took place that bore frightening similarities to the offence for which David Lashley was sentenced to eighteen years in 1977. A woman sales representative, travelling alone in Wales, was abducted at knife-point and held captive in her own car for more than three hours. During this time she had her clothes cut off her with a knife and was indecently assaulted. Finally, in a remote mountain forest, her attacker first attempted to strangle her, then slit her throat with the knife and left her for dead.

Miraculously, she survived, and in court gave what the judge called a 'quite extraordinary total recollection' of her ordeal. Her attacker was found guilty of assault and attempted murder. Yet Mr Justice Hutchinson sentenced him to only ten years in jail. If he earns the full remission for good conduct, he will be free again by March 1991 – after only six years and eight months.

LOST WITH ALL HANDS.

On the afternoon of 24 November 1941, two weeks before the Japanese attacked Pearl Harbor and invaded Malaya, the Shell tanker *Trocas* was heading for Fremantle in Australia when she sighted a rubber raft crammed with 25 men, survivors from the German merchant raider *Kormoran*. In all, a total of 293 other survivors were captured and on interrogation they revealed that *Kormoran* had been lost in action with the Australian cruiser *Sydney*. Not one of *Sydney*'s crew was ever seen alive again. *MICHAEL MONTGOMERY*, whose father was her navigator, spent four years investigating the loss of *Sydney* and found that the official story did not match the evidence – but the reasons for accepting it led all the way up to President Roosevelt in Washington

Below: on 10 February 1941, after her recall from the Mediterranean to counter the Japanese threat, HMAS Sydney *arrives at Circular Quay, Sydney. Below right: five days after the engagement between* Sydney *and* Kormoran, *on 24 November 1941, survivors from the German ship are taken aboard the British tanker* Trocas

THE troopship *Zealandia*, carrying men of the Eighth Australian Division and her escort, the Australian cruiser HMAS *Sydney*, steamed into the Sunda Strait between Java and Sumatra on 17 November 1941, just three weeks before the Japanese invaded Malaya and attacked the American fleet in Pearl Harbor. Due to a go-slow by *Zealandia*'s engineers, the two ships were a day late for their rendezvous with HMS *Dunbar*. After handing over the troopship to her new escort, *Sydney* steamed at speed towards her home port, Fremantle in Australia. *Zealandia* and *Dunbar* continued from the Sunda Strait to Singapore. When they reached their destination a message was sent to Australia to warn the Naval Board of the delay, and accordingly *Sydney* was not expected to reach Fremantle until 21 November. On 23 November there was still no sign of her. The Naval Board ordered *Sydney* to report her position by radio. There was no reply.

On the same day, at 6am Western Australian Time, the ex-Cunard troopship *Aquitania*, bound from Singapore to Sydney, sighted a life-raft floating 150 miles (240 kilometres) due west of Carnarvon on the Western Australian coast. *Aquitania* was unescorted and, fearing a trap, she stopped only briefly to pick up the 26 men on board the raft before sailing on. They turned out to be survivors from the disguised German merchant raider *Kormoran*, sunk in action with a cruiser four days earlier. The prisoners said nothing to suggest that the cruiser itself had also been lost, and

How had *Kormoran* managed to sink a battle-tried cruiser that had destroyed several enemy warships?

Aquitania's captain, W. S. Gibbons, decided not to risk breaking radio silence by reporting the incident. Forty-five miles (seventy kilometres) to the north-east on the following afternoon another boatload of survivors from *Kormoran* was sighted by the Shell tanker *Trocas*, which was heading for Fremantle with a load of Javanese oil. This second life-raft also contained several milk bottles with Japanese markings.

Captain S. L. Bryant of *Trocas* reported the sinking of *Kormoran*, but since none of his crew was able to speak German and the only prisoner with a good knowledge of English was too weak to talk, a proper interrogation was impossible. By now, the hunt for *Sydney* was already under way. It seemed likely that she had been lost. But despite an intensive search in the area, involving several ships and a number of aircraft, no trace of the cruiser was found and not one of her crew of 645 men was ever seen alive again.

The crew of *Kormoran* were luckier. Between 24 November and 26 November, several of *Kormoran*'s life-rafts were picked up at sea and two more made landfalls to the north of Carnarvon. A total of 318 men were rescued out of a complement of 398, including three Chinese prisoners who had been retained for laundry work. The accounts the survivors gave agreed that *Sydney* and *Kormoran* had engaged in battle on 19 November and both ships had been sunk. But how had *Kormoran* – which had been designed to prey only on unescorted merchant ships – managed to sink a battle-tried cruiser that had destroyed several enemy warships? And why had none of *Sydney*'s crew survived?

The first official announcement of the cruiser's disappearance was issued to the Australian press on 3 December by Prime Minister John Curtin. He stated that the two ships had met at dusk 300 miles (480 kilometres) from the coast, and that *Kormoran* had been flying the Norwegian flag. *Sydney* had cleared for action and closed to investigate her identity; the two ships had opened fire simultaneously. *Kormoran* knocked out *Sydney*'s bridge, and *Sydney* started a fire in the raider's engine room. The crew of *Kormoran* claimed they had fired a number of torpedoes, but they did not know if any of them had struck. After darkness fell *Kormoran* was abandoned and eventually blew up. The survivors had watched from their boats as the burning *Sydney* disappeared over the horizon.

This statement was followed by another, two days later, that differed from the first report in a number of details. It was largely based on an account given by one of *Kormoran*'s officers, Sub-Lieutenant W. Bunjes, who had been picked up at sea by the minesweeper *Yandra* on 26 November. The new details were adhered to thereafter by *Kormoran*'s officers, and eventually this version of events was officially adopted.

According to this new version, the ships had met at 5pm, and not at dusk – which would have fallen at 7pm. They were only 125 miles (200 kilometres) from the coast, and *Kormoran* was flying the Dutch flag rather than the Norwegian. She had radioed a 'Q' (suspicious ship) signal giving her identity as *Straat Malakka* – a Dutch freighter that was often in the area, although at the time she was

Above: the German submarine U-124 takes torpedoes aboard from Kormoran *in the Atlantic during March 1941.* Kormoran *left Gotenhafen (Gdynia) in German-occupied Poland early in December 1940. She slipped through the Allied blockade in Denmark Strait and spent some months in the Atlantic, during which time she sank or captured eight Allied merchantmen and supplied the German U-boat fleet, before steaming round the Cape of Good Hope and into the Indian Ocean where she continued to hunt Allied merchantmen with devastating success. Top right:* Kormoran *taking on stores in Kiel Harbour, where she had recently been converted from a merchantman intended for the Hamburg-Amerika Line into a merchant raider. Right: four of* Kormoran*'s officers on the bridge. From left to right: Commander Foerster, Lieutenant-Commander Oetzel, Lieutenant Goesseln and the ship's captain, T.A. Detmers*

thousands of miles away. When *Sydney* asked for the ship's international call sign, *Kormoran*'s signaller fumbled the flags in order to draw her in closer. By 6.25 she had come in to less than a mile on *Kormoran*'s starboard quarter with all guns and torpedo tubes bearing and, when she was almost abeam, *Sydney* signalled 'IK', the two inner letters of *Straat Malakka*'s secret call-sign IIKP. This was the next stage of the Admiralty challenge procedure. The merchant ship was supposed to reply with the two outer letters, but Commander Detmers of *Kormoran* — not knowing the secret call-sign — realised that the game was up and gave orders to hoist the German ensign and open fire.

The first salvo, the statement claimed, scored a hit on *Sydney*'s bridge. The cruiser's almost simultaneous reply went harmlessly over, but her second salvo found the engine-room fuel tanks of *Kormoran* and started a fire. *Kormoran* meanwhile had fired two torpedoes, one of which struck

***Kormoran*'s guns continued to score hits until *Sydney* was out of range**

Sydney under her two forward turrets and put them out of action. Frantic efforts were made to launch *Sydney*'s Walrus seaplane, but it was shot to pieces by *Kormoran*'s anti-aircraft gun. *Sydney* then tried to ram, but passed narrowly astern, and on to the raider's port side. Her two rear turrets were still firing independently, and she launched four torpedoes but they all missed. *Kormoran*'s guns were also still in action and they continued to score hits until *Sydney* was out of range. Both ships were then heavily on fire. *Kormoran* had stopped moving, but *Sydney* continued southwards at about five knots. At 8pm Detmers sent most of *Kormoran*'s company into the life-rafts and three hours later Detmers and the other officers abandoned ship after setting scuttling charges. The glow of fire on *Sydney* could be seen after darkness fell, but by midnight the ship had disappeared from view completely.

The two accounts of the engagement disagreed not only over its location and timing but also over the disguise the *Kormoran* had adopted and the events of the action itself. What was the origin of the discrepancies?

The crew of *Kormoran*, except for those on *Aquitania*, were reassembled at Fremantle for further questioning. When that was completed they were transferred to Victoria, where they spent the rest of the war in prisoner-of-war camps before being repatriated to Germany in 1947. During their interrogation the prisoners repeated the 'Bunjes' account of the action, varying only in minor details. Before that, however, what they had told their individual captors had differed very considerably. Three of the lifeboats had not contained officers, which made the evidence of their occupants especially interesting.

Sub-Lieutenant Bunjes was the second officer on board the lifeboat that was picked up by *Yandra*. His superior, Lieutenant J. von Goesseln, had been responsible as adjutant for recruiting *Kormoran*'s crew and was noted as being 'fanatically Nazi-minded'.

Goesseln refused to answer any questions whatever, although after the war he boasted that he alone had been with Detmers on the bridge throughout the action. Bunjes on the other hand was a natural choice as the officers' mouthpiece. Unlike the others he was not a Kriegsmarine regular – he had been conscripted from the merchant marine and so was more likely to be believed.

Another key witness who refused to comment at the time was Dr F. List, the ship's official war correspondent and propaganda officer, and a personal friend of Dr Goebbels. With twelve other officers, he succeeded in reaching land at Red Bluff, 70 miles (110 kilometres) north of the small town of Carnarvon. A second life boat had already made a landfall nearby at 17-Mile Well. The Germans on board the two boats – including the majority of *Kormoran*'s officers – were discovered on 25 November and taken into the jail to await transport to Fremantle. While they were there a local Volunteer Defence Corps guard, J. A. Robotham, made his own search of the prisoners and found Dr List's diary recording that their boat had met up again with von Goesseln and Bunjes' lifeboat on the morning after the action. Therefore, Bunjes must have been able to confer

Is it conceivable that he was lured and then fired on by *Kormoran* while she was disguised?

with the other officers before being picked up and interrogated on 26 November.

One of the key points at issue is the nationality of *Kormoran*'s disguise on the day of action. At first, all the evidence taken from the ordinary seamen spoke of the disguise being Norwegian. The boat that landed at 17-Mile Well had no officers on board. One of its survivors – a former steward with the Hamburg-America Line who spoke fluent English – described how *Kormoran*'s crew had hung a board over the side with the word 'Norge' painted on it.

Robotham also found a diary belonging to Petty Officer H. Kitsche, containing a dramatised account of the action that had Detmers, when he first identified *Sydney* as a warship, saying: 'Hoist the Norwegian flag, lieutenant'.

What of the officers' story? The claim that *Kormoran* was disguised as the Dutch ship *Straat Malakka,* and had radioed a 'Q' signal accordingly, is quite implausible. First, *Straat Malakka* had a counter stern as opposed to the cruiser stern of *Kormoran*, a difference that Captain Burnett of *Sydney* would hardly have missed at a distance of less than a mile (1·6 kilometres). Secondly, on 19 November *Straat Malakka* happened to be anchored four thousand miles (6500 kilometres) away in Beira and so could not have been on the list of 'Vessels in Your Area', issued to *Sydney* every 24 hours.

The standard procedure for a warship checking out the identity of a merchant ship that failed to answer the challenge correctly was either to put a shot across her bows, or to put down a boat with a boarding party while standing

Below: survivors from Kormoran *come ashore at Fremantle. Below right: three Chinese prisoners who were retained on board* Kormoran *for laundry work. They were the only non-German survivors, and their version of the events on 19 November 1941 differed substantially from the officers' account. Far right: two of* Kormoran's *lifeboats reached land north of Carnarvon in Western Australia. From top to bottom: 17-Mile Well; the cave at Red Bluff where the propaganda officer aboard the ship, Dr List, claimed to have buried his camera; the beach at Red Bluff showing* Kormoran's *lifeboat; the cave at Red Bluff where survivors from* Kormoran *lived for two days before being found*

some distance away, bows-on, and order the merchant ship to approach the boat. The warship would, of course, be at action stations throughout. But the weight of evidence from *Kormoran*'s survivors gave a quite different impression — several of them spoke of seeing *Sydney*'s pantrymen 'lining the rails to get a better look'. Burnett, though by all accounts he was cautious and a stickler for procedure, would appear to have broken every rule in the book. Is it conceivable that he was lured and then fired on by *Kormoran* while she was disguised?

Supposing that, far from being obliged to open fire as a last resort when her bluff had been called, *Kormoran* had launched a surprise attack while still flying a neutral flag, it would be easy to explain many of the new details of the officer's story. Such an action was in contravention of international law, and if proved would have theoretically rendered every *Kormoran* survivor liable to summary execution as a common pirate. They had every motive for claiming that *Sydney* had signalled the letters 'IK', that they had been disguised as the Dutch *Straat Malakka*, and that not knowing the proper response, they had raised the German ensign and fired on *Sydney*.

If Burnett did *not* signal 'IK', how could Detmers have known later that these letters represented part of the *Straat Malakka*'s secret call-sign, which was supposedly unknown to him? Six months earlier he had met his sister raider *Atlantis*, which had captured top-secret documents from the British freighter *Automedon*. These had included a list of secret call-signs to be issued to Dutch merchant ships operating in the Far East, and as a result Detmers immediately changed his disguise to *Straat Malakka*. This is apparent from his logbook, a copy of which was sent back to Japan on *Kulmerland* in October. In 1947, Detmers admitted to prisoner-of-war camp commandant Major Heinrich Schrader that he had indeed known *Straat Malakka*'s secret call-sign all along. Had *Kormoran* really been disguised as *Straat Malakka*, Detmers could have replied correctly to the

Below: 'The Destruction of HMS Hood', by John Hamilton. On 24 May 1941 the battle-cruiser Hood *– one of the Royal Navy's oldest capital ships, launched in 1918 – and the battleship* Prince of Wales *(foreground) engaged the German battleship* Bismarck *and the heavy cruiser* Prinz Eugen *in the icy waters off Greenland. Eight minutes after the battle began,* Hood *received a whole salvo of 15-inch shells from the German flagship. Immediately there was an explosion of 'incredible violence', followed by others as the magazines exploded.* Hood *sank soon afterwards. Although the explosions and sinking followed the initial hit very quickly, there were still three survivors. Yet, six months later, when* Sydney *sank – much more slowly and with less violence – in the warmer waters off Australia, not one of her crew survived. Right: a Supermarine Walrus seaplane of the kind carried by* Sydney, *in flight immediately after being catapulted from* HMS Mauritius. *Below right:* HMAS Sydney *in service in the Mediterranean in 1939. She still carries the British recognition markings on her 'B' turret that date from her service in the Neutrality Patrol at the time of the Spanish Civil War*

challenge.

Kormoran's original 'Q' signal was picked up in a faint and heavily distorted form by Geraldton radio station and by the tug *Uco*, 100 miles (160 kilometres) away. Both were able to make out the phrase '1000 GMT' (6pm local time) and some unintelligible figures which seemed to indicate the sender's position, but neither received anything resembling a ship's identity.

A statement made by Wireless Operator H. Linke, the man who transmitted the signal, provides an answer. According to him its purpose had not been to add to any deception about *Kormoran*'s identity, but to distract attention. Raider wireless operators were thoroughly trained in 'throwing' signals – that is, in making them appear to be coming from elsewhere – by deliberately distorting them. If this was what was being practised here – and the form in which it was picked up by the *Uco* only 100 miles (160 kilometres) away suggests that it was – Linke was saying in effect that the object of the 'Q' signal was to make Burnett believe that somewhere over the horizon an Allied merchantman was signalling the presence of a 'suspicious ship', which would in turn persuade him to abandon his inspection of *Kormoran*.

Evidence that Burnett did indeed interpret it thus comes from none other than Detmers himself, in a document entitled 'Action Report', which was found on him at Fremantle before he had been able to compare notes with the other officers, and which refers to *Sydney* drawing away on the starboard beam at 6.15 – ten minutes after the signal was sent. This contrasts with the claim of the officers' story

Sydney the brave

At the outbreak of the Second World War *Sydney* and her sister ships *Perth* and *Hobart* were the most modern cruisers in the Royal Australian Navy. Their design was based on the Royal Navy's 'Leander Class' cruiser – a class that included the famous *Ajax* and *Achilles* – but the plan had been changed slightly. To reduce the risk of a single hit destroying both boilers, the boiler and engine rooms were placed alternately and there were therefore two funnels instead of one.

Sydney was originally built for the Royal Navy as HMS *Phaeton* by Swan Hunter and Wigham Richardson at Wallsend-on-Tyne. She was bought on the stocks by the Australian government and commissioned in 1936. Her main armaments consisted of four six-inch (15-centimetre) twin turrets – two forward and two aft – with a maximum effective range of 22,000 yards (20,000 metres). Her Walrus seaplane was launched by means of a catapult located between the two funnels and it could be recovered by means of a crane.

In May 1940, with her complement of 550 officers and men, *Sydney* was sent to join Admiral Cunningham's Eastern Mediterranean fleet. The following month she was involved in the sinking of the Italian destroyer *Espero*. On 19 July, off Crete, she sighted two Italian cruisers that were giving chase to four British destroyers. Her captain, John Collins, immediately turned to engage the cruisers, and quickly disabled the *Bartolomeo Colleoni* (claimed to be the fastest cruiser in the world) with a hit in the engine room. The destroyers were then able to finish the first cruiser off with a torpedo attack. *Sydney* continued to fire at the *Giovanni Delle Bande Nere* until she ran out of ammunition. *Sydney*'s vital victory enabled a much freer flow of supplies to Montgomery's beleaguered Eighth Army in Egypt.

In the same month, *Sydney* took part in the Battle of Calabria, and in September 1940 she was one of a group of ships that bombarded enemy torpedo boat bases in the Dodecanese Islands. She was recalled to Australia in January 1941 to counter the growing menace of Japan. After a tumultuous welcome and a spell in dry dock in her home port, she was transferred to Fremantle under the command of Captain J. Burnett and assigned to troopship escort duty, mainly on the run from Fremantle to the Sunda Strait, between Java and Sumatra.

HMAS Sydney

Type Light cruiser
Dimensions Length 555 feet (154 metres); beam 56¾ feet (17·3 metres)
Maximum speed 32½ knots
Armour Side-belt 2-4 inches (50-100 millimetres; decks, 2 inches (50 millimetres); main turret 1 inch (25 millimetres)
Armament 8 x 6-inch guns; 8 x 4-inch guns; 8 x 21-inch torpedo tubes; 12 x 0·5-inch anti-aircraft machine-guns; 1 Walrus seaplane

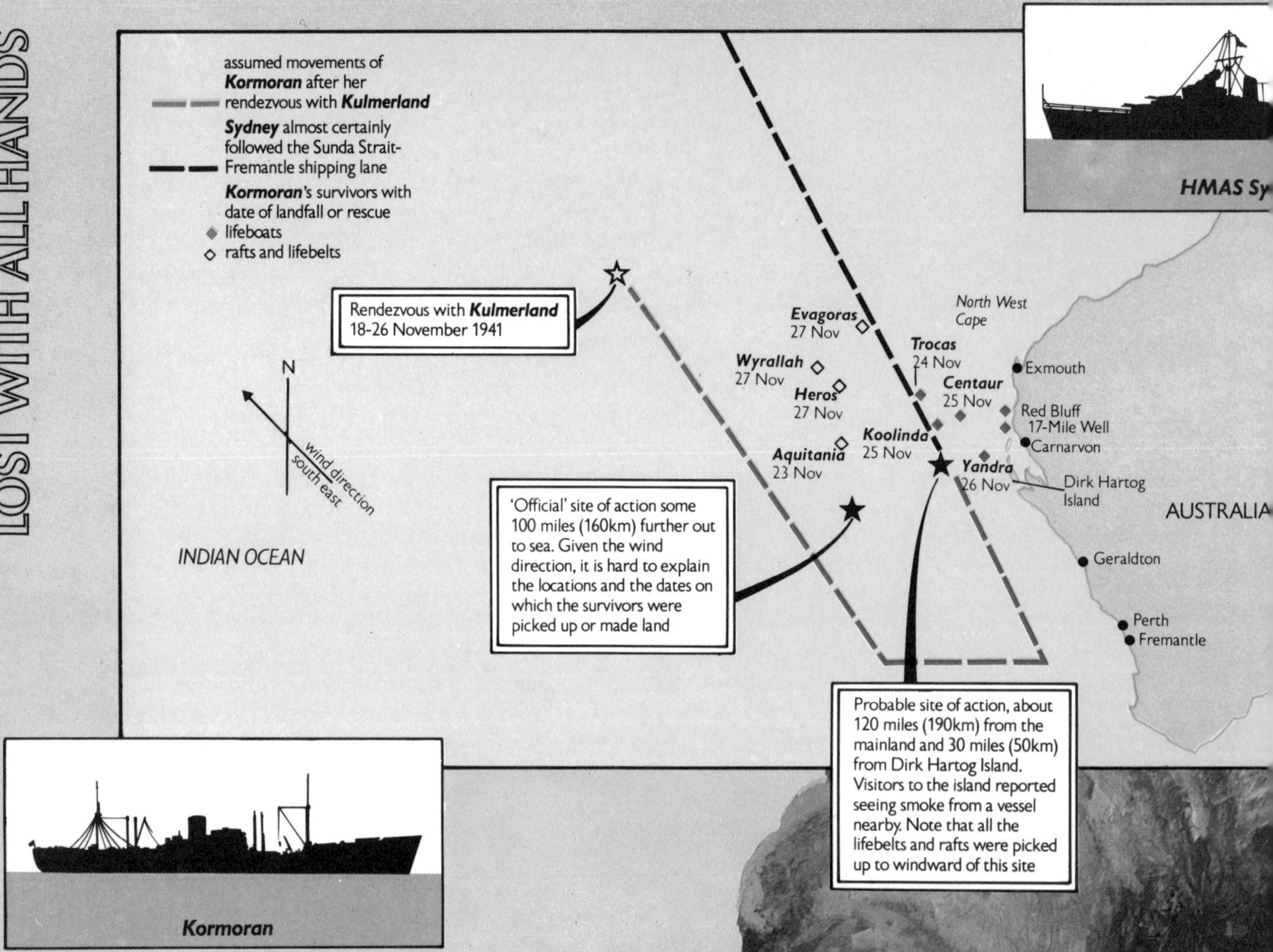

assumed movements of **Kormoran** after her rendezvous with **Kulmerland**

Sydney almost certainly followed the Sunda Strait-Fremantle shipping lane

Kormoran's survivors with date of landfall or rescue

◆ lifeboats

◇ rafts and lifebelts

Rendezvous with **Kulmerland**
18-26 November 1941

N

wind direction
south east

INDIAN OCEAN

Evagoras 27 Nov

Wyrallah 27 Nov

Heros 27 Nov

Aquitania 23 Nov

Trocas 24 Nov

Centaur 25 Nov

Koolinda 25 Nov

Yandra 26 Nov

North West Cape

Exmouth

Red Bluff

17-Mile Well

Carnarvon

Dirk Hartog Island

AUSTRALIA

Geraldton

Perth

Fremantle

'Official' site of action some 100 miles (160km) further out to sea. Given the wind direction, it is hard to explain the locations and the dates on which the survivors were picked up or made land

Probable site of action, about 120 miles (190km) from the mainland and 30 miles (50km) from Dirk Hartog Island. Visitors to the island reported seeing smoke from a vessel nearby. Note that all the lifebelts and rafts were picked up to windward of this site

HMAS Sy

Kormoran

Previous page: Kormoran *(left) and* Sydney *engage. Above, left to right: the sinking of the Italian cruiser* Bartolomeo Colleoni, *believed to be the fastest ship in the world, after encountering* Sydney *off Crete on 19 July 1940. At this time,* Sydney *was attached to the Eastern Mediterranean Fleet. She distinguished herself in several engagements. Below: a shell hole in* Sydney*'s funnel – the only hit she received during the engagement with* Bartolomeo Colleoni. *Right:* Sydney *takes on survivors from the Italian cruiser*

that at 6.15 she 'was almost abeam with all her guns and torpedo tubes trained'. At that stage less than an hour of daylight remained and Burnett's only hope of tracking down the 'suspicious ship' lay in launching his seaplane. It seems that the heavy swell decided him against it, for several accounts spoke of the Walrus being swung out on its catapult and then in again.

The next entry in Detmers' 'Action Report' reads '6.25 Morse signal "Hoist Your Secret Call-sign", cruiser stops engines thus had not the least suspicion'. This not only makes no mention of the letters IK, but it also flatly contradicts the officers' account that the two ships now 'proceeded parallel to each other 1300 yards (1200 metres) apart'. Several other accounts confirm that not only *Sydney* but also *Kormoran* hove to at this point. Kitsche, for instance, stated specifically that *Sydney* signalled the raider to 'close up to half a mile and heave to'. Detmers replied with the answer 'Understood' and said to his companion on the bridge: 'We will keep them busy when we have got them within half a mile.'

The 'Q' signal by itself would hardly have been enough to persuade Burnett of *Kormoran*'s innocence. What else, then, could have induced him to approach within point-blank range of a ship that he had not identified nor even properly challenged, to pull in alongside, stop engines and lower a boat – all without even taking the elementary precaution of closing up to action stations? He would certainly not have done so for the purpose of putting a boarding party across, the procedure for which, as we have already seen, demanded that the warship stood bows-on at a distance

with all guns bearing. Such behaviour could only be explained, though, by the assumption that he was answering a distress call.

When he was interrogated on this point, Wireless Operator Linke denied that he had ever put out a false SOS call, explaining that 'it was too dangerous'. Nothing could have presented a greater danger than the sight of an enemy cruiser, however, and such a ploy was a recognised part of a raider's repertoire — ten months earlier the merchant raider *Orion* had used it successfully to decoy a merchant ship off Nauru in the Pacific. Several others spoke of *Kormoran* having made a lot of smoke as *Sydney* approached, which would also have helped to create an impression of distress. Indeed, it might even have led Burnett to believe that she was the recent victim of the same 'suspicious ship' indicated by the 'Q' signal.

If so, he was the victim of a vastly more elaborate deception than the mere false identity and flag-fumbling of the official history. The sending of false SOS calls would have been, of course, against international law.

The officers' account of the action itself is also at variance with other evidence. The order in which *Kormoran*'s weaponry was allegedly fired — main armament, anti-aircraft gun, torpedoes — is exactly the reverse of what one would have expected, given the need for total surprise if she was to have any hope against such a formidably superior enemy. Even at cruising stations each of *Sydney*'s gun turrets would have had a crew who would have needed just a few seconds to fire a first round.

Kormoran's six 5·9-inch guns were concealed either by

Below: Steiermark *before her conversion to the German merchant raider* Kormoran. *Below right:* Kormoran *stands by as one of her victims sinks. Right: one of* Sydney's *bullet-riddled life-rafts — all that remained of the pride of the Royal Australian Navy. Are the bullet holes a clue to the fate of* Sydney's *crew?*

counter-weighted plates in the sides or by false hatches on the holds and took at the very least a full minute to be uncovered and aimed. The anti-aircraft gun was hidden behind a screen on the bridge and required fifteen to twenty seconds before it could be brought to bear. By contrast, it needed only the removal of a simple flap to expose the two torpedo tubes above water, while the underwater tube could fire — and strike the target — without being revealed at all.

Neither Detmers nor any other of the officers made any mention of the underwater tube ever being fired, obviously in order to avoid adding to the suspicion that they had opened fire under a neutral flag, but there is no lack of evidence to this effect from other sources. A number of survivors picked up by the Blue Funnel freighter *Centaur* stated specifically before they were landed at Fremantle that *Sydney* was first hit by a torpedo fired underwater, while the Vichy magazine *Sept Jours* reported that when *Kormoran* was ordered to heave to 'she replied with a torpedo'. Once it had gone home Detmers would have immediately followed up with the above-water tubes. Shu Ah Fah, one of the three Chinese survivors — the only independent witnesses — told the captain of *Yandra* that *Sydney* had been hit by three torpedoes in quick succession. He was

Merchant raider

Kormoran was originally built at Kiel as the 8736-ton merchantman *Steiermark* for the Hamburg-Amerika line, but was promptly handed over for conversion into a merchant raider at the outbreak of war. Her four diesel-powered engines gave her a top speed of eighteen knots, although persistent trouble in one of them effectively reduced this. Her main armament was provided

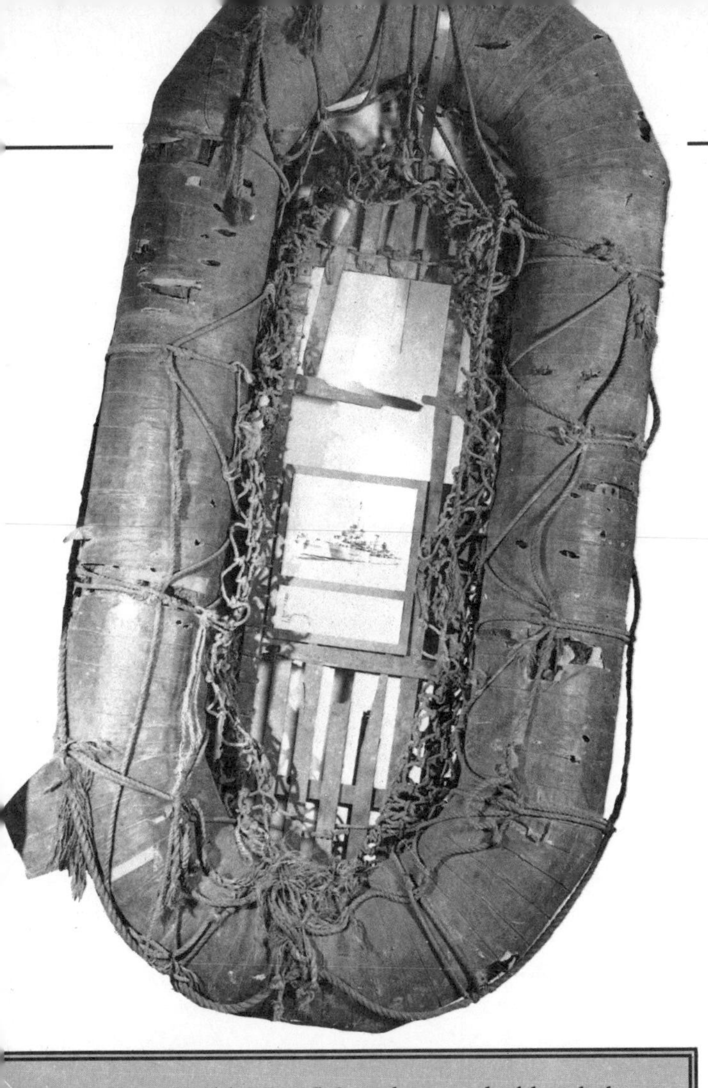

by six First World War 5·9-inch guns hidden below deck, two on either side and two in concealed central holds giving her a four-gun broadside. Two 3·7-inch anti-aircraft guns were mounted at either end of the bridge and there were a number of machine-guns variously located. Each side of the *Kormoran* was fitted with two torpedo tubes above the water-line and one below it.

Kormoran set sail on 3 December 1940 from Gotenhafen (Gdynia), a port near Gdansk in German-occupied Poland. She was disguised as a Soviet ship and, successfully evading the allied blockade of the Denmark Strait, she sailed into the Atlantic. *Kormoran* underwent several changes of paintwork and altered the nationality of her disguise almost daily. After sinking seven merchant ships and capturing another as a prize, she sailed into the Indian Ocean in April and sank three more ships there. She took on supplies from a Japanese freighter in July and was supplied again in mid October by the blockade runner *Kulmerland*. She then steamed towards the Australian coast.

On 19 November the atmosphere on *Kormoran* was relaxed, in celebration of the Lutheran Day of Atonement. The holiday had been marked by a special 'Farmer's Breakfast' for the whole crew, and most of those off duty were sleeping it off below decks in the sub-tropical warmth – until the lookout suddenly reported: 'Two masts ahead.' He had sighted the Australian cruiser *Sydney*.

interviewed again on landing in Fremantle and, even though his account was noted as differing radically from that of *Kormoran*'s officers, naval intelligence did not see fit to keep a record of his evidence.

All accounts are at least agreed that the first torpedo struck *Sydney* below her two forward turrets. This by itself would probably have been sufficient to disable them from the outset, and the devastating effect of the anti-aircraft gun from such short range would have ensured that they were unable to get a round off before being knocked out altogether by *Kormoran*'s main armament. Her reply would thus have been confined to her two rear turrets.

It was at this juncture that, according to the officers' story, *Sydney* attempted to ram and passed aft of *Kormoran* onto her port quarter, whereupon *Kormoran* 'swept her starboard side devastatingly'. But a diagram of the action drawn by F. Treber while on board *Aquitania* suggests that *Sydney* did not try to ram – an unlikely tactic given that she had been torpedoed in the bows.

According to Detmers, *Kormoran*'s turn to port shown in Treber's second sketch was made in order to clear the gunsights of smoke rising from the fire in the engine-room, but before it could be completed the engines failed. In attempting to get the engines started again, *Kormoran*'s two engineering officers and seventeen others were killed. The hit on the funnel had also sparked off some aviation fuel, starting an even more serious fire – in the words of one survivor who was interviewed later in Germany, 'the whole ship was burning like a cellulose factory'. It is thus unlikely that the ship was abandoned in the orderly manner the officers described.

The officers' story painted a picture of *Sydney* making off after the action at five knots, and last being seen six miles (nine kilometres) away. Yet Treber shows her 'stopped and swinging in the wind' at a distance of only 8000 yards (7000 metres) at 6.45pm, and List wrote in his diary that at 7.15pm she was 'gesenkt' (sunk). Several others spoke of actually seeing her explode and sink; two described her as turning turtle. None was more graphic than G. Albers, *Kormoran*'s range-finder operator: 'Suddenly there was a burst of flame. She had blown up! The smoke on the horizon cleared. Then there was nothing at all of the cruiser except a little wreckage floating.'

The evidence is thus overwhelmingly against the official version of *Sydney* limping away over the horizon never to be seen again – but what were the motives underlying this fabrication?

The only items ever recovered from *Sydney* were two lifebelts and two Carley floats. The first of the latter was found peppered with machine-gun bullets by the auxiliary vessel *Heros* on 27 November. The second, also riddled with bullet holes, was found just off Christmas Island on 6 February 1942; it contained the remains of a body dressed in a Royal Australian Navy-issue boiler suit and boots. Christmas Island lies in the direct path of the prevailing current from the site of the *Sydney-Kormoran* action. Yet naval intelligence have always maintained that the boat could not have come from *Sydney*, even though at that date no other Royal

Above: T. A. Detmers, captain of Kormoran. He was a rigid disciplinarian and dedicated to the aims of the Nazis. Below: J. Burnett, captain of Sydney from 1941. He was known to his superiors as a cautious officer and 'a cool customer in a crisis'

Australian Navy ship had lost a single man in action within 7000 miles (11,000 kilometres) of Christmas Island.

The angle of entry and the distribution of bullet holes in both floats strongly suggested that they had been in the water rather than still on board *Sydney* when they were fired on. Both the lifebelts had been inflated, something that was not done until just before the wearer's entry into the water. Were survivors from *Sydney* deliberately mown down in the water by machine-gun fire after the battle? Such an act would constitute an atrocity.

In 1943 a series of innocent-seeming sketches drawn by List were found on Ship's Doctor S. Habben just before his repatriation to Germany on an exchange of medical personnel. When they were examined by an expert in German shorthand, he was able to decipher a number of phrases concealed in them: 'A terrible deed. . . if under. . . special sacrifices. . . if alive.' In the light of the evidence already quoted, it would not seem over fanciful to reconstruct from them a sentence such as 'it was *a terrible deed*, but *if under* extreme threat one is justified in making *special sacrifices* in view of the consequences *if* they had been allowed to remain *alive*'.

It is now readily apparent why *Kormoran*'s officers might have gone to such lengths to paint a picture of *Sydney* disappearing over the horizon two hours before they themselves abandoned ship. If this had really been the case, it would effectively remove any suspicion that they had been party to firing on survivors in the water. A similar wish to explain the absence of survivors could well lie behind the improbable claim that *Sydney* had attempted to ram and had thereby allowed herself to be 'devastatingly swept' by gunfire. But if the officers' story is so improbable, one larger question remains to be answered – why did the Australian authorities so willingly accept it, in spite of the glaring inconsistences, and allow it to pass into official history?

In the diary of Rear-Admiral Crace, the admiral commanding the Australia squadron, the entry for 24 November 1941 records that the Naval Board were very worried about *Sydney* on the grounds that she had been torpedoed and sunk by a submarine. The actual wording gave the board's opinion as being that 'a Vichy submarine escorting a Vichy ship had torpedoed her [*Sydney*]'. But at that time, as a signal to the Admiralty would have very quickly confirmed, no Vichy submarine was operating any nearer Australia than the Mediterranean – 7000 miles (11,000 kilometres) away. The Naval Board must have known this – so what could they have meant? No German or Italian submarines entered the Indian Ocean until 1943. This left only Japan as the possible origin of such a vessel, and, though Japan was not yet officially in the war, there had already been eight 'probable' sightings of Japanese submarines in Australian waters.

The best possible source of such a suspicion would of course have been *Sydney* herself; and the apparent inability of even one of her four radio rooms to get off an Enemy Engagement signal has always been one of the most improbable aspects of the whole story. But even if *Kormoran*'s opening shot somehow succeeded in simultaneously silencing all four radios, which were widely dispersed around the ship, there were still good grounds for the board to suspect the presence of a Japanese submarine. It had long been known that Japan harboured territorial designs on Australia, as demonstrated in the plan of invasion captured in China in 1940. As recently as 28 October 1941 Townsville fisherman E. Dodd had reported to naval intelligence that he had seen a submarine off the Great Barrier Reef launching a seaplane — at that time, a capacity only the Japanese 'I' class submarines were known to have.

Left: one of Dr List's sketches, now in the Australian national archives. When it was examined by an expert in German cryptography, he deciphered the following message — 'a terrible deed. . . if under. . . special sacrifices. . . if alive. . .' Below: a diagram based on a plot of the action between Kormoran *('No. 41') and* Sydney *drawn by F. Treber while aboard* Aquitania. *The prisoners picked up by* Aquitania *had no officer among them, and the points at which their accounts differ from the officers' account of the action are therefore particularly interesting. Treber's diagram indicates that* Sydney *never attempted to ram* Kormoran *and throws doubt on Detmer's claim to have 'swept her starboard side devastatingly' with close range fire — a claim that may have been prompted by the need to explain the absence of survivors from* Sydney. *And finally, Treber's drawing indicates that* Sydney *did not limp away over the horizon; she was stopped at 8000 yards (7000 metres) and drifting into the wind*

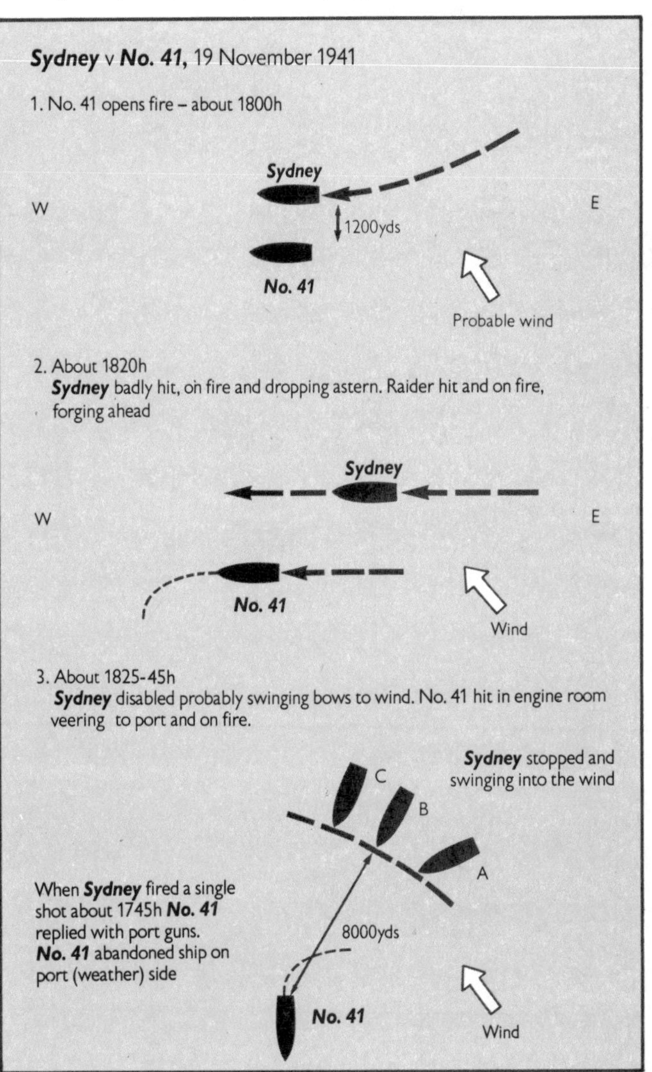

Japan was not yet at war, but the decision to attack had already been taken. The contingency of an encounter with a naval unit was covered by the Number One Order to the Japanese fleet, issued on 5 November, which instructed that 'in the case of discovery within 600 miles (1000 kilometres) of the countries against whom war is to be declared, make immediate preparations to attack and destroy the unit responsible'. Any Japanese submarine involved in the action with *Sydney* on 19 November would have had no compunction about ensuring that no witnesses survived to tell the tale.

When List's sketches were discovered in 1943 one of them contained the most specific evidence of all for Japanese involvement in *Sydney*'s destruction. It was deciphered to read: 'Until reinforcements arrived. . . in the evening conquered the victim. A Japanese gunfire attack from Japan itself.' The phrase 'in the evening' fits not only the timetable of events, but also what one would expect of such a combined operation — the submarine would of course have had to come up to periscope depth to fire its torpedoes, and it would hardly have risked doing so in daylight.

One of the official interrogators of the *Kormoran*'s survivors, Lieutenant-Commander G. B. Salm of the Royal Netherlands Navy, was later employed on a similar assignment in Sydney, where a naval intelligence officer confided to him that it was accepted that List's sketches 'gave the full story'. Further evidence of this surfaced in, of all places, the official diary of the German naval war staff in Berlin, which recorded in connection with Dr Habben's report on his repatriation in 1943 that 'in the opinion of Australian specialists *Kormoran* was co-operating with a submarine and it was the submarine which was responsible for sinking the cruiser'. What this admission amounted to was an acknowledgement that Japan had committed an act of war three weeks before any formal declaration. Such an event would clearly have carried the gravest political implications. Prime Minister Curtin had already been warning London for months of the impossibility, without full American military assistance, of defending Australia against a Japanese attack.

In the main Churchill-Curtin correspondence file there is a gap of over three weeks running from early in November 1941 until 27 November, a week after the sinking, when Churchill cabled his 'deepest sympathy on the feared loss of the *Sydney* so close to Australian shores'. The Churchill-Roosevelt correspondence also appears to have been similarly doctored. On 25 November the United States War Council had approved the terms of a three-month 'modus vivendi' to be offered to Japan whereby America would resume exports of embargoed oil and certain other raw materials to Japan on condition that Japan reduced her forces in Indochina to 25,000 men. But in the early hours of 26 November a cable was sent to Churchill: 'Negotiations off. Services expect action within two weeks.' Such an immediate change of policy, without any explanation, points to Churchill as having been the source of the intelligence item that provoked it.

The relevant file in London contains a telegram from Churchill purportedly sent at 3.20am on 26 November to the United States Embassy in Grosvenor Square, London, that reads: 'Your message about Japan [detailing the terms of the proposed modus vivendi] received tonight. Of course it is for you to handle this business and we certainly do not want an additional war.' It goes on to voice some concern about the effect of negotiations with Japan on China's position, but ends with an expression of confidence that Roosevelt would take this fully into account. It is hard to see how anything as non-committal as this would have caused the change. The phrase 'received tonight' – referring to Roosevelt's telegram, which was sent on 24 November – proves beyond argument that Churchill's reply was also sent on 24 November, and not on 26 November. There is no doubt, however, that Churchill sent Roosevelt another telegram at 3.20am on 26 November, because another file contains a

Below: Japanese markings on milkbottles recovered from one of Kormoran's *lifeboats. Bottom: a Japanese I-Class submarine off Tokyo in 1940. Was a submarine of this type involved in sinking* Sydney?

Enter Japan

In November 1941 Japan – an empire of some 72 million people – was at peace with Britain and the United States. But it was an uneasy peace. It was known in Europe and America that 49 per cent of Japan's budgetary expenditure during 1941 had been devoted to armaments. The Japanese air force numbered 4000 aircraft. The navy had 10 battleships, 10 aircraft carriers, 38 cruisers, and 112 fleet destroyers, together with some 65 submarines. Many of these were armed with a new 24-inch torpedo with a 100-pound (45-kilogram) warhead.

The Japanese army consisted of 54 divisions. Thirteen of these faced the Red Army in Manchuria where a Japanese puppet state had been set up, but they were not yet engaged; since 13 April, when the Soviet-Japanese Non-Aggression Pact had been signed, the two nations had avoided going to war. Further south, the situation was different: 27 Japanese divisions were fighting the Nationalist Chinese forces under Chiang Kai-shek who, since the beginning of the war, had been supplied by the western allies via Burma and French Indochina.

Within two months of the fall of France, in June 1940, the Japanese had turned French Indochina into a vassal state and established military bases there that threatened the British colonies of Burma and Malaya, and the Dutch East Indies. This made relations with Britain and the United States, already strained because of the attempt to impose Japanese rule in China, even worse.

The Japanese prime minister, Prince Konoye, hoped for a diplomatic settlement and on 12 October he called a cabinet meeting to discuss the problem. The war minister, General Tojo, criticised Konoye's view that a diplomatic solution was possible and insisted that war was inevitable; the cabinet agreed and on 16 October they passed a vote of censure against the prime minister. Emperor Hirohito immediately appointed Tojo to take his place. At a second cabinet meeting on 1 November, it was decided to pursue negotiations but that failing a settlement by the end of the month Japan would go to war.

Ambassador Kurusu arrived in Washington for the negotiations on 16 November, and four days later tabled his proposals. The Americans made counter-proposals on 26 November – a week after the sinking of *Sydney* – calling for a complete Japanese withdrawal from China and Indochina. But it is clear that by now they, too, were convinced that war was bound to break out.

Whether or not the sinking of *Sydney* had been discussed at the American defence committee meeting of 25 November is not known. But on Sunday 7 December 1941 the Japanese launched their attack on the United States fleet in Pearl Harbor. And a dozen Japanese divisions began the lightning conquest of the Philippines, the East Indies, Malaya, Thailand and Burma.

Below: Japanese soldiers march triumphantly through Malaya. Singapore fell in February 1942

What information could have been contained in the suppressed telegram that would cause Roosevelt to break off negotiations and expect war with Japan?

covering letter sent with it from Churchill's private secretary to the senior officer on duty at the embassy. The letter reads: 'I enclose a Telegram from the Former Naval Person to the President for dispatch as soon as possible. I am so sorry to trouble you at this hour.' This suppressed telegram did transmit a vital piece of intelligence, for had it not done so the telegram could have been sent up to nine hours later, because of the time difference between London and Washington, and it would still have reached Roosevelt before the start of his next working day; therefore it must have contained intelligence that admitted no delay. This can scarcely correspond to the non-committal telegram now filed as having been sent on 26 November at 3.20am – the original must have been suppressed. What information could have been contained in the suppressed telegram that would cause Roosevelt to break off negotiations and expect war with Japan?

Given the eleven-hour time difference between Canberra and London, the Australian Naval Board had almost three clear days in which to convey its suspicions to London before Churchill passed them on to Roosevelt on 26 November. Churchill's aim in doing this would clearly have been to persuade Roosevelt that the Japanese were not negotiating in good faith and that America was therefore as much at risk from them as anyone else. The president's response represented the *de facto* commitment to enter the war on the Allies' side that Churchill had so long sought, and which Roosevelt had until now consistently refused to give him. If the sinking of *Sydney* did involve a Japanese submarine as well as *Kormoran*, as the evidence suggests, then it is easy to see why the authorities so readily accepted the unlikely story given by *Kormoran*'s officers. That the Japanese involvement, weeks before the declaration of war, was used to push Roosevelt into committing himself to enter the war on the side of the Allies would be something that everyone concerned in the affair would not want to become public knowledge.

A son's quest

One of the officers who was lost when *Sydney* went down was Lieutenant-Commander C. A. C. Montgomery. Montgomery was *Sydney*'s navigator and, like most of her officers, he had served throughout the ship's Mediterranean tour. His son Michael, just four years old when his father disappeared, has embarked on a quest to find out what really happened to the *Sydney*.

He began his research in Australia in 1977. Royal Australian Navy officers assured him that the loss of *Sydney* had been thoroughly investigated but he was encouraged to continue by the families and friends of his father's shipmates. The surviving officers of *Kormoran* were unhelpful, but over a period of four years he interviewed many of the ordinary seamen. Every one of them diverged from the official story in one or more important respects.

In London, Montgomery read the relevant files at the Ministry of Defence – but five of the most important were withheld. When he pursued the matter with his MP, he was given a reply from the Minister of State for Defence stating: 'The files concerned contain information which I am satisfied it would be in neither the Ministry of Defence nor the national interest to be disclosed publicly at present.'

Above: Captain J.A. Collins and navigating officer Lieutenant-Commander C.A.C. Montgomery

MURDER WITHOUT MOTIVE

Sir Jack Drummond, a well-known English scientist, his wife Ann and their ten-year-old daughter Elizabeth were on holiday in southern France in the summer of 1952 when they were discovered brutally murdered at their roadside camping spot. Despite an intensive investigation by the French police, no motive could be found for the violent killings. One family in particular emerged as the most likely suspects, but finding out which of its members had actually committed the murders proved difficult. Hampered by an energetic and impenetrable family conspiracy, the police had a tough job establishing any of the facts, and the uncertainty as to whether the right man was convicted still persists. This week *CLARE TAYLOR* examines the crime and reports on the investigations

Ann Drummond (right), née Wilbraham, the second wife of Sir Jack Drummond (below, far right). Following their murders and that of their daughter Elizabeth (below right) at the Grand'Terre farm (below), it was Sir Jack's first wife — from whom he had been divorced — who inherited his wealth. The ten-year-old Elizabeth had been her father's pride and joy; he wrote of her shortly before their last tragic holiday: 'She has always had a morbid fear of physical pain: she cannot bear the thought of an injection or a vaccination. She imagines fearful pains and sometimes wakes up in tears crying for help.' He added: 'She is wild with joy at the idea of the trip we are going to take to France'

IT had been a beautiful day, the weather was warm and the scenery impressive. Ahead of the travellers lay the valley of the Durance, but the evening was drawing in and it was time to find a suitable camping spot. Sir Jack Drummond, his wife Ann and their ten-year-old daughter Elizabeth were on holiday in France in the summer of 1952.

They were travelling back to Villefrance to rejoin some friends after attending a bullfight in Digne. The family had left Digne quite late and they had not gone far before it was time to settle down for the night. Sir Jack noticed a triangular patch of gravel just off the side of the road and decided that it was as good a place as any to set up camp. The site overlooked a farm called La Grand'Terre and Sir Jack thought that they may be able to get some provisions early in the morning before they set off again.

La Grand'Terre was the property of the Dominici family. Gaston Dominici, the 75-year-old patriarch of the family, had worked hard all his life to make something of the land

and was proud of his achievements, but he had relinquished the responsibility of farming the land to his nine children and now spent most of his time wandering over the hills with his goats. Water was scarce in this area during the summer and the local farmers had devised a system whereby they took it in turns to water their crops. The previous day it had been the turn of the Dominicis and the fields were watered by Gustave Dominici who, although not Gaston's eldest son, had taken over the running of the farm. Gustave had been over-anxious to give the land a good soaking and this had resulted in a heavy landslide onto the Marseilles–Digne railway line that skirted the farm. It had taken Gustave nearly a whole day to clear the track of mud and he had then gone to the nearest village to report the incident to the railway foreman, Faustin Roure. Roure had assured Gustave that he would inspect the area the following morning. Little did he realise the scene he would face.

At around 5.45 on the morning of 5 August factory worker Jean-Marie Olivier was riding home on his motorcycle after having completed his night shift. He was just passing the Dominici farm on the Route National 96 when Gustave Dominici ran out into the road and stopped him. Gustave was shouting and seemed to be in great distress; he told Olivier that there was a body on the bank of the river and he thought that there was murder involved. Olivier left immediately to inform the gendarmes in Oraison.

Faustin Roure arrived to survey the damage caused by the landslide at about 7am. He decided that it was not too serious and that he would return in the afternoon with a small party of workmen to clear the remaining mud from the track. Roure was walking back to the road when he met Clovis Dominici, the eldest son of Gaston and a plate-layer for the railway, with Marcel Boyer, another linesman. 'Have you seen it?' asked Clovis. Roure, assuming that he was referring to the landslide, told him that it was nothing to worry about. He then noticed that Clovis was staring at something on the bank. 'Look,' he said, 'she's dead.' A small girl lay on the bank, her head a mass of blood. After a moment all three returned to the road and it was there that they discovered the bodies of a man and a woman near to a car. Faustin Roure said that he had noticed the car on his arrival but thought nothing of the general clutter that surrounded it, assuming that the campers had simply gone down to the river to bathe or wash up.

Clovis Dominici and Boyer were riding their bicycles towards Grand'Terre, so Roure decided to follow to see whether the police had been informed and to ask the family if they had any idea about what had happened. By the time Roure reached the courtyard of the farm there was a spirited discussion going on between Clovis, his mother Marie, Gustave and his wife Yvette, and Boyer. Yvette announced that they had heard shots at about one in the morning, but had assumed they came from poachers. Roure asked if the police had been informed of the massacre and Clovis replied that Gustave had stopped a motorcyclist on the road earlier that morning and asked him to go for the police.

It was about 7.15am before the first policeman arrived at the scene of the crime. Police Sergeant Louis Romanet and

Right: Gaston Dominici, the patriarch of the Dominici clan. Below right: Gaston's daughter-in-law Yvette (left), wife of his son Gustave, with her ten-month-old son Alain and one of Gaston's daughters. They are sitting in the farmyard, two days after the murders were committed, watching the police investigation. Yvette told the police that she had been up feeding the baby when she heard the shots, and that the family had been too scared to venture forth and find out what had happened. This statement was not regarded as satisfactory by the police

Romanet was shocked when Gustave informed him that there was yet another body – on the bank of the river

a gendarme called Bouchier were approaching the scene when they were met by Aimé Perrin, whose brother was married to a Dominici daughter. The family had apparently grown anxious at the length of the time it was taking the police to arrive and had despatched a search party to see if they were coming. Once they reached the spot, Romanet began by examining the car. The green Hillman Estate had a GB plate and the registration number NNK 686. It was parked on the side of the road on a gravel patch underneath a larger mulberry tree. The inside of the car was in total disarray, but when the policeman examined the exterior of the vehicle he was surprised to find no obvious sign of any fingerprints. He did, however, notice a shred of flesh that had been caught in the rear bumper. Together with Bouchier, Romanet made a complete inventory of the articles lying around the car. It was obvious that whoever the occupants of the car had been, they had settled here for the night: there was a camp-bed with some rugs draped over it, two seats, a child's hat, some money and a note book with some English writing in it. Bouchier and Romanet then began examining the bodies of the victims.

The first body that they saw was that of a woman. She was partly covered by a rug which concealed the upper half of her body. The woman was in her forties, brown-haired and stockily built. She was wearing a red flowery dress and her arms and legs were bare. Under one arm there was a large bullet wound; rigor mortis had already set in – so she had been dead for some hours. The second body was that of a man, lying under a camp-bed on the other side of the road. He was about sixty and had thinning fair hair, a small moustache and a gaping bullet wound in his chest. Romanet carefully recorded the positions of the two bodies – a detail that was to prove very important in the ensuing investigations. The man was lying with his head towards La Brillanne in the direction of Marseilles; his body was hunched up and a trail of blood could be followed from a water

'He saved our babies'

The murdered Drummonds were no ordinary family of tourists. Sir Jack Drummond was a distinguished and well-known British scientist, famous for solving the nation's war-time dietary problems. British newspaper headlines announcing the Drummond murders proclaimed: HE SAVED OUR BABIES.

Jack Cecil Drummond was born in 1891. He followed an academic career and taught biochemistry at the University of London until 1939 when he joined the Ministry of Food. There he made a major contribution to the nation's war effort, first working on food rationing for armies in the field and then for the civilian population when Germany's invasion of Europe and blockade of Britain forced the country to rely on its own food production and whatever could be brought in from the United States.

Drummond's best-known – and most successful – innovations included the 'National Loaf' (a wheatmeal bread fortified with vitamin B and calcium salts); the introduction of free fruit juices in schools; the reorganisation of school meals to base them on vitamin content and the 'Drummond mixture'. This was a blend of pre-digested proteins, glucose and vitamins for intravenous injection. It saved the lives of many concentration camp victims who could not digest the food stuffs necessary to save them. In May 1945 Drummond himself travelled into Nazi-occupied Holland to give aid to the starving Dutch population.

At the end of the war Drummond was knighted, decorated by the Dutch and Americans and elected to the august institutions of his field of work. In 1946 he left government service to act as technical adviser to Boots the Chemist at their Nottinghamshire headquarters. He settled quietly in this county with his second wife, Ann, who was fifteen years his junior and one of his former students. They collaborated on a successful book, *The Englishman's Food*. In 1942 Ann gave birth to their daughter, Elizabeth.

sprinkler on the other side of the road where he had obviously tried to escape from his assailant. The woman was lying to the left of the car and at a right angle to it.

It was only after having taken down these details that Romanet became aware of the presence of Gustave Dominici. 'What a night,' said Gustave, 'We were very frightened.' The full significance of this remark took time to hit the policemen. Why should Gustave have been frightened? Had he seen something of the nocturnal happenings? Was he somehow involved in the incident? Romanet was shocked when Gustave informed him that there was yet another body — on the bank of the river.

As Romanet went down the stony path he noticed various objects strewn along the way and wondered if robbery had been the motive of the crime. He then came across the body of a young girl about ten years old, who was lying on her back, her arms and legs spreadeagled in the form of a cross. She had sustained the most appalling injuries to her head, which had been smashed by some kind of blunt instrument. She, too, had been dead for some time.

On the way back to the car Romanet discovered another notebook on the ground; this one bore an inscription on the first page, it read 'Drummond, Jack Cecil, Director, born 12 January, 1891, at New Caster'. Suddenly the whole affair turned into a matter of some urgency — the murder of three English tourists would attract far more attention than a local murder. It was essential that the Chief of the Forqualcier Police was informed of the situation right away. Romanet made the relevant telephone call and carried out another search of the immediate area, discovering several spent cartridge cases around the bodies as well as one undischarged bullet near to the water sprinkler. He soon identified these as having come from an American carbine. He also found some footprints down by the river, leading both to and from the body of the child.

By this time the murder spot was beginning to attract attention and passers-by were continuously having to be moved on. Gustave was still present and the policeman asked him for a preliminary statement. Gustave did not appear in the slightest bit worried and maintained a detached, distant manner throughout the entire interview. Police officers interviewing him in the following months were so infuriated by this attitude that some of them were tempted to strike him.

Gustave said that he had first seen the English family at about 8.30 the previous evening when he had gone down to check on the state of the railway line. He had passed the car but noticed nothing unusual. He had then returned home and gone to bed. Romanet asked him if he had heard any shots but Gustave avoided answering the question by telling him that at about 11.30 three people — a man, a woman and a child — had driven into the courtyard of the farm. The man had called out in some foreign language and Gustave said that he had ignored him because he did not understand what was said. The shouting did not persist so Gustave went back to sleep. The policeman asked again about the shots and Gustave told him that he had heard five or six shots coming from the Route National at about one in the morning but had not got up to investigate, as

he assumed they came from poachers' guns. He said that he had not discovered the body of the little girl until he had got up the following morning and had once again gone down to the railway track to make sure the bank had held through the night. It appeared to Romanet that Gustave did not seem terribly shocked by the sight of the girl's body. Gustave knew that her parents were camped only a short distance away and yet he did not rush to tell them what had happened to their daughter, or even to see if they themselves had come to any harm.

At 8.30am Police Doctor Dragon arrived and was busy examining the bodies when he noticed an old man strolling towards him, wearing dark velvet trousers, a striped shirt, and an old broad-brimmed hat. This was Gaston Dominici, a man whose distinctive appearance was to become well known to the public. Gaston told the doctor that he had been shocked by the events. He had first been informed of the murders by his daughter-in-law Yvette on his return from taking his goats to their grazing land in the mountains. When Dr Dragon told Gaston that there was another body on the river bank — that of a small girl — Gaston replied that the whole affair was horrible. He then strolled down to take a look at the body, returning only a few minutes later with the suggestion that the child's face should be covered as ants were crawling over her. Despite claiming to be shocked, the old man did not appear to be perturbed by what he had seen or by the fact that his land had been invaded by hordes of policemen. He simply leant against the mulberry tree and smoked his pipe.

The local police then sent for Superintendent Edmond Sébeille, a young officer who had a good record of success. He had headed fourteen murder investigations and had solved all of them. On 5 August 1952 he received a service telegram telling him that three bodies had been found at Lurs and that preliminary investigations had pointed towards robbery being the motive. A murder investigation is a very complicated affair – it takes four or five experienced officers to carry out a thorough investigation and in the middle of a holiday period four or five experienced officers were not easy to find. So although Sébeille received the communique at about 9.15am, he was not on his way to the scene of the crime until well after midday. The first few hours after a crime has been discovered are undoubtedly the most crucial, and in this case many important clues had been destroyed or rendered invalid due to the delay and the number of sightseers who had trampled the area by the time Sébeille arrived.

Once at the scene of the murders Edmond Sébeille quickly took stock of the situation. He confirmed that some cartridge cases that had been found had been fired from an American carbine, and allocated two officers to search the river in case it had been discarded there by the killer in the hope that the currents would carry it away. As Sébeille was examining the car Gustave Dominici approached him, introduced himself and pointed out that his fingerprints would probably be found on the car; he said that he had helped a policeman when the rear door had stuck. This struck Sébeille as being slightly odd, and when he questioned the officer in question later, the latter denied that anything of the kind had occurred. A thorough search of the area around the bodies uncovered a chip of wood from under the child's head. Sébeille was sure that it had come from the gun, thereby suggesting that the child had been beaten with the butt of the gun when her attacker realised that he had run out of bullets. The gun was later recovered from under the carcass of a sheep in the river.

It was indeed a carbine, from the Rock-Ola factory in Chicago. It was in an extremely poor condition, parts of it being held together by means of an aluminium ring more commonly used to fix identity tags on to bicycles. The fact that the gun was in such bad condition convinced Sébeille that the murderer was a native of the area – if a person had come into the area with the specific aim of murdering someone, he would have been expected to have at least carried a reasonable firearm. Sébeille was also convinced that now they had the murder weapon, the murderer would soon be caught. A gun like that was fairly easy to identify, and he felt sure that someone would soon recognise it – as he said, 'the gun will speak'. There was one fact, however,

Left: Gustave Dominici is sentenced to two months' imprisonment for having failed to give aid to a person – Elizabeth Drummond – in peril of death. Gustave, who ran the family farm and had been out early on the morning of 5 August, found the child's body on the riverbank – and apparently saw her arm move and heard a noise from her throat. But by the time help had arrived she was dead – and it was considered that Gustave Dominici had acted negligently. He faced no further charges, however, and the weight of incrimination eventually fell on his father, Gaston. Below left: Clovis Dominici leaves court after the sentence had been passed on his father. Clovis was the only member of the family to adhere to his original story

The wrong men

The Dominici family were by no means the only people the police were interested in in their hunt for the murderer of the Drummond family; they were following up numerous leads throughout the inquiry and their investigative net was cast as wide as possible. There was great excitement at the discovery of an abandoned uniform in a copse near to the murder scene. The uniform was quickly identified as belonging to a deserter from the French Foreign Legion. A search began immediately to find the owner but when he was located in his native Italy he was able to prove that he had been there since 15 July.

Soon after the murder a tramp, who had been seen spending foreign money in the cafes around Digne, came to the attention of the police. Fortunately for him he was able to prove that on the night in question he was almost 10 miles (16 kilometres) from Lurs. Another tramp who came under the same suspicions was able to prove his innocence by producing a railway ticket which he had failed to surrender – the ticket had been issued in Nice on 5 August.

An unsuccessful search was mounted for two men who had forced another British tourist to stop around Aix-en-Provence; they had threatened the man with revolvers but had been frightened off by the sounds of an approaching car.

This succession of false trails inevitably cast suspicion back on to the Dominicis themselves who seemed to know so much yet gave away so little.

that still bothered him; if the attacker had been a poacher, for example, why had the little girl run towards the river rather than towards the farm where she could have raised the alarm? The more Sébeille thought about it the more convinced he became that the murderer was not only a native of the area, but a member of the Dominici family.

There had been a number of curious things that had led Sébeille to conclude that one of the Dominicis was guilty. Gaston's behaviour had been extremely suspicious. He had been walking up the path with Sébeille after having

Above left: on the morning of 12 November 1953 the police surrounded the Dominici farm to carry out a reconstruction of the crime. The car (above) was re-sited at the original scene and the witnesses were called to re-enact their parts in the proceedings. Below left: the scene of the murder is unchanged today — the mulberry tree still stands and the occasional traveller still camps by the roadside

searched the area where the little girl had fallen, and as they approached the mulberry tree, Gaston had pointed to it with his stick and, obviously without thinking, said, 'There, that's where the woman fell. She didn't suffer.' Then, having noticed the policeman's surprise, he carried on, apparently unbothered, with the words: 'I say that, but I'm only supposing.' Another incident for which no reasonable explanation had been given took place when Officer Girolami, another member of the investigation team, went over to Grand'Terre to ask the family some questions. As he entered the farmyard he caught sight of a pair of trousers hanging on a wire line outside the house. They had only recently been washed as they were still dripping, and the police officer marvelled at the fact that life apparently went on as normal at the farm despite the upheaval at the end of the garden. His curiosity aroused, the policeman asked Gaston who did the washing at the farm. Gaston eventually told him that his eldest daughter collected the washing every week and took it home, bringing it back clean and dry. Girolami indicated to the trousers drying on the line, 'What about those?' he asked. Gaston looked slightly uncomfortable and told the policeman that he had better ask Gustave as the trousers had nothing to do with him. When Girolami asked Gustave about the trousers, he seemed puzzled. It took him a long time to answer the question, and when he eventually did it was only to say that he wore blue trousers and that his father wore velvet ones so they must belong to Gaston. Girolami was confused by this and reported it right away to the Superintendent. Sébeille was too busy to take much notice of what the officer was saying and decided that the incident bore no relevance, so it was not mentioned again.

The first solid indication the police had that the Dominici family were not telling the whole truth came when one of the police officers staged a watch on the farm throughout the night. Yvette had told the police in her statement that they had heard the shots at about one in the morning as she was feeding the baby, and that although the lights had been on the family had been too scared to look out of the window to see what was happening. This in itself was a curious statement — why would they have been scared if, as they had previously stated, they had assumed the shots had been fired by a poacher? On the night of the watch, however, no lights were seen in the farmhouse at any time. It was hardly likely that the baby had decided not to bother with an apparently customary early morning feed. If a child is used to receiving food at a certain time his or her stomach becomes a most reliable alarm clock. It was, therefore, far more reasonable to assume that the baby's parents had been up for some other reason on the night of the murders — perhaps because his father had in fact been out at the time, at the scene of the crime?

The first solid indication the police had that the Dominici family were not telling the whole truth came when one of the police officers staged a watch on the farm throughout the night

It soon became obvious to the police that at some stage between the discovery of the bodies and the arrival of the authorities the Dominici family had had a conference and had agreed unanimously on the story they were going to give the police. It looked distinctly as if each had formed an alibi for the other, making the entire evening's affair so

Below: a picture taken during the reconstruction of the Drummond murders. The chief suspect, Gaston Dominici, is seen holding his walking stick in one hand and the murder rifle in the other. A few minutes later Gaston astounded the police by taking off at a run and attempting a suicide leap from the railway bridge (right)

convoluted that it was almost impossible for the police to extract the truth from the web of lies.

Meanwhile Superintendent Sébeille remained convinced that the gun would eventually lead him to the murderer. He showed the gun to each member of the Dominici family and was told by each of them that it had never been seen before. Sébeille decided to stage a surprise for Clovis whom he had already discovered was not quite as much a part of the family as the others. In fact, it had come to light that Clovis and his father had had some fairly passionate arguments and that there was still a certain amount of animosity between the two men. The Superintendent placed the gun on top of a wall and covered it with a newspaper; he then called Clovis over and suddenly uncovered the gun in front of him. The result was astounding: Clovis fell to his knees, his mouth dropped open and his eyes opened wide in an expression of horror. Sébeille told Clovis that if he recognised the gun he must tell him to whom it belonged. It was fairly obvious that the sight of the gun had shocked Clovis, but to Sébeille's astonishment he said that he had never seen it before in his life. Clovis was then taken to the Perius town hall where he was interrogated to no avail for over two hours.

Meanwhile Gustave was having difficulty supporting his original statement. First, the police had discovered from a statement taken from Jean-Marie Olivier that Gustave had hailed him from *behind* the car; although Gustave still maintained that at this stage he had only just discovered the body of the child and had immediately run into the road some distance from the car to find someone to alert the police. Eventually Gustave admitted that he had been lying. He had discovered the body and had run towards the road, allowing the first vehicle he had seen to pass as it bore a Swiss number plate and probably had a foreign driver. He then started to walk towards the car when he saw Olivier coming along the road on his motorcycle. He was adamant he had hailed Olivier before he had reached the car.

Gradually the police were beginning to piece together the evidence for the investigation. It seemed to Sébeille that whichever direction he turned he was confronted with yet another lie from a member of the Dominici family. One of the most vital discrepancies in Gustave's story had come to light while the police were questioning a man by the name of Paul Maillet. Maillet had been the leader of the local Resistance group and had fallen under suspicion of the Drummond murders when the police had discovered some guns which he had kept hidden in his kitchen since the war. The police had promised to make things very difficult for him if he did not co-operate. Maillet said that he had gone to the farm to see if Yvette could sell him any potatoes. He had noticed that Gustave was looking very tired and drawn, and when Yvette went to check her stock Maillet asked Gustave if he was feeling all right. It was then, Maillet said, Gustave had told him that he had heard screams on the night of the murder and when he discovered Elizabeth the following morning the child had not been dead; in fact, it was the movement of her arm that had drawn his attention to her in the first place. He said that he had then heard a rattling sound coming from the child's throat and had gone over to her. There had been no further movement so he had gone back to the road and alerted the motorcyclist.

Sébeille wasted no time at all – he organised a confrontation between Maillet and Gustave Dominici. On 15 October 1952 the two men were brought to Digne's police station at six in the morning and interrogated separately.

Above: a member of the French Resistance, which continued to fight the Germans after the Occupation

The police even went to the extent of wrapping an officer in the rug to take the place of Lady Drummond's body

For the first few hours Gustave denied that the child had been alive when he first saw her, but when he was confronted with Maillet he eventually admitted that it was true. The foundations of his story were beginning to crumble. Gustave was formally charged with having failed to give aid to a person in peril of death. He was tried, found guilty and sentenced to two months' imprisonment and the equivalent of about £5 costs. Gustave admitted nothing more during his internment. He was released on 16 December having completed his sentence.

More than a year after the murders had been committed the police were not really any further forward in their investigations than they were on the morning of the discovery of the crime. Sébeille decided that the time had come to stage a reconstruction at the scene, in the hope that it might jog someone's memory. The Dominicis, he decided, were to be the last people to know of this action – surprise could prove to be the essential element in the proceedings.

The date was set for 12 November 1953, a day that dawned cold and grey. Barriers were erected each side of the area and all traffic unconnected with the case was diverted away from the area. The Drummonds' motor car was driven to the spot and parked where the family had camped. The articles that had been scattered along the path and around the car were present and the camp-beds were placed where they had been found by the police. The police even went to the extent of wrapping an officer in the rug to take the place of Lady Drummond's body. All the witnesses had been called, including one Jean Ricard who had not been questioned since the morning of the murders. Along with Ricard there were Sergeant Romanet and Gendarme Bouchier, Faustin Roure and Jean-Marie Olivier. Roure was the first to be accompanied to the scene; he followed the course that he had taken the morning of the crime and commented on the position of the body. It was, he said, in exactly the same position as he had seen Lady Drummond – parallel to the car and covered by the rug.

Next it was the turn of Jean Ricard, who on the morning of 5 August had been walking along the road to catch his bus. He had noticed the disarray surrounding the car, had gone for a closer look and had also seen the body lying parallel to the car. The two policeman, however, were equally sure that when they first saw the body it had been lying at right angles to the car. Lady Drummond's body had obviously been moved between the time of its supposed discovery at 7am and the time of the arrival of the police at 7.30am.

During this time the police had gone to fetch Clovis Dominici who had been working at the railway station in Lurs. If the Dominici story was to be believed, Clovis had first seen the body at 7am in the morning and Sébeille now asked him if the body was lying at the correct angle. Clovis was looking very anxious by this stage, as though he was not quite sure of what to say for the best. Eventually he told the police officer that the body had been lying at right angles to the car when he had first seen it – thereby contradicting the other witnesses. When Clovis was confronted with the other witnesses he became unsure of his story and

Secret weapons

The American carbine that was used to kill the Drummond family was a relic of the Second World War. How did it fall into the hands of the Dominici family?

Although much of France was effectively occupied after the armistice of 1940 in the Second World War, many of the French continued to fight the German invaders. General Charles de Gaulle, undersecretary of state for war, escaped to England in 1940 to form the Free French movement. The movement grew over the next few months, and made connections with the various Resistance groups that had sprung up in France. As the groups gained in strength arms, ammunition and money were dropped to the Resistance fighters. These illicit arms became even more abundant when the American troops passed through the area during the Liberation.

The 45th US Infantry Division was the first to reach the region on their way along Napoleon's route to Grenoble. The soldiers were tired and hungry and were more than willing to exchange their guns and hand-grenades for the comforts of life they had been without for many months. And so it was that the local farmers acquired guns in exchange for eggs, and hand-grenades for perhaps a bottle of wine or a chicken. These arms lay hidden in the barns and outhouses of the farms, used by a few of the farmers for an evening's poaching but ignored by many others for fear of discovery. The gun in the Drummond murder case was almost certainly one of these.

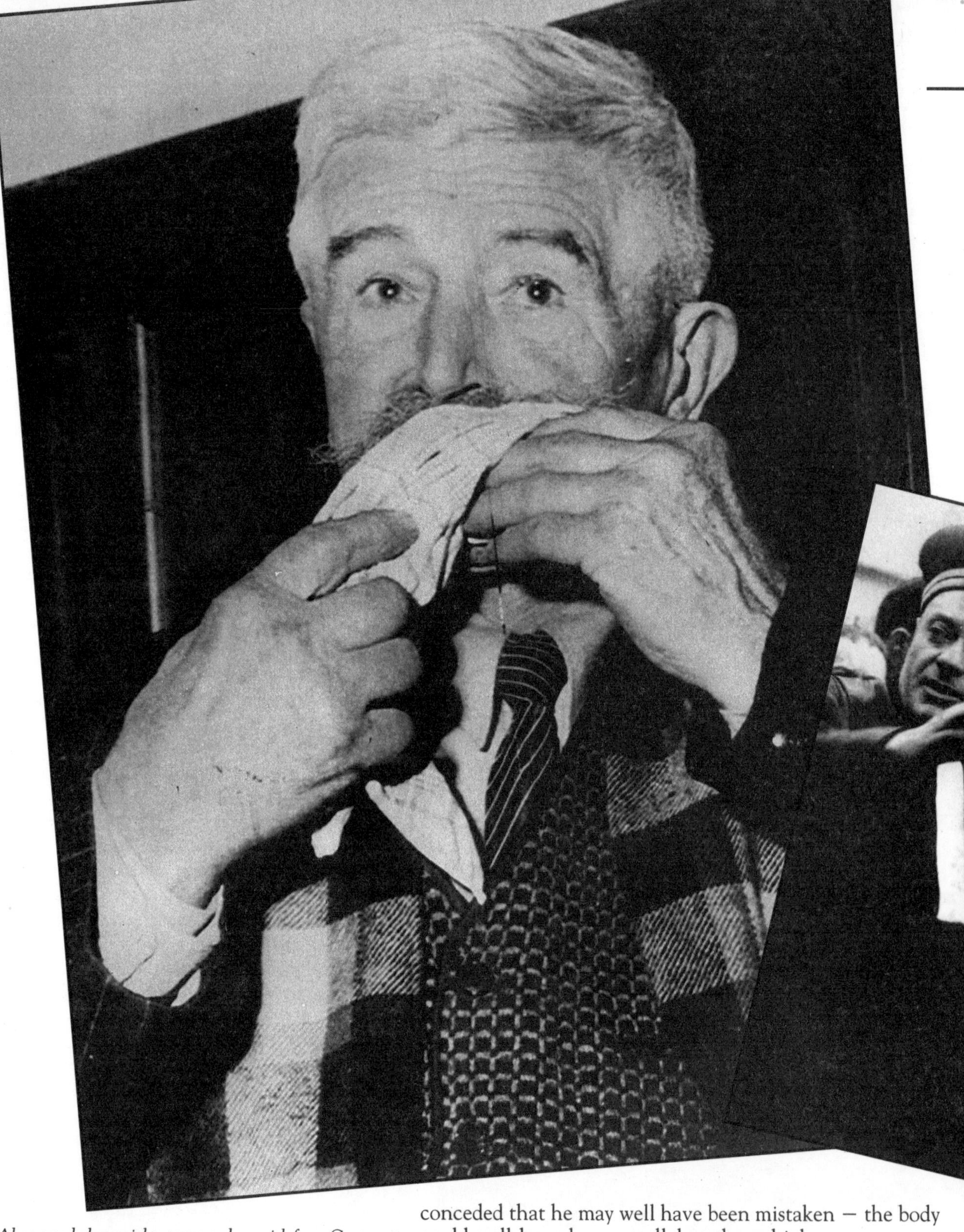

Above and above right: tears and anguish from Gaston Dominici during his trial. The old man was capable of controlling his emotions to his advantage and of winning the jury's sympathy

conceded that he may well have been mistaken — the body could well have been parallel to the vehicle.

Gustave Dominici was then brought from Grand'Terre to the scene of the crime. Jean-Marie Olivier was asked to ride around the bend in the road as he had on the morning of 5 August and Gustave was told to show the police exactly where he had stopped Olivier. Gustave walked some distance from the car and when Olivier came around the bend began waving his arms to attract his attention. Olivier showed a gesture of annoyance and skidded to a halt, claiming that Gustave had been nowhere near the place where he had stood on the morning of the crime. Olivier walked back towards the car and stopped just in front of the Hillman's bonnet. It was

Sébeille was convinced that, at last, after months of failure, he was going to receive a confession from Gustave

here, he said, that Gustave had waved him down. When Sébeille gave Gustave the rug and told him to place it where he had first seen it, Gustave lost his temper and refused point blank to do so. Sébeille threw the rug at him and informed him that he had no choice in the matter; he would remain at the murder spot all day if necessary. Eventually Gustave agreed and positioned the rug by the ditch where he claimed to have discovered the body – at right angles to the car. As far as Sébeille was concerned this was the evidence he needed to convince him that it had been Gustave who had moved the body on that morning. It was already obvious that Gustave had lied about his position in relation to the car when he had stopped Olivier. Whatever Gustave had heard, seen or done that night, the time had come for him to be subjected to some serious questioning. He was accompanied to the farm to get a jacket and his family's reaction to his being taken in for questioning was one of apparent panic. Gaston lost all sense of calm, cursing everyone. Yvette and Gustave's mother sobbed in the kitchen, and when it was announced that Clovis was also to be questioned there was further hysteria.

The interview took place at the Palais de Justice in Digne. Gustave was led to the library and Sébeille questioned him solidly for twelve hours during which time Gustave admitted that he had lied about not hearing the screams, but had not told the police as he had not wanted any trouble. He also admitted that it was he who had moved the body of Lady Drummond. Sébeille was quite satisfied with the outcome of the interview and after he was sure that Gustave was not going to reveal anything further he allowed the man to have something to eat and to sleep until the following day. The questioning recommenced early the next morning – the policeman was still not happy with the reasons Gustave had given for moving the body. Gustave had said that he had moved the woman's body to discover whether or not she was still breathing. Sébeille was not convinced by this as Gustave had not thought it necessary to do the same with Sir Jack's body when he had discovered that. After Gustave had been questioned quite extensively about this, Sébeille was not surprised when the witness slumped back into his chair, his eyes filled with tears and he broke down. Sébeille was convinced that, at last, after months of failure, he was going to receive a confession from Gustave. When Gustave spoke, however, it was not to admit his own guilt, but rather to condemn his father.

Gradually Gustave told his version of the events that took place that August night. He told Sébeille that he had heard the shots at one in the morning. He was unable to go back to sleep afterwards and had gone downstairs when he heard his father getting ready to take the goats to the mountain. He had asked Gaston whether he had heard the shots and Gaston replied that it was he who had fired them. Gustave said that he had asked his father what he had been doing. Gaston replied that he had gone out to do some poaching, had got into an argument with the man and had ended up shooting the entire family. Sébeille was stunned; this was not what he had expected at all. He took

Above: the accused, in the dock, listens to the speech of his counsel, Mr Pollak. Above right: Judge Périès (standing) consults the Procureur de la Republique Mr Sabatier. Right: during the trial the advocate general Calixte Rozan was equipped with a loud-speaker system with which to make his speech, as he had lost his voice

Gaston said that he had been shocked and scared by Sir Jack and had begun to shoot indiscriminately, killing the entire family

Gustave straight down to the magistrate's office where the still sobbing man made his formal confession. It took Gustave a while to sign the written account of the admission and after he had the magistrate started questioning him about some points on which he thought Gustave was rather vague. He asked if Gustave had known about the gun but Gustave still maintained that he was ignorant of its existence. The magistrate also found it hard to believe that Gustave had spent two months in prison to protect his father. When he asked Gustave whether or not his father had thanked him for this Gustave shouted bitterly that the old man did not care who went to prison for him. Gustave also told the police that Clovis was aware of the fact that his father was the murderer, but had, like him, been sworn to secrecy.

When Clovis was brought before the police, he too broke down and admitted that his father had told him that he had murdered the campers but, unlike Gustave, he said that he had known of the existence of the gun, which he had seen in a shed on the farm some years earlier.

On Friday 13 November the police went to Grand'Terre to arrest Gaston, who was taken to the same place as his sons and subjected to the same questions as them. Gaston remained adamant about his innocence and appeared distraught when Sébeille told him that both his sons had accused him of the murders. Both Gaston's sons were presented to him during the day and both of them repeated their accusations to his face — Clovis with a sad confidence, and Gustave with a great deal of hesitation and stam-

mering. The questioning went on until the following day.

A young policeman called Victor Guérino was appointed to guard Gustave. He had been chatting with Gustave for a while when he noticed that the old man was crying. Guérino asked him what was wrong and could not believe his ears when the old man replied that he was crying because his sons had told the truth. It was he who was the murderer. The police officer kept quiet while the old man poured out his tale. He had, he said, taken a walk that morning to check the state of the railway line as he was worried the landslide might cause an accident. As he approached the Drummonds' camping site the man had taken him for an intruder and attacked him. Gaston said that he had been shocked and scared by Sir Jack and had begun to shoot indiscriminately, killing the entire family.

Guérino knew that he must get this information to his superiors as soon as possible before the old man composed himself and denied the story. Gaston refused to tell Sébeille his story but he would, he said, tell the magistrate what had happened. The magistrate was sent for and Gaston repeated his confession to him, developing the story. He had hidden behind the mulberry tree and watched Lady Drummond undress. Sir Jack had spotted him and it was this that caused the argument. Eventually Gaston agreed to tell his story to Sébeille and further embellished the tale. Gaston had gone out with the sole intention of watching Lady Drummond; he had got as far as touching her before he was spotted. Gaston appeared to be quite at ease with his story and was not really worried by the prospect of going to prison. He asked for and was assured receipt of some wine, some tobacco and a rather large amount of money from the farm. He spent a comfortable night in the Palais de Justice and was apparently unperturbed when he was informed the following morning that there was to be a further reconstruction of the crime, following which the magistrate would decide whether or not to charge him.

Once again Route 96 was closed to unrelated traffic, and this time the police hoped it would be the last time that it would be closed in connection with the Drummond murders.

There were still a few points of fact to clarify; for instance, was Gaston capable of chasing a young girl fast enough to catch her? The first priority, though, was to establish exactly where the murder weapon had been hidden on the farm since the war. Gaston led them to a shed near the forge on the farm and took them inside, pointing out the shelves where he had originally kept the gun. This complied with the evidence given by Clovis and also Gustave — who had once again changed his story and admitted that he had seen the gun before in the shed where the farm implements were stored. Gaston then led the police to the scene of the murders, to re-enact them. The police took the part of the victims with Dominici telling each of them what to do. When it came to the killing of the child one officer took off at a run towards the river with Gaston following at a sedate walking pace. When he was ordered to run as he had on the night of the crime, the old man took off at such speed that for a moment the officers did not realise what was happening.

Below: the murder weapon, found at the scene of the crime. The gun was an American carbine, and the magazine held fifteen rounds. Three shots were fired at Sir Jack and three more were needlessly ejected; another four shots were fired at Lady Drummond, with four more ejected, making a total of fourteen, which along with the one cartridge found jammed in the gun accounts for all fifteen. However, only four cartridges were recovered from the scene of the crime — two fired and two unfired — so where had the other cartridges gone? Had the murderer taken them with him, or had Gustave removed them during one of his dawn visits to the site? Right: the old man, a picture of composure, is led into the courtroom at the start of his trial. Below right: Marie, wife of Gaston, and his daughter-in-law Yvette leave the court house in Digne during an intermission in the trial

Rather than running over the railway bridge Gaston was running towards the edge of the bridge with the obvious intention of hurling himself onto the track below. He was caught just in time and for the police any doubts that he was guilty were dispelled. They were further convinced by the way Gaston used the gun that he was apparently unaware, as the murderer had been, that the gun was in fact a semi-automatic and that he had wasted a cartridge every time he had reloaded.

Gaston was therefore charged with the murder of the Drummond family and was taken to the prison in Digne. The police were more or less satisfied that they had caught the murderer, even if there were still a few points of contention in the old man's statement. None of the police really believed that Gaston had actually had any kind of sexual contact with Lady Drummond; they thought it much more likely that Sir Jack had challenged him, having taken him for a robber. Also the police doctors were of the opinion that Elizabeth had been hit several times while she was lying on the ground, while Gaston had said during the reconstruction that he had hit her only once while she was kneeling on the ground. Gaston also said that he had only shot Ann Drummond once, while the evidence showed that she had been hit by three bullets, not one.

The police should have realised that nothing would be that simple where the Dominici family was concerned. Gaston talked to his lawyers, and by the time the case came

to court he had taken a leaf from his son Gustave's book and changed his story. He had, he said, gone to bed early on the night in question, had risen at 4am to take his goats to the mountain and was unaware of any crime until his return home at 8am.

Meanwhile Gustave had succumbed to family pressure and had also retracted the statement in which he had accused his father of the murders. Clovis was the only member of the family to stick to his original story, even though this course of action caused him to be ousted from the safety of the Dominici family's protective circle.

The date of Gaston's trial before the Basses-Alpes Assizes at Digne was set for the 17 November 1954, over two years after the crime had been committed. It was a particularly arduous trial, especially since those present were still being forced to contend with the lies of Gustave and displays of fury from his father. The trial lasted for eleven days and nobody was sorry when the jury retired to consider their verdict. When the verdict was read out, the court was packed with people, most of whom did not doubt in their own minds that the old man was guilty, and it was no surprise when the jury returned the same verdict. Gaston was sentenced to death and was led stunned from the court room. As he passed his lawyers he leant towards them and reaffirmed his innocence: he had confessed only to protect his sons, he was an old man and it was better for him to spend what little was left of his own life in prison than to condemn his sons to perhaps fifty years of internment.

As soon as Gaston had been taken to Les Baumettes Prison an appeal was made by his defence lawyers. They claimed that Gaston had revealed some important evidence from his cell. An order was made for Gaston to be questioned in the prison and members of the Paris Sûreté went to Digne to carry out further investigations. Gaston's lawyers insisted that the evidence disclosed by their client was crucial and demanded a confrontation between Gaston and Gustave as soon as possible. The meeting of the two men took place on 8 March 1955.

Gaston claimed that a few days after the murders he had overheard a conversation between Gustave and Yvette, in which the word jewellery was mentioned and the death of the child referred to. Gustave denied that such a conversation had ever taken place, and to any other questions he simply replied: 'I know nothing, and my father is innocent.' He offered no explanation as to why his father should have made a new statement and apparently none was asked for. No official record was made of this confrontation between Gaston and Gustave: yet another blunder by the police. They had already erred in the matter of the shred of flesh that was found on the car bumper, and thought to have been torn from Sir Jack's hand in his efforts to escape his murderer; this was assumed to have been lost between the scene of the crime and the police laboratories until Sébeille admitted in his memoirs that he had actually kept the flesh as a memento of the case. The police had also assumed that the murderer had wasted one cartridge in two because he was not aware of how to use the gun, but subsequent investigations have shown that there was in fact some obstruction in the weapon preventing the other

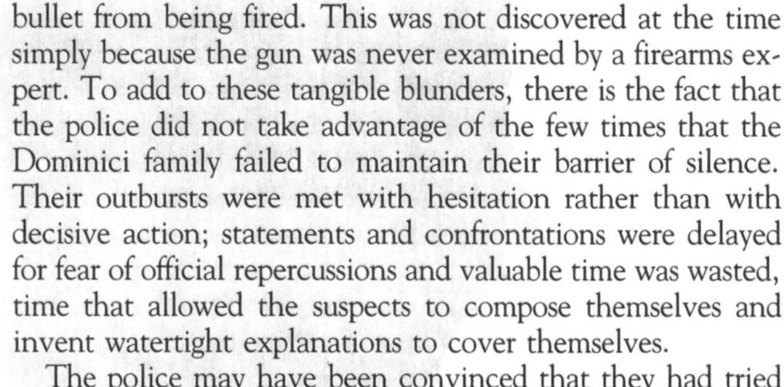

bullet from being fired. This was not discovered at the time simply because the gun was never examined by a firearms expert. To add to these tangible blunders, there is the fact that the police did not take advantage of the few times that the Dominici family failed to maintain their barrier of silence. Their outbursts were met with hesitation rather than with decisive action; statements and confrontations were delayed for fear of official repercussions and valuable time was wasted, time that allowed the suspects to compose themselves and invent watertight explanations to cover themselves.

The police may have been convinced that they had tried and convicted the right man but the public certainly was not. In 1960 a television station interviewed Gaston in his prison cell; the old man once more pleaded his innocence and one very important viewer was convinced by what he saw. President Charles de Gaulle issued a statement of clemency soon after the programme, offering no explanation of his motions but using his prerogative of silence.

Gaston thus ended his days a free man, not at Grand' Terre, but living comfortably in an old peoples' home nearby. Gustave and Yvette sold the farm to a hotelier but the business failed and the 'rooms vacant' sign now hangs creaking in the wind. The mulberry tree still stands on the roadside by the gravel patch; it is thicker and more gnarled today than it was then but it still offers shelter to the odd passer-by. The scene has not changed, and neither have the opinions of the local people; they still believe that the true murderer of the Drummonds escaped. Even the Superintendent at the Marseille Gendarmeria is prepared to say that he felt Gaston was innocent. But the surviving Dominicis continue to maintain a stubborn silence.

Below: a picture of Gustave Dominici taken in 1967 after his divorce from Yvette. Bottom: Gaston Dominici on his release in 1960. Bottom right: a fitting epitaph – 'They were lovely and pleasant in their lives and in their death they were not divided.' The grave of the Drummond family in the cemetery at Forcalquier

HOMICIDE IN HOLLYWOOD

The killing of film director William Desmond Taylor, whose body was discovered by his manservant in his Los Angeles bungalow on the morning of 22 February 1922, shocked the Hollywood community. Within hours Taylor's studio, Famous Players-Lasky, fearing a major scandal, had instigated a cover-up. Vital clues went missing and the case was never solved. Who killed Taylor, a debonair ladies' man with a shady past? Was he shot by an assassin hired by a drugs ring? What was the involvement of Taylor's brother and of Mrs Shelby, the mother of film star Mary Miles Minter? *JACK LODGE* unravels the most baffling of Hollywood's murder mysteries

CLASSICAL murder mysteries seldom occur in real life; the necessary ingredients are lacking. There must be a generous cast of suspects, a variety of motives, people who are not what they have always seemed to be, an alibi or two, some macabre element in the actual crime. Real murders are usually nasty, brutal . . . and dull. But with the killing of William Desmond Taylor on 21 February 1922 reality made amends. It was an affair worthy of Raymond Chandler, but sadly no Philip Marlowe ever walked the Hollywood streets to solve it.

In 1922 William Desmond Taylor was a leading director at the Famous Players-Lasky studio, the producing arm of Paramount Pictures. He had been in the industry since 1914, had made his name with a popular serial, *The Diamond From the Sky*, and moved on to features. He directed the last three films that Mary Pickford made before she left Famous Players in 1919, and when the studio tried to build up their new blonde *ingénue*, Mary Miles Minter, into a second Pickford, it was natural that Taylor be allotted her films, too. In all, Taylor and Minter completed four films together. Taylor had become a distinctive figure in the film capital. No one knew much about his origins, but he was English, sophisticated, a bit of an intellectual, and a ladies' man. Later on, the columnist Adela Rogers St John would describe him as 'the sort of man that revived your faith in the sex'. He could clearly have been a star himself, had he chosen. In fact, he did act a little at the start of his career, playing the lead in Vitagraph's *Captain Alvarez* in 1914. That brief appearance before the cameras would have certain repercussions, but by 1922 it was well behind him. He was firmly settled as a prosperous director, and living in a bungalow court on Alvarado Street, in the Westlake Park district of Los Angeles.

On the morning of 22 February 1922, at around 7.30, Taylor's manservant Henry Peavey entered the bungalow's living room, and found his master lying on the floor, dead. A chair had fallen across his legs. Taylor's face was composed. His body lay straight, his arms at his sides. Someone had laid out an impressive tableau, its good taste marred only by the chair.

When police examined the body, it was found that Taylor had been shot. The bullet – from a ·38 revolver – had passed through his right lung and lodged in his neck. The bullet holes in his clothing did not match with the one in the body – the result, and the proof, of the killer's careful tidying up. And at this early stage, robbery could be ruled out. Taylor was still wearing his gold watch, worth $2000, and a diamond ring, and had $75 in cash on him. The police proceeded to interrogate Henry Peavey.

Peavey described what he knew of the previous evening. At 6.30 he had told Taylor that dinner was ready. At that time Taylor was working on his income tax forms. During dinner the telephone rang, and while Taylor was on the telephone, the film star Mabel Normand arrived. According to Normand, Taylor had rung her in the afternoon and told her that he now had a book that he had promised to get for her. She was, in fact, doing a course in reading under Taylor's guidance. Taylor told her that the telephone call

Left: William Desmond Taylor (left) on set with Mary Miles Minter. In 1922 Taylor was a successful and well-to-do director at the Famous Players-Lasky studio where he directed four films starring Minter, the Famous Players replacement for Mary Pickford, who had left them in 1919. On 21 February 1922 Taylor was murdered, and the scandal arising from this unsolved crime and the liaisons with several women that it exposed had dire consequences – not least for Mary Miles Minter herself. Although the sophisticated Taylor could have pursued an acting career, he chose to appear in only one film – Vitagraph's Captain Alvarez *(below), made in 1914. In view of his mysterious past, Taylor may have later felt it wiser to achieve success in a way that did not involve displaying himself to the public on the cinema screen*

concerned his tax, but the actor Antonio Moreno later claimed that he had rung Taylor at this time. In any case, Normand was still there when Henry Peavey left at 7.30. Normand filled in a little more: she had stayed only until 7.45 and Taylor had walked with her to her car, leaving the front door open. He was in an extremely cheerful mood, teasing her as she left about her carrying a volume of Nietzche under one arm and one of Freud under the other, and obviously going in for some heavy reading that winter. Studio publicity men reissued this tit-bit, but not wishing to give audiences the impression that the delectable comedienne was too much of a blue-stocking, they tactfully changed Freud to Ethel M. Dell. As Normand left, Taylor said that he would ring her in an hour. He did not do so.

Below: William Desmond Taylor's house in a bungalow court on Alvarado Street in the Westlake Park district of Los Angeles. The urbane Taylor led a most comfortable life (bottom) and was very attractive to women

Two other celebrated movie figures lived in that court. One was Charles Chaplin's leading lady, Edna Purviance. According to some accounts, it was she who had introduced her friend Mabel Normand to Taylor the previous year. Now Miss Purviance said that she had noticed that at some time after midnight the light in Taylor's bungalow was still on. Beyond that, she had seen and heard nothing. But opposite Taylor's house lived the actor/producer Douglas MacLean, a very popular light comedian of the Twenties, and his wife Faith. The MacLeans had seen and heard quite a lot. Between 8pm and 8.15 there had been what they described as 'a shattering report' from the Taylor house (no one else seems to have heard this noise). Faith MacLean went to her window and saw a figure emerge from Taylor's bungalow. The figure wore a cap and muffler, and Mrs MacLean was unable to determine its sex, but thought that it had an effeminate walk.

Attempts to trace this person's moves were inconclusive,

but reports came in of a man who had boarded a street-car in nearby Maryland Street at 8.30. He was said to have been about 26 years of age, with dark hair and light complexion, and to have been wearing a cap and a dark suit. And attendants at a petrol station in the area said that a man had asked them for directions to Alvarado Street at around 7.30. Richly suggestive as all this was, the trail petered out.

Told in a telephone call from Edna Purviance of what had happened, Mabel Normand went to the bungalow. She made contradictory statements about her reasons, saying first that she went there to recover her letters to Taylor, fearing that 'terms of affection might be misconstrued', but later that she had gone simply to help the police, for with her knowledge of the household she could see whether furniture or anything else had been disturbed. She found none of her letters, but later missives from sundry ladies were discovered concealed in a riding-boot (which turned out to belong to Mabel Normand). Taylor seemed to have been conducting a number of affairs, but these letters were returned to their writers, and the investigators declared them irrelevant to the case. Taylor's library yielded a more interesting find — a breathless letter from his recent star, Mary Miles Minter. A handkerchief embroidered 'MMM' also came to light, and with the letters in the boot there was a monogrammed pink nightgown. There is some dispute about this nightgown, for when the case was reopened years later Miss Minter vehemently denied that the nightdress had ever been in Taylor's bedroom. This was in 1937, and by that time, relevant evidence or not, the nightdress had been

Below: Mabel Normand, one of Taylor's most intimate female friends, surrounded by young suitors in Samuel Goldwyn's 1920 film The Slim Princess, *directed by Victor Schertzinger. Mabel was the first great Hollywood screen comedienne and she helped to spot and develop the talents of men like Charles Chaplin and Roscoe 'Fatty' Arbuckle. Her own career was ruined by drug-dependency and the scandals surrounding the murders of Taylor and Hollywood millionaire Cortland S. Dines in 1923*

Tom Ince's last voyage

Just two years after William Desmond Taylor's death, Hollywood was shocked by the passing of another, greater film-maker. By 1924 Thomas Harper Ince, pioneer director and producer, was not quite the dominating figure in the industry that he had been a decade earlier, but he was still big enough for newspaper tycoon William Randolph Hearst to want him for Cosmopolitan Pictures, a concern that Hearst had founded mainly to produce films starring his mistress, Marion Davies (a brilliant comedienne who didn't in the least need a rich man's patronage). Ince for his part wanted the rights to certain stories published in Hearst's *Cosmopolitan* magazine. Hearst had also invited Ince to a weekend party on his yacht, the *Oneida*. Because Ince had to attend a premiere, he arranged to take the night train to San Diego and join the yacht there. He would be on board in time to celebrate his 43rd birthday on Sunday 16 November. Mrs Ince did not accompany her husband.

On the Monday Mrs Ince received a telephone call asking her to come at once to Del Mar, a town thirty miles north of San Diego, where her husband was lying ill. The caller was Dr Daniel Carson Goodman, head of Cosmopolitan Pictures and a guest on the yacht. Ince had apparently suffered some form of heart attack. Mrs Ince went to Del Mar, with her son Bill and the family physician, one Dr Glasgow. Glasgow took over from the local doctor who had been called, and arranged for Ince to return home in a private car attached to the Los Angeles train. Ince reached his house in Benedict Canyon, but at 5.30am on the Wednesday, he died. His body was cremated – and then the rumours started.

Gossip spoke of heavy drinking on the yacht. As this was during the Prohibition period, it was perhaps not surprising. But there was also rumour of some involvement of Hearst in Ince's death, and even, remarkably, of a shooting. The District Attorney of San Diego, Chester Kemply, felt obliged to investigate. It was in Kemply's power to still the rumours for good, if they were false, or to take action if there was any evidence of crime. But he made the fatal error of calling only one witness from the yacht – Dr Goodman, an employee of Hearst – and of declaring himself satisfied on his evidence alone that there had been no foul play.

Goodman's story was simple and totally credible. All it lacked was support from the other guests. On the Sunday, said Goodman, Ince had complained of tiredness, had discussed the production agreement with Hearst, and retired early. On the Monday, Ince and Goodman had risen before the other guests to catch the train for Los Angeles. Ince had suffered from indigestion during the night, and on the way to the station had felt a pain in his heart. This became worse, and Goodman took Ince from the train at Del Mar and to a hotel. Goodman summoned the local doctor, Truman Parker, and stayed until the afternoon. Ince said these attacks were an old story with him. Goodman suspected acute indigestion. Ince told Parker that he had

Above, from left to right: Thomas Harper Ince in 1916 — Ince died suddenly after a weekend on William Randolph Hearst's yacht; Hearst's mistress Marion Davies (right) and Charles Chaplin (with Gloria Swanson) were also aboard; Davies and Hearst in 1951

eaten and drunk a good deal on the Sunday, and Parker diagnosed a heart attack. Then Mrs Ince and her doctor arrived.

The account that gossiping tongues spread was rather different. The most lurid version suggested that Hearst suspected another guest, Charles Chaplin, of conducting an affair with Marion Davies, that he caught the couple together, fired a shot at Chaplin, and hit Ince by mistake. This take was given renewed life when it appeared in Kenneth Anger's scurrilous book *Hollywood Babylon* (1975), but the only supporting evidence was that a secretary of Chaplin's was said to have observed a bullet hole in Ince's head as he was carried off the yacht. It is fair to add that Anger does not wholly accept the tale, but it is disturbing that in as scholarly a work as Ephraim Katz's *International Film Encyclopedia* (1979) it is categorically stated that 'Ince was mysteriously and fatally injured aboard William Randolph Hearst's yacht'.

These books have been widely read. Far less widely read was an article in a relatively obscure film buff's magazine, *The Silent Picture*, for this piece should have settled the Ince affair for good and all. It consisted of a letter, printed in the magazine's sixth number, in 1970, and written some years before, by Mrs Ince herself, to the film historian George Pratt of the Eastman House film archive. Elinor Ince says that she is writing 'owing to the many rumours and false statements and ignorant gossip regarding Mr Ince's death'. She supports Goodman, with added details. She did not accompany Ince because one of their sons was taken ill at the last moment. Ince told her before he died that he had drunk a certain amount, against his doctor's orders (he suffered from an ulcer). He said, too, that contracts for the deal with Hearst had been arranged. Furthermore, Mrs Ince refers to an examination of the body carried out under the eye of the Los Angeles Chief of Homicide. No marks of any kind were found.

Not even the powerful Hearst, surely, could have contrived a cover-up of such proportions. But, conversely, it is easy to see how enemies of Hearst — and he had many — could have seen in the events of that weekend with its sad consequence a splendid opportunity to spread a little poison. And in a gossip-ridden atmosphere a little poison could spread a very long way.

Thomas Ince, the man who made movies as good as *The Italian*, and *Civilization*, and *Hell's Hinges*, deserves, at last, a little peace.

Below: film star Edna Purviance, who lived in the same bungalow court as William Desmond Taylor and who had rung their mutual friend, Mabel Normand, to warn her of Taylor's death and the presence of the police in his house. Edna was Charles Chaplin's leading lady between 1915 and 1923 and the pair were lovers for a brief period in 1916. Right: the ecstatic and compromising love-note from actress Mary Miles Minter that was found in Taylor's library. Below right: Mary Miles Minter, Famous Players' darling, whose career was shattered by her association with the murdered director

lost, and may indeed be part of the mythology that grows up around such sensations.

The police investigated Taylor next, and what they turned up stood the case on its head. For William Desmond Taylor was indeed a William, but he was not a Desmond Taylor. The police discovered that he was William Deane Tanner, vice-president of the English Antique Shop in New York City, a man who had vanished without trace on 26 October 1908, leaving a wife and daughter behind him. A certain amount of his earlier history became clear. He was born in County Cork in Ireland in 1877 and educated at Clifton College in England. By 1895 he was working in the theatre in Manchester. He next turned up in Kansas, possibly shipped abroad by a respectable family alarmed at the way the boy was turning out. He then made his way to New York and entered the antique business. He married Ethel May Harrison, and her uncle helped him to establish himself in business. 'Taylor' paid off this debt before his disappearance. Some of this history corresponds with the accounts of Taylor's career issued by the studio as routine publicity.

Dearest –
I love you – I love you – I love you – – –
XXXXXXXXX
X
Yours always!
Mary

This had him born in 1877, at Mallows in Cork, made him son of an English colonel and an Irish girl, and agreed on Kansas, but also claimed that he took part in the Alaska Gold Rush of 1898, served as a private in the Canadian army, and rose to captain.

Just before Taylor vanished from New York he had been to see the Vanderbilt Cup yacht race at Newport, gone on some kind of spree lasting a week, then returned, taken $500 from his office, and disappeared.

There are scattered indications of Taylor's whereabouts in the years between 1908 and his entry into films. At one time he was stage manager of a vaudeville theatre in Dawson City in the Yukon, and was apparently accompanied by a sister. Other witnesses placed him in Alaska and in Cheyenne, Wyoming, and Telluride, Colorado, in these last two as night clerk in a hotel. If true, these humble occupations serve only to deepen the mystery of why he threw up his comfortable life in New York.

Another strange happening in the Tanner clan came to light. In 1912, four years after William's departure, his brother, Dennis Deane Tanner, left his wife Ada and two children in his turn and vanished from his New York home. And this was an even more successful vanishing act than William's, for no certain trace of Dennis was ever found. For a while, however, he was very much in the forefront of inquiries into the Taylor murder case because of the 'Sands' link. A man called Edward F. Sands had been engaged by William Desmond Taylor as his secretary in or around 1920, and soon afterwards jewellery and clothes began to disappear from Taylor's house. He reported the matter, but at that point Sands was not suspected. Then Taylor went on a trip, returning some six months before his death. He found that Sands had forged cheques on his account, run up a number of bills in his name, stolen more property, and then staged the third disappearance in this story – but not before wrecking two cars belonging to his employer. That Sands also uttered threats against Taylor is a colourful addition to the picture, but although this features in some accounts, it barely makes sense. When Taylor left, they were on good enough terms for him to leave Sands in the house. When he came back, Sands had gone. So when could he have made those threats? Sands was never traced.

He can scarcely have been the figure seen leaving the bungalow after the murder, for he was well known to the MacLeans, and that it might be Sands seems not to have crossed Faith MacLean's mind. He was also much older than 26, and so unlikely to have been the man on the streetcar. For a while the police toyed with the theory that Sands and Dennis Deane Tanner were one and the same. One vanished mystery man rather than two was neater all round, and somewhat more credible, and would moreover explain why Taylor had given shelter and employment to someone who was not quite the perfect secretary. This theory seemed to be confirmed when Dennis Deane Taylor's wife received a letter containing a number of pawn tickets. The tickets were for jewellery belonging to Taylor, and they were in Sands' name. If he were not Dennis, why should he send them to Dennis' wife? And how did he obtain her address?

Fatty's fall

A major Hollywood scandal was already in the headlines at the time of William Desmond Taylor's death. On Saturday 3 September 1921 the film comedian Roscoe 'Fatty' Arbuckle left Los Angeles for San Francisco accompanied by two friends, director Fred Fischback and actor (later director) Lowell Sherman, for a well-earned rest. Arbuckle had moved into full-length comedies before any of his rivals, had a Paramount contract worth $3 million over three years, and had completed nine films under that contract. He was universally popular, and widely respected. And he was not the gross fat man of legend: he was fat indeed, but as his films show, he moved with an astonishing delicacy and grace. Yet this weekend was destined to destroy him.

On the Monday, 5 September, there was a wild party in Arbuckle's suite at the St Francis Hotel. A great deal of bootleg liquor was consumed; girls were invited, two of them at least of doubtful repute, and the whole affair was certainly nothing to be proud of. For a man with so much to lose, Arbuckle had indeed been supremely foolish, yet no degree of wisdom could have foretold the consequences of that afternoon. One of the guests was a 27-year-old film actress and model named Virginia Rappe. She had achieved little in the movies,

Top: Roscoe 'Fatty' Arbuckle with Mabel Normand; they starred together in a series of comedy films. Above: Arbuckle's luxurious, custom-made Pierce Arrow car which he drove to the fateful party in San Francisco. Right: 'Fatty' at the height of his fame with a bevy of Mack Sennett Bathing Beauties

and was currently the mistress of the comedy director Henry Lehrman, who at the time was away in New York.

When Arbuckle went to his bathroom wearing pyjamas, intending to leave the party to take a drive, he found Virginia Rappe on the floor, vomiting and groaning. Arbuckle spent ten minutes trying to help, giving her water, and putting her on the bed in the adjacent bedroom. Then he returned to the party and told two of Virginia's companions, Maude Delmont and Zey Prevon, what he had seen. When the three went back to the bedroom, Virginia was tearing off her clothes and screaming that she was dying. Other guests came in and crude methods of remedy were tried, including dipping the girl in a cold bath and applying a lump of ice to her body. When this proved useless, the hotel doctors were belatedly summoned. These doctors did little or nothing, and on the Tuesday evening, after Arbuckle had returned to Los Angeles, Maude Delmont, who had stayed to look after Virginia, summoned a Dr Rumbold, whom she knew. His first diagnosis was alcoholism, but two days later he became worried, suspected gonorrhoea, realised that she was pregnant, and had her removed to a maternity hospital, where the following day she died.

Maude Delmont, who posed as Virginia's life-long friend, although she had met her for the first time two days before the party, had by now seen her chance. She spoke to reporters, telling them such spicy inventions as that Arbuckle had dragged Virginia into the bedroom, and kept her there for an hour. She claimed that Virginia had said that he had tried to rape her, thrown his considerable weight (of 19 stone) upon her, and hurt her dreadfully in so doing. She also, as emerged much later, sent telegrams to two attorneys saying: 'We have Roscoe Arbuckle in a hole here. Chance to make some money out of him.' Moreover, she swore out a formal complaint to the police.

At first the San Francisco District Attorney, Matthew Brady, wished to indict Arbuckle for murder in the first degree, but the police court and grand jury proceedings compelled him to reduce the charge to manslaughter. Brady was soon in trouble. He realised that his principal witness, Maude Delmont, had told a string of lies, and could not put her on the stand. Forced to rely on the testimony of Zey Prevon and another girl, Alice Blake, he played very foully indeed, keeping both girls under virtual arrest for a long period and subjecting them to intense pressure to say that in their hearing Virginia Rappe had claimed that Arbuckle had killed her. In the event, neither would go that far, but the

continued on next page

Below: Virginia Rappe, whose death followed an alleged sexual assault by 'Fatty' Arbuckle. Bottom: on 4 October 1921 Arbuckle was released on $5000 bail and the charge against him reduced to manslaughter. After three trials he was fully acquitted

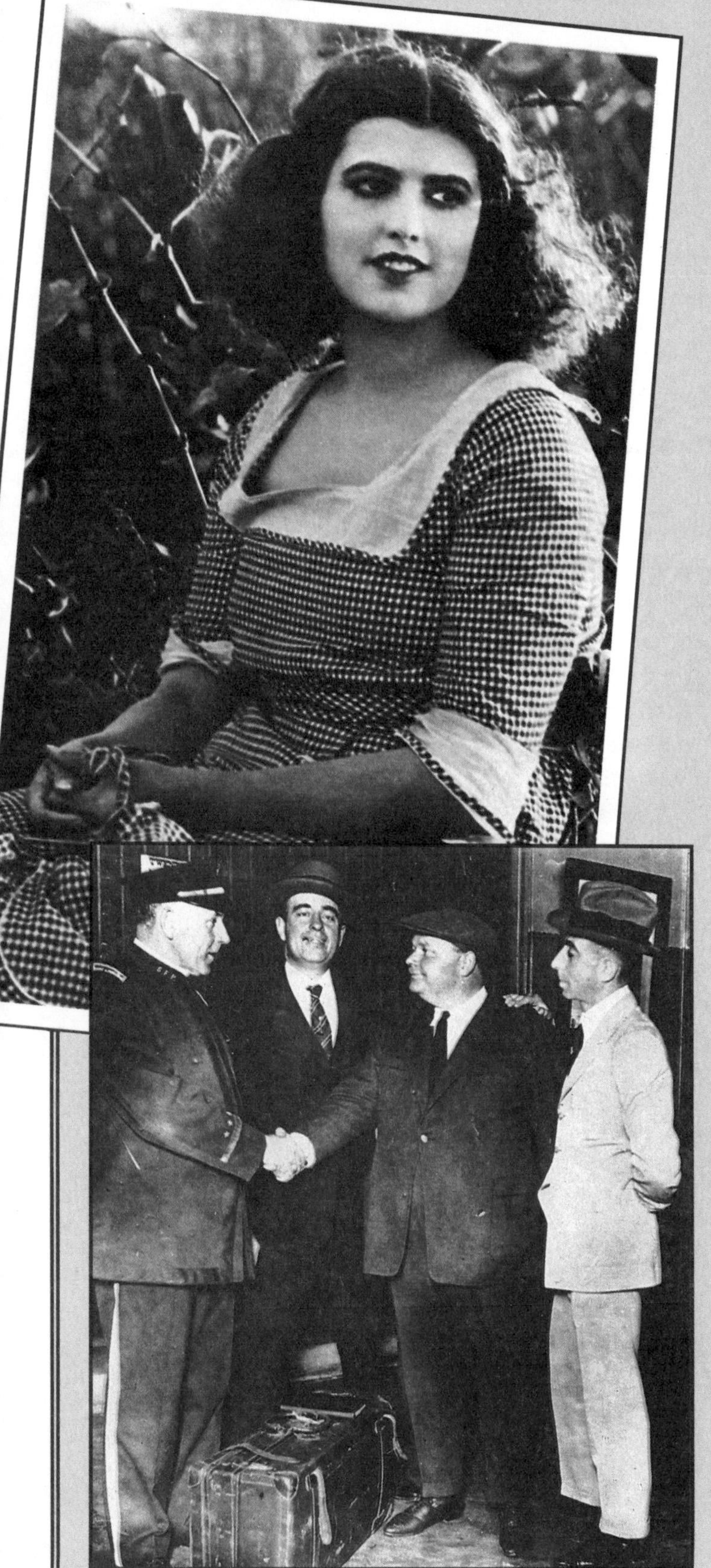

girls were compelled to say that Virginia had accused him of 'hurting' her.

Arbuckle himself gave evidence at the first trial, was cross-examined harshly for three hours, but told his simple story clearly and consistently. The jury voted ten to two in favour of acquittal, but majority verdicts were not acceptable, and a new trial followed. This time, with some over-confidence, the defence lawyers felt it unnecessary to submit their client to the ordeal of giving evidence, and this may have affected the jury, who now voted ten to two for guilty. A third trial brought entire vindication – Arbuckle testified on this occasion. The prosecution, curiously, brought out evidence of Virginia Rappe's past life. (The defence had long known that she had had five abortions by the time she was 16, but had declined to blacken her character.) This time the jury had no doubts; they were out for a mere five minutes, and not only acquitted Arbuckle, but made a statement which began: 'Acquittal is not enough for Roscoe Arbuckle. We feel that a great injustice has been done him. We feel also that it was only our plain duty to give him this exoneration, under the evidence, for there was not the slightest proof adduced to connect him in any way with the commission of a crime.' That was on 12 April 1922 but to Roscoe Arbuckle the verdict brought no relief.

What had happened to Virginia Rappe had been clear for some time. She was now known to have suffered from chronic cystitis, and this had caused a rupture of the bladder and peritonitis. Less clear are the reasons for Brady's dogged persecution of Arbuckle. Civic pride may have had something to do with it, for San Francisco resented Los Angeles, and would not gladly see itself contaminated by its licentious rival. Political ambition was present too – Brady aimed at governorship, which he never got. But more powerful was the climate of repression that had already harassed aliens and radicals, outlawed alcohol, and in its attempt to impose 'morality' would have loved to outlaw the movies, too. 'Vigilante' women had packed the courtroom for the trials, and in the end they had their victim. Four days after the first trial ended, the most powerful film magnates invited Will Hays, President Harding's Postmaster General, to become head of what would in time become the Hays Office, in charge of 'cleaning up' Hollywood. Thus the film industry would be shielded from public criticism, at the cost of an often destructive censorship. And Paramount threw Arbuckle to the wolves. Soon after the case broke, they withdrew his films. Six days after his final acquittal, Hays banned him from the screen.

Arbuckle lived on, obscurely, until 1933. He directed some films under a pseudonym; he appeared in vaudeville. In 1932 Warner Brothers gave him the chance to act in some two-reel shorts, to test public reaction. These little films went well, but before he had the chance to do more, Roscoe Arbuckle died of a heart attack on 29 June 1933. He had spent twelve years in the shadows – a stiff punishment for one reckless weekend.

That at least has an answer. Sands spent time with Taylor and in Taylor's house, and Taylor had by no means severed his connection with his family as completely as was at first supposed.

One day in 1914 Mrs Dennis Deane Taylor had gone to the cinema and to her astonishment seen her missing brother-in-law in the film *Captain Alvarez* (other versions have it as a newsreel, which seems less likely). She at once told William's wife, who then admitted that she knew perfectly well where Taylor was, and had even been receiving a monthly cheque from him for some time. She had, however, divorced him in 1912. Later, Taylor made some provision for Dennis' wife, too, and so it would not have been difficult for Sands, even if he was not Dennis, to have discovered that address. This promising line of inquiry was taken up periodically until 1937, when a photograph of Dennis was finally obtained and it seemed clear that he and Sands were not the same person. It is mildly odd that so elementary a step was not taken at once, but perhaps Dennis' wife had not been in the mood to keep reminders of her departed husband about the place.

From the beginning the murder attracted lurid publicity, and this of course centred on the involvement of the two popular stars Mabel Normand and Mary Miles Minter. The heads of the film industry were alarmed. For them, the murder had come at the worst possible time. On the very day of the crime, Roscoe 'Fatty' Arbuckle, the popular film comedian, was undergoing his second trial for manslaughter in San Francisco. Will Hays had only a month or two before been brought in (as head of the Motion Picture Producers and Distributors of America) to restore respectability to the movies, threatened as they were by reformers and increasing censorship, the Arbuckle calamity, and bad publicity resulting from rumours of orgies and drug addiction. And then the Taylor scandal erupted. No wonder that, as time went on and no arrest was made, talk of a cover-up increased. Cover-up or no, the studios did all they could to parade their stern views on wrongdoing. Just as, a few months later, the innocent Arbuckle was to be banned, so Mabel Normand's latest picture, *Molly O*, was withdrawn, and when an exhibitor in Massachusetts voluntarily removed a Mary Miles Minter picture from his programme, the bells were tolling for Mary as well: by 1923 she had starred in her last film, *The Trail of the Lonesome Pine*.

The happy screen personality of Mabel Normand makes the bitterness of her last years all the sadder to recall. Although she was shown beyond doubt to have had no connection with Taylor's death, she had been there on his last evening alive, and that was not forgotten. She was also widely rumoured to be addicted to drugs, and the final blow came when on New Year's Eve 1923 her chauffeur, Horace A. Green, was found standing over the body of the millionaire Cortland S. Dines, a warm pistol in his hand – a pistol that belonged to Mabel Normand. After that, she made one or two two-reel comedies, and had a doomed marriage with the actor Lew Cody. Each was desperately ill, Cody of a heart condition, Normand of tuberculosis. She died in 1930, he in 1934.

Below: Mary Miles Minter in her last film, The Trail of the Lonesome Pine, *in which she starred with Ernest Torrence and Antonio Moreno (right), the actor who claimed to have telephoned William Desmond Taylor the night he was murdered*

Below: Mary Miles Minter's family before the scandal arising from the William Desmond Taylor murder. Left to right: Juliet (Mary), Mrs Charlotte Shelby and Margaret. Charlotte was the manipulative Hollywood mother of legend – and was sued by both her daughters in the mid-Thirties for mismanagement of their financial affairs. It was rumoured at the time of Taylor's death that Charlotte may have wanted to protect Juliet's reputation from her entanglement with him. Right: William Desmond Taylor in 1920 – a photograph personally inscribed to Mary Miles Minter. Far right: Mary Miles Minter in Anne of Green Gables *(1919), one of four films in which she was directed by Taylor*

Mary Miles Minter survived the scandal and lived quietly in California until her death in 1984. She was born on 1 April 1902. Her name was Juliet Reilly, and she was the daughter of Mr and Mrs Homer Reilly. The birthdate is sometimes given as 1892, but that is an absurdity. She appeared in her first film, as a child, in 1912, and in *The Ghost of Rosie Taylor* (1918), the only Minter film modern audiences are likely to see, she looks perhaps 20, but is clearly 16 rather than 26. Soon after her birth, her mother Charlotte left Mr Reilly and took the name Shelby. As Juliet Shelby the little girl became a popular child actress on stage, particularly in a famous Civil War melodrama, *The Littlest Rebel*. There is a story that on one occasion the municipal authorities in Chicago, suspecting that an under-age child was being used for stage work, descended on Charlotte Shelby, who pacified them by producing the birth certificate of Juliet's elder sister, Margaret. So little Juliet Shelby made that first film in 1912, and three years later, still only 13, she began her career as Mary Miles Minter. That was rather young for a leading lady, but the child-heroine was a popular figure in early movies, and to play adult roles at 15 or 16 was not unusual. The name Mary Miles Minter was euphonious and catchy enough, and not quite an invention: it was borrowed from Mrs Shelby's elder sister, Mary Miles, who had married a Mr Augustus Lafayette Minter. Charlotte Shelby, very much the dominating mother of Hollywood tradition, lived with Margaret and Juliet, and did her best to guide Juliet's career. They lived at 56 Fremont Place, a house that had once belonged to Mary Pickford, the star whose place Mary Miles Minter was expected to fill.

Mrs Shelby seems to have wanted to run her younger daughter's life as well as her career. The actress Colleen Moore is quoted as saying that Juliet would leave the house for the evening with a rich young man, dutifully playing his part, and then go on to join Mabel Normand (or others of whom Mrs Shelby presumbly disapproved). Charlotte, according to Miss Moore, had 'a personality that grated'. It was a wretched household, as the lawsuits that followed showed. On the evening of 21 February, when William Desmond Taylor died, Charlotte Shelby was at home alone. Juliet and Margaret were out together, visiting their grandmother, Mrs Julia Branch Miles, at her house on Hobart Street. So Juliet had an alibi that would stand up well. Charlotte Shelby had no alibi. She also owned a ·38 revolver, the calibre of the gun with which Taylor was shot. So did thousands of others, and it must be emphasised that no evidence of any kind implicates her beyond the mere facts of the revolver and the lack of alibi, but this did not stop people speculating at the time. Charlotte Shelby might well have tried to intervene had she known, or suspected, that her nineteen-year-old daughter was conducting an affair with a man in his middle forties, but that is not the same thing at all.

When she heard of Taylor's death, Mary Miles Minter had hurried to the bungalow, where the police had refused to admit her. Eager to defend her reputation, she issued a statement saying that her engagement to Taylor was to have been announced that week. It sounds as though the

studio was behind that one; more convincing is another remark attributed to her to the effect that in view of the age difference between them, Taylor had never encouraged her. That has the ring of honesty.

Frustrated in their investigation, the police accused the studios of organising a cover-up, a claim that would be repeated by many people down the years. At the beginning there had certainly been a hasty attempt at a partial whitewash, for before the police were notified either Henry Peavey or someone else from the court informed Famous Players-Lasky, and the studio's general manager, Charles Eyton, made a rapid visit to Alvarado Street and cleared the bungalow of its supplies of illicit liquor. If Eyton searched for more incriminating evidence, he missed the letters, the handkerchief and, if it was there, the nightgown.

From time to time in the years that followed, the case briefly came to the surface. That the peddling of drugs was in some way involved was a recurrent theme. Taylor is known to have sought the help of the United States Attorney with regard to a young actress who was in the power of a dope ring. Perhaps this was Mabel Normand. Some have suggested that Taylor in fact informed on Normand's suppliers, and was killed by them in consequence; others, with as little proof, maintained that Taylor had replaced the ring as her supplier, which could have been as good a motive for disposing of him. A convict in Folsom Prison said that another convict known to him had killed Taylor, hired to do so by an actress whose supply of drugs he was trying to stop. Other rumours attributed the crime to a 'jealous actress', to the husband of one of Taylor's mistresses, and to an unnamed starlet. In 1929 an ex-Governor of California, F.W. Richardson, said that in 1926 he had been told that a leading actress had killed Taylor.

The first district attorney to struggle with the complexity of the Taylor case was Thomas Lee Woolwine. He achieved nothing, and a year or so later resigned. His successor, Asa Keyes, made the headlines in 1926 by declaring that an arrest was imminent. It never came, and a disconsolate Keyes alleged that crucial evidence had been stolen from a locked cabinet in his office. Soon afterwards, the wretched man went to jail himself, found guilty of accepting a bribe in an oil company investigation.

In 1930, the year of Mabel Normand's death, a candidate for political office returned to the cover-up theme, repeating that an actress had been guilty. A year later, Henry Peavey died. But the Shelby family was still there, and in the mid-Thirties the bitterness that had been kept under cover in that household broke out. Mrs Shelby had managed Mary Miles Minter's financial affairs in the days of her stardom, and now Mary sued her mother for a million dollars. The courts awarded her $200,000, and a man to whom Charlotte had entrusted a great deal of Mary's money, and who had lost some $450,000 of it on the stock market, was jailed. Mary's sister Margaret (now Margaret Fillmore), feeling equally aggrieved, sued her mother for a relatively modest $48,000, the balance, according to her account, of $133,000 that she had been owed since 1923. These unedifying family battles would be of little interest but for the

Above: in 1937 Mary Miles Minter appeared with her mother before a special grand jury in a sudden re-opening of the investigation into the fifteen-year-old William Desmond Taylor murder case. Left: a cartoonist's view of politician Will Hays, who in the wake of a series of Hollywood scandals was invited by the most powerful film magnates to act as the guardian of America's morals. Above left: Mary Miles Minter in 1919 — the 'new Pickford'

way they suddenly brought the Shelby family slap up against the now fifteen-year-old Taylor case. As Margaret Fillmore's suit proceeded, the District Attorney, Buron Fitts, came across an undated statement made by Margaret saying of her mother, 'I protected her in the Taylor case'. Margaret also referred to two diaries kept by Mary. Charlotte's response was to try to get her daughter certified insane. She lost on all counts. There was no certification, Margaret was awarded $20,000 and Charlotte was evicted from the family's Laguna Beach house.

Fitts now had his chance to become the man who solved the Taylor mystery. He authorised a search of Charlotte and Mary's possessions, and discovered the diaries. A special grand jury was convened, and Charlotte, Margaret and Mary were questioned before it. They gave evidence in camera, and no details have ever been released. Charlotte was asked, it is said, about the pearl-handled ·38 revolver that she owned, but nothing conclusive emerged, and no one was charged. At this time Buron Fitts was waylaid on a lonely road, shot, and wounded — but not fatally. Was someone issuing him a stern warning? His final step in the case was to issue a statement absolving Mary and Charlotte from all blame. (It was Fitts, incidentally, to whom in 1937 Ada Tanner belatedly showed her husband's photograph.)

In 1938, Margaret Fillmore died. Needless to say, there was a legal dispute over her will. Charlotte Shelby lived on until 1957. In that same year, Mary Miles Minter married Brandon Hildebrandt, an interior decorator and real estate man. The marriage lasted until his death in 1966. In 1959 Faith MacLean, who had probably seen the murderer, died.

There were a few bizarre footnotes. In February 1970, as part of a crime series written by Rod Serling, CBS television put out a programme on the case. Three years later, Mary Miles Minter sued CBS for $350,000, alleging invasion of privacy. She lost. Many people have written about the case; a few have attempted an independent investigation. One of these, Anne Etheridge, worked on the affair in the summer of 1978, but was warned off by the Los Angeles police. Another, Stephen Zito, was simply told that all records had been lost. Was someone still covering up?

The director King Vidor suggested that this could have happened. In David Yallop's book on Arbuckle, *The Day the Laughter Stopped* (1976), he quotes Vidor on Taylor's death: 'Bribes were handed out all over the place in the Taylor case. The cover-up was entirely organised by Hollywood. To fight it was like taking on the United States government. Remember, these men were all-powerful, you could not fight them.'

It is unlikely that any more evidence in this case will emerge. Yet certain impressions remain. It seems likely that Edward Sands, whether he was Taylor's secretary, or butler, or valet (and writers have variously described him as all three), was in fact Dennis Deane Taylor. The posting of the pawn tickets to Ada points straight to that conclusion, and the production of the photograph fifteen years after the murder is hardly convincing. As to the killing, perhaps the answer does somehow lie in Taylor's involvement with drugs. The man in Folsom Prison spoke of a hired assassin.

Garage of death

Another of Hollywood's unsolved death mysteries concerns Thelma Todd, the 'ice-cream blonde' star of comedy and occasional drama. She had been a schoolmistress in Massachusetts, won a beauty contest there, went to Hollywood, and appeared in films from 1926 onwards. She died in December 1935 in circumstances that baffled everyone. She had interests outside films. In partnership with her lover, the film director Roland West, she ran a restaurant, Thelma Todd's Roadside Rest, on the coast between Santa Monica and Malibu.

Left: Thelma Todd in the Marx Brothers film Horse Feathers, *directed by Norman Z. McLeod in 1932. Below left: Captain Bert Wallis of the Los Angeles Police Homicide Squad views Thelma Todd's body, which was found in her garaged car on 16 December 1935. Below: 'Lucky' Luciano (between detectives) arriving at the New York City Supreme Court building in June 1936. Thelma Todd's lawyer maintained that she had been murdered on the instructions of Mafia boss Luciano*

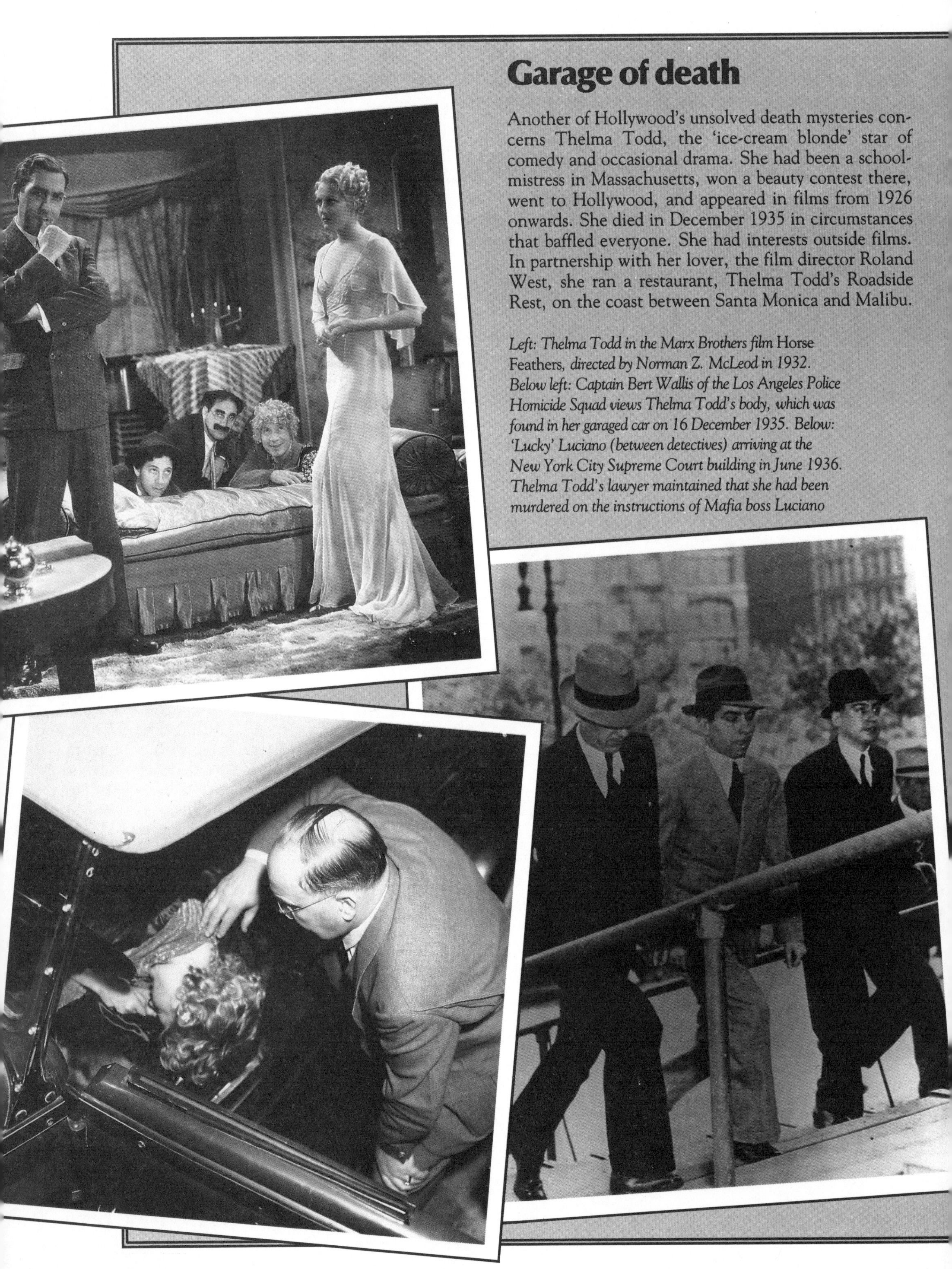

She and West lived in separate apartments above the restaurant. West also had a house on the nearby Pasetano Road. That house had a garage, and in that garage Thelma Todd's body was found at 10.30am on Monday 16 December.

The body was found by Thelma's maid, who had gone, as was her custom, to bring the car round to the restaurant. It was lying on the front seat of the car, an open Packard Convertible. The ignition switch was on, but the engine dead, and there were still two gallons of petrol in the tank. There was blood on Thelma's face, mouth, and cheeks, and some on the evening dress and mink coat she was still wearing. More blood was found on the car and on the garage floor. The garage light was off and the door shut, but a window was open. When and how did she die?

The official view was that she had died some time early on the Sunday. An inquest, and a grand jury, returned a verdict of carbon monoxide poisoning. That left a great deal unexplained. Thelma's movements that weekend were clear – up to a point. On the Saturday evening she had been a guest at a party, at the Trocadero on Sunset Strip, given by the English actor Stanley Lupino, whose daughter Ida had just begun a Hollywood career. Thelma had met the Lupinos when making a film in England. Also present was Thelma's divorced husband, the agent Pat de Ciccio, who had been invited by Ida, then declined the invitation but nonetheless turned up accompanied by the actress Margaret Lindsay. Roland West spent the evening in his rooms above the restaurant. Between 2 and 2.30am the cinema owner Sid Grauman telephoned to say that Thelma would be home in an hour. West's accountant, a man named Smith, was with him until late that night. Smith had a room above the garage. He would say later that he read until 2.30, and heard nothing. West walked his dog at 3.30, went to bed, woke up again, unlocked the dividing door, found no Thelma, and assumed that she was spending the night at her mother's.

Evidence given by neighbours challenged that account, and gave rise to one of the more ludicrous theories about the affair. These neighbours reported hearing, in the small hours, a violent quarrel at the restaurant door between Thelma and West, which culminated in West's shutting her out. The theory is that the quarrel was staged with another girl posing as Thelma, who had previously been killed. Its proponents might well consider why a man who had just committed a murder should draw attention in this way to his quarrel with his victim.

Evidence also arrived to challenge the police theory of a death in the garage that Saturday night. At least six people saw Thelma alive and well on the Sunday. The wife of actor Wallace Ford said that Thelma telephoned her about a cocktail date, said she had not been to bed, and asked if she could come in her evening clothes, bringing a man. She did not arrive. West's wife, actress Jewel Carmen, saw Thelma in her Packard that Sunday morning, at the junction of Hollywood and Vine, with a dark man. The owner of a liquor store on Figueroa Street, one W.F. Person, said that Thelma had come into his place that morning, hatless and coatless, wearing her blue evening gown, her speech slurred. She asked to use his telephone, did so, left, joined a man, and sat for a while on some church steps opposite. Who this companion was is not known, but at the party Thelma had admitted to Ida Lupino that she had embarked on an affair with a businessman from San Francisco.

Complicating matters yet further, there was a gangster connection. Thelma Todd's lawyer maintained that she had been killed at the instigation of the notorious Mafia chief, 'Lucky' Luciano, the reason being that she had turned down his request that she allow him to take over the rooms above the restaurant as an illegal casino, into which restaurant customers could be enticed. Presumably if the death excited no suspicion, pressure would be put on West to play along with a cover-up. Behind this speculation there is a little hard fact. In the previous February, Thelma had received a threatening note. It read: 'Pay 10,000 dollars to Abe Lyman and live. If not, our San Francisco boys will lay you out. This is no joke.' Abe Lyman was a band leader, and allegedly a former lover of Thelma's. Thelma is said to have taken this seriously enough to hire a bodyguard for a while. And in August, Henry Schimanski, a New York commissionaire, was found guilty of attempting to extort $20,000 from Miss Todd.

There are a few more minor oddities. Pat de Ciccio's change of heart over the Trocadero party is one: Margaret Lindsay said that he had told her he had lunched with Thelma four days before. Thelma denied this when it was mentioned that evening. On the Sunday, de Ciccio left Los Angeles for New York. Another item was provided by Thelma's friend, ZaSu Pitts, who had lent Thelma a great deal of money for the restaurant venture which was never repaid. Miss Pitts said that she had gone with Thelma on the Tuesday to a dressmaker's, and Thelma had confided to her, mysteriously, that a great many changes would come into her life before the year ended.

Did she return home in the early hours of Sunday? She may have done so, quarrelled with West, and left in a huff. It seems certain that she was alive later that day, yet between the Sunday morning, when she was with the dark man, and the Sunday night, she reached the garage, and died there, or perhaps was killed elsewhere, and the stage set for the Monday morning discovery.

Roland West never directed another film. Perhaps not much should be made of that, for his last film had been in 1931. That film was a racketeering melodrama called *Corsair*, and it provides the final enigma. The heroine was played by an unknown named Alison Loyd. Look closely if *The Corsair* comes your way. Alison Loyd is Thelma Todd.

Someone that night asked the way to the bungalow court. Could the laying out of the body, neat and tidy for burial, have been a macabre Mafia touch? If drugs were at the heart of the matter, too, then the disappearances from New York of William and Dennis Deane Tanner could be an earlier episode in one long story.

When William Desmond Taylor died, his last two films had not been shown. One of them, *The Green Temptation*, had its New York premiere on 18 March 1922, less than a month after its director's death. It dealt with a double identity and a change of name. On 18 June of the same year, his last film, *The Top of New York*, was first shown. The mainspring of that film's plot . . . the pawning of jewellery.

Below: the New York Sunday American, *20 January 1924. The early Twenties saw a rash of sensational Hollywood scandals that ruined the careers of a number of film stars*

JAN 20 1924

Ruined Movie Stars

What the New and Exacting Code of Ethics for Screen Heroes and Heroines Has Cost Some of the Fallen Idols of the Films

"Fatty" Arbuckle Photographed in a Scene He Thought Was Funny and Other People Laughed at a Few Years Ago.

Mary Miles Minter, Over Whose Young Life the Cloud of Mystery of William Desmond Taylor's Murder Has Drifted.

Mabel Normand, Whose Face Has Been Barred from the Screens of the Motion Picture Theatres in Kansas Because, While She Had no Part in the Recent Shooting of Mr. Dines, Yet She Confessed She Had Been Drinking That New Year's Afternoon.

Edna Purviance, Whose Films Are Threatened in the Movie Theatres.

IN SEARCH OF AMELIA EARHART

At 8.43am on 3 July 1937 radio operators aboard the ship *Itasca,* anchored near Howland Island in the Pacific, tuned in to the voice of Amelia Earhart for the last time. The famous flier, who was on the last lap of her west-to-east flight around the equator, was clearly in trouble, and it is believed that shortly after her final frantic message her Lockheed Electra aeroplane went down. But where? Were Earhart and her navigator Fred Noonan claimed by the ocean – or did they make a forced landing on an island and become prisoners of occupying Japanese soldiers? If so, were they then executed as spies? *FRED GOERNER* reconstructs Earhart's last flight and confronts a mystery that has foxed America's top military observers

Below: Amelia Earhart (right) with her first flying instructor, Neta Snook, in 1920 when she was 22. Neta Snook was one of the pioneer women in aviation – the first ever female graduate from the Curtiss School of Aviation in California. Earhart explained her choice by saying: 'I felt I would be less self-conscious taking lessons with a woman instructor than with the men who overwhelmed me with their capabilities.' But Neta Snook was not able to see her protégée through: her training business went bankrupt and Earhart had to finish her course with a male instructor. Below right: the Fokker twin-float seaplane Friendship *in Southampton Harbour, after completing the flight from Newfoundland to Burry Port on the coast of Wales in 21 hours. The date was 17 June 1928, and Amelia Earhart had become the first woman to fly the Atlantic. Right: the crew of the* Friendship *come aboard at Southampton, with Earhart in her leather flying gear holding a somewhat incongruous bouquet. On the left is Mrs Frederick Guest, the American wife of the British Secretary of State for Air, who financed the trip and had originally intended to go on it herself. Next to Mrs Guest is the flight mechanic Louis 'Slim' Gordon, and on Earhart's left the pilot, Wilmer L. Stultz. Below, far right: Amelia Earhart is cheered by admirers on landing in Ireland in May 1932 in her single-engined Lockheed Vega. She had flown from Newfoundland in only 13¼ hours – which was then a record-breaking time*

PIONEER airwoman Amelia Earhart carefully taxied her Lockheed Electra 10-E twin-engined aircraft to the take-off stand at the runway at Lae, New Guinea. Behind the cockpit in the main cabin was Captain Frederick Noonan, her navigator. He had secured all loose items and cinched tight the safety belts attached to his seat.

It was 2 July 1937. Earhart was embarking on the first ever attempt at a flight around the world by the longest route – the equator, a distance of 27,000 miles (43,500 kilometres). Already she had become the first woman to fly solo across the Atlantic and the first pilot ever to fly alone from Hawaii to California.

The round-the-world attempt had begun on 17 March when Earhart and two navigators flew the 2410 miles (3880 kilometres) from San Francisco to Honolulu. But bad luck struck almost immediately. As the Lockheed Electra was taking off from Honolulu, it crashed and the landing gear collapsed.

On 1 June, Earhart started again. She had changed her plans, and set off from west to east, this time with only one navigator, Fred Noonan. (Captain Harry Manning, the other navigator, decided after the crash that he had risked his life enough in the interests of Amelia Earhart and returned to his sea command). Earhart and Noonan flew successfully over South America, Africa, Asia and Australia and then made the short hop from Darwin to Lae.

They had publicly acknowledged that the forthcoming stretch would be the most difficult and dangerous part of their well-publicised flight. Their course would take them over an expanse of Pacific Ocean never flown before – 2556 miles (4113 kilometres), mostly over open water – to tiny Howland Island, a fleck of land ¾ mile (1.2 kilometres) long by ½ mile (0.8 kilometres) wide, just north of the equator, where the US Navy, Army Air Corps and Interior Departments had recently scratched out a rudimentary air-field.

The US Navy and Coast Guard had each provided a guard vessel to keep watch on the flight. The navy's USS *Ontario* would be stationed in the open sea at the flight's mid-point and the Coast Guard Cutter USS *Itasca* would anchor near Howland Island. Both vessels would try to assist with

communications and both could serve as rescue ships should Earhart and Noonan have to attempt an emergency landing on the ocean.

Perhaps the most dangerous and difficult aspect of the endeavour would be the take-off. The aircraft was grossly overloaded with 1050 US gallons (3980 litres) of 86-octane fuel, together with 50 US gallons (190 litres) of 100-octane petrol to provide extra power for the initial lift.

It was exactly 10am New Guinea time as the Electra spun into take-off position. The bright controllable-pitch Hamilton Standard props whirled as the powerful 1500-horsepower (1120-kilowatt) Pratt and Whitney Wasp engines chewed great holes in the air. Earhart checked the revolutions and magnetoes, sending a hurricane blasting back against the vibrating 55-foot (16·8-metre) wingspan. Satisfied with the performance of both engines, Earhart throttled back. Then, with a smooth, positive motion, Earhart pushed both throttles forward to full open, slipped the brakes, and the Electra began to lumber forward. The roar of the engines alerted a small band of spectators at the Guinea Airways hangars. The group included J. A. Collopy, district superintendent of civil aviation for the Territory of New Guinea; Harry Balfour, senior radio operator at the Lae Aerodrome and the technicians and pilots of Guinea Airways.

Collopy later wrote in his official report to the Civil Aviation Board:

> The take-off was hair-raising as after taking every yard of the 1000 yard [900-metre] runway from the north-west end of the aerodrome towards the sea, the aircraft had not left the ground 50 yards [45 metres] from the

Below: the crew of the first attempt at the round-the-equator flight after landing at Honolulu in March 1937. On the left is the technical adviser, Paul Mantz. Next to Earhart stands Harry Manning, who dropped out of the flight on the second attempt, leaving only Fred Noonan (right) to accompany the pilot on the fatal trip. Bottom: the 'Flying Laboratory' passes over the still unfinished Golden Gate Bridge at Oakland, California, after the first take-off on 24 March 1937. Bottom right: Earhart and Fred Noonan at Batavia, Java, one of the last stop-overs on the flight before their disappearance. At Lae, New Guinea, according to the district superintendent of civil aviation, J. A. Collopy, Noonan had said that he was not a bit anxious about the flight to Howland Island and quite confident that he could locate it. Though Noonan was known to have drink problems, it is unlikely that he would have taken any risks on this flight — he had been married for just three weeks. He was a talented navigator, but he was by no means a skilled radio operator — if there had been a radioman in the crew, the flight might not have ended in tragedy

end of the runway. When it did leave it sank away but was by this time over the sea. It continued to sink to about five or six feet [1·5 or 1·8 metres] above the water and had not climbed to more than 100 feet [30 metres] before it disappeared from sight. It was obvious the aircraft was well handled and pilots of Guinea Airways were loud in their praise of the take-off with such an overload.

A few minutes after the Electra disappeared from the sight of Lae, radio operator Harry Balfour received the long-awaited weather forecast for the Earhart flight from the US Navy Fleet Air Base at Pearl Harbor. The message had been routed through American Samoa and Suva, Fiji, which is why it took so long to arrive. As Earhart and Noonan would be flying dead reckoning most of the day and night, it was vitally important that they know the wind directions to enable them to make navigational corrections for drift.

At 10.22am, 11.22am and 12.22am, Balfour transmitted the information by radiophone on Earhart's daytime frequency, 6210 kilocycles (kilohertz):

Partly cloudy skies with dangerous rain squalls about 300 miles [480 kilometres] east of Lae. Scattered heavy showers rest of route. Winds east-south-east about 25

knots to Ontario. Then east to north-east about 20 knots to Howland.

Balfour heard no acknowledgement from Earhart, but supposed she had got the message and had simply been too busy to reply.

Consumption of coal and water was already reaching a critical point

At approximately 3pm Lae time, Earhart's voice came through Balfour's receiver, clear and unhurried. The aeroplane was flying at 10,000 feet (3000 metres), but she was going to reduce altitude because of thick banks of cloud ahead.

Then, at 5.20pm, Earhart broke through again on 6210 kilocycles to announce they were currently at 7000 feet (2100 metres) and making 150 knots (280 kilometres per hour) speed. The position reported was latitude 4 degrees 33 minutes south, longitude 159 degrees 06 minutes east, a point about 785 miles (1265 kilometres) out from Lae and almost directly on course. The true ground speed was only about 111 knots (206 kilometres per hour), indicating the Electra was indeed bucking the headwinds mentioned in the US Navy weather forecast.

Earhart closed the broadcast by stating her next report would be on 3105 kilocycles, her night-time frequency. But Balfour radioed back that her signal was coming through strongly and that she should continue to use 6210. Earhart again did not acknowledge, and Balfour heard nothing more.

To US Navy Lieutenant Horace Blakeslee, the assignment as commanding officer and navigator of USS *Ontario* was both fascinating and frustrating. The *Ontario* was the US Navy's only remaining coal-burning vessel and serving as a guard ship for the Earhart flight stretched her capabilities to the maximum; in fact, she was no longer considered fit for patrol duty. To make the voyage of more than 1200 miles (1900 kilometres) to the mid-point of the projected Earhart flight, remain on guard station for as much as two weeks and then return to the US Navy Station at Tutuila, Samoa, Blakeslee fully loaded the *Ontario*'s coal bunkers and piled a reserve supply on her decks. By the time Earhart and Noonan took off from New Guinea, Blakeslee and his crew had been steaming up and down a small portion of Earhart's announced flight path for ten days. Consumption of coal and water was already reaching a critical point.

Blakeslee had no illusions that two-way communication between Earhart and the *Ontario* would be difficult to establish. The Electra had a low-frequency receiver, but no broadcast capability, and the *Ontario* had no high-frequency equipment. At the end of each minute, the *Ontario* was to broadcast the letter 'N' on 400 kilocycles with the ship's call letters. With a low-frequency receiver, Earhart could presumably estimate her distance from the *Ontario* by strength of signal. Her direction finder, restricted to high-frequency signals, would be of no use to home in on the ship.

With Earhart's 5.20pm reported position, the Electra was due over the *Ontario* at approximately 10pm. Blakeslee recalls (and this is substantiated by his ship's official log) that at 10pm the weather consisted of scattered banks of massed clouds (cumulus clouds), moving from east-north-east, and occasional showers. One of the watch officers believed he heard the sound of an approaching aircraft a few minutes

Above: in Newark, New Jersey, with Harry Manning (left), Amelia Earhart picks up her Bendix high-frequency direction finder. It had been specially adapted by radioman Joseph Gurr of the US Navy, and replaced the direction finder designed by Frederick Hooven that had originally been installed in the Electra. Gurr built a new type of antenna into the belly of the aircraft and also constructed a new antenna that could be used in a forced landing. For many years there were rumours that communications failed on the flight because Amelia left her Morse code key behind. But Gurr revealed that he had rigged the system so that she would not need one. What has never been made clear is why Hooven's direction finder was discarded in favour of the Bendix – the Hooven design went on to serve several generations of fliers, including most of the pilots of the Second World War, and was very reliable. Above right: Earhart in the cockpit of the Lockheed Electra. The all-metal aircraft was stripped of its eight passenger seats to make room for all the extra fuel tanks. Right: the Lockheed takes off from Honolulu on 21 March 1937. A few seconds later, it lurched to the left, swerved into a vicious groundloop and finally came to a stop in a shower of sparks with the fuselage actually on the ground. The landing gear had entirely collapsed, and the round-the-world flight would be delayed for three months. Earhart's prompt action in switching off the engine prevented a certain fire and ensured no one was hurt

after 10pm. The *Ontario* searchlight swept the sky but nothing could be seen for cloud.

By 1am the overcast had become complete and heavy rain squalls were buffeting the ship. Blakeslee radioed, asking for permission to return to base, which he received. The old ship had difficulty making it, 'scraping the bottoms of the coal bunkers'.

At the same time as the men of the *Ontario* believed the Earhart aeroplane to be passing overhead, the radio operator of the Nauru Island station to the north copied Amelia saying, 'A ship in sight ahead.'

The 250-foot (76-metre) Coast Guard Cutter USS *Itasca* steamed slowly by Howland Island, barely keeping way. The radio room was fully manned, and a satellite station ashore on Howland housing a new and top secret high-frequency radio direction finder was ready for action as well.

By midnight, the *Itasca* radio-room was crowded. The wire service correspondents jockeyed for position with the army men. William Galten and Thomas O'Hare, two coast guard radiomen, along with Chief Radioman Leo Bellarts, hovered over the transmitters and receivers. It was a long wait. Earhart's voice did not break through the static on 3105 kilocycles until 2.45am, and then all that could be clearly understood was 'Cloudy weather. . . cloudy'. An hour later, at 3.45, her voice was heard again, saying: '*Itasca* from Earhart. *Itasca* broadcast on 3105 kilocycles on hour and halfhour – repeat – broadcast on 3105 kilocycles on hour and half-hour. Overcast.'

The *Itasca* operators then transmitted on 3105, asking

Earhart to send on 500 kilocycles so that the ship's low-frequency direction finder could get a fix on her. Obviously no one on the *Itasca* knew that Earhart did not have the equipment to broadcast on 500 kilocycles.

Then, after another long wait, at 4.53am Amelia's voice was recognised again, but her signals were unreadable. The first real sense of worry began to permeate the radio room. At 5.12am, Earhart's voice came through again. This time it was much clearer. 'Want bearings on 3105 kilocycles on hour,' she said. 'Will whistle in microphone.'

The only high-frequency direction finder available that could take a bearing on 3105 kilocycles was the navy set ashore on Howland, and there the coast guard operator, Frank Cipriani, was in a sweat. Earhart was simply not staying on the air long enough for him to get a fix on her position. The whistling into the microphone helped, but it was too short. Another important factor was also disturbing Cipriani. The wet-cell batteries that powered the direction finder were beginning to run down. He could only pray that they would last long enough to give Earhart a proper reading.

Amelia broke in again, three minutes later, at 5.15, this time saying only, 'About 200 miles [320 kilometres] out.' Again, she whistled briefly into her microphone.

Another half-hour dragged by, and then again Earhart's voice was heard, this time with a note of pleading: 'Please take a bearing on us and report in half-hour. I will make noise in microphone. About 100 miles [160 kilometres] out.' She whistled again. On Howland Island, Cipriani made a note in his log: 'Her carrier is completely modulated. I cannot get a bearing.'

Nothing further came from Earhart until 7.30am. Her voice was strained and concerned. 'We must be on you but cannot see you but gas is running low. Have been unable to reach you by radio. We are flying at 1000 feet [300 metres].' The atmosphere in the *Itasca* radio room was heavy with alarm. The operators redoubled their efforts, still pleading with Earhart to transmit on 500 kilocycles.

At 7.57, still on 3105 kilocycles, Earhart's voice filled the radio room at the clearest level yet. 'We are circling but cannot see island. Cannot hear you. Go ahead on 7500 kilocycles on long count either now or on schedule time of half-hour.'

At this message, the *Itasca* operators looked at each other in amazement. Earhart was trying to use her own direction finder, but none of them had any idea that it ranged to

Right: on 24 August 1928, two months after her Atlantic flight in the Friendship, *Amelia Earhart made her first flight in a D H 60 Cirrus Moth aircraft. She landed at Northolt Airfield in west London, obviously in very high spirits*

7500 kilocycles. Quickly, the *Itasca* transmitter began to pour forth a stream of letter 'A's on the suggested frequency.

Almost immediately, at 8.03, Earhart replied: 'We received your signals but unable to get minimum. Please take bearing on us and answer on 3105 kilocycles.' This time she made long dashes by depressing the microphone button, but still the direction finder on Howland Island could not get a bearing. Cipriani shook his head in desperation. The batteries were almost completely discharged.

Forty miserable minutes dragged by in the *Itasca*'s radio room. Frustration etched every face. As one of the operators said later: 'It was like not being able to reach a friend who was falling over a cliff.'

At 8.43, Earhart's voice, which some later described as frantic, blurted: 'We are on the line of position 157-337. Will repeat this message on 6210 kilocycles. We are now running north and south.' Earhart was switching to her regular daytime frequency of 6210 kilocycles. The *Itasca*'s radio operators immediately monitored 6210 kilocycles but they were greeted with nothing but static.

Captain Warner Thompson of the *Itasca* waited until it was 10.30am, then radioed Honolulu that the Earhart aeroplane was probably down at sea and that he was going to begin a search operation.

Search, indeed. But where? What did '157-337' mean? It was probably a sun line that Noonan had been able to get a

Winning her wings

Above: Amelia Earhart and husband George Palmer Putnam at Newark, New Jersey, in 1931

There are roads, buildings, libraries and schools named after her. There are scholarships, statues, plaques and even a flower in her honour.

Amelia Earhart was born on 27 July 1898 in Atchison, Kansas, the daughter of a talented but unsuccessful lawyer. Her mother came from a wealthy legal family and the marriage was never very good. Finally, in 1924, the marriage ended in divorce, due in no small part to her father's alcoholism.

Amelia grew up determined to be successful and, above all, independent. 'Many divorces', she would later say when she was a counsellor to women students, 'are caused by the complete dependence of the female. . . . We must earn true respect and equal rights from men by accepting responsibility.'

She studied medicine, but flying was her real love. She began to learn in 1920 and made her first solo flight in 1921. She loved the role that flying enabled her to play: one of daring, courage and independence. In 1922 she bought her first aircraft – a sports bi-plane in which she practised spins, forced landings and flying without instruments. She had accidents, but always managed to escape uninjured.

The late Twenties saw a series of 'firsts' in aviation: in 1927 Colonel Charles Lindbergh made the first solo flight from New York to Paris. Amelia, a highly-skilled flier, was the right age at the right time. In 1928 she was invited to be a member of a crew flying a tri-motored Fokker aircraft across the Atlantic from Newfoundland to Burry Port, Wales. She was the first woman ever to

make the crossing, which somewhat made up for her disappointment at being only a passenger.

Her part in the Atlantic flight — instigated by the influential American publisher George Palmer Putnam, to whom she was married in 1931 — brought her instant, world-wide fame. It was the beginning of a long series of record-breaking achievements in aviation that was to end so dramatically with her disappearance in 1937. She was the first woman to fly the Atlantic alone in 1932, and the first pilot since Lindbergh to make the dangerous crossing at all. She set aircraft speed and altitude records, and convinced a whole generation of Americans that air travel was safer than motoring. She was the first person ever to fly solo from Hawaii to the mainland of America, landing at Oakland, California, on 12 January 1935. The same year she became the first person to fly from Los Angeles to Mexico City and from Mexico City to Newark, New Jersey.

She wrote books and magazine articles, counselled students and gave many lectures on the coming age of air travel. She usually wore boots and khaki trousers, with a scarf wrapped round her throat and folded inside a leather flying jacket that was properly aged with the right amount of grease; dresses and high heels were seldom seen at the airports of the Twenties and Thirties. Amelia Earhart not only competed in a man's world, but she also won — against all the odds — a unique place in the history of a brand new skill. Her image is as strong today as it was that day in 1937 when she disappeared forever.

bearing on just before Earhart's last radio transmission. But a sun line was no good without a reference point. The aircraft could be anywhere along 2000 miles (3200 kilometres) of that sun line. On a compass reciprocal, '157-337' could represent a south-east to north-west line through Howland Island itself. Thompson reasoned that since the weather front to the north-west might have stopped Earhart and Noonan from seeing Howland Island, he would search in the area immediately around the island first.

The disappearance of the world's most famous flier was headline news in America and in most of the rest of the world. President Franklin D. Roosevelt, who had arranged for US government co-operation with the flight, and whose wife had flown with Earhart during Roosevelt's presidential campaign, immediately ordered the battleship USS *Colorado*, which was on a reserve training cruise near the Hawaiian Islands, to proceed at top speed to the Howland Island area to assist with the search. The *Colorado* carried three catapult observation aircraft that could cover wide areas of ocean. And on the evening of 3 July 1937, the president ordered the navy aircraft carrier USS *Lexington* and three destroyers to proceed from the west coast of America to the vicinity of Howland Island to augment the search.

It was clear it would take at least ten days for the *Lexington* and the accompanying destroyers to reach the scene, and there was considerable grumbling in navy circles and in Congress about 'spending millions of dollars and disrupting navy training schedules to search for a couple of stunt fliers'.

In the first days following the disappearance, many sources reported radio distress signals received from what was believed to be the downed Earhart areoplane. Two amateur radio operators in Los Angeles claimed to have heard two SOS calls followed by Earhart's call letters, 'KHAQQ'. On 4 July, three radio operators at the Wailupe Naval Radio Station in Honolulu, Hawaii, took the message: '281. . . north. . . Howland. . . KHAQQ. . . beyond north. . . don't hold with us much longer. . . above water. . . shut off.' At the same time, an amateur radio operator in Oakland, California, heard: '281. . . north. . . Howland. . . can't hold out much longer. . . above water. . . shut off.'

On the strength of the two specific messages, the navy and coast guard asked the *Itasca* and a passing freighter, SS *Morby*, to search the area 280 miles (450 kilometres) to the north of Howland Island. The effort was futile.

The next day in Los Angeles, Paul Mantz, who had been technical advisor for Earhart's first attempt at the round-the-world flight, dropped a small bombshell. He told the press that he had learnt from sources in Lockheed Aircraft that Earhart's aeroplane was incapable of broadcasting from the surface of the water. This statement had immediate and disastrous effects. All the messages so far received were discounted as hoaxes, the cruel work of charlatans and damnable publicity seekers.

But Mantz, in fact, did not know the state of Earhart's radio equipment, and neither did the people at Lockheed Aircraft. Mantz had been dropped from the flight team after the Honolulu crash, and was not even in California when

the second attempt at the flight began.

There was only one man who knew for certain about the Electra's radio gear – Joseph Gurr, who had been assigned, alone, to the task of adapting a Bendix-built US Navy high-frequency direction finder for Earhart's flight and making sure the rest of her equipment would function properly. Gurr believed it possible that signals from the downed Electra in the vicinity of Howland Island could have been heard 3750 miles (6030 kilometres) away in the United States. 'Signals can skip great distances and play some crazy tricks,' he says.

On 5 July 1937, most newspapers carried a brief story alluding to possible signals from the Earhart aeroplane being received at Honolulu, on Midway Island and on Wake Island by high-frequency direction finders owned by Pan American Airways. The bearings from those signals indicated that the aircraft might be down in an area several hundred miles south-east of Howland in the vicinity of the Phoenix Islands. But this story was quickly discounted by the US Navy and coast guard for security reasons. One of the most important aspects of military intelligence communications was strategic direction finding, particularly in the high-frequency range. America did not want the rest of the world, particularly Japan, knowing what her capabilities in that arena were. The disguise concealed grave weakness. The US Navy would later learn as the Second World War got under way that England, Germany and even Japan were far more advanced

Below left: Amelia Earhart's projected world trip, as depicted in the New York Herald Tribune. *Earhart set off the first time from east to west, but after the crash at Honolulu she decided to take the other direction. She started again from California and completed more than two thirds of the journey over land, leaving the hardest stretch over the Pacific to the last. Bottom: the coast of New Guinea and the Pacific islands. Clearly, for the Lockheed to have gone down anywhere near Saipan in the Marianas, Earhart would have to have been badly off-course. Below: the reefs and sandbars around the Phoenix Islands are still largely uncharted; those marked with a broken line still count as 'doubtful data'*

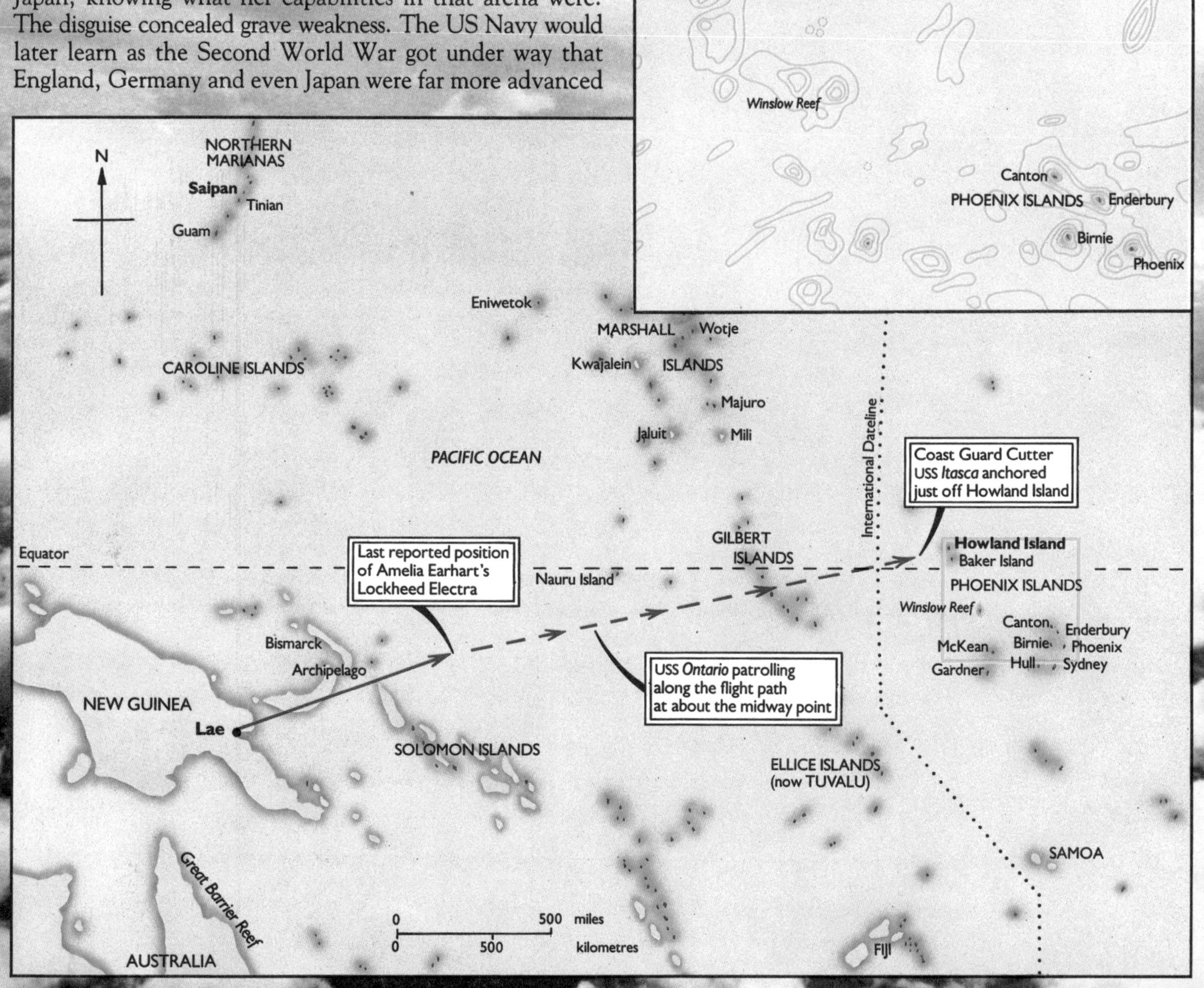

The plane maker

Many aviation experts call him a genius – the most successful innovator since the famous brothers Orville and Wilbur Wright in the early years of the century. Clarence 'Kelly' Johnson has personally directed the design and production of more than forty different types of aeroplane, including the F-80, America's first combat jet, the famed U-2 reconnaissance aircraft and the Mach 3 (three times the speed of sound) SR-71 'Black Bird' super-spy aircraft.

It is Johnson who is given the credit for convincing the RAF to order Lockheed's Hudson bomber in 1938, while, at the same time he was developing one of the most effective US fighter aeroplanes of the Second World War, the twin-boom P-38 Lockheed Lightning. In more recent years, he has played an important role in the creation of spy satellites, electronic jamming and other espionage technologies.

Clarence Johnson was a graduate of the University of Michigan where he studied aeronautical engineering. He landed a job with Lockheed in the depression year of 1933, and it was he who suggested the twin tail for the new all-metal Electra, Lockheed's first passenger aircraft to sell in large numbers.

In 1937 Johnson assumed the role of behind-the-scenes advisor to Amelia Earhart on her round-the-world flight. He was extremely proud of his association with Earhart.

Below: the Lockheed Electra designed by Clarence 'Kelly' Johnson. Right: Johnson with Earhart at the Lockheed airfield

In the interests of security, the navy quashed the story of Pan Am's direction finding bearings on possible signals from Earhart

in direction finding development; indeed, as early as 1937 the Japanese had a string of direction finding stations in the Marshall Islands to the north of Earhart's flight path. They could track her aeroplane better than the Americans could.

Pan American Airways and US Navy communications, which had become partners in the Pacific, were still relying on the Adcock direction finder, which was of British origin. Pan Am provided an excuse for developments on strategic islands in the Pacific that could, and did, have military application. So, in the interests of security, the navy quashed the story of Pan Am's direction finding bearings on possible signals from the Earhart aeroplane. The records of those bearings were later picked up by navy intelligence officers at the Pan Am communications headquarters in Alameda, California, but they remained sequestered from the public until the early Seventies.

But George Palmer Putnam, Earhart's husband, had seen the reports, and when the navy direction finding base on Howland Island reported on 6 July that it had got a bearing on 'KHAQQ', which could either be south-east or north-west, he begged the navy to instruct USS *Colorado* to begin its search to the south-east of Howland and extend it to a group of eight small coral atolls, known as the Phoenix Islands. He urged that a particular effort be made to locate several small coral reefs plotted on the hydrographic charts as being approximately 165 miles (265 kilometres) south-east of Howland.

The 14th Naval District at Honolulu agreed, and so did Captain Wilhelm Freidell, the commanding officer of the *Colorado*. He made a rendezvous with Captain Thompson and the *Itasca* at 6am on 7 July, and the navy then took charge of the search. By mid-morning the *Colorado* was on course for the general area of the reefs. At 2.30pm three

Left: Amelia Earhart at Lockheed in 1932, with her car and the single-engined Lockheed Vega in which she made her record-breaking solo Atlantic crossing to Ireland. She was quite frank about her motives for the flight, and did not profess that it would do any good to anyone or anything. 'I did it really for fun,' she said, 'not to set up any records or anything like that.' After the dramatic and successful flight, she was fêted in England, France, Belgium and Italy, and was given a flying decoration by the United States

He called her 'a fine pilot who could follow directions to the letter'. He was proud of her Electra, too. 'It had a still-air range of 4500 miles [7200 kilometres],' he said, 'and could reach a ceiling of 25,000 feet [7600 metres] at half gas load. It carried oxygen, you know.'

Johnson went on to say that he had personally taught Earhart how to manage heavy-load take-offs, and had given her exact instructions on how to get the greatest distance out of the aircraft. He does not believe the rumours that Earhart had aerial cameras aboard the Electra or that she was on any kind of spy mission: 'I think she and Noonan were badly lost far north of their proper course, and finally ran out of gas. I have never seen anything that would indicate they were captured by the Japanese.'

In 1969, when asked what he felt the degree of US government involvement was in the Earhart flight, he said he was not at liberty to discuss it. Johnson repeated his position in a letter written in 1970 and reiterated it again in 1978 and in 1982: 'I know of no connection', he wrote, 'between our government and Miss Earhart or her advisors.' Johnson was recently awarded America's National Security Medal by President Ronald Reagan.

Below: the Japanese bomb the American fleet at Pearl Harbor, Hawaii, on 7 December 1941. The surprise attack marked the start of the Pacific war and was the climax of years of secret preparation by the Japanese in the mandated Pacific islands. Japan's military headquarters in the islands was on Saipan, which the Americans finally gained after a long drawn-out offensive on 9 July 1944. Right: Fleet Admiral Chester Nimitz, commander of the American naval forces in the Pacific during the Second World War. At the time of the war, Nimitz was not concerned about the rumours he heard connecting Amelia Earhart with the Japanese mandated islands he was so desperate to conquer. But later he became vitally interested in the story, providing the author with suggestions for research. Below right: President Franklin D. Roosevelt in Sicily in 1943. His use of civilians as covert spies has led many people to wonder whether Earhart was on an espionage mission

young pilots, Lieutenants John Lambrecht, William Short and Leonard Fox, were launched from the ship in their 03U-3 observation open cockpit bi-planes.

At 500 feet (150 metres) they swept an area 10 miles (16 kilometres) square around the charted positions of the reefs, and when nothing was found they flew west-south-west 12 miles (19 kilometres) into an area covered by a large rain squall. They still saw nothing but open ocean. They returned to the ship just after 5pm, landing alongside in the water to be winched aboard.

After debriefing his fliers, Captain Friedell came to the conclusion that the charted reefs probably did not exist at all, and a decision was made to begin searching the Phoenix Islands themselves the following day. Friedell made a note for his report that it was not the most comfortable thing in the world to be prowling about in waters where there could be reefs in uncertain locations. He decided to post extra lookouts that night and to use the ship's searchlight in case they might be passing Earhart and Noonan in the dark.

During the following five days, the *Colorado* aviators

averaged four flights of three aircraft each day. Each aircraft flew for more than 21 hours and together they covered an area of more than 25,000 square miles (65,000 square kilometres). They searched Enderbury, Phoenix, Birnie, Sydney, McKean, Gardner and Hull Islands, and then finally Canton, the northernmost island in the Phoenix group. All were uninhabited, save Hull Island where Lambrecht landed in the lagoon and was greeted by the British resident commissioner and a boatload of natives who had paddled out to get a close view of this wonder. None of them had even heard of Amelia Earhart, let alone seen her.

Friedell and his crew left the Phoenix Islands relieved to be out in open, charted waters again. Perhaps they would not have felt so comfortable if they had known that the 'missing' reefs certainly did exist and would be charted again in the years to come. But to this day, none of them have ever been investigated at close range but only from aerial reconnaissance. Could the Electra still be wedged on one of them or buried in a sandbar?

Friedell and his men might have contemplated another search of the area had they known that amateur radio operators in northern California had picked up two more messages on the night of 7 July. One read: 'Plane on reef. . . 200 miles [320 kilometres] south. . . Howland. . . both OK.' The other was: 'SOS. . . KHAQQ. . . east. . . Howland. . . lights tonight. . . can't hold. . .'

At 7am on 12 July 1937, the *Colorado* met and refuelled the destroyers that were leading the aircraft carrier USS *Lexington* to the search scene. After refuelling, the *Colorado* was detached from the search and returned to port.

The carrier USS *Lexington*, with sixty aircraft, began its search to the north and north-west of Howland Island on 13 July. Ocean currents in the area are generally to the north-west and the reasoning was that a drifting aeroplane could now be hundreds of miles from the place where it went down.

Japan had serious cause for concern about United States intentions in the search for Amelia Earhart. Japan had occupied the Marshall, Caroline and Mariana Islands during the First World War, and had maintained control of the area under a League of Nations mandate after the war. But, beginning in 1934, Japan had gradually sealed off the islands from the rest of the world. It was believed that the Japanese were building airfields, fuel depots and expanded harbour and communications facilities in preparation for a Pacific war with the United States, in total contravention of the conditions of the League of Nations mandate.

The Japanese-mandated Marshall Islands lie only 550 miles (880 kilometres) north and west of Howland Island, and the construction of an American airfield on Howland was most disconcerting to the Japanese. They had repeatedly sent surveillance vessels to Howland to try to determine from offshore the extent and progress of the construction.

By 18 July, the *Lexington* aeroplanes were searching areas almost touching the Marshalls, and over the years there have been allegations that some of the *Lexington* pilots made deliberate detours over selected Japanese-held islands to take illicit photographs. The *Lexington*'s official

Women in the clouds

Top: the Duchess of Bedford at the cockpit of her aircraft. She disappeared in her Moth aeroplane on 22 March 1937. Above: Jean Batten about to climb into her aeroplane in Sydney in 1935, her new record for the England-Australia trip proudly inscribed on the side of the cockpit. Left: Amy Johnson, Britain's own 'Queen of the Air'

The arrival of controlled, powered air flight was exactly contemporary with the beginning of the twentieth century – a coincidence of chronology that brought to air travel a special kind of symbolism: it literally seemed to represent the modern world. The famous Wright brothers made their first motor-powered flight in *The Flyer* near Kitty Hawk, North Carolina, in December 1903. It was the first time in history that a machine heavier than air had been successfully flown, and a new era had dawned.

As with most mechanical inventions, the new aeroplanes soon found a role in warfare: the development of aviation during the First World War was very rapid. And the war encouraged another social development, too – the increasing liberation of women into active roles on the public stage. The real era of expansion of air travel, the Twenties, coincided with the period in Europe of greatest change in the lives of women. Those women who had got their hands dirty working on their first motor cars and who had driven ambulances on the battlefields of the Somme were not going to be left out of one of the greatest adventures of the century.

Amelia Earhart encountered opposition and ridicule from men when she first learnt to fly, but it did not daunt her. Her persistent refusals of marriage led to rumours that she was 'unfeminine' – and that did not daunt her either. When she did decide to marry, at the age of 32, she made sure it was to a man who approved of her career and could provide financial support.

Most of the women who were obsessed with flying and able to indulge their interest were wealthy. The amiable and eccentric Duchess of Bedford, who took up flying with enthusiasm at the age of 61, was for twelve years one of Britain's most famous aviators. She flew to India in 1928, got lost over the Sahara and landed among lions in Uganda. Increasing deafness did not diminish her enthusiasm, but the prospect of a frail and inactive old age depressed her. One day in 1937 she set off for a perfectly ordinary flight from her home – and was never seen again. Ten days later bits of her aircraft were washed up on the east coast near Yarmouth. Whether she flew out to sea and crashed deliberately, or met her death by accident, was never discovered.

Younger and more professional women aviators were busy at the same time making and breaking records. The New Zealander Jean Batten was the first woman to fly the South Atlantic, from England to Brazil, in 1935; she followed it the next year with the fastest solo flight from England to Australia, and went on to New Zealand, becoming the first aviator ever to make the journey.

But perhaps the best known of all the 'Queens of the Air' was Amy Johnson, who in 1930 became the first woman to fly from England to Australia. Unlike other women fliers, she was not wealthy and had no major financial backing. She was not only a flier, but also a qualified engineer who had studied direction-finding, meteorology and signalling. As with Earhart, it was her uncompromising professionalism, her courage and her modesty that endeared her to millions the world over.

log and search report, however, do not support such contentions, nor do the recollections of officers who participated in the search. Former Admiral Felix B. Stump, who was navigator for the *Lexington* in 1937 and who later became head of Air America (the CIA's airline), told the author: 'We did not violate Japanese air space over the Marshalls. Although, now, I wish we had.'

After the air search on 18 July, the *Lexington* set a course for San Diego, California, while the destroyers *Drayton*, *Lamson* and *Cushing* headed for Pearl Harbor, Hawaii. Aeroplanes from the *Lexington* had covered 151,556 square miles (392,530 square kilometres) of ocean without finding any trace of Earhart or Noonan or any wreckage from the Electra.

Straightaway, the rumours began to spread. One had it that Earhart had been working for the United States government at the time of her disappearance. Another was that she had purposefully lost herself so the US Navy could search the Japanese-controlled islands. The most dramatic speculation – not taken seriously by the American public – was that she and Fred Noonan had been forced to land on or near one of the islands and that they were being held prisoner by the Japanese.

The *Oakland Tribune* in May 1938 began a series of articles about the Earhart disappearance by reporter Alfred Reck. Somehow, Reck had managed to gain access to the then highly classified coast guard files. In the first article he alleged that Earhart and Noonan had been lost because of the failure of the US Navy direction finder on Howland Island, and that Richard Black, the US Department of Interior representative who had brought the navy direction finder aboard the *Itasca*, had supplied the wrong kind of batteries, so that the equipment failed at the very moment it was needed most. Immediately the navy, coast guard and Black brought their full authority to bear on the *Oakland Tribune* and reporter Reck. The remaining articles were censored.

Also in 1938, the popular *Smith's Weekly* newspaper, published in Sydney, Australia, printed a lengthy article alleging that the United States had used the Earhart disappearance as a pretext to fly over the Japanese-held islands and that Australia's defence establishment had been informed of the plan and of its results: 'So when Amelia Earhart went down and her faint distress signals located her aeroplane around the Phoenix Islands, the search gave the needed excuse. Sentiment comes second to secret service.' One Republican senator felt that the primary motive of the article 'may have been to stimulate ill feeling between Japan and the United States'. But the Japanese sinking of the American gunboat USS *Panay* in the Yangtze River two months later effectively buried his concern. Ill-feeling had now become outright hostility. With the surprise attack by Japan on the US fleet at Pearl Harbor on 7 December 1941, Amelia Earhart's fate was, not surprisingly, virtually forgotten.

Rumours about the fliers' disappearance continued to circulate, however. In 1944, on Majuro Atoll during the invasion of the Marshall Islands, Vice Admiral Edgar A. Cruise learned from a native interpreter that two American fliers, a man and a woman, had been picked up and brought to the Marshalls in 1937. At almost the same time, Eugene

Above: during the bitter conquest of Saipan in July 1944, US Marines keep watch on Tanapag Harbour to prevent the Japanese from attempting to escape from the island by boat. The Japanese were driven to the northernmost point of the island where, with no hope of escape and surrender unthinkable, the soldiers urged on their women and children who threw themselves off the cliff onto the rocks below. The soldiers then followed or blew themselves up with hand grenades. Above right: the interior of the cell in the ruined Garapan prison where Amelia Earhart was reportedly held until she died, possibly of dysentery. Right: one of the fathers of the Catholic Mission on Saipan with a native, Jesus Bacha Salas, who told the author that before the war he had occupied a cell in the prison in Garapan next to that of an 'American woman flier'. Many other witnesses thought that the fliers had come down somewhere near the Marshall Islands and had been brought for interrogation to Saipan by ship, their aircraft in tow

F. Bogan, the senior military government officer at Majuro, interviewed a Marshallese native who told the same story.

Four other Marine Corps and navy officers turned up similar information: an American man and woman, fliers according to the Japanese, had been brought into Jaluit in the Marshalls, then transported to Majuro and Kwajalein, also in the Marshalls, and finally taken to Saipan in the Marianas. Saipan was Japan's military headquarters in the Pacific islands before and during the Second World War. All these men filed reports, which still remain classified.

During the invasion of Saipan in June 1944, the possibility of the capture of Earhart by the Japanese became stronger with the testimony of Saipanese natives that two Americans, a man and a woman, identified by the Japanese as fliers, had been brought to the island in 1937 and detained. The woman had died of dysentery and the man reportedly had been executed some time after her death. They had been buried in unmarked graves outside a native cemetery.

In 1964 two former US Marines, Everett Henson Jr and Bill G. Burks, came forward to say they were part of a group of Marines who recovered the remains of Amelia Earhart and Frederick Noonan on Saipan in July 1944. They had found remains, they said, in an unmarked grave outside a small graveyard and placed them in metal canisters for transport to the United States. To this day, the US Marine Corps will neither confirm nor deny such an event ever occurred.

It was not until 1960 that a real investigation began, and that investigation was civilian. The Columbia Broadcasting System in San Francisco sponsored four expeditions to Saipan Island in the Marianas and two more to Majuro Atoll in the Marshalls to try to find answers to the Earhart mystery. Several hundred natives on Saipan were questioned and more than thirty individuals told stories that supported the theory that two American fliers, a man and a woman, had lived and died on Saipan before the war.

When the Freedom of Information Act became law in the United States in 1968 a number of files began to appear and more and more pertinent material has been found and declassified since. From 1968 to the present day, well over 20,000 pages of records concerning the Earhart flight from seven different departments of the US government and the military have been released, and there is certainly a great deal more to be revealed.

One revelation is the close involvement of the government in the preparations for the flight. The idea for a round-the-world flight had begun at the Purdue Research Foundation at Purdue University in Lafayette, Indiana. Amelia Earhart had served the university for brief periods as a lecturer and counsellor to women students. The foundation, formed to seek 'new knowledge in the field of aviation, with particular reference to National Defense', was in close communication with the US War Department, Army Air Corps and Naval Aviation. The foundation provided the funds for the purchase of Earhart's Lockheed Electra on the understanding that the aeroplane would be used 'for the purpose of improving radio direction finding equipment'.

Earhart first planned to fly the Pacific from east to west and refuel in flight over Midway Island with the assistance of a specially equipped US Navy aircraft. Techniques such as mid-air refuelling were then in their infancy and extremely risky. Then the pilot's needs and those of the military coincided. Earhart needed a safer method for crossing the Pacific, and the navy and Army Air Corps needed an excuse to build an airfield on an island near the equator. America had agreed with Japan at the Naval Treaty Conference in Washington in 1923 that military construction on most of the Pacific islands controlled by each nation would be prohibited. The United States had long believed that Japan was violating that treaty in the mandated islands, but could not prove it. America had played the same game on Midway and Wake Islands through co-operation with Pan American Airways. Now, Earhart provided a purely civilian reason for building an airstrip on Howland.

From the records that have now been released, Earhart does not seem to have been conducting an overt spy mission during the world flight, though, at one time, that did look possible. There is, however, evidence and testimony that she and Noonan were gathering what is called 'white intelligence'. As civilians they were quite legitimately going to visit and fly in and out of places seldom, if ever, visited by the US military, and observation of these areas would be valuable.

Nothing in the records released so far proves that the

There is strong testimony that two American fliers were picked up by Japanese military units

Japanese captured Earhart and Noonan, though the testimony gathered from Marshallese and Saipanese native witnesses is very strong. Nor is there anything documentary to substantiate the claim that the remains of Earhart and Noonan were recovered on Saipan in 1944 by US Marines.

There *is* evidence that Roosevelt and naval intelligence suspected that Earhart and Noonan might have fallen into the hands of the Japanese. The Office of Naval Intelligence arranged in December 1937 that an American working with the Korean underground against the Japanese, Kilsoo Haan, should sneak several of his agents into the Japanese mandated islands 'to determine whether Miss Earhart and Captain Noonan are alive or dead'. Was that mission ever carried out? If so, its results have never been made public.

In recent years, two Americans have come forward with information that proves that the Earhart saga is far from ended. Thomas McKeon says that, as an officer with the 441st US Army Counter Intelligence Corps Unit in Tokyo, he read the Japanese files on the case and even talked with a former Japanese officer who had served as an interpreter when Earhart and Noonan were questioned. Carroll Harris was, from 1942 to 1945, one of the navy personnel responsible for the 'Security Room' of the Chief of US Naval Operations, Ernest King. In the top-secret vault in the room in Washington, there was, he claimed, an extensive file on Amelia Earhart. Its information went as far back as pre-First World War navy involvement in the Pacific, and included material picked up during the invasion of various Japanese-held islands in the Second World War. Harris recalls that the records were carefully boxed and sent to the US Naval Supply Depot at Crane, Indiana, towards the end of the war in 1945. So far, the records referred to by McKeon and Harris have not been found.

After 23 years of research, twelve trips to Saipan and four to Majuro Atoll, the author has arrived at certain conclusions that might offer a solution to the mystery. Namely, at the time of their disappearance, Earhart and Noonan were co-operating with their government and there is strong testimony that two American fliers were picked up by Japanese military units somewhere in the Pacific and taken to the Marshalls and then to Saipan.

But just where the Electra landed is very much a matter for conjecture. If the Japanese know, they have said nothing. If Earhart and Noonan were off course considerably to the north of Howland Island, they may have landed at Mili or one of the other islands in the southern Marshalls. If they were blown off-course to the south (which could have happened if they did not receive the weather forecast predicting significant winds from the north-east), the Phoenix Islands would surely have been their choice. Until the mysterious and uncharted reefs lying between Howland and the Phoenix Islands are thoroughly searched and the lagoons of those islands are plumbed, the possibility remains that the wreckage of the Electra could still be found.

Below: every twist and turn in the saga of the missing Electra was widely reported in the world's press, such as in this front page article which features a smiling Earhart before the flight indicating to reporters how big she thought Howland Island was. In the end all the hopes raised by reports of signals from the aircraft were cruelly dashed. Eventually, after sixteen days of the largest air-sea rescue operation in history, the search was called off. The epitaph for Amelia Earhart and Frederick Noonan was 'two civilian fliers lost at sea'. But Earhart's former secretary was only one among many who held another view. 'President Roosevelt knew about everything,' she told the author in the early Sixties. 'When one does the things Amelia was doing, one can't expect to receive justice. She knew that. She talked to me about it'

THE WEATHER
Saturday and Sunday generally fair and warmer

Columbus Evening Dispatch

VOL. 67, NO. 3. Telephone—MAin 1234

OHIO'S GREATEST HOME DAILY

SATURDAY, JULY 3, 1937.

14 PAGES

Wirephotos
Associated Press
International
News Service

AMELIA'S VOICE, CALLING S-O-S, IS HEARD BY LOS ANGELES RADIO MAN; SIGNALS SPUR SEARCH

FLYER'S OWN STORY WRITTEN BEFORE LAST TAKEOFF

By Amelia Earhart

LAE, NEW GUINEA, JULY 2. — "Denmark's a prison" and Lae, as attractive and unusual as it is, appears to two flyers just as confining. The Lockheed Electra is poised for our longest trip.

It is weighted with gasoline and oil to capacity. There is only one runway and a parallel is needed to take off. However, the wind is blowing the wrong way and threatening clouds conspired to keep her on the ground today.

In addition Frederick Noonan, my navigator, has been unable, because of radio difficulties, to set his chronometers. Any lack of knowledge of their fastness or slowness would defeat the accuracy of celestial navigation. Howland is such a small spot in the mid Pacific that every aid to locating it must be available. Despite our restlessness and disappointment in not getting off yesterday morning, we still retained enough enthusiasm to do some exploring of native villages a few miles from Lae.

We commandeered a truck from the manager of the hotel and with Fred Noonan at the wheel because the native driver was ill with fever we set out along a dirt road. We forded a sparkling little river, which after a heavy rain so common in the tropics, can be turned into a veritable torrent, and drove through a lane of grass taller than the truck. We turned into a beautiful cocoanut grove before a village entrance. The natives grow the cocoanuts mostly for their

Operator Sure He Heard Flyer

Planes and Ships Rush to Hunt For Aviatrix, Down at Sea After Futile Attempt to Reach Howland Island.

LOS ANGELES, JULY 3.—(INS).—Amelia Earhart's voice came crackling over the Pacific today from her big airship drifting helplessly in mid-Pacific.

The voice was heard by a Los Angeles amateur radio operator.

"SOS, KHAQQ . . . SOS, KHAQQ . . ." she repeated. The rest of the message, probably giving her position, faded away.

Where Earhart Is Lost . . . . on Pacific Flight to . . . . Such a Tiny Island

FRED NOONAN

MISS EARHART JOKED ABOUT HOWLAND THEN

Fireworks

THE ZODIAC KILLER

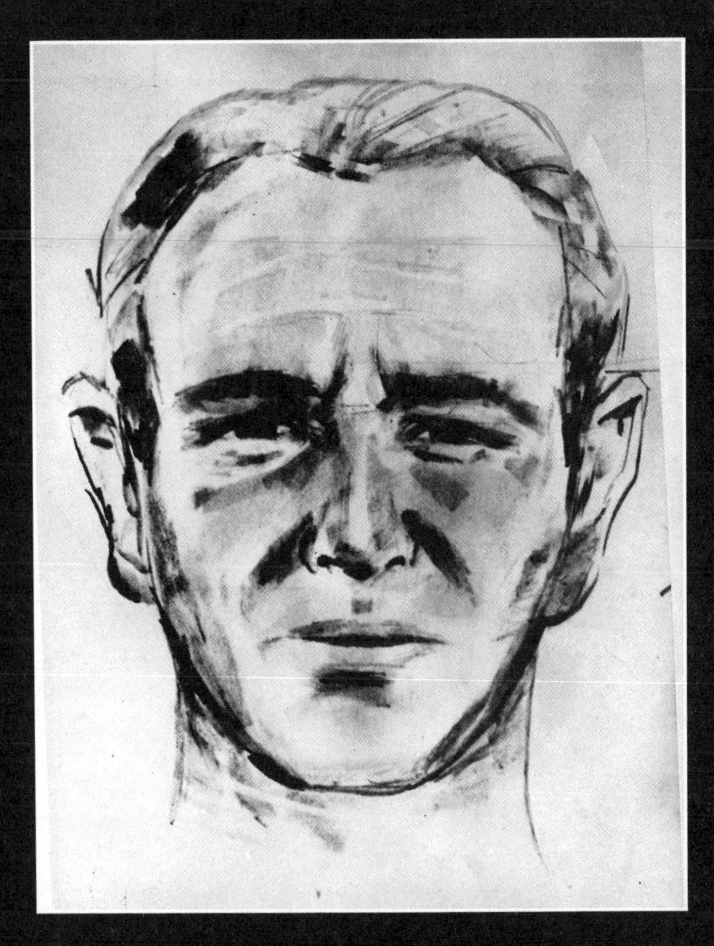

On a cold, clear evening in December 1968 a teenage couple on their first date parked their car at a well-known lovers' spot above a reservoir in San Francisco Bay, California. Within minutes they were both dead from gun-shot wounds in an apparently motiveless murder – the first known crime of an insane killer who terrorised California with random murders for the next ten months. In mocking letters and telephone calls boasting of his crimes to the police, he called himself 'Zodiac'; a letter in code using astro-logical symbols gave a chilling account of the pleasure he got from killing people – 'collecting slaves for my afterlife'. Yet despite the evidence of cartridge cases, fingerprints, descrip-tions, voice-identifications and handwriting, the police have never caught 'Zodiac'. *COLIN WILSON* tells the story of the maniac murderer from San Francisco

Sooner or later, this hunter of human beings would probably experience the urge to kill again

Right: David Farraday (top) and Bettilou Jensen, the teenagers murdered in their car on the evening of 20 December 1968. They were the first known victims of the killer who became known as Zodiac, though claims he made later that he had murdered eight people led police to wonder whether student Cheri Jo Bates, found stabbed and with her throat cut in autumn 1968, was in fact his first victim. Below right: the parking spot near a pump-house overlooking the Lake Herman reservoir in San Francisco (below) where David and Bettilou were shot dead

IT was the perfect night for young lovers: calm, moonlit and cold enough outside for the inside of the estate car to seem the most delightful place in the world. David Farraday and Bettilou Jensen were out on their first date on the night of 20 December 1968. They had spent most of the evening at the high school Christmas concert in nearby Vallejo, a small town about 20 miles (30 kilometres) north-east of San Francisco, California. Now, at 11.15pm, they had just parked near a concrete pump-house above Lake Herman reservoir. The heater blew warm air, the radio played pop music, and the seventeen-year-old boy and sixteen-year-old girl began to get better acquainted.

Suddenly, a man appeared at the window, and David Farraday found himself looking straight down the barrel of a gun. As the youth opened the door and started to climb out, the gun exploded. David Farraday fell dead instantly with a bullet wound behind his left ear. Bettilou flung open her own door and began to run. In the moonlight, it was impossible for the gunman to miss her; five shots ploughed into her back and she collapsed 75 yards (68 metres) from the car.

Only a few minutes later, another car drove past the pump-house. The woman driver saw the two bodies clearly in the headlights, but she did not stop; on the contrary, she put her foot down on the accelerator and drove fast towards the next town, Benicia, about 6 miles (9 kilometres) away, where she was going to meet her children from the Saturday evening cinema. A few miles further along the road she

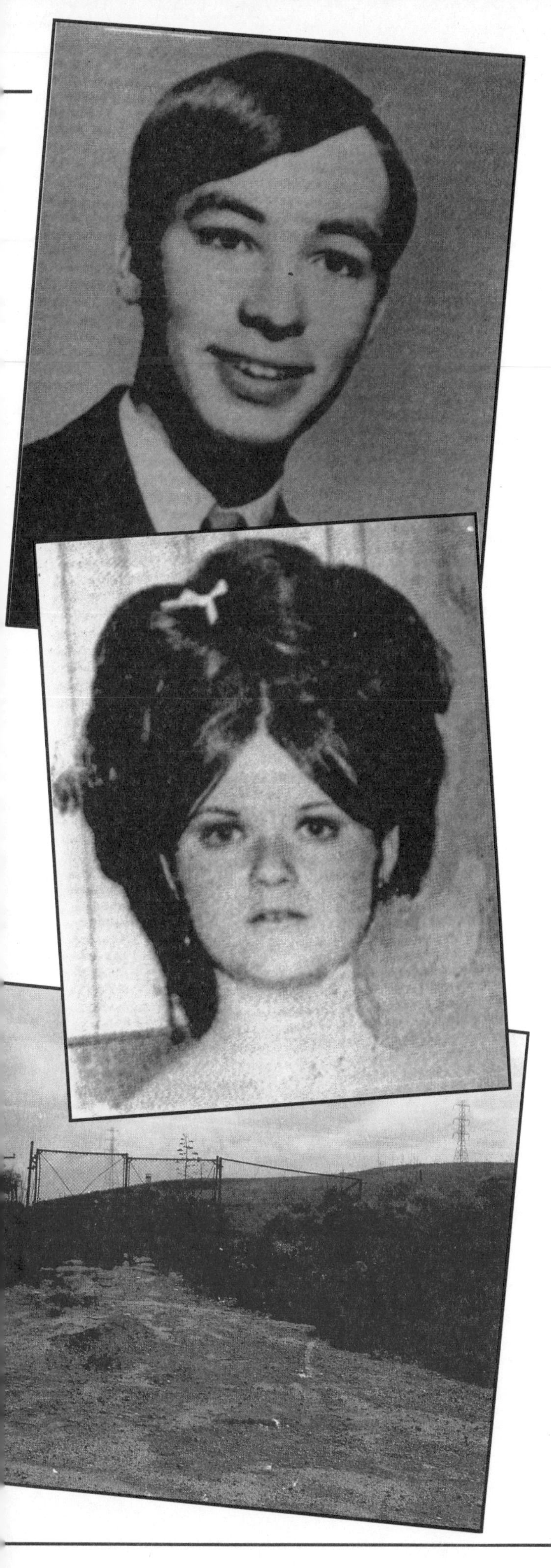

saw, with relief, the red, flashing light of an oncoming police car. Within minutes, two deputy sheriffs and a detective sergeant were on their way to the pump-house on the Vallejo-Benicia road.

The young couple were both dead, and the warmth of their bodies told Detective Sergeant Leslie Lundblad that they had died recently. But beyond that there seemed to be no clues. David Farraday's wallet was intact in his pocket. Bettilou Jensen lay exactly as she had fallen, and her clothing was undisturbed. This, however, did not entirely rule out sex as a motive – it was conceivable that the killer had been disturbed by the passing car and taken refuge temporarily behind his victims' car until it had gone. The woman driver had, it turned out, shown very good sense in not stopping to investigate.

There were two more possible explanations. The most obvious was jealousy. David Farraday was a good-looking young man; Bettilou was a pretty girl. Perhaps some rejected lover had followed them as they drove towards the lovers' lane. The other possibility was rather more disturbing: that the killer was not a rejected lover, merely a reject – and a man who hated *all* lovers.

Lundblad's investigations soon disposed of the jealousy theory. David and Bettilou were ordinary high-school students. Both had good scholastic records and David was a scout and a fine athlete. Neither had any 'secret life' to investigate. It became clear to Lundblad that the two victims must have been chosen at random. Their killer had probably been hiding near the pump-house – a well-known resort for young lovers – waiting, like a hunter, for someone to arrive. It seemed probable that he had parked his car out of sight and sat in it until David's estate car had arrived. Even that was only a guess; the ground was frozen too hard to show tyre tracks. Only one thing seemed clear: sooner or later, this hunter of human beings would probably experience the urge to kill again.

Six months passed and David Farraday and Bettilou Jensen became just two more statistics in California's huge file of unsolved crimes. It looked as though their murders were an isolated incident until, shortly before midnight on 4 July 1969, another young couple parked their car in Blue Rock Springs Park, Vallejo, only 2 miles (3 kilometres) from the place where David and Bettilou had died. The car, a brown Ford Corvair, belonged to the girl, 22-year-old Darlene Elizabeth Ferrin, a Vallejo waitress and mother of a young child. With her was nineteen-year-old Michael Renault Mageau, who worked for his father, a Vallejo businessman.

Soon after the couple drove into the car park, another car came and parked beside them. They were not particularly disturbed at this: there were various other cars in the park, the nearest of which contained several people. In any case, this second car soon went away, leaving them in peace. Ten minutes passed, and suddenly the same car returned, this time parking on the other side of the Corvair. A blinding beam of light, like a searchlight, shone through the window on the passenger side, which made the couple think that it was a police patrol car. A man opened the door and came over towards them. Suddenly there was an explosion of gunfire. Two shots struck Darlene Ferrin as she sat at the wheel; another ploughed into Michael Mageau's neck and went up into his mouth, causing him to scream with agony. Then the man turned and walked back to his own car. He paused and fired another four shots, then drove away, backing out so fast that he left a smell of burning rubber behind him.

Michael Mageau, still conscious, saw him drive away. By this time he was lying on the ground beside the car, trying to reach the nearest other car in the park. But before he succeeded, this car also drove away: the occupants were obviously anxious not to get involved. Michael Mageau lost consciousness.

At four minutes past midnight, the switchboard operator at the Vallejo Police Headquarters received a call. A man's voice told her, 'I want to report a double murder. If you go one mile east on Columbus Parkway to a public park, you will find the kids in a brown car. They are shot with a 9mm Luger. I also killed those kids last year. Goodbye.' Then the line went dead.

When the police patrol car arrived at Blue Rock Springs

Above right: Darlene Ferrin, a 22-year-old waitress who was shot dead by Zodiac in July 1969 while out with her boyfriend Michael Mageau. Mageau survived and was able to give evidence to the police. He described his attacker as having light brown hair and wearing spectacles. Other witnesses in the car park where the two were shot corroborated some of the details, including the information that the killer drove a brown car. Zodiac, quickly irritated by the lack of publicity given to the case, sent letters to three major newspapers on 1 August 1969, each containing a letter and a fragment of code that revealed some knowledge of astrological symbols (right). He signed the letters with a cross inside a circle – the sign of the zodiac, which gave him his name. The code defeated the cipher experts at the nearby Mare Island Naval Yard, but was eventually cracked (below) by a schoolteacher and his wife. Zodiac's promise that the code contained a clue to his identity proved false

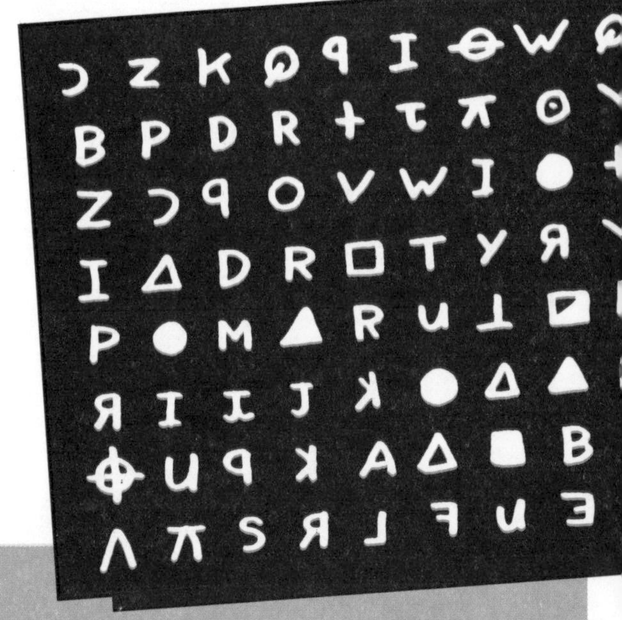

I L I K E K I L L I N G P E O P L

E B E C A U S E I T I S S O M U C

H F U N I T I S M O R E F U N T H

It was the signature on the letters – the circle with a cross inside it – that provided the killer with his nickname. The sign is the astrological symbol for the zodiac

Park, the officers discovered that the caller had been mistaken about one detail: it was not a double murder. Michael Mageau was still alive, although the bullet that had passed through his tongue prevented him from speaking. Darlene Ferrin was dead.

Michael Mageau slowly recovered. When he could speak, he was able to describe his assailant as a stocky, round-faced man, about 5 feet 8 inches (1.72 metres) tall, with light brown wavy or curly hair. His age was around thirty. The gun he had used was not the same one as in the previous case; this one was a 9mm whereas the other was a ·22. But the Solano County Sheriff's Department had little doubt that the caller was telling the truth when he admitted to killing David Farraday and Bettilou Jensen. And Lundblad now knew that his worst apprehensions were confirmed. The killer's motive was not robbery, rape, or jealousy. This was simply a 'nut', a homicidal maniac who killed at random.

Again, there were no clues. Even the discovery that the killer had used a public telephone booth in a garage 2 miles (3 kilometres) from the murder scene failed to provide a lead. The garage had been closed at the time, so no one had seen the caller. The likeliest inference was that the killer was an inhabitant of Vallejo, or was at least familiar with the town, and knew where the garage was and that it would be closed. And since Vallejo was a small town, that seemed a promising lead. Surely somebody would recognise Michael Mageau's description of the stocky, wavy-haired man who drove a brown car, probably a Ford?

But it seemed that no one did. And four weeks after the 4 July murder, the killer himself apparently became impatient with the police's lack of progress and decided to liven up the investigation. On the morning of 1 August 1969 the editor of the *Vallejo Times-Herald* received a crudely scrawled letter, signed with a circle containing a cross, which looked ominously like the telescopic sight of a rifle. The letter-writer described himself as the man who had shot both couples, giving details that made it clear that he knew more about the murders than had been made public. For example, he gave precise details of the type of bullets that had killed Darlene Ferrin. He also mentioned the clothing worn by Bettilou Jensen, evidence that he had taken a close look at her body before fleeing from the scene.

The letter contained an enclosure – a third of a sheet of paper, covered with a strange cipher. What had happened to the other two thirds? The answer soon came. They were enclosed in two more letters, sent simultaneously to the *San Francisco Chronicle* and the *San Francisco Examiner*. The letters to all three newspapers were identical; the code was not. But the letter-writer explained that if the three fragments of the ciphered message were decoded and joined together, they would reveal his identity.

It was the signature on the letters – the circle with a cross inside it – that provided the killer with his nickname. The sign is the astrological symbol for the zodiac, the circle of twelve heavenly constellations. From then on, the newspapers called the killer 'Zodiac'. All three letters contained the same threat: that if they were not published that same

'I will cruse around killing people who are alone until Sun night or until I kill a dozen people'

Below: policemen from two counties in the San Francisco Bay area compare notes in their search for Zodiac. A pile of 'Wanted' posters lies on the table, while behind the officers is the first, crude Identikit picture of the killer. The sign of the zodiac, with which the killer signed his letters to the newspapers and police, is drawn on the top left corner of the blackboard

Murderers on the move

Since the Zodiac murders in the late Sixties the USA has been plagued with a new type of criminal: the 'serial killer'. This, according to a US Justice Department report of January 1984, is someone who has killed at least ten people. During the Seventies there were at least seventeen such murderers and of this number nine have committed more than twenty murders each. According to *The New York Times* of 21 January 1984, 'Law enforcement officials say there have been isolated examples of such criminals in the past, including Jack the Ripper. . . . But after a study of homicide reports spanning the past few decades, the officials assert that history offers nothing to compare with the spate of such murders in the United States since the beginning of the Seventies.'

Why did it take so long for this to dawn on the Justice Department? The answer is that most 'serial killers' roam the country, often moving on quickly after committing murders in a particular area. Lack of cooperation between records departments in different states means that police may be quite unaware that a killer is travelling across the US leaving a trail of bodies behind him. In April 1979, 22-year-old Steven Judy was arrested in Indiana, charged with raping and murdering a young woman and killing her two children. Before his execution he told his stepmother that he had travelled around the country and had raped and killed more women than he could remember.

In the early Seventies the McCrary family – three men and two women – wandered from Florida to California, abducting waitresses and shop assistants whom they raped and murdered; their arrest in 1972 led the police to investigate 22 such crimes. Theodore Bundy, a plausible young law student, roamed the country and is believed to have killed more than thirty young girls. The 'freeway killers' of the Seventies specialised in murdering young men and dumping their bodies on roads; William Bonin was eventually charged with some of these killings, but another thirty or so are still unsolved. In 1983, George Stano admitted to having killed 31 girls in Florida alone. Patrick Kearney killed eighteen young men in California in 1980. And Henry Lee Lucas claimed that he and a partner killed a total of two hundred women and children in the Seventies.

'Something's going on out there,' said Robert Heck of the US Justice Department, 'It's an epidemic.' He estimates that 4000 Americans a year – at least half of them under the age of eighteen – are murdered by 'serial killers'; their bodies are dumped on hillsides or at the side of deserted roads and are never identified. Now the epidemic has been recognised, the solution may be brought nearer by computerisation of records departments of different counties and states, which will permit closer cooperation between police departments.

Above left: killer Danny McCrary under arrest in 1972. Left: Steven Judy, who claimed to have raped and killed more women than he could remember. Below: six faces of Theodore Bundy, charged with over thirty murders

day, 1 August, the writer would 'go on a rampage': 'This will last the whole weekend and I will cruse around killing people who are alone until Sun night or until I kill a dozen people.'

The letters were published – but not in their entirety. Certain details were withheld, including the murder threats. Most major murder cases provoke false confessions from the mentally ill; by withholding part of the letters, the police had a useful method of distinguishing between a harmless crank (who would not be able to say what was missing) and the real killer, if they were to make an arrest.

All three newspapers published the complete text of the cryptogram, together with a request that the letter-writer should provide more proof of his identity. Zodiac responded promptly, sending the *San Francisco Examiner* a letter beginning: 'This is Zodiac speaking', in which he gave more details of the crimes. But he provided no further clue to his identity.

Public attention now centred on the cryptogram. It was sent to naval code experts at the nearby Mare Island Naval Yard, but they failed to crack it. Amateur cryptanalysts all over the state experienced the same lack of success. But one

man – a schoolteacher named Donald Harden, who lived in Salinas, California – had the inspired idea of looking for groups of signs that might fit the word 'kill', on the grounds that this word would be used more than once. When he had found the suspected group of signs, he began the long, slow business of working out other letters that might be associated with it – for example, endings like '-ing' or '-ed'. It took Harden and his wife ten hours to decode most of the letter. It read:

> I like killing people because it is so much fun it is more fun than killing wild game in the forest because man is the most dangerous animal of all to kill something gives me the most thrilling experience it is even better than getting your rock off with a girl the best part of it is when I die I will be reborn in paradise and

Above: Bryan Hartnell and Cecilia Shepard, tied up and stabbed while picnicking on the shores of Lake Berryessa, California. Hartnell survived and was able to give police a description of the hooded killer's appearance and voice. Cecilia Shepard died without regaining consciousness. Left: the telephone booth in Napa used by Zodiac to inform the police of his crime. The receiver bore three fingerprints, but they did not correspond with any in the state criminal records. Above left: police with the door panel of Hartnell's car, on which the killer had written the dates and times of his attacks

> all I have killed will become my slaves I will not give you my name because you will try to slow down or stop my collecting slaves for my afterlife. . .

The decoding was made more complicated by the fact that the cryptogram was full of spelling errors (such as 'forrest' for forest and 'sloi' for slow), and it ended in an incomprehensible jumble: 'ebeori st me thh piti.'

But the threatened massacre (the 'rampage') did not materialise. Perhaps Zodiac was satisfied with the partial publication of his letter, or perhaps he never had any intention of going on a murder rampage on a weekend when every police officer in California would be looking for him. The threat was simply to cause the maximum amount of panic.

The public offered more than a thousand tips, and every one was checked by the police. Yet ten weeks after the murder of Darlene Ferrin, they were still apparently no closer to solving the crimes. The long, blazing hot summer drew to a close. On the afternoon of Saturday 27 September, two students from Pacific Union College, a Seventh Day Adventist institution above Napa Valley, went out for a picnic on the shores of Lake Berryessa, about 13 miles (20 kilometres) north of Vallejo. Bryan Hartnell was twenty years old, and Cecilia Shepard was 22. They had just finished eating at about 4.30pm when they heard a noise behind them. From the shadow of a tree, a hooded figure stepped out. On the part of the hood covering the figure's chest was a zodiac sign, drawn in white. The short, pudgy figure advanced towards them, a gun in one hand and a knife in the other.

In a gruff voice, the man asked Hartnell for money, and the young man said he was welcome to the small amount he had on him. The hooded man then declared that he was an escapee from Deer Lodge State Prison in Montana, where he had killed a guard, and said that he needed to take their white sports car so that he could get to Mexico. Then he produced a length of plastic clothes-line and proceeded to tie them both up. As he tied Hartnell's hands, the young man was able to see through the eye-slits in the hood that their assailant wore glasses and had brown hair. When he had tied both victims by the wrists and ankles, the man announced: 'I'm going to have to stab you people.' Hartnell replied, 'I'm chicken. Please stab me first – I couldn't bear to see her stabbed.' 'I'll do just that,' said the man, and plunged the knife again and again into Hartnell's back. Sick and dizzy with pain, Hartnell then watched the man attack Cecilia. This, obviously, was what the killer had been looking forward to. After the first stab he went into a frenzy, driving the knife again and again into her back. Then he turned her over and stabbed her repeatedly in the stomach. When he had finished, he went over to their car, took out a black felt-tipped pen and wrote on the passenger door. Then he left.

Fighting off unconsciousness, Bryan Hartnell managed to struggle over to Cecilia and undo her wrist bonds with his teeth. It made no difference; she was too weak to move. But fortunately help was already on the way. A fisherman on the lake had heard their screams and had seen the two

Right: the corner of Washington Street and Cherry Street in San Francisco where taxi-driver Paul Stine (below, inset) was shot in the back of the head in October 1969 by a customer who stole his takings. Police regarded it as a straightforward armed robbery until the following week when a newspaper received a letter from Zodiac claiming to be the murderer. To prove it, he enclosed a piece of bloodstained shirt that exactly matched the torn shirt found on Stine's body (below). Below right: a new cryptogram, sent with a second letter to the same newspaper a month later, which Zodiac enclosed with another piece of Stine's shirt as proof of his identity. No translation of the cipher has been released to the public

bodies lying on the shore. He rowed straight to the headquarters of the park ranger and within half an hour Ranger William White was kneeling by the two victims, who both looked close to death. They had just been rushed off to hospital when the Napa police arrived. They, however, had not been summoned by the fisherman or the ranger. They had been alerted by an anonymous telephone call, a man with a gruff voice telling them: 'I want to report a murder. No, a double murder. They are two miles north of park headquarters. They were in a white Volkswagen Karmann Ghia. I'm the one that did it.' There was no click to end the call; the man had apparently left the telephone to dangle off the hook.

Bryan Hartnell and Cecilia Shepard arrived at hospital in Napa; neither was able to speak. Cecilia died two days later without recovering from her coma; Bryan Hartnell recovered slowly, and was later able to describe their attacker. But by then the police already knew they were dealing with Zodiac. They found his sign on the passenger door of the sports car. He had also written two dates, 20 December and 4 July, the dates of the first two attacks; and a time, 4.30, the time of

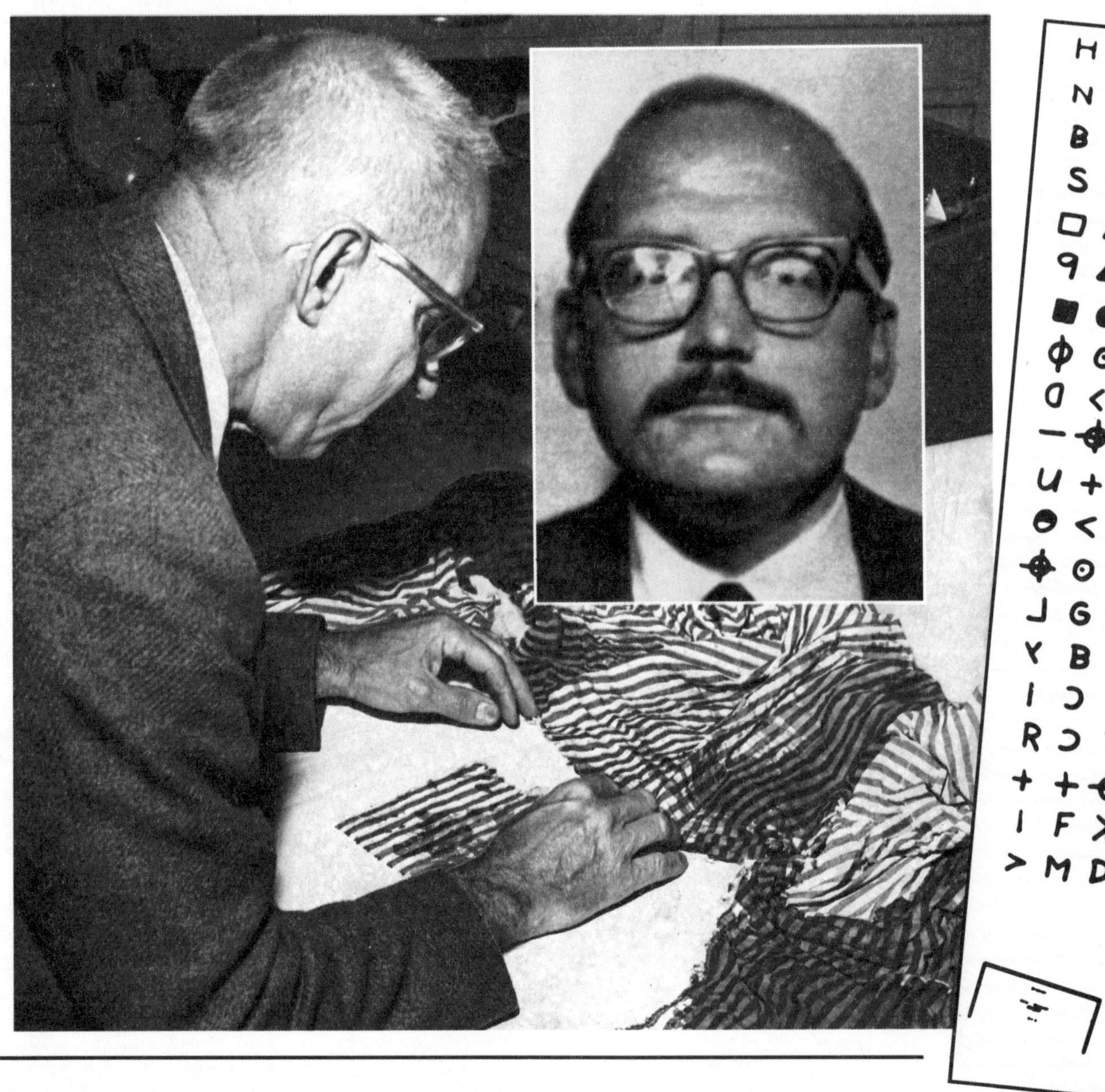

the third attack.

Only six blocks from the police headquarters in Napa, the police found the public telephone from which Zodiac had made the call; the telephone receiver was still hanging off the hook. Technicians found three fingerprints on it, but this clue also led nowhere. The killer's prints were not on police records in California; apparently he had no criminal record in the state. A check with Montana's Deer Lodge State Prison revealed what the police already took for granted: the killer's talk about escaping and killing a guard there was pure fantasy.

Two weeks later, on the evening of 11 October 1969, a student and part-time taxi-driver named Paul Stine picked up a passenger near the Fairmont Hotel on Nob Hill in San Francisco; he was a stocky man with brown hair and horn-rimmed glasses. A quarter of an hour later, two youths standing at the intersection of Washington Street and Cherry Street heard the sound of a gunshot. It came from a yellow cab that had pulled in to the kerb. As they watched, a man got out of the back seat, and leaned through the window into the front of the cab. There was a tearing noise, then the man began wiping the cab with a piece of cloth. Suddenly aware that he was being watched, he left the cab and began to walk rapidly along the street towards the great open space called the Presidio.

The youths alerted the police, who were at the spot within minutes. Paul Stine was slumped forward over the wheel of the cab. The 29-year-old student of San Francisco State College was dead, shot in the back of the head. The motive was robbery – his wallet was missing and so was the cash from previous fares. The tearing noise the witnesses had heard had been Stine's shirt, which the killer had used to wipe the cab, presumably to eliminate fingerprints.

It looked like a typical armed robbery, the kind that often occurs in San Francisco on a Saturday night. The only unusual feature about this particular crime was its sheer ruthlessness – the driver had been killed when he could just as easily have been left alive. It was not until the following Tuesday that the police realised that they had come close to catching Zodiac. The *San Francisco Chronicle* received a letter that began: 'This is Zodiac speaking. I am the murderer of the taxi driver over by Washington and Maple Street last night. To prove this here is a bloodstained piece of his shirt. I am the same man who did in the people in the south bay area. The S.F. [San Francisco] police could have caught me last night if they had tried. . . '

The letter went on to jeer at the police for not making a thorough search of the Presidio, and commented on how much the killer detested the sound of the police motor cycles. It continued: 'Schoolchildren make nice targets. I think I shall wipe out a school bus some morning. Just shoot out the tyres and then pick off all the kiddies as they come bouncing out.'

The letter was signed with the mark of the Zodiac. By that time, a check on the bullet that had killed Stine showed that it came from the same ·22 that had killed the first two victims ten months before. There could be no doubt that the letter was genuine. The bloodstained piece

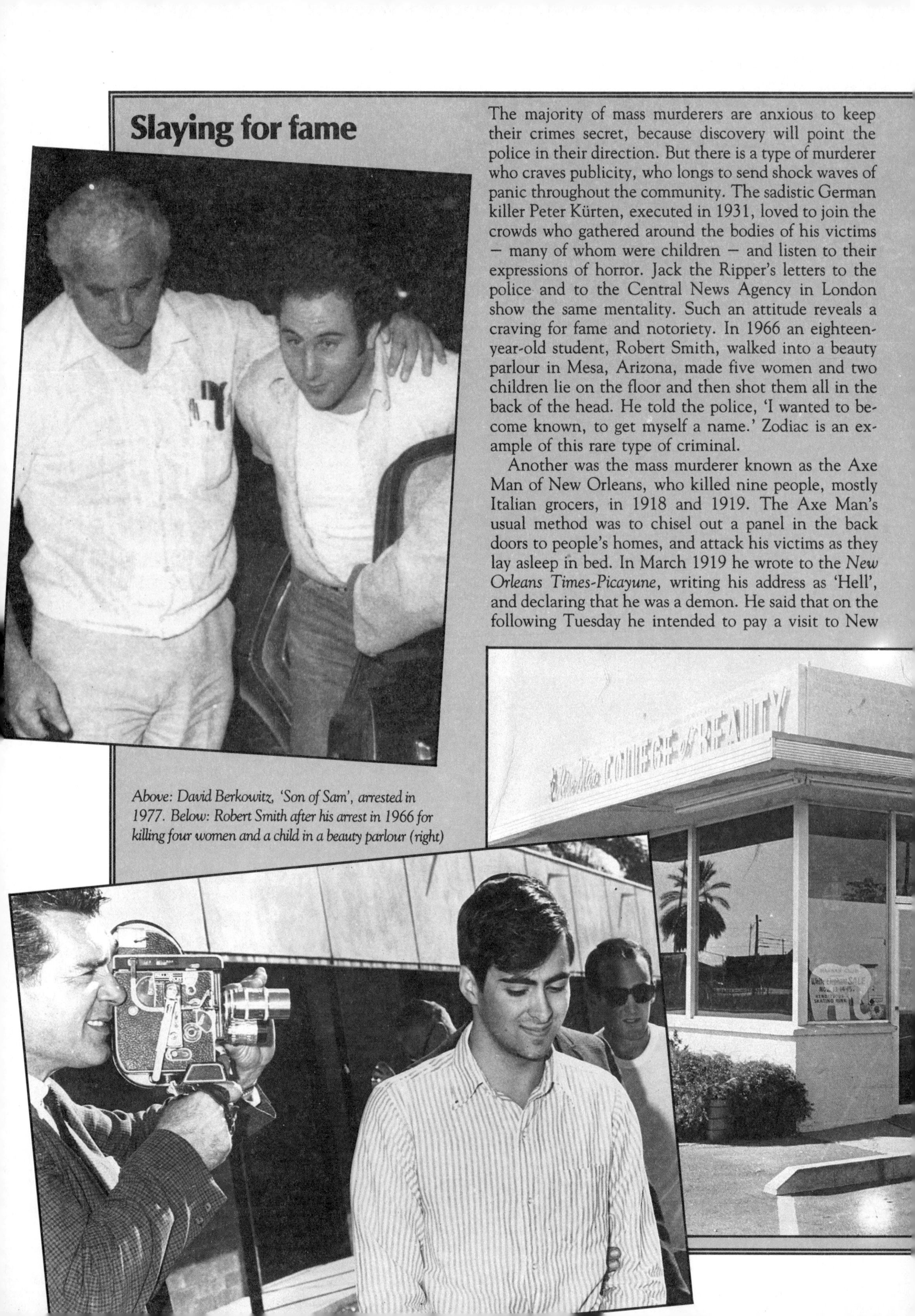

Slaying for fame

The majority of mass murderers are anxious to keep their crimes secret, because discovery will point the police in their direction. But there is a type of murderer who craves publicity, who longs to send shock waves of panic throughout the community. The sadistic German killer Peter Kürten, executed in 1931, loved to join the crowds who gathered around the bodies of his victims – many of whom were children – and listen to their expressions of horror. Jack the Ripper's letters to the police and to the Central News Agency in London show the same mentality. Such an attitude reveals a craving for fame and notoriety. In 1966 an eighteen-year-old student, Robert Smith, walked into a beauty parlour in Mesa, Arizona, made five women and two children lie on the floor and then shot them all in the back of the head. He told the police, 'I wanted to become known, to get myself a name.' Zodiac is an example of this rare type of criminal.

Another was the mass murderer known as the Axe Man of New Orleans, who killed nine people, mostly Italian grocers, in 1918 and 1919. The Axe Man's usual method was to chisel out a panel in the back doors to people's homes, and attack his victims as they lay asleep in bed. In March 1919 he wrote to the *New Orleans Times-Picayune*, writing his address as 'Hell', and declaring that he was a demon. He said that on the following Tuesday he intended to pay a visit to New

Above: David Berkowitz, 'Son of Sam', arrested in 1977. Below: Robert Smith after his arrest in 1966 for killing four women and a child in a beauty parlour (right)

Orleans to look for victims, but that he would bypass all houses in which jazz music was being played. That Tuesday evening the whole of New Orleans rocked to the sound of jazz. The Axe Man failed to appear, and his identity was never discovered.

Another mass murderer whose crimes bear a curious resemblance to those of Zodiac is David Berkowitz, better known as 'Son of Sam', an insane killer who terrorised New York for thirteen months in the mid Seventies. Like Zodiac, 'Son of Sam' walked up to cars and fired at random, often choosing courting couples. Caught purely by chance in August 1977 when a policeman came to stick a parking ticket on his car while he was committing his sixth murder, Berkowitz proved to be 'a mouse of a man' — plump, smiling, very polite, a boring nonentity. Like Zodiac, Berkowitz also liked to write letters to the police, using phrases like, 'I love to hunt. Prowling the streets looking for fair game — tasty meat. The women of Queens are prettiest of all. . . . ' Berkowitz was intensely shy and probably a virgin; his crimes were a way of asserting his masculinity. Although judged sane (and sentenced to 365 years in jail), Berkowitz was undoubtedly mentally retarded. In view of the soft-voiced caller who identified himself as 'Sam' on Jim Dunbar's show, it may be more than coincidence that Berkowitz decided to call himself 'Son of Sam': was the Zodiac killer of the late Sixties his hero?

of cloth was from the tail of a shirt, and it fitted the torn shirt left on Paul Stine.

Was the killer serious about shooting children from a school bus? Probably not — he had never, so far, taken any real risk; he liked to kill stealthily, then run away. But the threat could certainly not be ignored. Armed deputies started to ride on all school buses, not only in San Francisco but in all the surrounding towns. Drivers were instructed not, on any account, to stop even if shots were fired; they were to drive on at top speed, sounding the horn and flashing the lights.

But all these precautions proved unnecessary. The murder of Paul Stine was the last officially recorded crime of the Zodiac killer. The murderer may well have felt that the hunt was getting too close; the police by now had good descriptions of him, and had issued 'Wanted' notices showing a man with a crew-cut and horn-rimmed glasses. Police from Napa to San Francisco were permanently on the alert; and there was a noticeable drop in the number of courting couples using lovers' lanes at night. The team hunting Zodiac now believed they were getting close, and that it would only be a matter of time before their net snared the man whose fingerprints matched those found on the telephone. But this optimism proved to be unfounded.

Zodiac had decided to stop killing, but his craving for publicity was unsated. In the early hours of 21 October, ten days after the murder of Paul Stine, the switchboard operator of the Oakland Police Department heard a gruff voice saying, 'This is Zodiac'. He went on to make a number of remarks that later convinced police that he was the man who had so far killed five people. What he really wanted, said the caller, was to give himself up. He would do that on condition that he was represented by a famous lawyer — preferably F. Lee Bailey or Melvin Belli, both well-known lawyers at the time. He would also, he said, like to speak on a famous television talk-show that went out on breakfast television.

The requests sounded absurd, but the Zodiac squad decided that it was worth a try. They immediately contacted Melvin Belli, who had an office in San Francisco, and asked if he would be willing to try to help them trap Zodiac. He agreed without hesitation. Then they asked the chat-show host, Jim Dunbar, if he would reserve space for a telephone call on his show at 6.45 that morning. The police then got in touch with the only three people who had heard Zodiac's voice: victim Bryan Hartnell and the two switchboard operators who had taken Zodiac's calls.

When the show went on the air at 6.45am, silver-haired Melvin Belli was sitting beside the presenter Jim Dunbar. Dunbar told his audience that they were hoping for a call from the Zodiac killer, and asked them to keep the telephone lines clear. The audience cooperated. Those who saw the opening moments of the show rang their friends to tell them what was happening and, as a result, the show reached a record audience for that time of day in the San Francisco Bay area.

Almost an hour went by, while Belli and Dunbar discussed the murders. Then, at 7.41am, a soft, boyish voice

The letter seemed to indicate that the writer's mental state was deteriorating – there was a note of desperation that sounded genuine

Right: a Napa detective shows an Identikit picture of the Zodiac killer to students in September 1969. Below right: the poster issued by the San Francisco Police Department in October 1969 using an improved Identikit on the left and a further amended version on the right. Below, far right: an extract from one of Zodiac's letters, referring to his second cryptogram (page 819) and offering a tantalising clue to his identity. Below: Jim Dunbar (left), host of a television chat show, waits with lawyer Melvin Belli for Zodiac to ring in to the programme on 21 October 1969. Belli finally persuaded the caller who claimed to be Zodiac to meet him at an arranged place, but he failed to turn up

came on the line. He rang off immediately, but rang back five minutes later. This time he identified himself as Zodiac, but said he preferred to be called Sam. In the studio, Bryan Hartnell and the two switchboard operators shook their heads. Unless Zodiac had been deliberately lowering his voice when they heard him, this call was a hoax.

Sam rang off and rang back fifteen separate times. He stated that he had been suffering from headaches 'since I killed that kid last December', and he frequently groaned with pain, explaining, 'it is the headache speaking'. Belli tried twice to persuade Sam to give himself up, without success. But finally, with the broadcast sound cut off so that the television audience could not hear, Belli persuaded the caller to meet him in front of a shop in Daly City, south of San Francisco.

Predictably perhaps, the mysterious caller failed to arrive. Members of the Zodiac squad hidden at various points near the shop told themselves in consolation that they did not believe the caller was Zodiac anyway. Yet that conclusion is by no means as obvious as it looks. If the caller was a hoaxer, then it would seem logical to expect that the real Zodiac would lose no time in denouncing him. Nothing of the sort happened. And when, that Christmas, the lawyer Melvin Belli received a letter from a man who called himself Zodiac, it began 'Dear Melvin', as if he and Belli were old acquaintances. To confirm his identity, the writer enclosed another piece of Paul Stine's bloodstained shirt. Handwriting experts confirmed that this letter bore strong resemblances to the earlier ones. The letter seemed to indicate that the writer's mental state was deteriorating. The spelling was worse than usual, and there was a note of desperation that sounded genuine: 'The one thing I ask of you is this, please help me. I cannot reach out for help because of this thing in me won't let me. I am finding it extremely difficult to hold it in check and I am afraid I will lose control and take my ninth and possibly tenth victim. Please help me I am drowning. . . '

The claim that he had killed eight people, not five, led to frenzied activity in the San Francisco Police Department, where records were checked and re-checked for other possible Zodiac murders that had gone unrecognised. The only unsolved case that seemed to fit Zodiac's pattern was the murder of an eighteen-year-old student, Cheri Jo Bates, who had been found dead in her car in the college car park with her throat slashed. If she was a Zodiac victim, then

WANTED

SAN FRANCISCO POLICE DEPARTMENT

OCTOBER 18, 1969

WANTED FOR MURDER

ORIGINAL DRAWING

AMENDED DRAWING

Supplementing our Bulletin 87-69 of October 13, 1969. Additional information h
developed the above amended drawing of murder suspect known as "ZODIAC".

WMA, 35-45 Years, approximately 5'8", Heavy Build, Short Brown Hair, possibly
Red Tint, Wears Glasses. Armed with 9 MM Automatic.

Available for comparison: Slugs, Casings, Latents, Handwriting.

ANY INFORMATION:
Inspectors Armstrong & Toschi
Homicide Detail
CASE NO. 696314

THOMAS J. CAHILL
CHIEF OF POLICE

This is the Zodiac speaking
By the way have you cracked
the last cipher I sent you ?
My name is —

A E N ⊕ ⊗ K ⊗ M ⊗ ⊥ N A M

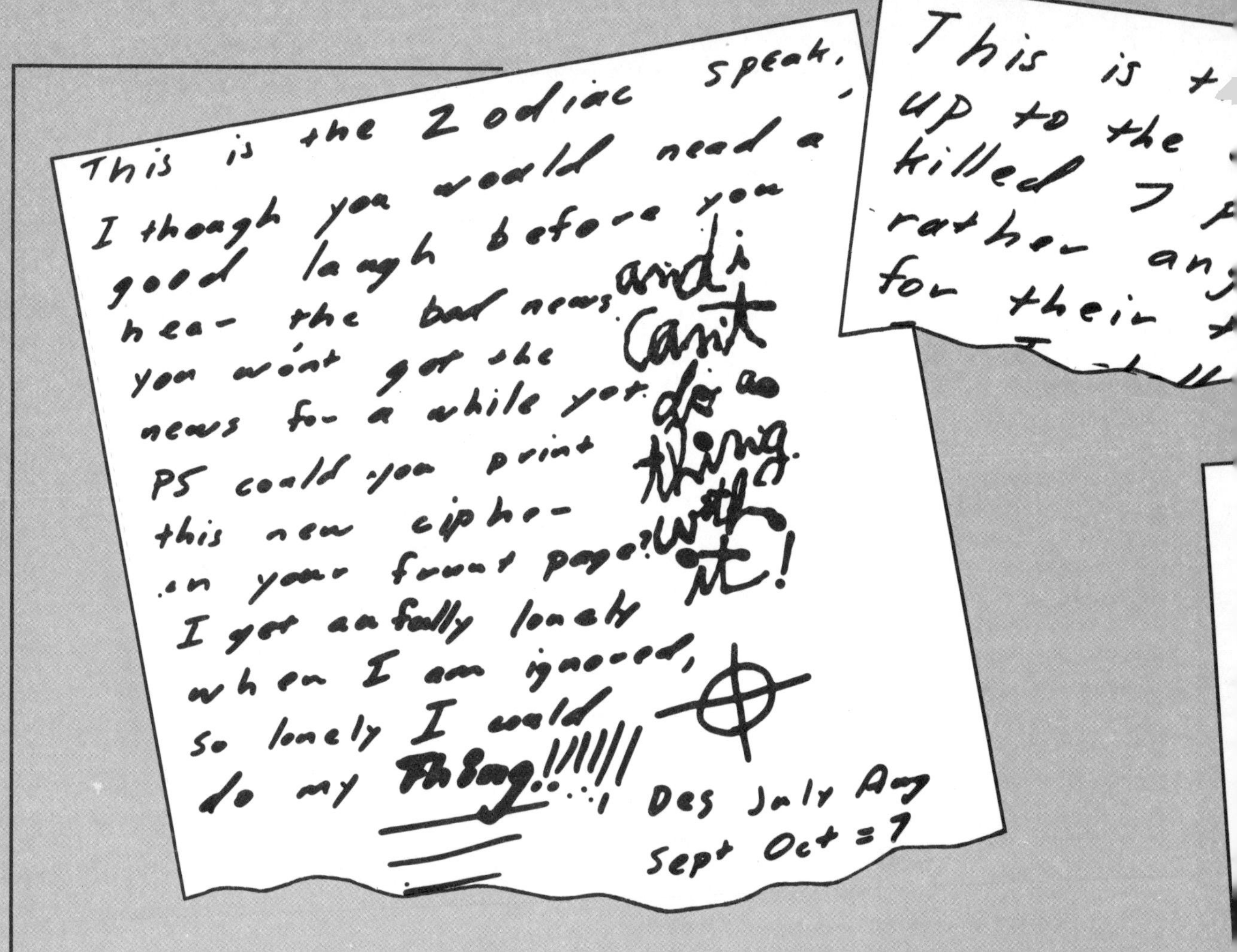
This is the Zodiac speaking,
I though you would need a
good laugh before you
hear the bad news
you won't get the
news for a while yet.
PS could you print
this new cipher
on your front page?
I get awfully lonely
when I am ignored,
so lonely I could
do my Thing!!!!!!
Des July Aug
Sept Oct = 7

and I can't do a thing with it!

This is t
up to the
killed 7
rather an
for their

Selections from Zodiac's written communications to the police and various newspapers. Above: in November 1969 the killer claims seven victims. Above right: Zodiac's response to police insistence that he had killed only five people, not seven. Right: details of a threatened bomb attack, with Zodiac's 'score' at the bottom: 'Zodiac = 10; San Francisco Police Department = 0.' Below right: a letter received by the Los Angeles Times *in March 1971 – the last sentence reveals the killer's pathological need for publicity. Below: a handwriting expert compares letters claiming to be from Zodiac*

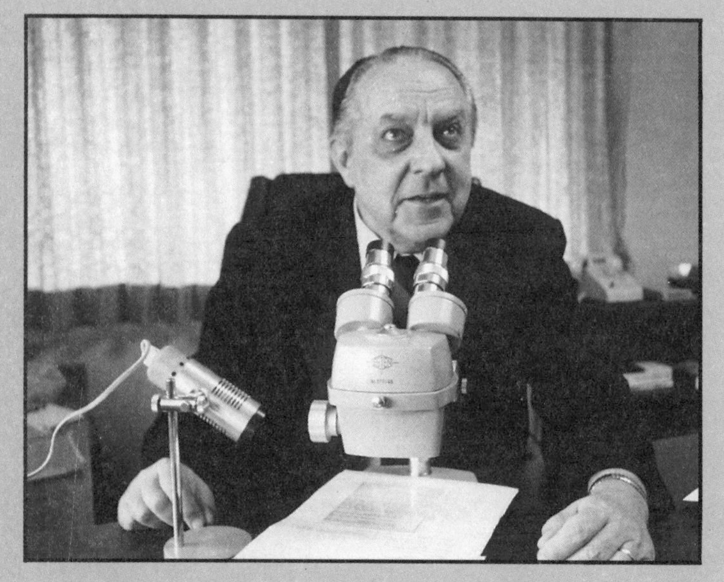

she predated all the others, and it seemed odd that Zodiac had not taken the opportunity to boast about this crime at some time, as he had done about the others. If Cheri Jo Bates was the first victim and Zodiac was counting the two men who had recovered, that would explain the 'eight' mentioned in his letter.

One big problem for the police was that hoaxers and mentally disturbed people were jumping on the Zodiac bandwagon; some of these showed a disturbing note of sadism. In one letter, the writer threatened to torture his victims before he killed them by tying them over anthills to watch them squirm or driving splinters under their nails. In some cases, the writers snipped out letters or words from newspapers and glued them to postcards. One read: 'The pace isn't any slower! In fact it's just one big thirteenth. Some of them fought. It was horrible.' But police were able to dismiss most of these; the real Zodiac usually went to some trouble to prove his identity. On 16 March 1971 the *Los Angeles Times* received a Zodiac letter, postmarked from Pleasanton, near Los Angeles, in which the murderer taunted the police for being unable to catch him. This letter included the figure '17+' – an attempt to imply that the death toll was rising.

Three years passed. In January 1974 Zodiac was still hungering for attention; a letter postmarked San Francisco hinted that the number of his victims had now reached 37; it added that he would 'do something nasty' if the letter was not publicised. Internal evidence suggested that this time the letter was genuine – and there were others, too, which

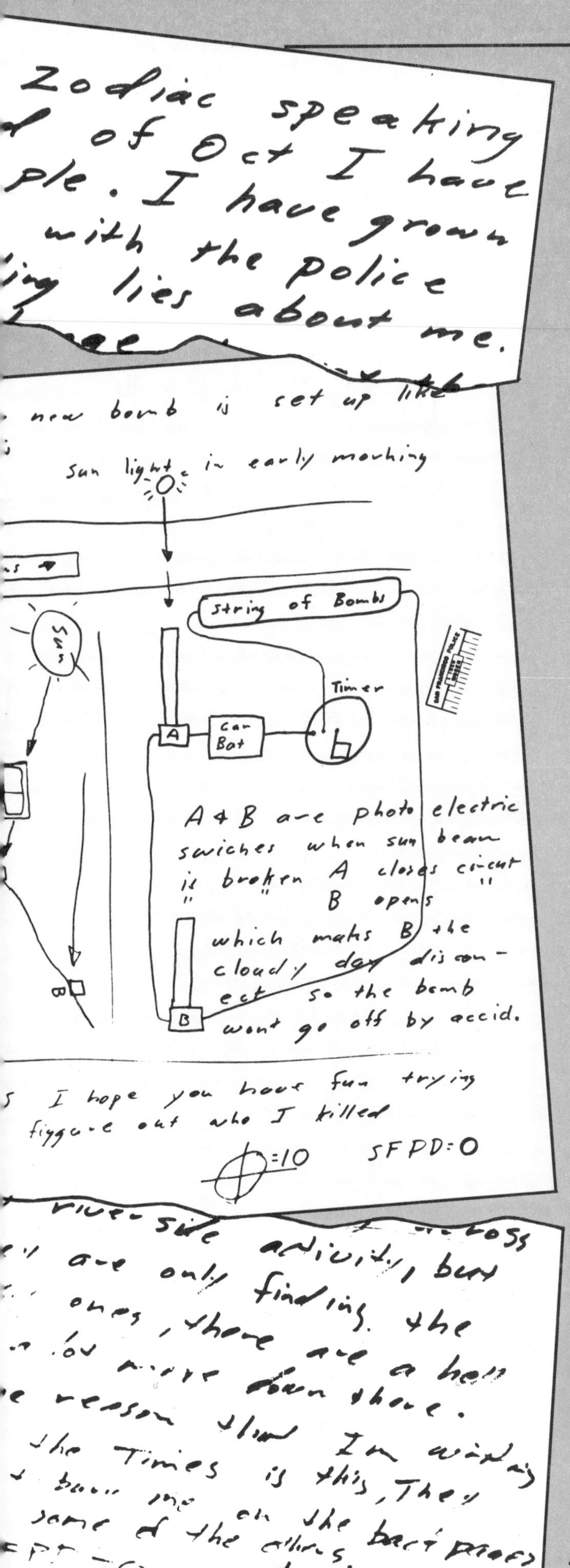
Zodiac speaking
d of Oct I have
ple. I have grown
with the police
ing lies about me.

new bomb is set up like

I hope you have fun trying figgure out who I killed
=10 SFPD=0

river-side activity, but
are only finding the
ones, there are a hell
more down there.
reason that Im writing
the Times is this, They
bury me on the back pages
same of the others.
SFPD—0
—17+

appeared to be authentic communications from the killer.

The 1974 letter is, in its way, as significant as any of the crimes themselves. What it reveals is a man whose deepest craving is for attention; he clamours for it like a badly behaved child. This point was noted by one of the USA's top psychiatrists, Dr Laurence Freedman, who commented, 'He kills senselessly because he is deeply frustrated. And he hates himself because he is an anonymous nonentity. When he is caught he will turn out to be a mouse, a murderous mouse.' He added that he was convinced that Zodiac was insane.

Freedman's psychological portrait of Zodiac is based on the crimes themselves which, studied closely, reveal a certain pattern. The first element is a complete lack of courage. It appears that Zodiac ordered David Farraday out of the car, then started to shoot almost immediately, as if afraid he himself might be attacked. He approached the car containing Michael Mageau and Darlene Ferrin and began to shoot immediately; then he jumped into his own car and drove off so fast that he burnt the rubber of his tyres.

It is also significant that two of his male victims survived. In the case of Bryan Hartnell, it is obvious that the killer's real interest was in his friend Cecilia Shepard, who was a beautiful girl. He stabbed Hartnell only in the back. But when he began to stab Cecilia he lost control, stabbing her repeatedly in the back then turning her over and stabbing her another 23 times in the stomach. In all probability, this violence brought him some kind of sexual satisfaction, but there was no evidence of rape or attempted rape in the case of any of his three female victims. This seemed to suggest a man who was repressed and inhibited in his relations with women.

The case of the taxi-driver Paul Stine again illustrates the same combination of nervousness and extreme caution. It took place at a late hour on a foggy night, and he ordered the driver to pull up in a deserted street. The motive was robbery, but he was not willing to risk simply holding him up and taking his money; he preferred to guard against being identified by shooting his victim in the back of the head. When he realised he was being watched, he fled instantly. The next day, his courage restored, he wrote the police a jeering note and enclosed a fragment of his victim's bloodstained shirt.

As significant as the killer's cowardice is his craving for attention. After the first double murder, he drove off hastily, perhaps alarmed by the headlights of the oncoming car whose driver noticed the bodies only minutes after they had been shot. He made no attempt to contact the police or to publicise the murders. Yet immediately after shooting Michael Mageau and Darlene Ferrin, he rushed to the nearest telephone to inform the police of what he had done. And it was after this shooting that he wrote the letters to three newspapers, including one in code, and threatened to go on a murder rampage and kill twelve people. By then he was convinced he had got away with it and wanted to boast, to defy authority, to make people cringe. He was no longer an 'anonymous nonentity'. He would force the world to pay attention.

If, in fact, the telephone caller to the Jim Dunbar show

Return of Zodiac?

Above: Paul Avery, who studied the Zodiac case

In February 1971 Sheriff Earl Randol of Napa County found it necessary to assure newsmen that the Zodiac killer was not at work again. The newsmen were far from convinced. Paul Avery, a *San Francisco Chronicle* journalist who had been studying the crimes for three years, told his readers that there was a good chance that two more cases were the work of the same man.

On the morning of 25 February 1971 twenty-year-old Sharon Wilson, a student of Humboldt State College in Arcata, California, drove off to relax on the nearby Mad River beach. When she failed to return, fellow students alerted the police. Sharon's car was found abandoned on a remote dirt road; her spectacles and lipstick were found on the edge of the river. On the same day, 200 miles (300 kilometres) south in 'Zodiac country', another twenty-year-old college student, Lynda Kanes, stopped her car on a hilltop road to look at the view. When the car was found the radio was still playing. Lynda's bra and coat were on the seat, but the girl had vanished. When the police in Napa County heard about Sharon Wilson's disappearance, the word 'Zodiac' began to be mentioned.

One of the volunteers who helped to search the Mad River area for Sharon Wilson was eighteen-year-old Philip Kohler, a dairy worker; it was he who stumbled on Sharon's fully-clothed body lying in the water. She had been stabbed repeatedly.

A week later, the body of Lynda Kanes was also discovered, buried under branches in a ravine close to the

Right: Inspector Dave Toschi of the San Francisco Police Department, who was in charge of the Zodiac case. Far right: a letter from Zodiac to the San Francisco Chronicle, *in which he derides Toschi for not being good enough to catch him. This time he does not give his total number of murders, but invites the public to guess at it. The letter was received on 25 April 1978, eight and a half years after the last murder that the police definitely attributed to Zodiac. Interest in the case continues to run high: a book on it, called simply* Zodiac, *by Robert Graysmith, was published in the USA in 1984*

spot where her car had been found. It was not far from the place where Zodiac had killed Cecilia Shepard eighteen months before. Footprints of 'a very big man' were found in the area.

One puzzle in the case was why Lynda had chosen to drive to her work as a waitress in a country club over Howard Mountain Road when there was a much more direct route. Friends told the police that she disliked a 57-year-old woodcutter, Walter Boyd Williams, whose house she had to pass on the more direct road. In Williams' home police found bloodstained clothing; he was arrested and charged with Lynda's murder.

Police in Humboldt County had also been finding out about Philip Kohler, the youth who had discovered Sharon's body; it turned out that he had spent some time in the state asylum after molesting girls. When Kohler was taken in for questioning, another college girl went to the police and told them that two days before Sharon had vanished Kohler had attempted to rape her at knifepoint on the very spot where her car had been found. The friend identified Kohler in a police line-up, and he was charged with Sharon Wilson's murder.

So in both these cases the scare that Zodiac was at work again was defused before it had had time to cause too much panic. And Paul Avery, the *San Francisco Chronicle* reporter who had first started the rumour, was one of those who publicly expressed relief that he had been mistaken.

was Zodiac – and the later letter to Melvin Belli makes this highly probable – then this episode is rather ironic. The 'anonymous nonentity' had caused shock waves all over California; he had had the satisfaction of knowing that hundreds of people were trying to puzzle out his cryptogram – it must have felt rather like being a best-selling author. He had certainly achieved a kind of fame. The murder of the taxi-driver brought him yet more publicity, and after the threat of an attack on a school bus, he was the most talked-about man in the USA. When he rang the San Francisco Police Department on 21 October, he undoubtedly wanted to appear on Jim Dunbar's show. The fact that the caller to the show had a 'boyish voice' is no proof that he was not Zodiac. Various other people described Zodiac as having a gruff voice, but any man can lower his voice to make it sound gruff – in fact, this is the easiest way of disguising the voice. And if 'Sam' was not Zodiac, then who was he? One thing that seems fairly certain is that if Zodiac had changed his mind about ringing through to the programme and a hoaxer had taken his place, Zodiac would have lost no time in denouncing the phoney; his sense of publicity would have guaranteed that.

Yet all this fame was ultimately self-defeating since, though he could walk along a street and think, 'I am famous', nobody knew him – he was still an anonymous nonentity. He could address the famous lawyer as 'Dear Melvin' – but he did not dare to sign his own name. He tried to keep the excitement alive with more letters, hinting at more killings, but he was crying wolf too often and the newspapers eventually relegated him to the back page.

This is the Zodiac speaking I
am back with you. Tell herb caen
I am here, I have always been here.
That city pig toschi is good · but
I am ~~bu~~ smarter and better he
will get tired then leave me
alone. I am waiting for a good
movie about me. who will play
me. I am now in control of all
things.

yours truly :

⊕ - guess

Above: one of the final Identikit pictures issued of Zodiac; a similar one showing him without spectacles appears on page 809

The only way of keeping the excitement alive would be to commit more murders, but next time he might be caught. Besides, being a temporary 'celebrity' had released some of the frustration that had turned him into a killer. As it was, the police had come dangerously close, with an accurate description of him and three fingerprints. So the 'murderous mouse'— unless he has since been arrested and jailed for another crime, perhaps in another state where he was not recognised — has presumably lapsed back into obscurity, telling himself that at least he had made the world sit up and take notice of him. Other police theories are that he is in hospital or has died. The Zodiac killings could be used to illustrate one of Freud's most disturbing assertions: that if a child only had the power, it would destroy the world.

There is one more speculation. In his first letter, Zodiac asserted that the decoding of the cipher message would reveal his identity. It did not do so. The logical assumption is that the killer never meant to reveal his identity, but intended the claim to act as bait and cause widespread effort to crack the code. Yet one thing that may strike anyone who looks at the first few lines of the cipher message is that Zodiac sometimes used the letter 'Z' to signify an 'E'. Might the killer have, in fact, hidden his own name in the message, and could the solution to the case now lie in the hands of another cryptanalyst?

The Ripper syndrome

Few writers on the Zodiac case have been able to resist the temptation to compare the killer to the unknown maniac who killed five prostitutes in the East End of London in 1888 and who wrote jeering letters to the newspapers signed 'Jack the Ripper'. Partly because the Ripper was never caught and partly because of the horrific nature of his crimes — he was the first 'sex maniac' in our modern sense of the word — the case still excites as much interest as it did almost a century ago. But most writers on the case add that, with the use of up-to-date police methods, a modern Jack the Ripper would infallibly be caught.

Does the evidence bear out this claim? The answer, regrettably, is no. San Francisco police had an accurate physical description of Zodiac, as well as three of his fingerprints. More than a decade after the murders, his identity still remains a mystery. So does that of the sex maniac known as the Moonlight Murderer of Texarkana, Texas, who killed five people in 1946. So does that of the Texas Strangler, who murdered and mutilated twelve women, and abducted two others whose bodies were never found, between 1968 and 1971. The victims included barmaids, a schoolteacher and a go-go dancer, and the motive in all cases seems to have been rape, although in one case the strangler left a note saying, 'Got wrong one — sorry'. In mid 1984, the Los Angeles slasher, who murdered at least eight tramps in the slums of Los Angeles, was still uncaught; he always slit his victims' throats, and the ferocity of the crimes indicated a sexual motive.

Although he was finally caught, Peter Sutcliffe, the 'Yorkshire Ripper', provides another case in point. Sutcliffe knocked his victims unconscious with a hammer blow, then mutilated them with a knife. Between October 1975 and November 1980 he killed thirteen women in the north of England. A massive police operation, which included elaborate checks on all cars seen more than once in red light districts, failed to catch Sutcliffe although he was interviewed nine times. He was finally caught by accident, when police found him sitting in a car with a prostitute and discovered that the car had false number plates. A hammer and knife found nearby finally revealed him as the mass murderer. If Sutcliffe had not made the mistake of using false number plates, he might still be at large.

After the Yorkshire Ripper hunt, it was generally agreed that the police's main problem was poor co-ordination of the vast body of evidence and that if a computer had been used efficiently Sutcliffe would probably have been caught a great deal sooner. In the USA, a similar insight is dawning on authorities searching for 'serial killers' who travel from state to state selecting victims at random. In San Francisco, centre of the search for Zodiac, the introduction in 1984 of a fingerprint computer, which can check fingerprints against those of known criminals in seconds, has led to an astonishing increase in the number of crimes solved. Since Zodiac's prints are still on the San Francisco police file, it is conceivable that even at this late date his crimes may yet be solved.

DEATH OF A HERO

In May 1935 'Lawrence of Arabia' was involved in a fatal motorcycle crash and the coroner's verdict was 'accidental death'. But the shock of the death, the security surrounding it and the conflicting evidence at the inquest inevitably gave rise to imaginative rumours. Some thought that Lawrence had committed suicide; others that he had been assassinated or that his death was staged. COLIN SIMPSON considers these theories in the context of Lawrence's life and adventures, and in a careful reinvestigation of the accident offers the most likely explanation for a fifty-year-old mystery

Above: the last picture of T. E. Lawrence, taken at his home at Clouds Hill. He is seated on the motorcycle, a Brough Superior that he crashed, killing himself, on 13 May 1935. This motorcycle was originally on trial as a dispatch rider's bike for the Seventh Hussars at Catterick. Lawrence saw it, was impressed and bought it. Above right: Lawrence at Carchemish, a dig organised by D. G. Hogarth, Keeper of the Ashmolean Museum, Oxford, for the British Museum. Carchemish was a small Hittite site of modest interest beside the Euphrates river and some 70 miles (120 kilometres) north of Aleppo, Syria. Arriving in 1911, Lawrence spent four years on the dig, which closed down during the heat of the summer months. At these times he would wander off into the hinterland of Turkey, Persia and Arabia, sometimes alone, sometimes with a young Arab donkey boy called Salim Dahoum. Right: Carchemish site workers – Dahoum is the fair-skinned boy on the left. During the war he acted as an agent or courier for Lawrence and died in his arms, of typhoid, in September 1918

AT 11.22am on Monday 13 May 1935, T. E. Lawrence, who found fame as 'Lawrence of Arabia', had a motorcycle accident. He was in a coma for six days and died the following Sunday, just after 8am. Within minutes of learning of the accident, the government of the day took the most extraordinary security precautions. The War Office imposed a total ban on all information to the press, security guards ringed the hospital and special branch officers remained at his bedside until he died.

The evidence at the inquest was both inaccurate and conflicting. The only adult eyewitness stated that, from the sound of Lawrence's motorcycle, it was travelling between 50 and 60 miles per hour (80 and 100 kilometres per hour), when it was known to all concerned that the machine was recovered locked in second gear, which had a maximum at full revolutions of 38 miles per hour (61 kilometres per hour). The same witness attributed the accident to Lawrence swerving to avoid a large black car that appeared to crowd him off the road. Yet two young boys who were on their bicycles ahead of the accident denied having seen or heard a car of any sort.

The coroner advised the jury that the presence of a car was irrelevant. 'Lawrence,' he said, 'had either had an accident on his motorcycle or he had not.' Thus prompted, the jury recorded that 'Mr T. E. Lawrence had died from injuries received accidentally'. In a somewhat unseemly rush, the man who was the nation's hero was packed into his coffin and buried within two hours of the verdict.

The mysterious circumstances of the accident, the remarkable reactions of the authorities and the rushed funeral sparked off a spate of rumours that continue to this day. Many believed it was murder by either French, German or Arab agents. The *Daily Express* offered one unchallenged reason, even as Lawrence lay unconscious in the closely guarded sick bay of Bovington Army Camp. The newspaper claimed that 'Lawrence has the plans for the defence of England in his head'. There were other explanations. It has also been suggested that Lawrence was killed because he had designs to become absolute ruler of England, a notion apparently encouraged by the author – and fascist – Henry Williamson, who advised Lawrence to 'seize power while' he was 'still a hero in the public eye'. One group of people believed that he was not killed at all, but that the secret service faked his death so as to allow him to undertake, incognito, important work in the Middle East during the approaching Second World War, and that he died of old age in Tangiers, Morocco, in 1968. Others suspect that Lawrence committed suicide because life no longer held any appeal for him. The most widely held belief of all is that he was victim of his love of speed and a personal death-wish, both of which

were expressed in a poem he wrote for a friend shortly before the accident:

In speed we hurl ourselves beyond the body.
Our bodies cannot scale the heavens, except in a fume of petrol.
Bones. Blood. Flesh. All pressed inward together.

It was a prophetic verse, almost matching the autopsy report, which reported a 9-inch (23-centimetre) gaping hole in the back of his head where his skull had been crushed. The death certificate described Lawrence as: 'Thomas Edward Shaw', an 'aircraftsman (retired)', and gave as the cause of death: 'Congestion of the lungs and heart failure following a fracture of the skull and laceration of the brain, sustained on being thrown from his motorcycle when colliding with a pedal cyclist.' The coroner did not comment on the fact that the cyclist with whom Lawrence allegedly collided at 'between 50 and 60 miles per hour [80 and 100 kilometres per hour]' received only the most superficial grazes, which did not require anything more than a piece of sticking plaster, and he also left unanswered the vital questions. Why, and how, did the accident happen?

To answer the first question, we must look at the man himself. Who was Lawrence? Why should such a mystery have grown up around his death?

Thomas Edward Lawrence was born at Tremadoc in Caernarvonshire, Wales, in the early hours of 16 August 1888. He was the second of four illegitimate sons sired by an Anglo-Irish country squire called Thomas Chapman. Chapman had deserted his wife and four daughters and run off with the girls' governess, Miss Sarah Madden, who herself was

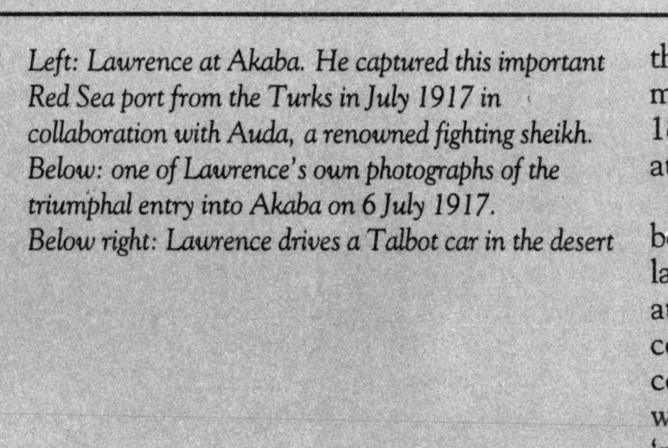

Left: Lawrence at Akaba. He captured this important Red Sea port from the Turks in July 1917 in collaboration with Auda, a renowned fighting sheikh.
Below: one of Lawrence's own photographs of the triumphal entry into Akaba on 6 July 1917.
Below right: Lawrence drives a Talbot car in the desert

the illegitimate child of a Norwegian seaman and an English mother. Chapman changed his name to Lawrence and in 1896 he and his somewhat eccentric *ménage* made a home at 2 Polstead Road, Oxford.

Chapman was not a scholarly man. 'He never touched a book nor wrote a cheque,' Lawrence proudly told a friend in later life. He was a dignified, quiet man, a regular worshipper at the local evangelical church, a member of the church committee, and he took great pains to conceal his antecedents. The boys' mother was equally secretive, but riven with guilt. She could never bring herself to use the words 'my husband', and always referred to him as either 'Tom' or 'the boys' father'. The family kept to themselves, and those who remember them were familiar with the sight of the four boys, all dressed in identical striped jerseys, cycling in single file to and from Oxford High School.

The young Lawrence was a loner. A former master described him as 'self-possessed, purposeful, inscrutable'. He took long, solitary cycle rides; he developed an interest in archaeology and military history, and spent holidays grubbing around Roman forts and battlegrounds. He gained enough knowledge of medieval history to win a history exhibition to St John's College, Oxford, in the autumn of 1907.

He was not a typical undergraduate. In those days, most Oxford students were wealthy and went up to university to do just as much work as was required to get a degree and devoted the rest of their time to pleasure. His contemporaries remember him as elusive, contrivedly enigmatic, yet generous with offers of reconciliation if his sarcasm cut too deep. In short, he acquired the classic defences of a shy, acutely intelligent and sensitive boy embarrassed by his background.

Below: Lawrence took this photograph of Feisal, the military leader of the Arabs, with his bodyguard on 3 January 1917. Lawrence (bottom) recommended that Britain should support the Arab Revolt and was attached as liaison officer to Feisal to ensure the revolt went in Britain's favour. Lawrence said: 'Had I been an honourable adviser I would have sent my men home and not let them risk their lives for such stuff.' Right: Arabia before the revolt and (inset) today's national divisions. One theory at the time of Lawrence's death was that his influence on the political reshaping of Arabia might have made him a candidate for assassination by several disappointed national groups

At an age when most young men were discovering the sensual side of life, he deliberately withdrew himself from it. Any act of physical sex or of obtaining physical pleasure from food or drink disgusted him. One of his nicknames was 'the mad monk', and it was a role he exploited to the full, blending the monastic life with playing to the gallery.

His peculiar talents had been recognised in Oxford, even before he went up to the university, by one of the most remarkable men of his time and one of the founders of the British intelligence service. This was D. G. Hogarth, who was then the Keeper of the Ashmolean Museum. He became Lawrence's mentor, father substitute and financial backer. Hogarth led a double life. Outwardly he was a respected archaeologist and orientalist, with an international reputation as a scholar. He was also the organiser of a private intelligence service that kept him remarkably close to successive foreign secretaries and prime ministers. Hogarth sought out 'dedicated men of special knowledge, in it for neither pay nor honour'. Outwardly, they would be academics or consuls, archaeologists or even businessmen, but secretly they would serve the British Empire by gathering and interpreting intelligence and manipulating people and events — Hogarth had a strong contempt for democracy. He was ever anxious to find such men to carry the torch, and it was to Lawrence that he handed it.

Lawrence's training as a new recruit to what Hogarth called 'the Great Game' was meticulous. He acquired a complete grounding in military history and was encouraged to develop supreme physical fitness. Lawrence tested his endurance by going without food for two or three days, made midwinter cross-country marches by compass, swimming, or climbing every obstacle so as not to deviate from the

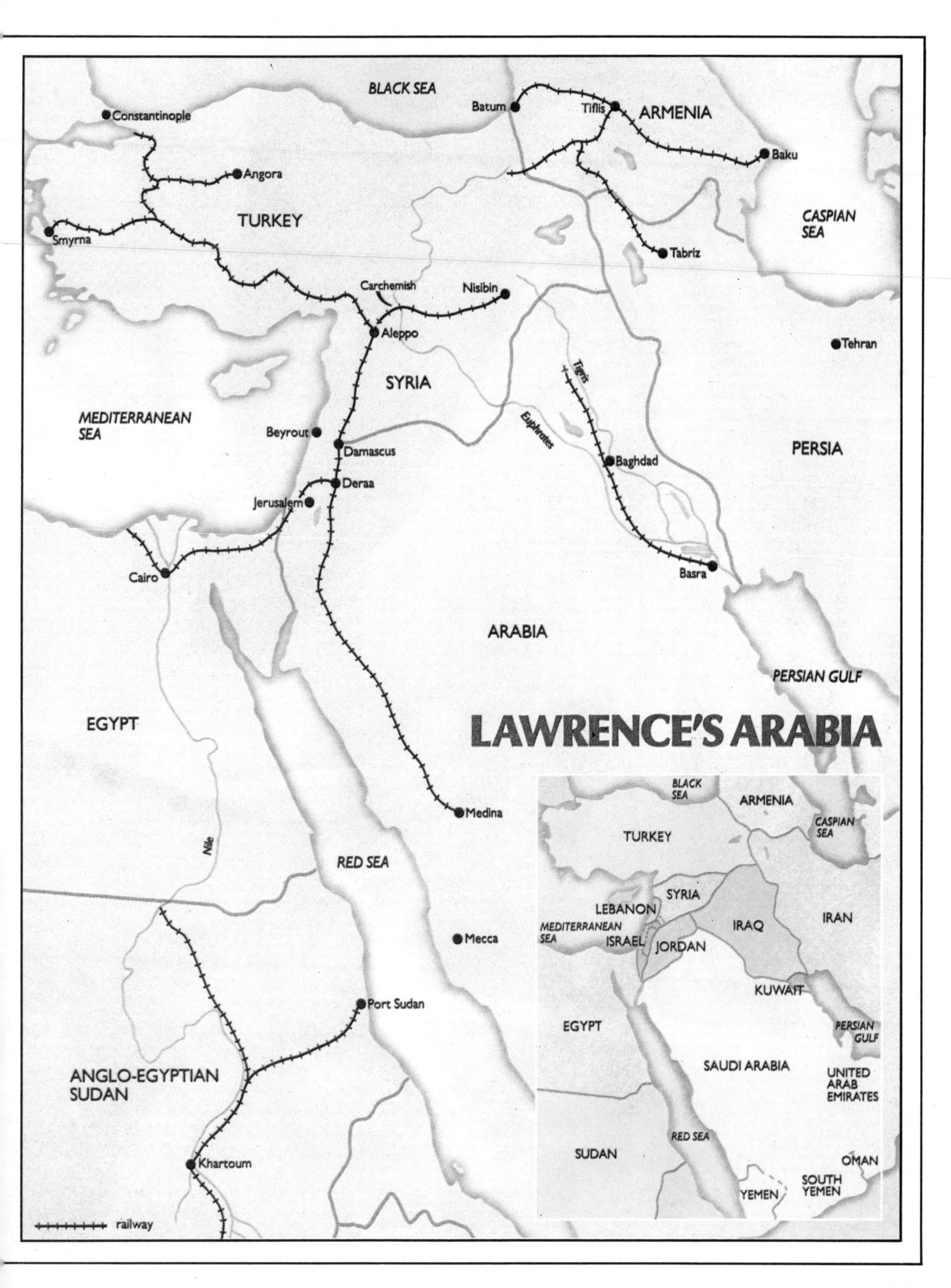
BLACK SEA
Constantinople
Batum
Tiflis
ARMENIA
Baku
Angora
TURKEY
CASPIAN SEA
Smyrna
Tabriz
Carchemish
Nisibin
Aleppo
Tehran
SYRIA
Tigris
MEDITERRANEAN SEA
Euphrates
Beyrout
Damascus
PERSIA
Baghdad
Deraa
Jerusalem
Cairo
Basra
ARABIA
PERSIAN GULF
EGYPT
LAWRENCE'S ARABIA
Medina
Nile
RED SEA
Mecca
Port Sudan
ANGLO-EGYPTIAN SUDAN
Khartoum
railway
BLACK SEA
ARMENIA
TURKEY
CASPIAN SEA
SYRIA
LEBANON
MEDITERRANEAN SEA
ISRAEL
JORDAN
IRAQ
IRAN
KUWAIT
EGYPT
PERSIAN GULF
SAUDI ARABIA
UNITED ARAB EMIRATES
RED SEA
SUDAN
OMAN
SOUTH YEMEN
YEMEN